Contents

COGNITIVE MODELS OF MEMORY

Studies in Cognition

Editor: Glyn Humphreys
University of Birmingham

COGNITIVE MODELS
OF MEMORY

EDITED BY
MARTIN A. CONWAY
UNIVERSITY OF BRISTOL

The MIT Press
Cambridge, Massachusetts

First MIT Press edition, 1997
© by Martin Conway and contributors, 1997

Library of Congress Cataloging-in-Publication Data

Cognitive models of memory / edited by Martin A. Conway.
    p. cm.
  Includes bibliographical references (p.   ) and index.
  ISBN 0-262-03245-7 (hardcover : alk. paper). — ISBN 0-262-53148-8
(pbk. : alk. paper)
  1. Memory. 2. Mental representation. I. Conway, Martin A.,
  1952– .
BF371.C574 1997
153.1′2—dc21   96-43748
                                     CIP

Cover painting *Still life with flask* (Tempra) by Ian Hopton

Printed and bound in the United Kingdom by Biddles Ltd, Guildford and King's Lynn.

Contributors

John Ainsworth, Department of Psychology, University of Manchester, Oxford Road, Manchester, M13 9PL, UK.

Stephen J. Anderson, University of Bristol, Department of Psychology, 8 Woodland Road, Bristol, BS8 1TN, UK.

Gordon A. Brown, Department of Psychology, University of Warwick, Coventry, CV4 7AL, UK.

Paul Burgess, Department of Psychology, University College London, Gower Street, London, WC1E 6BT, UK.

Martin A. Conway, University of Bristol, Department of Psychology, 8 Woodland Road, Bristol, BS8 1TN, UK.

Peyman Faratin, Department of Psychology, University of Manchester, Oxford Road, Manchester, M13 9PL, UK.

Jonathan Foster, Department of Psychology, University of Manchester, Oxford Road, Manchester, M13 9PL, UK.

Alan Garnham, University of Sussex, Experimental Psychology, Biology Building, Falmer, Brighton, BN1 9QG, UK.

Susan E. Gathercole, University of Bristol, Department of Psychology, 8 Woodland Road, Bristol, BS8 1TN, UK.

James Hampton, City University, Department of Psychology, School of Social Sciences, Northampton Square, London, EC1V 0HB, UK.

Tim Perfect, University of Bristol, Department of Psychology, 8 Woodland Road, Bristol, BS8 1TN, UK.

Gabriel A. Radvansky, Department of Psychology, University of Notre Dame, Notre Dame, Indiana 46556, USA.

Tim Shallice, Department of Psychology, University College London, Gower Street, London, WC1E 6BT, UK.

David Shanks, Department of Psychology, University College London, Gower Street, London, WC1E 6BT, UK.

Jon Shapiro, Department of Psychology, University of Manchester, Oxford Road, Manchester, M13 9PL, UK.

Philip Smith, Department of Psychology, University of Reading, Building 3, Earley Gate, Whiteknights, Reading, RG6 2AL, UK.

Rose T. Zacks, Department of Psychology, University of Notre Dame, Notre Dame, Indiana 46556, USA.

Series Preface

Over the past 20 years enormous advances have been made in our understanding of basic cognitive processes concerning issues such as: what are the basic modules of the cognitive system? How can these modules be modelled? How are the modules implemented in the brain. The book series *Studies in Cognition* seeks to provide state-of-the-art summaries of this research, bringing together work on experimental psychology with that on computational modelling and cognitive neuroscience. Each book contains chapters written by leading figures in the field, which aim to provide comprehensive summaries of current research. The books should be both accessible and scholarly and to be relevant to undergraduates, postgraduates and research workers alike.

Glyn Humphreys
27 May 1997

CHAPTER ONE

Introduction: models and data

Martin A. Conway

Memory, in one form or another, enters into virtually all cognition. Because of this it is not possible to generate research projects or design cognitive models that deal with memory as a self-contained cognitive faculty. Instead, and in order to explore tractable research questions, memory researchers have typically focused their research efforts on specific aspects of memory. The chapters in the present volume reflect this "regional" approach to research and modelling: they evaluate models of the short-term retention of knowledge, conceptual knowledge, autobiographical knowledge, transitory mental representations, the neurobiological basis of memory, and age-related changes in human memory. At the centre of each chapter is a concern with the *problem of representation* and with the associated problem of psychological validity. The problem of representation concerns how the mind represents reality and, in the case of memory, how and in what ways experience can be represented, retained and reconstructed. Of course, many representational schemes have been suggested by researchers (cf. Rumelhart & Norman 1983, Boden 1988) and a critical question is: which representational schemes are the most psychologically plausible? The chapters in this book deal with the problem of psychological plausibility or validity by evaluating the performance of a variety of models against empirical findings and against what is currently known concerning brain function and architecture.

Gathercole, in the opening chapter on models of short-term memory (STM), identifies a group of empirical findings that any plausible model of STM must explain. For instance, a particularly robust phenomenon in STM research is the *word length effect* in which serial recall of short words with comparatively brief articulation times, exceeds serial recall of longer words with longer articulation times. Other well known phenomena are the *phonological similarity effect*, in which words that sound the same are more difficult to recall immediately than words that sound different, and the effect of *articulatory suppression* in which STM performance is reduced when a rememberer is required to repeat aloud an irrelevant word while studying a list of to-be-remembered items. Gathercole appraises a series of different models but concludes that no current single model can account for these three effects. She also notes that they fail to accommodate findings relating to the lexicality of to-be-learned items and to the critically important issue of long-term learning. These models fail whether they are expressed in a nonformal way, such as the phonological loop (Baddeley 1986), or presented as detailed connectionist (Burgess & Hitch 1992) or mathematical models (Brown & Hulme 1996). However, the shortcomings of each model are in themselves instructive. Taken together they suggest that a more complete account will have to find a way in which to model the interaction of STM with long-term memory (LTM). Such an integrated model would hold out the possibility of successfully modelling a more complete range of fundamental properties of STM.

Brown's chapter is also concerned with the type of phenomena that must be explained by models of serial order. Serial order in immediate recall tasks reflects one of the fundamental abilities of STM, namely the ability to retain order information. Errors in serial recall, e.g. *transpositional errors* in which the correct items are recalled but in the incorrect order, constitute one of the main features that any (psychological) model of order effects must simulate. The focus of this chapter is on formal models of serial recall that can be expressed mathematically and implemented in computer programmes. Brown describes the basic representational scheme used in most models: items are represented as vectors (a list of numbers), and are combined by various algorithms for associating vectors, such as Hebbian, backpropagation, and convolution. In some respects the choice of an algorithm for associating vectors is independent of the general architectural assumptions based on the (nonformal) cognitive theory of a model. In the models evaluated by Brown either of the three forms of association could be used. However, and most importantly, the choice of a means to associate vectors places powerful constraints on the psychological plausibility of a model. So, for instance, only the backpropagation procedure can be used to learn how to represent items. But backpropagation takes many trials to learn to represent a set of items whereas human STM does this with a single exposure to a list. Hebbian learning and convolution represent the items in vector form directly and so overcome the problem of single-trial learning, but at the cost of having any learning mechanism at all. Clearly, even at this most basic level assumptions about representation do not satisfy the constraint to be psychologically plausible. Nevertheless, when placed in the context of a formal model of human STM serial recall, simulations can have a surprising degree of isomorphism with human performance patterns for both correct and incorrect responses. Promising though this is, Brown shows that current models cannot fully simulate human performance. Nevertheless development continues in modelling this fundamental attribute of STM and further progress appears highly likely.

The next two chapters deal with the representation of conceptual knowledge and with various attempts to find ways in which to model the astonishing diversity of human conceptual knowledge. There are five commonly acknowledged approaches to conceptual representation. The *classical view* holds that concepts have definitions; the *probabilistic view* denies that concepts have definitions and instead argues that concepts are interrelated by means of similarity of features; the *exemplar view* proposes that classification is based on remembered instances rather than definitions or feature comparisons; the *theory-based view* argues that concepts are set in the context of a theory or mini-theory of knowledge and what types of knowledge comprise each particular concept, and finally, and most recently, the *essentialist view* claims that every concept has an essence. Essences may be unknown to an individual but nevertheless they exist and, perhaps, can only be identified by experts.

Hampton critically appraises these theories and the models to which they have given rise, pointing to findings that call each view into question. For instance, interest in the classical view waned when various philosophers pointed out that there were many concepts for which a definition could not be generated. Wittgenstein (1953) used the concept "game" as an example of this. The category "game" refers to many activities as diverse as chess, water polo, and solitaire. Although all are games there is no defining feature that all share. Instead, argued Wittgenstein, the exemplars in the category "game" are bound together because they share a *family resemblance* i.e. exemplar "X" shares some features with exemplar "Y" that in turn shares some features with exemplar "Z", although "X" and "Z" themselves share no features. This feature-based approach underlies both the probabilistic and exemplar accounts of long-term conceptual knowledge. But a fundamental problem with the feature-based approach is how to identify a feature and, once identified, how to compare its similarity to other features of other concepts. Thus, for instance, virtually any concept can have an indefinitely large, or at least very long, list of features, the list only being limited by our ingenuity and motivation. A "robin" for example, has wings, a red breast, has a nervous system, is larger than a mouse, and smaller than an emu, often appears on Christmas cards, and so on. The question is where: do such features come from? One answer is that there is some more abstract knowledge that guides the computation of features and it is this that is fundamental in human conceptual knowledge. The theory-based approach openly rejects classification on similarity of features and instead proposes that concepts have attached to them theories that specify what they are. Of course the problem then arises as to where such theories, if they exist, come from. The essentialist view appears to be a new form of the classical view with the caveat that although we do not know what the essential (defining) features of many concepts are, we may do one day when experts have identified them for us. But the difficulties pointed out by Wittgenstein remain, and one wonders what domain of expertise could ever establish the essence of a concept such as "game".

Shanks emphasizes an important function of categorical knowledge, that of generalization. A category supports the generalization of functions to those items it contains. Knowing that a set of objects are foods allows the generalization that they can *be eaten*. This is an efficient form of knowledge representation because not all information must be stored with all items in a category. Shanks further introduces an interesting distinction between categories and concepts. A concept, he suggests, is a representation of objects that are grouped by some principle, rule, or set of rules, rather than by perceptual similarity. This chapter favours an exemplar account of categories, in which items are grouped by similarity, and a rule/abstract or theory-based account of concepts. Various models are then evaluated against these distinctions including connectionist models of conceptual representation. An additional and welcome emphasis is the discussion of the relation between conceptual knowledge and behaviour.

Chapters in the third section take a different and comparatively new approach to human memory. This approach is based on the concept of *mental models* (Johnson-Laird 1983) that originally emerged from investigations of reasoning and text comprehension. Garnham provides a thorough treatment of the development and current state of the mental models approach. In Craik's (1943) original formulation of mental models, a model was a simulation of some state of affairs in the world, especially of how some sequences of activities might evolve.

Memories of experienced events could also be viewed as simulations but simulations of how some states of world were in the past rather than of how they might be in the future or are at the present. Indeed Radvansky & Zacks develop this idea in some detail in their chapter. They refer to mental models as *situation models* which are representations of specific situations. By this view a situation is composed of specific entities that have relations to each other. However, each model represents a single unique situation and so situational models differ from categories and concepts that represent abstract and general information about groups of items. Moreover, situation models are analogues in that their representational structure directly models a specific situation. Consequently, situation models do not rely on verbal-linguistic encoding. Radvansky & Zacks distinguish two types of situation models: states-of-affairs models are static and model a single specific situation, e.g. an image of some scene, whereas, and in contrast, course-of-events models represent unfolding action sequences, e.g. a series of images of a sequence of scenes. Situational models are temporary and transitory mental representations that are represented dynamically, perhaps in working memory (cf. Kahneman & Miller 1986, Ericsson & Kintsch 1995). One great advantage of the mental model approach is that it leads to models in which knowledge can be represented in a dynamic, flexible and evolving form; which is surely how memory is used in everyday cognition.

Anderson & Conway evaluate various models of autobiographical memory (AM) against a set of criteria drawn from empirical observations. For example, autobiographical memories are difficult to construct; retrieval of memories takes considerably longer than verification of factual knowledge; memories contain both general and specific autobiographical knowledge; memories vary in their clarity, and appear to be more available from certain periods of life than others. Any psychologically plausible model of AM must adequately account for these well documented attributes of AMs. They favour a model in which memories are constructions of central control processes. Memories are transitory mental representations (highly similar to mental models) that must be effortfully maintained in working memory if they are to endure for more than a few brief moments. Importantly, Anderson & Conway also suggest that aspects of the self may act as control processes, and they propose that the self constrains the current interpretation placed on a constructed memory, while reciprocally a constructed memory constrains what forms the current self can take. The general architecture considered by these authors is one in which output from a complex and layered knowledge base, perhaps in the form of a connectionist distributed memory system, is modulated by control processes. Various developments of this view allow the authors to account for their critical list of empirical findings.

Burgess & Shallice also focus on the role of executive functions or control processes in memory. Their focus is on both autobiographical memory and prospective memory and the relation between the two. As they point out, it has often been maintained that autobiographical memory and prospective memory are unrelated. However, if executive processes play an important role in memory construction and also in remembering to perform future actions then the two should be closely related, as both rely heavily on control processing. The model of AM developed by Burgess & Shallice is similar in its architecture to the model favoured by Anderson & Conway, although it differs quite markedly in its details. Burgess & Shallice show their model can be applied to both autobiographical and prospective memory. Then, interestingly, they report several studies of patients with frontal lobe damage (a brain region known to mediate control processing) and patients with damage to their temporal lobes (a region known to support memory processes). Their intriguing findings are that patients with frontal damage cannot perform prospective memory tasks but, nevertheless, have apparently unimpaired autobiographical memories. Set against this, patients with retrograde amnesia (but no frontal impairment) cannot perform prospective memory tasks. This latter finding suggests that autobiographical memory may be of some critical importance to prospective memory. It seems that without a long-term memory knowledge base that represents one's personal history, there is no knowledge that can be used to plan future actions. Burgess & Shallice explore how this interrelation between autobiographical and prospective memory could occur within their model of AM.

The chapter by Foster and colleagues assesses a mathematical model of hippocampal function by implementing it in a formal programme. The hippocampus, a structure in the limbic system situated below the neocortex, is considered to play a central role in the formation of memories. In particular, the hippocampus, which receives input from the later stages of many sensory processes, is thought to configure these sources of information into an outline or skeletal memory (Squire 1992). The hippocampus, however, is not the storage site of memories. Instead it retains the outline memory for only a short period of time. The assumption is that the configured information is passed on to sites in the neocortex where it is stored in a more durable form. Understanding how circuits/networks in the hippocampus mediate memory formation is, then, of some considerable significance. Foster et al. describe their attempts to implement a mathematical model of the CA3 hippocampal network (Treves & Rolls 1992). CA3 has excitatory connections to the entorhinal cortex (a closely related structure) and the dentate gyrus (part of the hippocampus itself). This trisynaptic pathway is thought to be critical in representing configurational information of an event. The attempt of Foster et al. to implement this important hippocampal circuit in various connectionist models is particularly instructive. And it becomes apparent that modelling a single neural network is unlikely to be successful unless the effects of other networks can also be included in the model. The message at bottom is simple: brain networks do not do what they do in isolation. The modelling, however, indicates ways in which the influence of other networks might also be taken into account in future models.

The two final chapters both consider age-related changes in memory but from two very different perspectives. Perfect evaluates the current evidence suggesting that age-related changes in memory arise from neurological degradation of the frontal lobes. One common finding with the elderly is that there is a decline in the ability to recall information while recognition memory is preserved. Recall involves control processing more extensively than recognition, and if the site of executive function is in the frontal lobes then degradation of that brain region should first affect recall rather than recognition. Moreover, the neurological evidence supports the notion that neurons are progressively lost from the frontal regions and, in some respects, individuals over the age of about 80 years often have memory performance profiles that can be likened to those of younger individuals who have suffered neurological injury to frontal regions. However, the data do not support a simple analogy between frontal impairment and age-related changes in memory. As Perfect demonstrates, the pattern of findings are far more complex than that, showing signs of powerful individual differences in age-related memory changes and striking variations in the extent of global versus local changes in memory processes. What is required is a more complex and detailed model that can accommodate variable degrees of change in different groups of aging individuals.

Smith's chapter is more challenging for the student of models of memory, as it presents a fairly detailed application of connectionist modelling to both aging and emotion. Smith is concerned with how connectionist networks settle into stable patterns of activation. A problem here is that a network somehow has to find the optimal state in which to represent knowledge and in doing this has to avoid local maxima. Smith makes the analogy with the problem-solving strategy of hill-climbing. If a person were climbing a hill blindfold, then each time they reached a minor peak they might conclude they had scaled the hilltop. Similarly, in a network (connectionist or neuronal) once a stable but nonoptimal state has been achieved learning may cease. But as the optimal state has not been achieved such learning will ultimately prove ineffectual. Smith suggests that in human memory one of the functions of emotions may be to ensure that such states are avoided. He also suggests that in aging the ability to avoid nonoptimal states of representation may be slowly degrading. So, for instance, in memory retrieval (which he, along with Anderson & Conway and Burgess & Shallice, views as a problem-solving activity) the retrieval processes may terminate too early, leading to general and vague memories rather than vivid and detailed recollections. Smith illustrates how these ideas about changes in memory might be implemented in a connectionist network.

Taken together the chapters in this volume are intended to provide the reader with a broad perspective on current trends in modelling various aspects of human memory. All the contributors focus on problems in the representation of knowledge and evaluate the models they review against empirical findings. The constraints of data on cognitive models of memory are paramount, and without taking research findings into account psychologically plausible models cannot be created. But even when a model has the aim of simulating some aspect of remembering, it still does not follow that the model will be psychologically valid. For example, the adoption of a vector-based type of representation, although allowing many nonformal models to be expressed mathematically and implemented computationally, may nonetheless not correspond to the way in which knowledge is represented in neuronal networks in the brain. Moreover, if the way in which neurons encode knowledge were known, a complete account of human memory would still require an explanation of how represented knowledge was combined into knowledge structures such as memories and mental models.

In conclusion then, an important point to emerge from each of the chapters in the present collection is that modelling raises fundamental issues and compels the researcher to scrutinize the assumptions of their (nonformal) theorizing: two effects that make modelling an especially useful practice for the researcher.

REFERENCES

Baddeley, A. D. 1986. *Working memory*. Oxford: Oxford University Press.

Boden, M. 1988. *Artificial intelligence and natural man*, 2nd edn. Sussex: Harvester.

Brown, G. D. A. & C. Hulme 1996. Modelling item length effects in memory span: no rehearsal needed? *Journal of Memory and Language* **34**, 594–621.

Burgess, N., & G. J. Hitch 1992. Toward a network model of the articulatory loop. *Journal of Memory and Language* **31**, 429–60.

Craik, K. 1943. *The nature of explanation*. Cambridge: Cambridge University Press.

Ericsson, K. A. & W. Kintsch 1995. Long-term working memory. *Psychological Review* **102**, 211–45.

Johnson-Laird, P. N. 1983. *Mental models*. Cambridge: Harvard University Press. Harvard Massachusetts

Kahneman, D. & D. T. Miller 1986. Norm theory: comparing reality to its alternatives. *Psychological Review* **93**, 136–53.

Rumelhart, D. E., & D.A. Norman 1983. Representation in memory. *CHIP technical report* (no. 116). San Diego: Centre for Human Information Processing, University of California.

Squire, L. R. 1992. Memory and the hippocampus: a synthesis from findings with rats, monkeys, and humans. *Psychological Review* **99**, 195–231.

Treves, A. & E. T. Rolls 1992. Computational constraints suggest the need for two distinct input systems to the hippocampal CA3 network. *Hippocampus* **2**, 189–99.

Wittgenstein, L. 1953. *Philosophical investigations*. New York: Macmillan.

PART ONE
Short-term memory

CHAPTER TWO

Models of verbal short-term memory

Susan E. Gathercole

Our capacities to remember linguistic material such as sequences of unrelated words or telephone number-like lists of digits has been extensively researched by cognitive psychologists. The amount of material that can be remembered has been found to be lawfully related to many variables such as the familiarity of the memory items, the length of the memory list, the spoken duration of the memory items, and the degree of overlap in the sounds of the different stimuli in the list (see Baddeley 1996, for review). Research into verbal short-term memory, which commenced in the late 1950s and continued apace until the present time, has established that even simple immediate recall tasks called upon complex mechanisms and processes.

Despite this long-standing interest of experimental psychologists in the nature of verbal short-term memory, a complete theoretical account has yet to be provided. Significant progress in understanding short-term memory has undoubtedly been achieved in the past few decades of research, with the *working memory* model introduced by Baddeley & Hitch (1974; see too, Baddeley 1986, 1990) emerging as the dominant theoretical approach. However, the working memory model provides a broad characterization of key components of short-term memory rather than a detailed specification of the component processes and mechanisms. In an exciting development in the area, several research teams have recently turned their attention to the extent to which verbally specified theories such as the working memory model can be implemented in computational form (e.g. Burgess & Hitch 1992, Brown & Hulme 1996, Hartley & Houghton 1996). This computational approach has been particularly influential in identifying the degree of underspecification of models expressed only in verbal form, which had previously gone largely undetected.

The aim of the present chapter is to introduce a selection of current models of verbal short-term memory, and to assess the extent to which they accommodate the large body of experimental research on short-term memory. Before these models are considered, some of the key findings in the area of short-term memory are introduced.

INFLUENCES ON SHORT-TERM MEMORY PERFORMANCE

In this section, five key features of verbal short-term memory are briefly described. The first three features concern phenomena that have been linked closely to the development of the phonological loop component of the working memory model (see Baddeley 1986, 1990, and Gathercole & Baddeley 1993, for reviews). A further two empirical characteristics of verbal short-term memory, concerning the lexicality of memory items and the close associations between short-term memory and long-term learning, have emerged more recently as core features that need to be addressed by any complete theoretical models of short-term memory performance. Later in the chapter, the extent to which each model of short-term memory can satisfactorily accommodate each of these features of immediate memory performance will be evaluated.

WORD LENGTH

Serial recall of unrelated sequences of verbal items is substantially better for lists containing items that are short in articulatory duration (e.g., one-syllable words such as *sum*, *wit*, *hate*) than long (e.g., *university*, *opportunity*, *aluminium*). This phenomenon is known as the word length effect, and was first investigated by Baddeley et al. (1975). They established that the word length effect occurs both for memory lists presented auditorily (spoken by the experimenter) and for lists presented visually (in the form of printed words).

This phenomenon has been found to be remarkably robust, and despite its conventional label of "word length effect", the same sensitivity to the spoken duration of the items in the memory list is found when non-words instead of words are used as the stimuli (Hulme et al. 1991). When the memory sequence is presented in auditory form (with the experimenter vocalizing the list items), the word length effect in recall has been found in children as young as four years of age (Hulme et al. 1984).

Baddeley et al. (1975) argued that the word length effect is a product of the precise spoken duration of the memory items, rather than the amount of phonological information or number of syllables *per se*. They compared serial recall for lists of two-syllable words with either relatively short spoken durations (such as *wicket* and *bishop*) or long durations (such as *harpoon* and *Friday*). Recall was significantly better for the "short" than the "long" items, indicating the importance of spoken length of memory items for recall.

Despite this result, the precise contributions of spoken duration and amount of phonological information to the word length effect remain rather unclear. Caplan et al. (1992) challenged the assumption that it is the spoken duration of the items to be remembered that is critical, presenting evidence that the word length effect disappears when the numbers of phonemes and syllables in words containing either short or long vowels is controlled. This debate continues, and remains as yet unresolved (Baddeley & Andrade 1994, Caplan & Waters 1994).

The word length effect has been traditionally tied to the rehearsal process. This account is presented in detail in the later section on the working memory model. In brief, Baddeley et al. (1975) argued that rehearsal involves the subvocal articulation of memory items in real time, and therefore that lengthy items take relatively longer to rehearse and hence are more likely to be lost from memory in between successive rehearsal than short items. However, findings arising from an ingenious series of experiments reported by Cowan et al. (1992) point to the spoken recall process as a possible alternative source of the word length effect. In these experiments, memory lists were presented in which the spoken length of the items in the first and second halves of the lists were independently varied rather than being the same as in the original word length paradigm. Thus in some lists short words followed long words, and in other lists long words followed short words. Recall of individual words in the memory lists was found to be strongly influenced by the amount of time taken by subjects to recall the earlier items in the sequence, rather than by the length of the words *per se*. These findings suggest that the word length effect arises, in part at least, from the greater opportunity for decay of memory representations during recall of lists containing long rather than short items. Similar conclusions were reached by Avons et al. (1994).

A further complication for rehearsal-based accounts of the word length effect arises from studies of individuals who are unable to speak. Baddeley & Wilson (1985) investigated the short-term memory characteristics of an adult patient who had acquired language normally, but who as a result of acquired brain damage became anarthric (completely unable to produce discriminable speech sounds). Bishop & Robson (1989) studied a group of individuals with congenital anarthria resulting from cerebral palsy at birth; these individuals had never be able to produce speech. In both cases, memory performance for these individuals shows the normal sensitivity to word length. The word length effect, and so by implication rehearsal, therefore cannot be located in the operation of explicit articulatory processes.

In summary, the word length effect is a substantial and robust phenomenon in immediate serial recall. Its origins appear to be related to the amount of speech information in the memory items.Although traditionally linked closely with rehearsal, it is becoming increasingly apparent that the word length effect is not simply due to subvocal articulatory activity during presentation of the memory list, and that a contributory factor is probably the different delays involved in recalling lists containing long and short memory items.

ARTICULATORY SUPPRESSION

Immediate serial recall of memory lists is significantly diminished if subjects are required to repeat aloud an irrelevant sequence such as "hiya, hiya, hiya" continuously during presentation of the memory list (Murray 1967, Peterson & Johnson 1971). This technique is known as "articulatory suppression" and, like the word length effect, has been widely attributed to the rehearsal process. Specifically, it has been argued that articulatory suppression prevents the subjects from actively rehearsing the list items during presentation. Consistent with this view, Baddeley et al. (1975) found that when memory lists were presented visually (as printed words), the word length effect disappears when subjects engage in articulatory suppression during presentation of the memory sequence.According to the rehearsal interpretation, this finding arises because the benefits to rehearsing short over long words are lost when subjects are prevented from rehearsing by engaging in articulatory suppression.

Findings when memory lists are presented auditorily are rather more complicated. Recall of auditory lists is depressed under conditions of articulatory suppression, but to an extent that is equivalent for lists of short and long words (Baddeley et al. 1975); in other words, the word length effect remains intact. Subsequent investigation has, however, established that if the period of articulatory suppression is extended throughout recall, the word length effect disappears even with auditorily presented sequences (Baddeley et al. 1984).

PHONOLOGICAL SIMILARITY

Recall of memory lists is poorer if the items are similar to one another in sound structure (e.g. *B, C, T,* or *cat, rat, mat*) rather than phonologically distinct (e.g. *R, F, H,* or *man, egg, boat*). This phonological similarity effect was first reported by Conrad & Hull (1964) with lists of letters presented visually to the subjects, ruling out problems of acoustic discriminability as a possible source of the phenomenon. The effect contrasts with the relative insensitivity of serial recall to increases in the orthographic or semantic similarity of the memory list (Baddeley 1966).

Like the word length effect discussed above, the phonological similarity effect is removed under conditions of articulatory suppression, provided that the lists are presented visually (Levy 1971, Peterson & Johnson 1971). In contrast to the length effect, though, the similarity effect persists with articulatory suppression for auditory memory lists, even if the suppression activity continues throughout the recall as well as the presentation of the memory list (Baddeley et al. 1984).

LEXICALITY

It has been known for some time that serial recall is superior for memory lists containing words rather than nonwords. This lexicality effect has recently been the subject of systematic experimental investigation, with the aim of specifying the detailed mechanisms or processes underpinning the higher levels of recall for words than for nonwords. Across a series of studies, Hulme, Brown and colleagues (Hulme et al. 1991, Roodenrys et al. 1993) have provided convincing evidence that the lexicality effect is due to the beneficial consequences of familiarity with the phonological structure of the words rather than knowledge of the meanings of the words. This account fits well with much earlier findings of the relative insensitivity of memory span to the semantic characteristics of memory lists (Baddeley 1986).

The influence of knowledge about the phonological structure of familiar words has even been found in immediate memory tasks involving nonwords. Using a paradigm in which individual nonwords such as "blonterstaping" are presented to a child for immediate repetition, Gathercole et al. (1991) reported a significant positive correlation between the accuracy with which young children (aged 4 to 6 years) repeated nonwords and adult ratings of the "wordlikeness" of the individual nonwords. Thus, nonwords rated high in wordlikeness such as "defermication" tended to be repeated more accurately than unwordlike nonwords such as "loddernapeish". In a further study, it was shown that this "wordlikeness effect" in nonword repetition cannot be attributed to differences in the amounts of phonological information between the nonwords of low and high rated wordlikeness (Gathercole 1995). A wordlikeness effect has also been demonstrated in adults' memory for pairs of nonwords (Gathercole & Martin 1996).

Together, both the lexicality effect and the wordlikeness effect in nonword repetition establish that short-term memory is strongly influenced by knowledge concerning the phonological structure of the language. Any complete theoretical account of short-term memory will therefore need to specify the ways in which long-term knowledge contributed to immediate memory performance.

LONG-TERM LEARNING

Cognitive psychologists have long been interested in the function of short-term memory, as well as in identifying the specific mechanisms and processes underpinning performance in laboratory tests of verbal short-term memory. The view advanced by Butterworth et al. (1986: 707) that "it seems ecologically implausible to postulate a structure or process whose sole function is to mediate the immediate recall of strings of unrelated items" was shared by many.

Considerable progress in identifying the function of verbal short-term memory has been made in the past ten years or so. There is now very strong evidence that verbal short-term memory plays a critical role in the long-term learning of new phonological forms involved in acquiring new vocabulary. Many of the relevant findings have come from use of the paired-associate learning paradigm to simulate natural vocabulary acquisition (e.g. Baddeley et al. 1988). In the critical version of this task, subjects are presented with a set of word–nonword pairs such as "table–pilkatu" in a series of trials; the experimenter tests their learning of the nonwords by cueing the subjects with the associated word (e.g., "table– ?"). Subjects' abilities to learn word–nonword pairs in this paradigm appear to be constrained very directly by factors influencing verbal short-term memory, whereas the learning of word–word pairs (e.g., "table–donkey") is independent of such factors. Nonword learning is influenced by variables such as word length, phonological similarity and articulatory suppression, in much the same manner as tests of immediate verbal memory (Papagno et al. 1992, Papagno & Vallar 1992). Also, individuals with diminished verbal short-term memory capacities, as a result of either acquired brain damage or a developmental disorder, have been shown to have highly selective impairments in nonword learning (Baddeley 1993, Baddeley et al. 1988, Baddeley & Wilson 1993).

There is also a wealth of evidence linking individual differences in children's verbal memory skills with their abilities to learn new words. Young children's scores on immediate memory tests such as nonword repetition are excellent predictors of their natural vocabulary knowledge (Gathercole & Baddeley 1989, Gathercole et al. 1992, Michas & Henry 1994), of their abilities to acquire a foreign language (Service 1992), and of their speed of learning nonwords in an experimental setting (Gathercole & Baddeley 1990, Michas & Henry 1994).

The strength of this association between verbal short-term memory and long-term phonological learning has led some researchers to propose that one of the primary functions of the immediate memory system is to support word learning in the native language (e.g. Gathercole & Baddeley 1993). A critical requirement of a full model of short-term memory is therefore that it provides an account of how short-term memory mediates long-term phonological learning.

MODELS OF VERBAL SHORT-TERM MEMORY

In this section, four current theoretical accounts of short-term memory are considered. The models differ notably in their formal presentation: two accounts are expressed in purely verbal form (Baddeley 1986, Gathercole & Martin 1996), one is a neural network model (Burgess & Hitch 1992), and the final model is a mathematical implementation of a verbal account of short-term memory (Brown & Hulme 1996). Despite these differences, all four accounts are similar in their intended scopes, aiming to specify the component processes and mechanisms contributing to performance on tests of verbal short-term memory. After summarizing each model, the extent to which the model provides a convincing account of the core empirical phenomena, reviewed in the previous section and summarized in Table 2.1, will then be evaluated.

THE PHONOLOGICAL LOOP AND WORKING MEMORY

The working memory model introduced by Baddeley & Hitch (1974) consisted of three principal components: the central executive, the articulatory loop and the visuospatial sketchpad. The functions of the central executive include the processing and storage of information, the regulation of the flow of information through the working memory system, and the retrieval of information from other memory systems.

TABLE 2.1
**Summary of the extent to which the four models of verbal short-term memory
can account for five core memory phenomena.**

Memory phenomena	Models of verbal short-term memory			
	Phonological loop Baddeley 1986	Network model Burgess & Hitch 1992	Trace decay model Brown & Hulme 1995	Interactive model Gathercole & Martin 1996
Word length	++	++	++	+
Articulatory suppression	++	+	+	?
Phonological similarity	+	+	?	?
Lexicality	?	?	++	++
Long-term learning	?	?	?	++

++ Excellent account; + Good but incomplete account; ? Beyond the scope of the model.

The articulatory loop and sketchpad are slave systems, specialized for the processing and maintenance of particular types of information. It is the articulatory loop component, specialized for the temporary storage of verbal material, that is of most relevance here. In the original working memory model, Baddeley & Hitch proposed that the articulatory loop consisted of an articulatory rehearsal loop with a capacity corresponding to the amount of information that could be articulated within about two seconds (see also Baddeley et al. 1975). This account was revised by Baddeley and colleagues (Baddeley 1986, Salame & Baddeley 1982, Vallar & Baddeley 1984), and is now known as the phonological loop (Baddeley 1990).

The phonological loop comprises two components, the phonological short-term store and the subvocal rehearsal process, as shown in Figure 2.1. The phonological store represents material in a phonological code that decays with time. A process of articulatory-like rehearsal serves to refresh the decaying representations in the phonological store and so to maintain the memory items. The rehearsal process is also used to recode nonauditory inputs, such as the pictures of nameable objects or the printed forms of words, into their phonological form so that they can be held in the phonological store. In contrast, heard speech gains direct access to the phonological store without requiring articulatory rehearsal.

It is difficult to overestimate the impact of the accounts of immediate verbal memory function provided by the working memory approach over the past 20 years or so. The approach has stimulated a large body of experimental research, and continues to do so. This relatively simple

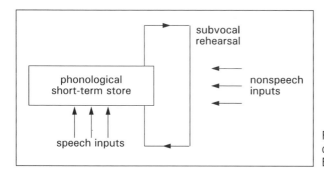

FIG. 2.1.   The phonological loop model, based on Baddeley (1986).

two-component account has proved extremely successful in accommodating a wide range of findings both from experimental studies of normal adult subjects and from neuropsychological investigations of patients with acquired brain damage (see Gathercole & Baddeley 1993, and Gathercole 1994, for reviews). The model has also been very useful in guiding the analysis of developmental changes in short-term memory function (see Gathercole & Hitch 1993, for review). It is this use of convergent sources of evidence from many different paradigms and subject populations that is one of the unique strengths and hallmarks of the working memory approach. For the purposes of this chapter, however, the principal focus is on the extent to which the phonological loop provides an adequate account of the empirical features of verbal short-term memory outlined earlier.

Word length and articulatory suppression

As the concept of the articulatory loop was specifically developed to account for data relating to the word length effect (Baddeley et al. 1975), it is perhaps unsurprising that it accommodates the data relating to immediate recall so well. According to the revised phonological loop model, the lower levels of recall on memory lists containing items of longer articulatory duration reflect the time-based operation of the rehearsal process. Lengthier items take longer to articulate subvocally, and so allow greater opportunity for decay of the phonological representations in the short-term store, between successive rehearsals. With increasing articulatory duration of the memory items, therefore, the probability of a representation in the phonological store decaying to a indiscriminable level is increased.

Articulatory suppression is assumed to occupy the mechanisms involved in articulatory production, thereby preventing the rehearsal of the contents of the phonological store and so allowing decay. This account readily accommodates the finding that with visually presented memory sequences, there is no word length effect under conditions of articulatory suppression (Baddeley et al. 1975). The reason for this is that without the opportunity for subvocal rehearsal, visually presented verbal material cannot even gain admission to the phonological store.

For several years the persistence of a word length effect with auditory lists even under articulatory suppression was problematic for this account, as according to the model outlined in Figure 2.1, rehearsal is blocked by irrelevant articulation irrespective of the mode of input. So, auditory material will gain access to the phonological store because of its privileged status, but there should be no rehearsal and hence no word length effect. The finding of Baddeley et al. (1984) that the word length effect for auditory lists is eliminated if suppression extends into the recall period provided a means of reconciling these findings with the phonological loop model. Baddeley et al. suggested that when subjects are required only to suppress during presentation of the memory list, there may be sufficient discriminable information remaining in the phonological store by the end of the list to give them the opportunity to rehearse prior to or during recall. This gives rise to the word length effect. By preventing rehearsal during the whole trial, this opportunity is denied and so the word length effect disappears.

So far, then, the phonological loop model provides a parsimonious account of the core findings relating to word length and articulatory suppression. The more recent findings of Cowan et al. (1992) that memory performance is directly related to the amount of delay prior to output do not, however, fit well with the strong claim that the subvocal rehearsal process is the sole basis of the word length effect in immediate recall. However, the data are compatible with a weaker claim that the rehearsal process is one possible source of the word length effect, and that decay prior to output can also contribute to the better recall of lists of short than long words. In fact, the "output decay" account alone also fails to provide a complete account of the available word length data. There have been many demonstrations of the absence of word length effects (for example, in young children with pictorial inputs, and with articulatory suppression) in the presence of spoken recall procedures (e.g. Baddeley et al. 1975, Hitch & Halliday 1983, Johnston et al. 1987). Spoken recall is therefore not a necessary condition for the occurrence of a word length effect. In short, it appears likely that the word length effect can arise from a number of sources, and that these sources include both the time-dependent rehearsal process and from decay during output.

A further problem for the phonological loop model concerns the occurrence of a normal word length effect in individuals who cannot produce speech, due to either congenital deficits (Bishop & Robson 1989) or to brain damage acquired in adulthood (Baddeley & Wilson 1985). This finding indicates that the source of the word length effect cannot be located in the processes of either planning or executing the articulatory commands corresponding to the production of speech, as these processes cannot be controlled by anarthric subjects. The articulatory basis of the rehearsal process is therefore in question, a problem acknowledged by Baddeley (1990) in his renaming the "articulatory loop" as the "phonological loop". One possible solution is that rehearsal consists of activating the mapping of phonological specifications (presumably within the phonological store) onto abstract motor commands, and that the capacity to map component speech sounds onto their motor equivalents is part of our biological endowment for language as outlined by the motor theory of speech perception (Liberman & Mattingley 1985). This possibility is discussed in more detail by Gathercole & Hitch (1993).

In summary, the current concept of the phonological loop accounts for many, but not all, of the findings relating to the word length and articulatory suppression effects in immediate recall. A weak version of the model, according to which word length effects may arise either as a consequence of rehearsal or of decay of the contents of the phonological store during output, fits the available data well. The problem of exactly what psychological processes are harnessed in rehearsal remains. We shall see later in the chapter, though, that this problem is shared by all current models in varying degrees.

Phonological similarity

According to the phonological loop model, the source of phonological similarity effects in immediate recall is the phonological store. It is argued that memory items that share a similar phonological structure will become more rapidly indiscriminable from one another due to decay than items with non-overlapping phonological structures. A simple example is provided by contrasting the consequences of loss of a single phoneme from the phonologically similar word pair "cat" and "bat", and the phonologically distinct pair "cat" and "bin". In the former case, the loss of the first phoneme from both words would leave the rememberer with no information on which memory representation corresponded to which item, leaving no opportunity but to guess at recall. In contrast, with the distinctive pair, loss of the initial phoneme in both cases would leave residual information that is sufficiently distinctive to provide the rememberer with a good chance of reconstructing the partial representation in the phonological store with the correct lexical item.

Articulatory suppression prevents rehearsal and therefore blocks access of visually presented verbal material to the phonological store, according to the phonological loop model. This model therefore readily predicts the finding that with suppression, there is no phonological similarity effect for visual inputs (Levy 1971, Peterson & Johnson 1971). It also accommodates the persistence of a phonological similarity effect for auditory lists under conditions of suppression, because auditory material gains obligatory access to the phonological store, which is the source of the similarity effect.

The account provided by the phonological loop model of the effects of phonological similarity on recall is therefore straightforward. The detailed interactions between phonological similarity, concurrent activity and modality of input are readily captured by the simple two-component model.

Lexicality

The phonological loop is by nature alexical. The phonological store maintains memory items in terms of their component phonological structure in a way that is entirely independent of whether their phonological forms correspond to familiar words or not. On its own, the phonological loop model therefore provides no account for either the superior recall of lists of words compared with nonwords (the lexicality effect; Hulme et al. 1991) or the better recall of nonwords with wordlike than unwordlike phonological patterns (the wordlikeness effect; Gathercole et al. 1991, Gathercole, 1995).

In order to provide an account of the lexicality and wordlikeness effects, the working memory model needs to identify a mechanism or process by which knowledge about the sounds structure of the language can be applied to the contents of the phonological store. One possibility is that the rememberer attempts to match the phonological representations in the phonological store with the stored phonological specifications of familiar words in the mental lexicon. This provides the opportunity for clean-up or "redintegration" (Schweikert 1993) of partially decayed phonological representations.

As yet, no explicit attempt has been made to extend the phonological loop model so that it can accommodate the influences of long-term knowledge on immediate recall. In principle, however, there is no reason why links between the phonological loop and more permanent knowledge bases cannot be specified in an elaborated version of the phonological loop model.

Long-term learning

Much of the research identifying short-term memory constraints on long-term learning has emerged from research teams exploring the ecological function of the phonological loop (see Gathercole & Baddeley 1993, for review). The current model of the phonological loop as it stands, however, fails to specify any means by which more permanent specifications can be constructed of phonological information held within the phonological store. The ways in which new sound patterns are learned on the basis of their temporary representations in the phonological store remain to be explained.

Summary

The model of the phonological loop provides simple and powerful accounts of three of the most extensively investigated phenomena within short-term memory research: the word length, articulatory suppression and phonological similarity effects. Despite continuing uncertainty about the precise nature of the rehearsal process, the two-component model provides an appealingly parsimonious account of a large convergent body of evidence. The main shortcoming of the model concerns its apparent dislocation from other memory processes and mechanisms. The working memory model specifies links only between the central executive and the phonological loop. However, it is becoming increasingly clear, first that the temporary storage provided by the phonological loop probably mediates long-term phonological learning, and second that immediate memory performance reflects a combination of temporary phonological storage and long-term knowledge concerning the structure of the language. In summary, then, the internal structure of the phonological loop captures well the findings from a large experimental literature on serial recall of word lists. The recent trend towards using nonwords as memory stimuli and the increasing interest on learning paradigms as well as single trial memory tasks has, however, made it clear that the phonological loop does not exist in isolation, and that it interacts in complex ways that have yet to be identified both with other memory systems and with language learning processes.

A NETWORK MODEL OF THE PHONOLOGICAL LOOP

In 1992, Burgess & Hitch presented a network model based on the phonological loop. In fact, the phonological loop model as described by Baddeley (1986) does not specify the mechanisms and processes underpinning the retention of serial order in sufficient detail to support a computational model, so the Burgess & Hitch model should be viewed as an implementation of a developed version of the phonological loop model rather than its computational equivalent. Burgess & Hitch devised a multilayered network model in which activation in units within each layer feed forward to successive layers. The capacity to accommodate basic experimental data was assessed across a series of simulations.

One of the major aims of Burgess & Hitch (1992) in designing their model was to specify in detail the way in which serial order is retained in immediate verbal memory paradigms. The concept of the phonological store has nothing to say about the way in which adjacent phonemes in a memory sequence are stored. Given that the majority of immediate verbal memory tasks require the retention of order as well as item information (i.e., the item not only has to be recalled, but recalled in the correct position), this is clearly an important issue. On the basis of existing human data on the detailed errors made in serial recall tasks (e.g. Conrad 1964, Wickelgren 1965, Bjork & Healy 1974), Burgess & Hitch proposed that recall is mediated by the retention of both item–item associations (often known as "chaining") and item–position associations.

The basic structure of the Burgess & Hitch model is summarized in Figure 2.2. Each of the layers in the model (the context nodes, input phoneme nodes, word nodes, competitive filter and output phoneme nodes) consists of a set of nodes with varying levels of activation. Activation feeds forward in the direction of the arrows shown in the illustration. The presentation of a memory item excites the phoneme nodes corresponding to the phonemes it contains; activation is then passed from the individual phoneme nodes to nodes in the word layer that contain those phonemes. The most active word node is selected by the competitive filter, and the output phoneme nodes corresponding to the word are immediately activated. This latter process of the selection of a word node and activation of its phonemes in the output phoneme layer corresponds to "articulation". Once a word node is selected by the

FIG. 2.2.   The basic architecture of the Burgess & Hitch (1992) network model of the articulatory loop. Copyright © 1992 by Academic Press, Inc. Reprinted with permission.

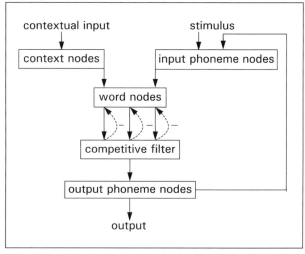

competitive filter, it is immediately inhibited to allow the articulation of a successive "word". The phonemic output for a word is fed back to activate the phonemic input for the next word in the list. This feedback loop operates by applying weights that link the phonemic output of one item with the phonemic input of the next item in the list during its original presentation; this process represents the operation of a chaining mechanism in which item–item associations are stored.

In addition, there is a layer of context nodes that are associated with each word at input, to provide item–position associations. The context for each item simply consists of a random pattern of activation across a subset of nodes within the context layer. An important feature is that this pattern of activation changes progressively during presentation of the memory list, with a subset of the nodes retaining the levels of activation over successive items. In this way, the contexts for the items are temporally correlated, with greater overlap in the context patterns for items closer together in the memory list.

The model therefore has three sets of permanent connections: the links between input phonemes and words, between nodes in the word layer and the nodes in the competitive filter, and between the filter nodes and the output phoneme layer. Basically, these connections represent the prelearned knowledge about the sound structure of familiar words and the ways in which they are articulated. During presentation of a memory list, temporary activation occurs at several points in the model. First, the active nodes in the context layer become associated with the word node excited by the input phonemes. Second, the most active word node is selected (and then immediately inhibited) and its output phonemes activated. Third, temporary associations are learned between the phonemes activated in the output phoneme layer and the subsequent input phonemes (i.e. the next word presented). In this way, the associations between successive items are learned. All of the temporary associations (weights) are subject to decay, producing imperfect levels of learning.

Recall or rehearsal (there is no distinction between the two) are initiated in the model by re-presenting the input phonemes and their associated context. Activation is then passed through successive layers on the network as described for the list presentation above. Excitation of the output phonemes leads to activation of a set of input phonemes that in correct recall will correspond to the next item in the sequence. However, the feedback weights decay with time (modelled as the number of active output phoneme nodes), and so will not result in perfect activation of the phonemic input of the next item. Correct recall of the next item is also aided by the existing pattern of activity in the context layer. As the context nodes associated with specific inputs are temporally correlated (i.e. more similar with increasing adjacency in the memory list), the context for a preceding item in the list will lead to partial activation of the word node associated with the next item in the sequence. In other words, the context primes the next word to some degree.

How does this architecture correspond to the structure of the phonological loop model? Burgess & Hitch equate the contents of the phonological store with the chaining weights that store associations between the output phonemes for one word and the input phonemes for the next in sequence. Like the putative phonological store, the chaining or feedback weights are subject to decay to a degree that is roughly proportional to the time to articulate the item. Rehearsal or articulation is represented by the selection of the most active word by the competitive filter.

Most of the simulations presented by Burgess & Hitch are based on the single presentation of a memory sequence and a single rehearsal or output. Below is considered the degree of success of this network model in capturing the core features of verbal short-term memory performance.

Word length and articulatory suppression

The model simulates the human data showing a linear relationship between level of recall and the length of the words in the memory list very effectively; recall declines systematically with increasing length of the memory item. The word length effect in the network model is due to the decay function on temporary weights between nodes in successive layers, which is proportional to the total number of phonemes output. Note that this source of the word length effect does not correspond to the part of the model that corresponds most closely, in phenomenal terms at least, to rehearsal, which is the selection of a single word by the competitive filter.

Articulatory suppression is mimicked in the Burgess & Hitch model by reducing to zero the feedback weights running from the output phoneme layer to the input phoneme layer. Thus, rehearsal is prevented by disabling the contribution of chaining associations to the retrieval of the next item. In this way, suppression and word length effects are attributed to different levels of activity in the network model. In the human data, articulatory suppression during list presentation eliminates the word length effect with visual but not auditory presentation of the memory list (Baddeley et al. 1975). The network model does not provide a particularly satisfactory simulation of either pattern of findings. With the feedback weights disabled, a diminished but nonetheless reliable word length effect remains. This is due to the increased decay of activation in the context layer as the number of phonemes in a memory item increases.

The model itself is modality-independent, and therefore does not address modality-specific aspects of the human data. It is, however, important to note that the residual word length effect under "articulatory suppression" in the model captures neither the visual nor the auditory data in normal human subjects.

Phonological similarity

The network model yields a good simulation of the experimental data on phonological similarity, producing a sizeable reduction in serial recall when phonologically similar rather than distinctive memory sequences are presented. The similarity effect in the model is due to the operation of the feedback weights running from the output phoneme layer to the input phoneme layer. The example provided by Burgess & Hitch is for the letter sequence a, b, f, c, q. For this list, positive weights will be learned that link the output phoneme for the "ee" sound (present in both the letters b and c) with the input phonemes corresponding to the sounds "e" and "f" as in f, and "k" and "you" as in q. So, when the letter b is recalled (i.e. its output phonemes activated), some of the input phonemes nodes for f will be excited, although to a lesser extent than the phonemes for the real adjacent item, q.

In the simulation data, this phonological similarity effect largely disappears under the "suppression" condition in which feedback activity from the output to input phoneme layer is prevented, because the sources of the effect are the input phonemes that now receive almost no activation and hence make little contribution to activation of word nodes. The model therefore provides an adequate simulation of the interactive effects of phonological similarity and articulatory suppression in human data (e.g. Peterson & Johnson 1971). Note, though, that the preservation of the similarity effect under conditions of suppression with auditory presentation in experimental studies cannot be captured by the network model, which has only a single modality-independent mode of operation.

Burgess & Hitch point out also that their model fails to yield the more detailed pattern of recall errors reported in an early study on phonological similarity effects by Baddeley (1968). In this study, serial recall of lists of phonologically similar and distinct letters was compared with that of lists containing alternating sequences of similar and distinct items (e.g. a, b, f, c, q, d). When recall for each individual list position was plotted, a sawtooth recall function emerged that zigzaged between the serial position curves for all similar or all dissimilar items. Thus recall of the similar items in the alternating lists corresponded approximately to recall of items in the similar-only lists, and so too recall of the distinct items was comparable in the alternating and pure lists. Burgess & Hitch's network model, in contrast, produces a smooth recall function for lists containing alternating similar and distinct lists that lies between the functions for the similar and dissimilar pure lists. The reason is that the effect of phonological similarity in their model is located within the feedback weights which serve to produce chaining associations between pairs of adjacent items in the memory sequence. This chaining works only on a pair-by-pair basis. Thus any factor that diminishes recall of one item will similarly impair the chances of correctly recalling the next item too. To reproduce the experimental data showing the scalloped effect in which it is the similarity of the item with non-adjacent items that determines recall, there would have to be some input of the contextual input (which serves the retention of item-position information) into the phoneme layers.

Lexicality

The network model of the articulatory loop was designed only to simulate recall of lists of words, as a starting point. Although the initial input to the model is in phonological form, the competitive filter acts simply to select the most active word node for activation of output phonemes. There is therefore no way that recall of nonwords can be simulated in the current version of the model, as they could never be rehearsed or output. And quite apart from this problem, the structure of the input and output phoneme layers is parallel rather than serial; thus the phonological input for the words "dog" and "god" would be equivalent in the present form of the model. Burgess & Hitch's decision to represent the phonemes in this way and to model recall of words only represents a simplifying assumption designed to allow a first attempt at modelling serial recall; they acknowledge these limitations, and make no claims to providing a complete account. Given the new impetus to explaining the ways in which memory for nonwords as well as words is achieved (Hulme et al. 1991, Gathercole 1995), this constraint on the network must however be considered to represent a significant limitation in the model's scope.

Some recent advances in extending the network approach to immediate serial recall from words to nonwords have been made by Hartley & Houghton (1996). Their network model has a rather different focus from that of Burgess & Hitch, being designed principally to simulate the contribution of syllable structure processes to constraining errors in nonword recall that would arise if nonword inputs were processed simply as phonological sequences. However, both of these network models adopt similar solutions concerning the way that serial order effects can be simulated in parallel processing structures, and could in principle be combined to produce a hybrid model in which both familiar and unfamiliar phonological forms could be output (Hartley & Houghton 1996). Both lexicality and wordlikeness effects should be emergent properties of such a model, as a result of (a) the beneficial consequences of both phoneme and lexical representations for words over nonwords, and (b) the greater (but incomplete) activation of lexical structures by wordlike than by unwordlike nonwords.

Learning

The domain of learning language structures has been shown to be particularly well served by parallel distributed processing models (e.g. McClelland & Rumelhart 1986; Pinker 1991). There should therefore be no reason in principle why the network approach to modelling serial recall could not be extended to accommodate the evidence of close links between short-term memory and long-term learning of new phonological forms reviewed earlier in the chapter. At present, however, the Burgess & Hitch (1992) model is designed only to simulate recall of word lists and therefore cannot process unfamiliar phonological forms, as discussed above. Moreover, although it can "learn" new associations within the memory sequence, the resulting weights do not result in the construction of new word nodes, as would be required if the model was to simulate word learning. According to Hartley & Houghton (1996), however, such a learning capability is well within the reach of a hybrid network model designed to handle nonwords as well as word inputs, such that "the acquisition of new lexical-phonological knowledge will depend upon the effective operation of the short-term component of the model".

Summary

The network model of the phonological loop developed by Burgess & Hitch (1992) provides an excellent start to specifying the detailed psychological processes and mechanisms that are required to support the retention of word lists. The model effectively simulates basic data on word length, articulatory suppression and phonological similarity effects, with some areas of further modification identified by the authors themselves. The scope of the model also extends beyond these phenomena, providing, in particular, very good accounts of the balance of item and order errors in immediate recall and of serial position functions. The phonological loop model of Baddeley (1986) is not sufficiently detailed to address this finer grain of detail in human recall data.

The model is less successful in accounting for the more recent bodies of evidence relating to lexicality effects and to short-term memory constraints on long-term learning. However, these limitations are more practical than fundamental, and arise largely because of the need to confine the area of experimental evidence that can be addressed by the first version of the model. There is every reason to believe that this network approach could be effectively extended to accommodate both human data on memory for nonwords and the long-term learning function of the immediate memory system.

A TRACE DECAY MODEL

Whereas Burgess & Hitch (1992) aimed to develop a relatively complete computational model based on the phonological loop that could simulate some classic phenomena from human short-term memory data, Brown & Hulme (1995) have recently put the computational approach to short-term memory to good use in a very different way. Their principal aim was to determine whether the word length effect in immediate recall can be an emergent property of a model that has no subvocal rehearsal process, thereby challenging the traditional working memory assumption that sensitivity to word length is necessarily an indicator of rehearsal activity (e.g. Baddeley et al. 1975, Baddeley 1986). In contrast to Burgess & Hitch, Brown & Hulme did not attempt to provide a complete model of short-term memory function. Their results nonetheless are extremely important in demonstrating the value of the computational approach as a means of providing simple tests of whether theoretical assumptions in verbally specified theories provide adequate accounts of human data.

Brown & Hulme constructed a mathematical model of the presentation and recall of verbal sequences which is illustrated in Figure 2.3. The model represents the memory trace for an item, in successive time slices corresponding to 0.1 second each. Thus a short word is modelled as four successive time slices, and a long one as seven 0.1-second units. The interval between successive items in the memory sequences is also represented in an appropriate number of time slices. Each time slice has an activation value that can vary between 0 and 1, and that can be interpreted as the trace strength of that component of the memory item or as its probability of correct recall. These activation values are

FIG. 2.3. Example of the temporal structure of the presentation and recall of a two-item memory sequence, in the Brown & Hulme (1995) model. Copyright © 1995 by Academic Press, Inc. Reprinted with permission.

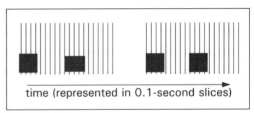

time (represented in 0.1-second slices)

updating every 0.1 second. The probability of correctly recalling an item is calculated by taking the product of activation values for each time slice in the item.

In the basic model, trace strength is lost via three processes. First, each segment has an initial activation value of 0.95. Second, a trace decay process is continuously applied to all segments until recalled; specifically, the activation value for each segment decays by 0.0001 every 0.1 second. Third, there is a 10 per cent chance that a segment is not recallable which is independent of its current trace strength. The purpose of this third process is to represent forgetting due to reasons such as distraction during recall which are independent of decay.

Word length

This model is capable of producing the classic linear relationship found in experimental data between memory span and the articulatory duration of the memory items: as the time taken to articulate memory items increases, the probability of correctly recalling all items in the series decreases. In subsequent demonstrations, Brown & Hulme established that the trace decay parameter alone was sufficient to give rise to this word length effect. In one case, the only source of loss of activation was the trace decay function, and the linear span-rate function emerged. In another demonstration, the trace decay parameter was omitted, so that trace strength was lost only as a consequence of the initial imperfect registration value of 0.95 and of the 10 per cent chance that any segment could not be recalled. Because there are more segments in the longer words (the values taken in this model were four segments for a short memory item and seven segments for a long item), the probability that all segments constituting a memory item would be recallable declines with the articulatory duration of the memory sequence.

The model therefore succeeds in providing a neat demonstration that the word length effect in immediate recall does not necessarily arise from subvocal rehearsal. Poorer recall of long compared with short words can arise as a consequence of trace decay during presentation and recall, providing a good account of the effects of recall delay on probability of recall reported by Cowan et al. (1992). Word length effects also occur in the model as a function of any process that leads to imperfect trace strengths of individual segments, as correct recall of lengthy items requires the accurate retrieval of more segments than recall of short items.

One of the notable features of Brown & Hulme's mathematical model is that it provides a reinterpretation of the normal word length effect data found in anarthric subjects (Baddeley & Wilson 1985, Bishop &

Robson 1989). The individuals tested in these studies could not articulate speech and hence presumably could not engage in the process of subvocal articulation conventionally assumed to reflect rehearsal. The simulation data from Brown & Hulme indicate that decay of the phonological memory trace in these subjects could be sufficient to give rise to their sensitivity to word length in recall. The issue of whether in "normal" subjects the source of word length effects is trace decay, subvocal rehearsal or some other mechanism of information loss that is sensitive to articulatory duration, however, remains an open issue.

Articulatory suppression

Requiring subjects to engage in irrelevant speech activity during a memory task is usually considered to disrupt recall by occupying the articulatory processes and mechanisms involved in rehearsal. How, then, can the simple trace decay model of Brown & Hulme, which has no rehearsal component, accommodate the disruptive effects of suppression on immediate recall? One possible solution adopted by these authors is to assume that suppression causes the memory traces to be degraded as a consequence of interference (see also Nairne 1990). Brown & Hulme implemented this process by degrading the memory trace by 0.5 per cent of its value for every 0.1-second time slice. Unsurprisingly, this adjustment led to a decline in memory span. More impressively, though, the effect of "suppression" in the model was to impair disproportionately the recall of short words. Sensitivity to word length was therefore diminished under suppression, showing some convergence with the human data. The reason for this effect of suppression in the model is that the gaps between presentations and recalls are longer for short words than long words, providing that presentation and recall are paced.

Thus the model is capable to some degree of capturing experimental effects of articulatory suppression. Unlike the word length effect, though, it is not a straightforward emergent property of the simple trace decay model and its implementation has a distinctly *post hoc* quality.

Phonological similarity

As Brown & Hulme acknowledge, their model is unable to accommodate the phonological similarity effect, as it does not "represent" the phonological structure of a memory item in any way other than the amount of time it occupies. Presumably, it would nonetheless be relatively straightforward to adjust the item recall probabilities just prior to recall by a value that was directly related to the degree of phonological similarity between list items. As in the case of articulatory suppression above, however, such a means of simulating the experimental data is arbitrary and offers little in the way of explanation for why memory span is so dramatically impaired for phonologically similar memory sequences.

Lexicality

One of Brown & Hulme's major aims in developing this model was to provide a simulation of the superior memory span for lists composed of words rather than nonwords. They attribute this lexicality effect to the process of "redintegration", by which the partial memory trace corresponding to an item is reconstructed prior to or at recall. The phonological specifications of familiar words are already stored in long-term memory, and can be used to reconstruct incomplete memory representations in the temporary memory system. For unfamiliar nonwords, in contrast, there is no such opportunity for redintegration.

Redintegration is achieved in the model in two ways. The first adjustment for lexicality involves incrementing the trace strengths for words by a greater constant value than nonwords, in order to simulate the benefits that follow from the availability of long-term phonological knowledge for a familiar item. This parameter itself is sufficient to give rise to a lexicality effect in span. It could also be extended to accommodate the wordlikeness effect in nonword recall, by incrementing wordlike nonwords by a value greater than that for unwordlike nonwords, but lesser than that for fully familiar words.

Interestingly, Brown & Hulme also provided a length-sensitive adjustment for lexicality that yields a benefit for lengthier items. The reason for this is that data of their own (Brown & Hulme 1992) indicate that the linear relationship relating articulation rate to memory span is considerably steeper for nonwords than for words, due to large progressive decreases in memory span with lengthier items. Thus for words, the cost on memory span of having lengthier items in the memory list is less than for nonwords. Brown & Hulme plausibly suggest that this is due to the greater phonological distinctiveness of typical long words compared with short words. For phonologically familiar items, redintegration is likely to be less successful if a single phoneme is lost for a memory trace corresponding to a short word (e.g., "?at" for "cat") than for the same amount of degradation for a lengthy word (e.g., "?ippopotamus"). For nonwords, though, the consequences of phoneme loss for the lengthier items will be just as serious as for short items, as there is no long-term knowledge with which to redintegrate the partial trace.

This process was simulated by incrementing the trace strength for an item by a value that was both weighted by the number of time slices occupied by the item and was sensitive to the degree of phonological familiarity. Specifically, trace strength was enhanced more for lengthy than for short words, but not at all for phonologically unfamiliar nonwords. Including this parameter in addition to the first length-independent lexical parameter, the model provided an excellent simulation of the lexicality effects, and the selective effects of articulatory duration on memory for words and nonwords, reported by Brown & Hulme (1992).

Learning
Learning the phonological forms of new words is beyond the scope of the Brown & Hulme mathematical model. It is therefore incapable of accommodating the close links between temporary storage mechanisms and the learning of new phonological forms.

Summary
Brown & Hulme have succeeded in demonstrating that the well documented sensitivity of memory span to the articulatory duration of the memory sequence can arise from trace decay alone. They establish that word length effects do not require a rehearsal mechanism for their emergence, and show that the greater decay during presentation of recall of long versus short items is itself sufficient basis to give rise to sensitivity to articulatory duration. A novel feature of this approach is that it incorporates a mechanism designed to give a "reverse" word length effect that benefits recall of long words over short words, as a function of their greater distinctiveness. There is indeed some experimental evidence for such an effect (Caplan et al. 1992).

Other qualitative characteristics of short-term memory performance, most notably the effects of phonological similarity and articulatory suppression, cannot be readily captured in this model except by applying arbitrary parameter values that provide little explanation for why the phenomena arise. Indeed, it is this feature of the mathematical modelling approach that is least satisfactory. The use of arbitrary values to accommodate quantitative relationships seems appropriate (as in the case of trace decay, which is a notion relating one quantitative measure to another, i.e. trace strength to passage of time). In the case of qualitative relationships, as in the differences between similar and distinct word lists, or between lists of words and nonwords, the use of numerical parameters to "explain" memory performance is of little value unless the precise mechanism that delivers the parameter is well understood. The contribution of the mathematical modelling approach therefore depends very much on its timing. As a means of discriminating between two well articulated theories (e.g. trace decay versus rehearsal), it is very effective. When little is known about the underlying architecture (as in the case of lexicality effects), it addresses few of the primary issues.

AN INTERACTIVE MODEL OF PHONOLOGICAL MEMORY

It is notable that the features of experimental data that cause most problems for the three models of short-term memory considered above are (a) the influences of lexicality on immediate memory performance, and (b) the close links between verbal short-term memory and the learning of the sound structures of new words. One of the principal reasons for the apparent inadequacy of these models to address these empirical phenomena is their relative recency: whereas word length, suppression and phonological similarity effects have each been well established for over 20 years, investigations of memory for nonwords and of the constraining influence of short-term memory on long-term phonological learning have emerged within the past six or seven years only. Models such as the phonological loop were simply not designed to address this new and developing database, and so inevitably require further development.

The final model of short-term memory to be considered in this chapter is, in contrast, designed specifically to accommodate the lexicality and learning data. A model recently advanced by Gathercole & Martin (1996) is summarized schematically in Figure 2.4. We propose that performance on verbal short-term memory tasks is not served by access to a specialized temporary memory system such as the phonological loop, but instead is mediated by the phonological representations resulting from speech perception. The representations may be conceived as patterns of activation across a phonological network (e.g. McClelland & Elman 1986), although this assumption is not critical for the present framework, which is precomputational. Gathercole & Martin suggest that these patterns of activation within a phonological network correspond functionally to the contents of the phonological store component of the phonological loop model. By this account, there is no separate temporary memory system.

Speech perception does not consist simply of a passive analysis of the incoming acoustic information; it is a highly interactive process in which sensory analysis is aided by at least two different sources of knowledge about the phonological structure of the language. One type of knowledge concerns the statistical properties of its phonological structure: this includes both its phonetic repertoire and phonotactic structure (e.g. Cole & Jakimik et al. 1980, Frauenfelder et al. 1993). Another source of knowledge concerns the phonological characteristics

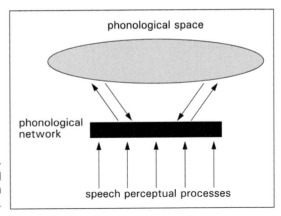

FIG. 2.4.   Schematic representation of the interactive model
proposed by Gathercole & Martin
(1996).

of words known by the listener: the mental lexicon (Marslen-Wilson & Tyler 1980, Lahiri & Marslen-Wilson 1991). By tapping the products of the speech perception process, performance on immediate verbal memory tasks will similarly reflect the contributions of stored knowledge of the language as well as sensory analysis procedures.

The full model is as follows. Temporary phonological representations of incoming speech are constructed on the basis of perceptual analytic processes developed for the native language in early childhood (see, e.g. Jusczyk et al. 1994). The strength of the activation patterns in the phonological network depend on three factors. One factor is the output of the perceptual analytic processes; incoming speech signals that have high signal:noise ratios will result in stronger patterns of activation in the phonological network than degraded input. A second factor is the pre-existing strengths of association between adjacent phonological elements. All languages have characteristic phonotactic properties, which are the constraints and probabilities governing the combination of their basic phonetic elements. Some phoneme combinations have much higher transitional probabilities within the language than others, because they occur in combination more frequently within the words of that language. Gathercole & Martin suggested that there will be resting levels of activation between the units in the phonological network that correspond to individual phonemes, and that the activation values will depend on the phoneme transition probabilities for the language. A third factor governing the patterns of activation within the phonological network arises from stored lexical representations of known phonological sequences. Lexical representations whose phonological structures are compatible with the patterns of activation within the phonological network will themselves receive activation through excitatory links running from the network to the lexical store, and this activation will feed back excitation down to the phonological layer. In this way, lexical knowledge will enhance the representation of an input in the phonological network.

One possibility we have considered, that is represented in Figure 2.4, is that lexical phonological representations are not held in a dictionary-type lexicon in which the phonological specification of a word is just one of many entries stored for each word, but instead are organized in "phonological space". Phonological space refers to a multidimensional system in which all legal phonological combinations of a language can be represented. Each word can be represented as a unique coordinate within phonological space. We have argued that phonological space may retain a permanent history of the occurrence of phonological events, such that the coordinates of phonological space corresponding to familiar words will have higher levels of activation. When an unfamiliar phonological structure is presented, it will result in an increase in the activation level (which may previously have been zero) of its place in phonological space. Activation within phonological space may also spread to adjacent locations in space.

When a previously experienced phonological form is once again encountered, the activation of its coordinate may provide a degree of top-down excitation of its component phonological features in the phonological network that is directly related to its previous history of occurrence. Frequent words will therefore excite their component phonemes in the phonological network in this downwards fashion more strongly than a word encountered only once before, for example. The recurrence of a particular phonological form in both cases will also increment the level of activation of its coordinates in phonological space, as well as transmitting activation back down to the phonological network.

Word length and articulatory suppression

This interactive model does not provide a direct account of the highly systematic effects of word length and articulatory suppression on immediate recall. It does not incorporate a rehearsal process, and so unlike the phonological loop model cannot account for the word length and suppression effects in terms of the operation and disruption (respectively) of a subvocal articulatory process. On the other hand, it is assumed that activation values for nodes in the phonological network decay with time. And on the basis of Brown & Hulme's (1995) implementation of a mathematical model of simple trace decay (see previous section), we know that decay alone is sufficient to give rise to the linear dependency between memory span and the articulatory duration of the memory sequence that is observed in human experimental data. But like the Brown & Hulme model, our interactive model does not provide an obvious source of the articulatory suppression effect and its related phenomena.

Note too that the dependency of the model on the products of speech perception strictly limits the model to accounting for the characteristics of short-term memory for auditory memory material. How, then, can the model accommodate the sensitivity of adults' memory span to word length for visually presented stimuli such as printed words and pictures of nameable objects? The model provides the necessary opportunity for activation of phonological representations in the links between stored lexical phonological representations (or "phonological space" in Figure 2.4) and the phonological network.

Phonological similarity

As the interactive model is not explicit on the issue of how the serial order of activated phonological elements is represented, it provides no explanation for the disruptive effects of phonological similarity between memory items.

Lexicality

One of the primary aims in developing this interactive model was to account for the two lexicality phenomena considered earlier: the superior recall of word compared with nonword lists, and the wordlikeness effect in nonword recall. The model readily accommodates both phenomena. The lexicality effect arises from the top-down activation of elements in the phonological network from stored phonological lexical representations (i.e. phonological space). Activated elements in the phonological network excite the relevant locations in phonological space which then feed back activation down to consistent elements in the network. In this way, speech inputs corresponding to familiar words will result in higher activation values in the phonological network than nonwords.

The wordlikeness effect in nonword recall may arise from either or both of two processes within the interactive model. First, unwordlike nonwords are typically composed of phoneme combinations with relatively low transitional probabilities, which will have correspondingly low pre-existing excitatory links between one another in the phonological network. In this way, higher levels of activation within the network will occur for nonwords of high than low wordlikeness. Second, the concept of interactive links between the network and phonological space allows for the spread of activation from the coordinates of phonologically unfamiliar stimuli (nonwords) to the immediate phonological neighbourhood. Because wordlike nonwords typically have phonological neighbourhoods that are more densely populated by lexical items than unwordlike nonwords, the spread of activation across phonological space will reach more words for the highly wordlike stimuli. As a consequence, the representations of highly wordlike nonwords in the phonological network will receive more top-down activation from lexical items.

Learning

Providing a coordinated account of both temporary storage of verbal memory items and how the learning of new phonological forms is supported was a further aim in developing this interactive model. The notion of direct excitatory bidirectional links running from the phonological network to phonological space provides a parsimonious explanation of both types of memory performance. The "learning" of new words consists of a cumulative record of activation in the unique point in phonological space occupied by the new word. Thus the stronger the activation in the phonological network, the greater the activation in the relevant location in phonological space; the two levels of knowledge have a highly reciprocal relationship with one another. In this way, the same factors that influence short-term retention of nonwords will inevitably constrain their long-term learning.

Summary

The interactive model of Gathercole & Martin uses the concept of a specialized speech perception system in which processing of sensory information and knowledge about the sound structure of the language are coupled to provide an account of both short-term memory and long-term learning. The system readily accommodates the influences of lexicality on immediate memory performance, too. It is not sufficiently explicit in terms of detailed mechanisms to provide accounts of the systematic effects of phonological similarity and articulatory suppression on recall, although Brown & Hulme's (1995) mathematical model establishes that time-based decay of phonological representations is sufficient to accommodate basic word length effects. This model provides a broader perspective on memory and learning than the other models considered in the chapter, but at a cost of detailed theoretical specification. It is our aim to develop a fuller account of the component processes involved in this system in the near future.

OVERVIEW

In this chapter, four models of the processes and mechanisms underpinning verbal short-term memory have been discussed and evaluated, with particular emphasis on the extent to which they accommodate five key features of human memory data. Although addressing a broadly common area of experimental literature, the four models are distinguished most notably by their contrasting levels of description. Whereas two of the models—the phonological loop model of Baddeley (1986) and in the interactive model of Gathercole & Martin (1996)—outline putative cognitive components and processes that are described in purely verbal form, both Burgess & Hitch (1992) and Brown & Hulme (1996) implement their models in computational form. These computational approaches have many beneficial features, providing detailed specification and assessments of how immediate memory performance is served. It is, however, important to note that the verbal and computational models have a close symbiotic relationship with one another: without the development of the original concept of the two-component phonological loop, Burgess & Hitch's network model would not have been possible, and Brown & Hulme's simulation of a trace decay model would have had little theoretical impact. Moreover, advances in modelling speech perception provide a substantial basis for the interactive model, presented in verbal form, of Gathercole & Martin.

This recent convergence of the computational with more traditional noncomputational accounts of short-term memory has already led to considerable advances in understanding the nature of immediate memory performance. With an increasing focus on combining the strengths of the alternative approaches, the prospects for more detailed and complete specifications of the structure of the human memory system in the near future seem very promising indeed.

REFERENCES

Avons, S. E., K. L. Wright, K. Pammer 1994. The word-length effect in probed and serial recall. *Quarterly Journal of Experimental Psychology* **47A**, 207–32.

Baddeley, A. D. 1966. Short-term memory for word sequences as a function of acoustic, semantic and formal similarity. *Quarterly Journal of Experimental Psychology* 18, 302–9.

Baddeley, A. D. 1968. How does item similarity affect short-term memory? *Quarterly Journal of Experimental Psychology* 20, 249–64.

Baddeley, A. D. 1986. *Working memory*. Oxford: Oxford University Press.

Baddeley, A. D. 1990. *Human memory: theory and practice*. Hove, UK: Lawrence Erlbaum Associates Ltd.

Baddeley, A. D. 1993. Short-term phonological memory and long-term learning: A single case study. *European Journal of Cognitive Psychology* 5, 129–48.

Baddeley, A. D. 1996. *Human memory: theory and practice*, 2nd edn. Hove, UK: Psychology Press.

Baddeley, A. D. & J. Andrade 1994. Reversing the word length effect: A comment on Caplan, Rochon & Waters. *Quarterly Journal of Experimental Psychology* **47A**, 1047–54.

Baddeley, A. D & G. J. Hitch 1974. Working memory. In *The Psychology of Learning and Motivation*, vol. 8. G. Bower (ed.), 47–90. New York: Academic Press.

Baddeley, A. D. & B. Wilson 1985. Phonological coding and short-term memory in patients without speech. *Journal of Memory & Language* **24**, 490–502.

Baddeley, A. D. & B. Wilson 1993. A developmental deficit in short-term phonological memory: implications for language and reading. *Memory* **1**, 65–78.

Baddeley, A. D., V. J. Lewis, G. Vallar 1984. Exploring the articulatory loop. *Quarterly Journal of Experimental Psychology* **36**, 233–52.

Baddeley, A. D., C. Papagno, G. Vallar 1988. When long-term learning depends on short-term storage. *Journal of Memory and Language* **27**, 586–96.

Baddeley, A. D., N. Thomson, M. Buchanan 1975. Word length and the structure of short-term memory. *Journal of Verbal Learning and Verbal Behavior* **14**, 575–89.

Bishop, D. V. M. & J. Robson 1989. Unimpaired short-term memory and rhyme judgment in congenitally speechless individuals: implications for the notion of "Articulatory Coding". *Quarterly Journal of Experimental Psychology* **41A**, 123–40.

Bjork, E. L. & A. F. Healy 1974. Short-term order and item retention. *Journal of Verbal Learning and Verbal Behavior* **13**, 644–55.

Brown, G. D. A. & C. Hulme 1992. Cognitive psychology and second language processing: the role of short-term memory. In *Cognitive approaches to bilingualism*, R. J. Harris (ed.), North Holland: Elsevier, 105–22.

Brown, G. D. A. & C. Hulme 1996. Modelling item length effects in memory span: no rehearsal needed? *Journal of Memory and Language* **34**, 594–621.

Burgess, N. & G. J. Hitch 1992. Toward a network model of the articulatory loop. *Journal of Memory and Language* **31**, 429–60.

Butterworth, B., R. Campbell, D. Howard 1986. The uses of short-term memory: a case study. *Quarterly Journal of Experimental Psychology* **38**, 705–37.

Caplan, D., E. Rochon, G. S. Waters 1992. Articulatory and phonological determinants of word length effects in span tasks. *Quarterly Journal of Experimental Psychology* **45A**, 177–92.

Caplan, D. & G. S. Waters 1994. Articulatory length and phonological similarity in span tasks: a reply to Baddeley & Andrade. *Quarterly Journal of Experimental Psychology* **47A**, 1055–62.

Cole, R. A. & J. Jakimik 1980. A model of speech perception. In *Perception and production of fluent speech*, R. A. Cole (ed.), 133–163. Hillsdale: Erlbaum.

Conrad, R. 1964. Acoustic confusions in immediate memory. *British Journal of Psychology* **55**, 75–84.

Conrad, R. & A. Hull 1964. Information, acoustic confusion, and memory span. *British Journal of Psychology* **55**, 429–32.

Cowan, N., L. Day, J. S. Saults, T. A. Keller, T. Johnson, L. Flores 1992. The role of verbal output time in the effects of word length on immediate memory. *Journal of Memory and Language* **31**, 1–17.

Frauenfelder, U. H., R. H. Baayen, F. M. Hellwig, R. Schreuder 1993. Neighbourhood density and frequency across languages and modalities. *Journal of Memory and Language* **32**, 781–804.

Gathercole, S. E. 1994. Neuropsychology and working memory: a review. *Neuropsychology* **8**, 494–505.

Gathercole, S. E. 1995. Is nonword repetition a test of phonological memory or long-term knowledge? It all depends on the nonwords. *Memory and Cognition* **23**, 83–94.

Gathercole, S. E. & A. D. Baddeley 1989. Evaluation of the role of phonological STM in the development of vocabulary in children: a longitudinal study. *Journal of Memory and Language* **28**, 200–13.

Gathercole, S. E. & A. D. Baddeley 1990. The role of phonological memory in vocabulary acquisition: a study of young children learning arbitrary names of toys. *British Journal of Psychology* **81**, 439–54.

Gathercole, S. E. & A. D. Baddeley 1993. *Working memory and language*. Hove, UK: Lawrence Erlbaum Associates Ltd.

Gathercole, S. E. & G. J. Hitch 1993. Developmental changes in short-term memory: A revised working memory perspective. In *Theories of memory*, A. Collins, S. E. Gathercole, M. A. Conway, P. E. Morris (eds). Hove, UK: Lawrence Erlbaum Associates Ltd.

Gathercole, S. E. & A. Martin 1996. Interactive processes in phonological memory. In *Models of short-term memory*, S. E. Gathercole (ed.). Hove, UK: Lawrence Erlbaum Associates Ltd.

Gathercole, S. E., C. Willis, H. Emslie, A. Baddeley 1991. The influences of number of syllables and word-likeness on children's repetition of nonwords. *Applied Psycholinguistics* **12**, 349–367.

Gathercole, S. E., C. Willis, H. Emslie, A. Baddeley 1992. Phonological memory and vocabulary development during the early school years: a longitudinal study. *Developmental Psychology* **28**, 887–98.

Hartley, T. & G. Houghton 1996. A linguistically constrained model of short-term memory for nonwords. *Journal of Memory and Language* **34**.

Hitch, G. J. & M. S. Halliday 1983. Working memory in children. *Philosophical Transactions of the Royal Society, London* **B302**, 324–40.

Hitch, G. J., M. S. Halliday, A. M. Schaafstal, J. M. C. Schraagen 1988. Visual working memory in young children. *Memory and Cognition* **16**, 120–32.

Hulme, C., S. Maughan, G. D. A. Brown 1991. Memory for familiar and unfamiliar words: evidence for a long-term memory contribution to short-term memory span. *Journal of Memory and Language* **30**, 685–701.

Hulme, C., N. Thomson, C. Muir, A. Lawrence 1984. Speech rate and the development of short-term memory span. *Journal of Experimental Child Psychology* **38**, 241–53.

Johnston, R. A., C. Johnson, C. Gray 1987. The emergence of the word length effect in young children: the effects of overt and covert rehearsal. *British Journal of Developmental Psychology* **5**, 243–8.

Jusczyk, P. W., P. A. Luce, J. Charles-Luce 1994. Infants' sensitivity to phonotactic patterns in the native language. *Journal of Memory and Language* **33**, 630–45.

Lahiri, A. & W. Marslen-Wilson 1991. The mental representation of lexical form: A phonological approach to the recognition lexicon. *Cognition* **38**, 245–94.

Levy, B. A. 1971. The role of articulation in auditory and visual short-term memory. *Journal of Verbal Learning and Verbal Behavior* **10**, 123–32.

Liberman, A. M. & I. G. Mattingley 1985. The motor theory of speech perception revisited. *Cognition* **21**, 1–36.

McClelland, J. L. & J. L. Elman 1986. The TRACE model of speech perception. *Cognitive Psychology* **18**, 1–86.

McClelland, J. L., D. E. Rumelhart, and the PDP Group 1986. *Parallel distributed processing: explorations of the microstructure of cognition*, vol 2. Cambridge, Mass: Bradford Books.

MacNeilage, P. F., T. P. Rootes, R.A. Chase 1967. Speech production and perception in a patient with severe impairment of somasthetic perception and motor control. *Journal of Speech and Hearing Research* **10**, 449–68.

Marslen-Wilson, W. D. & L. K. Tyler 1980. The temporal structure of spoken language understanding. *Cognition* **8**, 1–71.

Michas, I. C. & L. A. Henry 1994. The link between phonological memory and vocabulary acquisition. *British Journal of Developmental Psychology* **12**, 147–64.

Murray, D. J. 1967. The role of speech responses in short-term memory. *Canadian Journal of Psychology* **21**, 263–76.

Nairne, J. S. 1990. A feature model of immediate memory. *Memory and Cognition* **18**, 251–69.

Papagno, C. & G. Vallar 1992. Phonological short-term memory and the learning of novel words: the effects of phonological similarity and item length. *Quarterly Journal of Experimental Psychology* **44A**, 47–67.

Papagno, C., T. Valentine, A. Baddeley 1992. Phonological short-term memory and foreign-language vocabulary learning. *Journal of Memory and Language* **30**, 331–47.

Parkin, A. 1993. *Memory: phenomena, experiment and theory*. Oxford: Blackwell Scientific

Paterson, L. R. & S. F. Johnson 1971. Some effects of minimizing articulation of short-term retention. *Journal of Verbal Learning and Verbal Behaviour* **10**, 346–54.

Pinker, S. 1991. Rules of language. *Science* **253**, 530–5.

Roodenrys, S., C. Hulme, G. Brown 1993. The development of short-term memory span: separable effects of speech rate and long-term memory. *Journal of Experimental Child Psychology* **56**, 431–42.

Salame, P. & A. D. Baddeley 1982. Disruption of memory by unattended speech: implications for the structure of working memory. *Journal of Verbal Learning and Verbal Behavior* **21**, 150–64.

Schweikert, R. 1993. A multinomial processing tree model for degradation and redintegration in immediate recall. *Memory and Cognition* **21**, 168–75.

Service, L. 1992. Phonology, working memory, and foreign-language learning. *Quarterly Journal of Experimental Psychology* **45A**, 21–50.

Vallar, G. & A. D. Baddeley 1984. Fractionation of working memory: neuropsychological evidence for a short-term store. *Journal of Verbal Learning and Verbal Behavior* **23**, 151–61.

Wickelgren, W. A. 1965. Short-term memory for repeated and non-repeated items. *Quarterly Journal of Experimental Psychology* **17**, 14–25.

CHAPTER THREE

Formal models of memory for serial order: a review

Gordon D. A. Brown

It is often the case that when we are required to remember a list of items, we can remember the items in the list but not the order in which they appeared. Consider for example the task of remembering an eight-digit number, perhaps a telephone number, for a short period of time. Many carefully controlled experimental studies have shown that, when the length of a list of words or numbers is close to the maximum that we can remember, many (often a majority) of the errors that subjects make involve them recalling the right items but in the wrong order. This is particularly likely to be the case when the items to be remembered sound similar to each other (Conrad 1965). Thus, for example, we might misremember the sequence C P T D E G as C T P D E G (here the second and third items have been changed round, and have been recalled in the wrong order, a "transposition error"). Thus, there is an important difference between remembering the items in a list, and remembering the order in which those items occurred. Not surprisingly, this distinction has received much experimental investigation for 30 years within the psychology of memory. However it is only more recently that there has been a resurgence of interest in building models of the psychological mechanisms that allow the sequential order of information to be represented in memory.

One reason for the considerable recent interest in memory for serial order is the increasing recognition that an understanding of the dynamic, temporal and sequential aspects of human cognition and behaviour is likely to prove central to a mature psychology (see, e.g. Oaksford & Brown 1994). In activities as diverse as speech perception and production, reading, walking, and cognitive reasoning, the order of the inputs and outputs cannot be ignored. Thus "Mary loves John" does not mean the same as "John loves Mary", and 6574 is not the same telephone number as 6547. Trivial though these examples may seem, well specified information-processing models that can account for our ability to represent and remember such distinctions have only recently begun to appear. Laboratory-based study of human memory for serial order has perhaps provided us with the richest database of empirical evidence on how knowledge about serial order is represented psychologically.

This chapter therefore provides a critical overview of formal models of memory, particularly those that specify how we can represent and remember memory for serial order. Formal models of memory are taken to include both mathematical and computational implementations of models of short-term memory. Throughout, one aim will be to show that formal models of memory have allowed us to understand things about human memory and its organization that we would probably not have been able to understand in any other way. We begin with a brief discussion of the role of formal modelling in the psychology of memory, and discuss some of the basic assumptions that are generally made in formal models.

WHY FORMAL MODELLING?

By a "formal model" of memory, we mean one which has been implemented in the form of a computer program, or that has been expressed mathematically. Why should we want to express a model in this way, rather than simply describing the model in words, as is more usually the case? In this section we review some of the reasons.

One important consideration is simply the complexity of the models that are now being proposed to account for human memory and other phenomena. Traffic flows through a city, or the complex interacting behaviour of a weather system, are too complex to predict without extensive computer simulation. It is likewise the case that some psychological models are so complex, often including very many interacting components, that it is simply not possible to predict what the model's behaviour will be under specific conditions *without* simulation. This applies particularly to models that attempt to show how known structural characteristics of the brain may give rise to behaviour.

This is related to a second major advantage of implementing models, which is that there can never be any doubt about what the predictions of the implemented model are. It is always possible to examine the behaviour of the model under changed inputs, and hence derive predictions from the model that can then be tested experimentally. It may not always be clear which predictions follow from the core theoretical assumptions of the model, and which follow from less central aspects of the model (those that have been incorporated simply to enable it to function at all). An implemented model nevertheless generally has a considerable advantage over one that has simply been given a verbal description, and perhaps been described in the familiar "box-and-arrow" notation, when it comes to unambiguously deriving testable predictions from the model. The more predictions a model can make, the easier it potentially is to prove the model wrong, and so the more powerful the model. Furthermore, the detailed specification of a model that is embodied in a computer program (or set of equations) avoids some of the problems that can otherwise result when high-level cognitive concepts such as "rules", "representations", or "strategies" are invoked in explanations of psychological phenomena, for there is always the danger that the internal constructs of this type are ill-defined and are in some way simply a covert redescription of the data to be explained.

Finally, the process of trying to build a working model of some psychological process is an exceptionally valuable tool in the process of coming to understand that process. It is very often the case that some assumed psychological mechanism seems workable until one actually tries to construct a model of it. It also frequently occurs that some component of a model can give rise to unexpected side-effects in the behaviour of the model; effects that would not have been predicted had they not actually been observed to happen in the developing implementation of a model. We can give an anecdotal example from our own work. A few years ago we decided to implement, in the form of a computer program, the well known and influential "articulatory loop" model of phonological short-term memory developed by Baddeley (Baddeley 1986). This model includes a passive phonological store, and a subvocal rehearsal process that can be used to refresh information within the store before the information is lost due to trace decay over time. The subvocal rehearsal process is assumed to be necessary to explain phenomena such as word length effects. We began our work by implementing a simple computational analogue of the phonological store, and incorporated the assumption that information decays passively over time. Much to our surprise, it turned out that the assumption of decay over time, along with some simple assumptions about reconstructive processing during recall, was sufficient to explain word length effects; we did not after all need to implement a rehearsal process in the model (Brown & Hulme 1995). This result was entirely unexpected, for we had made the common assumption that a rehearsal process of some kind would be necessary to explain such data. Thus the attempt to implement even a simple and widely accepted model led us to some unexpected conclusions.

ASSUMPTIONS MADE BY FORMAL MODELS

In this section we review some of the assumptions that are common to many of the specific models of memory that we describe below. These concern basic issues that must be resolved before any model can be formally implemented, and they are relevant to both connectionist models and many mathematical models. Two particular concerns are (a) how items are represented, and (b) how associations are formed between representations.

The representations of items

First of all, it is necessary to have some way of representing the items that are to be remembered in a memory task. The items need to be represented in some way that a computer program or a set of mathematical equations can store and transform. It is therefore common to make the assumption that items to be remembered in a memory experiment (such as words, numbers, or nonsense syllables) can be represented as vectors of features in some way. A vector can be thought of as a list of numbers, each of which provides a value on some relevant dimension. Thus a single phoneme can be represented by a vector of 0s and 1s, each equivalent to "on" or "off", where each 1 represents the fact that the phoneme in question has a particular feature (such as "voicing", e.g. the difference between the sound of "P" and the sound of "B"). A 0 represents the fact that the phoneme does not possess the feature signalled by that number in the vector. Thus a phoneme can be represented to a memory network as a vector of 0s and 1s, of the kind illustrated in Figure 3.1(a) (although a vector with more elements, around 35, would normally be

FIG. 3.1.   Two ways of representing items as vectors. (**a**) Every element is either "on" or "off". (**b**) Each unit has an activation value associated with it.

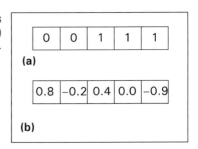

(a)

(b)

necessary to provide a good representation of phonemes). Alternatively, if the semantic properties of a word must be represented, each element of the vector could stand for a semantic property of the word, such as "animate" or "hairy." Sometimes, if it is not necessary for the semantic, phonemic or other structure of the items to be represented to the memory model, vectors of random numbers will be used (as in Fig. 3.1(b)). In this case, a different random vector may be used to represent each item. It is often assumed that item similarity can be modelled by making the vectors that represent the items similar to each other, in terms of the feature or element values that they share. Thus if two vectors have many elements in common, they are assumed to represent items that are similar to one another.

These vector representations assume that each item in a memory task, be it a phoneme, word, or whatever, is represented by a separate vector, where each vector contains several elements (i.e. is like a list of several numbers). However a simpler representation is sometimes used, in which just a single vector element is used to represent each of the items. In this case, each element of the vector stands for just one item. Thus, for example, the vector 1 0 0 0 could represent one item, and the vector 0 0 1 0 could represent another.

The vector representations described above are simply designed to enable the kinds of item that are used in human experimental memory tasks to be assigned some representation that can be used in a computational or mathematical memory model. However in connectionist models of memory, which we describe in more detail below, a further assumption is made. It is often assumed in connectionist models that the level of activity of a given "node" or "unit" can be seen as analogous in some simplified way to the rate of firing of a real neuron (or cluster of real neurons) in the brain. Thus, in a connectionist model, it may be assumed that an item in a memory task would be represented as a pattern of neuronal activity (usually distributed over many neurons), and in connectionist models of brain function these patterns of neuronal activity are represented as patterns of activity over a set of simulated artificial neurons, where each artificial neuron corresponds to one element in the vector that represents the item as a whole. However, the core assumption, that items can legitimately be represented in the model as vectors, remains the same.

In summary: a central assumption of many formal models of memory is that items in a list of to-be-remembered items can be represented as vectors of features. This is an assumption that is common to models with very different architectures, and in the present chapter we will not need to discuss how models differ in the precise assumptions they make about exactly how items are represented in memory. Instead, we focus on the higher level architecture of serial memory models: whether item representations (of whatever type) are associated to other item representations, or to representations of list position, or to something else. These architectural issues can be considered independently of exactly which representational scheme is adopted. First, however, we discuss a second "basic issue", concerning the basic mechanism that is used to form associations. Again, this can to some extent be considered independently of questions concerning higher level architecture.

The formation of associations

Just as any formal model of memory must make some assumption about how items are represented in memory, a formal memory model will also normally include some mechanism for forming associations between representations. This applies to both connectionist and mathematical memory models. The role of the associative mechanism, and the representations it acts on, depends on the architecture of the model. However, as we shall see below, it is important to realize that the decision as to which method of association will be used is to a large extent independent of the architecture within which the basic mechanism of association is embedded. Furthermore, in evaluating models, it becomes important to distinguish between properties of the model that result from the basic mechanism of association that the model makes use of, and properties that reflect the higher level structure, or architecture of the model. In this section, we briefly review some of the different methods that can be used to form associations between different vector representations. We consider just the three associative mechanisms of learning that have been most widely used in formal models of memory: Hebbian learning, backpropagation learning, and convolution. The first two of these both traditionally fall under the umbrella of connectionist models of psychological processing, and so it is to connectionism that we now turn.

Connectionism

Both Hebbian learning and backpropagation are normally presented within the connectionist tradition of research. Connectionist networks typically consist of a large number of computational units whose behaviour is in some respects assumed to be similar to that of neurons or neuronal clusters. Each of these units, or simplified "artificial neurons", is connected to some, although generally not all, of the other units in the network. Every unit is assigned a number that represents the "activation" level of that unit (just as, in the previous section, we described how each element of a vector can be given a number).

Connections can communicate the activation level of one unit to another, the amount of this communication depending on the "strength" of the connection. The level of activation of each unit is determined by all the activations that it receives from other units that it is connected to. In simplified terms, a unit's activation level will depend in some way on the amount that the total activation coming into that unit exceeds a "threshold" value. The influence that one unit has on another (if they are connected) depends on both the size of its own activation level and the strength of the connection between the two units.

As a result of these rather simple mechanisms, a pattern of activation over one set of units can give rise, via communication through the connections, to a pattern of activation over a different set of units. If each of these patterns of activation can be seen as representing an item, as described in the previous section, then the result can be interpreted as an association between two item representations (in the sense that provision of one item can lead to retrieval of another).

Some units in the network are normally considered "input" units, while others are referred to as "output" units. The activation levels of the set of input units could be thought of as representing one item in a pair of items that must be associated, while the pattern formed by the activation levels of the output units may be regarded as a representation of the other item in the pair to be associated. When the first item becomes represented on the input units, activation will spread through the connections in the network until some pattern of activity is established on the output units, the exact pattern being dependent on the strengths of all the connections in the network. Thus if the pattern of activity on the output units is to correspond to the desired pattern (i.e. one that represents the other member of the pair of representations to be associated) the connection strengths must be such as to cause this to happen.

Hebbian learning and backpropagation essentially represent different solutions to the problem of forming the appropriate set of connection strengths to allow an association to be represented correctly in the manner we have described. A central property of connectionist networks of the type we have been describing is that, given a particular input pattern, a learning mechanism can be used to change the connections between units in such a way as to cause a desired pattern to appear on the output units in response to an input pattern. In this way, the network can learn to associate one pattern with another. Furthermore, the network is not confined to representing just one input–output pair; rather, several different associations between pairs of patterns can be learned within the same set of connections.

Hebbian association. The Hebbian method of associative learning is the simplest. There are just two populations of units, as illustrated in Figure 3.2. If the task is to associate two item representations, the procedure is as follows. One of the vectors to be associated is represented on one population of units, and the other member of the pair of vectors to be associated is represented on the other population of units. Every unit in one group is connected to every unit in the other group in this network. The learning mechanism simply increments the strength of each connection to the extent that the units it connects have similar activations. Thus if both of two connected units are switched on, or both have a high level of activation, the connection between them is given a positive strength. If one of the connected units has a positive activation and the other has a negative activation, a negative connection strength is assigned.

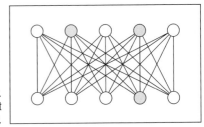

FIG. 3.2. A simple Hebbian associative network. Every unit in one layer is connected to every unit in the other layer.

There are several different versions of this learning algorithm, but all are capable of forming simple associations within a single trial of learning. Indeed, several such associations may be learned within the same network, with the connection strength changes that arise due to each new pair of items simply being added to make up the overall strength of each connection. Although there are various combinations of associations that cannot be learned by this type of simple associative mechanism, it nevertheless suffices for some of the most successful models of human memory for serial order, as we shall see below.

Backpropagation. A more complex learning mechanism is used widely in connectionist models of psychological processing, including models of memory for serial order. This is usually known as "backpropagation" or the "generalized delta rule" and is one member of a class of "gradient descent learning algorithms." For present purposes, the crucial differences between standard backpropagation and the varieties of Hebbian learning described briefly above are that: (a) backpropagation works by changing the connection strengths between units in such as way as to reduce the discrepancy between the pattern of activation that the network is producing on its "output units" and the desired pattern of activation, and, (b) backpropagation is normally an incremental learning procedure, in that each pair of associations to be learned must be presented to the network many times before the network will learn every required association, because only small changes are made to the connection strengths on each presentation of a pair of to-be-associated representations.

A typical backpropagation architecture is illustrated in Figure 3.3. Note that there is one important difference from the architecture in the Hebbian network described earlier; specifically, there is an intermediate layer of "hidden units" between the input units and the output units. This allows the learning of more complex mappings between inputs and outputs than is possible in a two-layer network, which is all that the Hebbian learning algorithm is normally used for (see Rumelhart et al. 1986, for extensive discussion).

We will not describe here the operation of the backpropagation learning algorithm in detail. The purpose of it is straightforward: to enable a connectionist network to form a set of connection strengths that will enable it to reproduce a given vector (representing, for example an item in a short-term memory task) on its output units when it is presented with a specified vector representation as its input.

It is important to re-emphasize that the network learns about associations between pairs of vector representations only by being repeatedly exposed to the pairs: all of the learning takes place by slow, gradual modification of connection strengths. At the end of learning the network is able to produce the correct output pattern in response to a particular input. Backpropagation networks have been used to provide

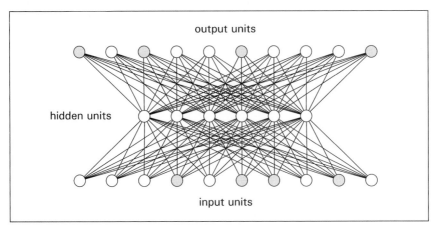

FIG. 3.3.   A simple backpropagation network.

psychologically interesting models of a variety of different behaviours, such as verb tense learning, speech perception and speech production, and reading development.

We now turn to a third method of forming associations in memory tasks: *convolution*.

Convolution

Mathematical models of memory that adopt convolution as the basic method of forming associations between item vectors are TODAM (Theory Of Distributed Associative Memory; e.g. Murdock, 1982, 1993; Lewandowsky & Murdock, 1989) and CHARM (Composite Holographic Associative Recall Model; Metcalfe Eich 1982, 1985). As in other models, items are represented as vectors of features. Convolution can be used to combine two items together into a third "memory trace" vector in such a way that either of the two associated items can be used to retrieve a vector that is an approximation of the other associated item from the "memory trace" vector. The retrieval operation uses correlation (mathematically the approximate inverse of convolution). Thus convolution can be used as a basic associative mechanism that associates two item vectors, e.g. **A** and **B**, into a memory trace vector **T**. The way this works is illustrated in Figure 3.4; this shows that every element of the memory trace vector is composed of the sum of products of certain pairs of the elements of the item vectors that are to be associated. This leads to a memory trace that "contains" information about the two associated item vectors.

The convolution and correlation operations are both described in more detail in Metcalfe Eich 1982; here the important point is that convolution is just another way of forming associations between vectors within a single trial[1].

FIG. 3.4.   The convolution method of association. Each element of the convolved vector is made up as the sum of products of elements of the item vectors that are to be associated.

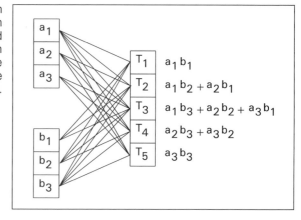

Several different associations (e.g. **A** with **B**, **C** with **D**, **E** with **F**) can be formed by convolution in the same way as illustrated in Figure 3.4, and the resulting convolutions superimposed into a composite memory trace (often referred to as **T**). This memory trace can then be "probed" with any of the original members of the associated pairs of vectors, leading to the retrieval of an approximation to the other member of the associated pair. So, in the example above, **T** could be probed with **E** and the result would be an approximation to **F**.

Summary

We have briefly outlined three basic methods of forming associations between vectors of features: Hebbian association, backpropagation, and convolution. Other schemes have been employed in some models, and some do not specify any associative mechanism at all. For alternative schemes, see, for example, Gillund and Shiffrin (1984), Hintzman (1986), Humphreys et al. (1989).

We have reviewed the various possible associative mechanisms without considering the higher architectures in which they have been, or could be, embedded. This is because the choice of the basic associative mechanism for a model is to a large extent independent of the architectural assumptions of the memory model within which the associative mechanism is embedded. So, for example, convolution, Hebbian learning or backpropagation could in principle be used to form item-to-item associations (e.g. Lewandowsky & Murdock, 1989) or item-to-context associations (e.g. Houghton 1990, Burgess & Hitch 1992) or item-to-list-position associations.

However the choice of associative mechanism is not arbitrary, even though they can all be used in any of several different model architectures. Different associative mechanisms do have different strengths and weaknesses (Brown et al. 1995a, 1996). For example, gradient-descent learning algorithms such as backpropagation, in which only small amounts of learning normally take place in response to each exposure to the data set, are not appropriate for characterizing the single-exposure learning that is often involved in human memory performance.

Hebbian learning or convolution can, in contrast to backpropagation, be used to model single-trial learning situations, but it has not been shown how an account of the development of learning could emerge within such a framework (see Brown et al. 1995b, for extensive discussion of this point). It is possible to explain the development of memory capacity in convolution-based models or Hebbian models if it is assumed that the quality of the representations of items improves over developmental time. However, none of the accounts above provide an account of "learning-to-learn"; that is, of how the ability to perform associations within a single trial could be gradually acquired. Such an account seems likely to be necessary if we are ever to account for the rich range of developmental data available from the study of memory in children. Furthermore, McClelland et al. (1994) have argued that it is computationally efficient to have at least two separate memory systems: one that enables fast one-trial learning and nonpermanent storage, and another that performs slower gradient-descent learning. The advantage of having a slow gradient-descent learning system, that perhaps uses a learning algorithm something like backpropagation, is that this facilitates generalization by allowing underlying regularities in the system to become represented; this is partly because the memory does not change its state very much in response to any single (and perhaps atypical) experience. McClelland et al. ascribe to the hippocampus the function of maintaining the temporary memories, and suggest that experiences stored in the hippocampus (on the basis of a single learning episode) may be "re-presented" to the slower learning but generalization-extracting cortex many times, allowing the gradient-descent learning to occur. They show how a two-store model such as this possesses many computational advantages, and also can be used to explain much amnesia data.

This leaves the question of how a developmental account of one-trial learning might be possible. Brown et al. 1996 have described a connectionist architecture that "learns to learn"; i.e. it gradually develops, using a gradient-descent learning algorithm a bit like the backpropagation system described above, the ability to perform associations within a single trial. In other words, after the "learning-to-learn" process is complete, it behaves rather like the convolution algorithm described above. Brown et al. (1995b) have shown how such an approach can give rise to specific developmental predictions (concerning, for example, the differing proportions of certain error types that should be made by children of different ages in a paired associate learning task). Although such predictions remain to be tested, an approach like this could in principle be used to model the development of memory using any of the architectures described below.

MODELS OF SERIAL ORDER

We have described some of the techniques and assumptions that underlie formal models of memory, and explained some of the different ways in which associations between items can be formed when those items are represented as vectors. Now we want to consider some of the ways in which the architectures of models of memory have accounted for our ability to represent the order of a series of items. We begin by briefly reviewing a wide range of options, and then focus on two general classes of model: those that may be termed chaining models, and context-based models. These are the two recent approaches that have been most concerned to specify the actual mechanisms that underlie memory for serial order. (We ignore some other classes of model, such as the "distinctiveness" models of Murdock (1960) and Bower (1971), see also Johnson (1991), which provide good mathematical characterizations of the shape of serial position curves but do not specify the underlying mechanisms that allow the internal representation of memory concerning serial order.)

In most of the examples below, we use the example of a six-item list, containing the items **A**, **B**, **C**, **D**, **E** and **F**. So correct recall of this list would be **A B C D E F**.

Slot-based models

An obvious simple possibility is to assume that there is some "slot" or "bin" corresponding to each position within a list. This is illustrated in Figure 3.5.

In such a model, items in a list would be put into successive bins or slot positions when the list is presented. When the list must be recalled, it is then a simple matter to examine the bins one-by-one, in the right order, and hence recall the items that appeared in each position. A simple model such as this could of course work, in that it would allow retrieval of a single list of items in the correct serial order. Indeed, such models have been proposed in the literature e.g. by Conrad (1965). In Conrad's version of the model, features of the items can be lost due to forgetting but items will not move to incorrect bins. The model is therefore faced with an apparent difficulty in accounting for "order errors", in which the right items are recalled but in the wrong order (e.g. **A B C** recalled as **A C B**). Conrad assumed that order errors (such as transpositions) arise simply due to the loss of good item representations: if some information is lost from an item's representation, then the subject will guess, and be likely to choose a similar item from the list if

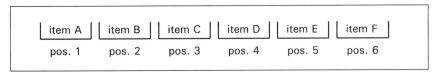

FIG. 3.5.   A simple "slot model" in which each list position is represented by a "bin" into which items may be placed.

one is available. In this kind of model there can be no separate representation of memory for items and memory for item order, so Conrad is forced to explain loss of order information as resulting from loss of item information. However such an account has difficulty in explaining the empirical observation that item memory and order memory can be differently affected by experimental manipulations (e.g. Murdock & vom Saal, 1967); the difficulty arises because, in the Conrad model, loss of order information is a secondary consequence of loss of information about the actual items, and therefore anything that affects memory for the items should also affect memory for their serial order.

To relate this kind of model to the types of associative mechanism we reviewed above, we could envisage a mechanism in which internal representations of list positions were used (these representations could be vectors, perhaps simulating patterns of neural activity). Learning a serial list would involve forming associations (using any of the methods described above) between each item and the relevant position-in-list vector. To recall the item that was in position 1 in the list, an attempt would be made to retrieve the item that was associated with the position-1 marker; to recall the item that was in position 2 in the list would involve an attempt to retrieve the item associated with the position-2 marker, and so on. Slot-based or position-based models have not been developed much further since the early versions just described, and so we will not discuss them at length here. However it is clear that they do not offer a real and satisfying explanation of how serially ordered information is maintained psychologically. The slot-based models take for granted an ability to search the bins in the right order during recall of a list of items; no explanation is provided about how this works. There is therefore an important sense in which models of this type assume the very ability that they are attempting to explain.

Estes' perturbation model

An alternative model involves the assumption that sequences of subsequences of items become associated to "control elements". Such a model was put forward by Estes (e.g. 1972) and is illustrated in Figure 3.6.

The central idea here is that associations are formed between items and control elements, rather than associations being formed between items themselves (as in the chaining models we review below). The control nodes can be seen as representing the context of learning. To the extent that associations are formed between items and the context of learning, retrieval of the items will be possible if the context of learning can be at least partially reinstated at retrieval (this involves reactivation of the relevant control nodes, whereupon the items that were

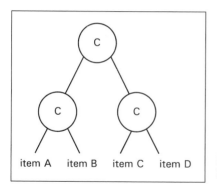

FIG. 3.6.   The Estes chunking model. Circles labelled "C" are list chunk nodes.

associated with that control node can be recalled). It is assumed that more than two items can be associated with each control node, although only two are shown in Figure 3.6. It is further assumed that a new control or chunk node is set up at each discontinuity in the input, and that a hierarchy of chunks is possible, as in Figure 3.6. Thus the low-level sequence elements might represent phonemes, while higher-level control nodes could correspond to higher-level units such as syllables or words.

The model as described thus far could potentially provide an account of how items are remembered, but not an account of how they can be recalled in the *correct serial order*. In the perturbation model, short-term memory for serial order is achieved by periodically reactivating the various connections between item representations and the list nodes are in sequence: this is a rehearsal process. The connections between items and control nodes are cyclically reactivated in the order the items were presented in, and this allows temporary maintenance of information about the presentation order. However the cyclic process is error-prone: it can happen that "perturbations" occur, with the result that the item-to-control node connections become reactivated in the wrong order. This can lead to "order errors" in which items are recalled out of sequence. Because small perturbations are more likely to occur than large ones, any item is likely to be recalled at close to its correct position in the sequence, even if not in exactly the right position. Estes (1972) provides a mathematical formulation of his perturbation model, and shows that it gives a good explanation of a wide range of results from studies of short-term memory for serial order.

The "cyclic reactivation" process described above is used solely for the short-term retention of order information; if sequential information is to be represented in the longer term then a pattern of inhibitory connections is set up between representations of different elements in the sequence. We explain this in more detail in a subsequent section.

It should be noted that this model does not specify the low-level mechanisms that give rise to the behaviour. It is not immediately obvious how such a model could be implemented at the level of item vector representations and basic associative mechanisms of the type discussed earlier. However the model is in many ways an attractive one, giving a good account for example of the nature and distribution of serial order errors in memory, and the separate encoding of item and order information. Furthermore, Nairne (1990, 1991) has shown that the perturbation model can be extended to account for data from studies of memory for serial order over longer timespans than those involved in immediate serial recall tasks. The model therefore appears to have wide generality. The model also has features in common with the context-based models to be discussed later in this chapter.

Chaining models

A third possibility is that memory for a list of items is stored as a set of pairwise associations. This is illustrated in Figure 3.7, for the list **A B C D E F**.

The basic idea here is that associations are formed between each successive pair of items in the list, effectively forming a "chain" made up of links between successive items in the list. Models that adopt some version of this scheme are therefore often described as chaining models. Thus the sequence **A B C D** would be stored as the associations **A–B**, **B–C**, and **C–D**. If each of the items **A**, **B**, etc. is represented as a vector of features, in the manner described earlier, then any of the associative mechanisms described earlier (e.g. Hebbian association or convolution) could be used to form each link in the chain of associations. Recall can proceed by "unwinding" the chain of associations, link by link. If the first item in the list, **A**, is available, perhaps because it has been associated with a "start-of-list" representation, then it can be used as a probe to recall the item with which it is associated, that is, item **B**. When **B** has been retrieved in this way it can be used as a probe to retrieve its associate **C**, and so on until the whole list of items has been retrieved.

A problem that is immediately apparent with this kind of chaining account is that recall of a list will stop whenever any item cannot be recalled correctly. Thus, for example, if item **B** in the example above cannot be correctly recalled, it will never be possible to recover item **C** (because **B** must be available to use as a probe if item **C** is to be recovered

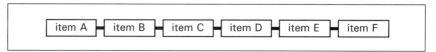

FIG. 3.7.   A chaining model.

via representation of the **B–C** association). This would mean that the probability of recalling an item could never be higher for an item late in the list than for an earlier item. However the reverse is of course observed to be true: items near the end of a list are generally more likely to be recalled correctly than items in the middle of the list (the "recency effect").

A recent chaining model developed by Lewandowsky & Murdock (1989) pointed to two possible solutions to this problem. First of all, it could be assumed that an approximation to an item could be success-fully used as a retrieval cue, even if it was not sufficiently good to allow output of the item itself. Thus in the example above, probing with the first item, **A**, might lead to retrieval of a vector that approximates the second item, **B**, but that does not resemble **B** sufficiently to allow **B** to be correctly recalled as the second item. However this retrieved approxi-mation to **B** might still in principle be good enough to be used as a probe for the correct retrieval of **C**. It is therefore possible that **C** could be cor-rectly recalled, even if **B** itself was not.

In the chaining model implemented by Lewandowsky & Murdock (1989), which is known as TODAM (theory of distributed associative memory) and uses convolution to form the pairwise associations between successive items in a list to be remembered, superior recall of items at the end of a list can occur because the pool of potentially recallable items gradually reduces as recall proceeds. This means that the chances of correctly recalling an item by chance alone increase as recall progresses through the list, and indeed this is the main mecha-nism that gives rise to recency effects in the model.

TODAM represents one of the most comprehensively explored formal models of memory for serial order in recent years, and it has been shown to fit a wide range of human data. However it has been criticized for a number of reasons. Pike (1984) has argued that the convolution approach in TODAM is neurally implausible, and convolution-based mod-els have recently been criticized both in terms of the functional nature of their associative and recall mechanisms (Nairne & Neath 1994, Brown et al. 1995a) and for the particular assumptions in the model of serial order (Mewhort et al. 1994). However one of the most serious criticisms is one that applies to any model that relies upon a chain of links between successive list items, and we return to this after a brief discussion of chaining-like connectionist approaches to modelling memory for serial order.

Connectionist chaining models
There has been considerable recent interest in how connectionist archi-tectures, often using backpropagation learning, can learn sequential

information (see Chater & Conkey 1994, for a review). Recently proposed sequential connectionist architectures are able to learn sequential information via recurrent links from output units (e.g. Jordan 1986) or hidden units (Elman 1988). Essentially, the addition of these links allows chaining-like associations to be formed between successive items in a list; each item in a sequence, when it is output by the network, can become part of the input that acts as a cue for retrieval of the following item.

A typical architecture is illustrated in Figure 3.8. The basic network design is identical to the backpropagation architecture described earlier, with one addition: recurrent links that project "backwards" from the output units to a subset of the input units. (In the Elman (1988) version, the recurrent links are from the hidden units rather than the output units.) These recurrent connections from the output units allow each output of the network to be copied onto the subset of the input units, and form part of the next input. (The subset of the input units that represents the last output is usually known as the "state" or "context" units, and these units may encode a decaying average of the last few outputs rather than just the last output.) The result of copying each output pattern back to the input units is that the total input (i.e. the pattern of activation over all the input units) can change as a sequence progresses thus allowing different outputs to be produced, even though the pattern of activation on the rest of the input units (often referred to as the "plan" units) remains unchanged throughout the sequence. A network like this is essentially learning a series of simple associations. When the first element of a sequence, **A**, must be output, there will be

FIG. 3.8. A sequential connectionist architecture.

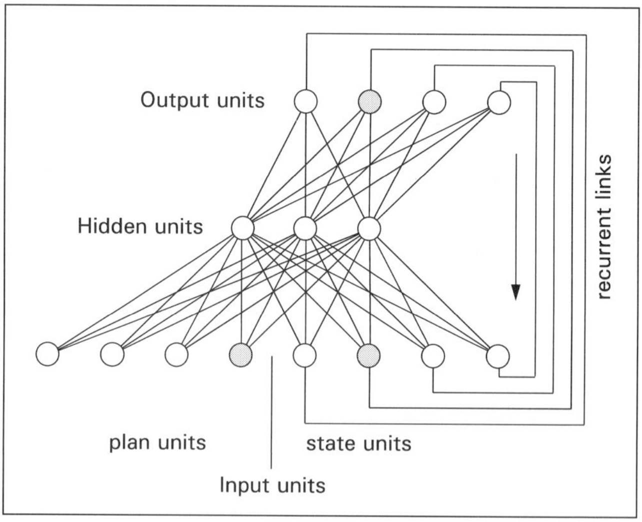

no activity on the state units. But when the second element of the sequence, **B**, is to be output, the pattern of activity corresponding to **A** will have been copied onto the state units. Thus the input to the network has changed, and this different input can be associated with the different output **B**. Thus, like the chaining models described above, these networks effectively rely on associations between successive items in a list to achieve sequential memory.

These networks are complex, and there are several different methods for training them. However Chater & Conkey (1994) have demonstrated that they suffer from severe problems in acquiring some types of sequential dependency. Although various types of recurrent network architecture have attracted much recent interest, they appear unsatisfactory as models of human memory for serial order. This is because all models that involve item-to-item associations suffer from one major problem, and it is to this that we now turn.

Problems with chaining models

A prediction that seems central to any chaining model follows directly from the fact that, during recall, each item in the list acts as a cue for the succeeding item. In the sequence **A B C D**, for example, **A** is the retrieval cue for **B**; **B** is the retrieval cue for **C**, and so on. Therefore, items that follow similar list items are likely to be confused in recall, because they both have similar retrieval cues. Assume for example that **A** and **C** are similar to one another. There should therefore be a tendency to make the incorrect recall **A D C B**, because the retrieval cues for **B** and **D** are similar. Although there was some early evidence that items that followed similar items were indeed more likely to be recalled incorrectly (Wickelgren 1965), it now appears clear that there is no such effect (Henson et al., 1996, see also Baddeley et al. 1991).

A second class of evidence casts serious doubt on chaining models. This concerns transfer effects. It might be expected that the learning of lists of item-to-item associations ("paired associate learning") might be facilitated if the pairs of associations to be learned contained items that were adjacent in a previously learned list. Paired associate tasks require subjects to learn which pairs of items go with each other: **A** goes with **B**; **C** goes with **D** etc. We might expect such a learning task to be easier if subjects had previously learned the same associations as part of a serial list learning task. For example, imagine that subjects are first required to learn the sequence **A B C D**. Subsequently, they are asked to learn one of two lists of paired associations. In one such list, the item pairs are **A B**, **C D**, and **B C**. In another, the pairs are **A C**, **B D**, and **A D**. If the sequence **A B C D** was represented by a series of pairwise associations between successive sequence elements, as assumed by chaining models, then we might expect the subsequent paired associate learning task to be easier if the item pairs were the same as had already been learned in the sequence learning task. In fact, this is not the case (e.g. Young 1968). This provides further evidence against the idea that the original sequence was learned as a chain of associations.

Thus the objections to chaining architectures, seen as models of human serial memory, are simple but effective: the most central predictions that would have to be made on the basis of such a model turn out to be incorrect. In recent years, therefore, attention has turned to other ways in which information about serial order could be represented.

Inhibition models and ecological approaches

In previous sections we have seen that the specific mechanisms that have been advanced as accounts of human sequential memory have largely failed to provide an adequate account of the relevant experimental data. More recently, however, there are signs that an alternative and more ecological approach may provide useful insights into human sequential memory. A central assumption is that a consideration of the simple forms of sequential behaviour exhibited by animals may provide ideas for explaining the more complex sequential behaviour displayed by humans.

One example concerns searching behaviour. Consider the need for an animal to make a systematic sequential search of locations in which food may be available, or to search locations in the visual field. There is a wealth of evidence concerning the sophisticated navigational strategies that animals may use to return to remembered locations (see, e.g. Gallistel 1990). However here we are simply concerned with the problem of conserving energy by not returning to recently searched locations (the same problem arises if there is a depletable food source that will yield no valuable energy). What sort of underlying mechanism could give rise to suitable behaviour? An obvious simple solution is to choose a location or food source to search at random, visit that location and search it, and then inhibit the representation of that location. Then when the next time comes to choose a location or food source to search, the representation of the recently searched location will not be active, and it will not be a candidate for selection in the choice of the next location to be returned to and searched. Similarly, after the second location has been visited and searched, its representation will be inhibited, and therefore when another choice of location-to-search is made, neither the first-searched nor the second-searched location is likely to be chosen, because their representations are both inhibited.

With the simple additional assumption that the inhibition that is applied to a given location's representation gradually wears off over time, we can see that this method can lead to a simple form of sequential behaviour, in which each location is searched in turn, and no location is searched until all others have been searched and the first-searched location is again the most active (because its inhibition has had the largest amount of time to wear off). A similar account can be given regarding sequential visual search of the environment: a systematic search of the visual field could be achieved by directing attention to a randomly chosen location, inhibiting that location's representation, and choosing another to search.

These examples show how a simple inhibitory mechanism can give rise to sequential searching behaviour. An obvious question is, therefore, whether inhibitory mechanisms of this type can be extended to account for the kind of sequential behaviour represented by human recall of a sequence of items. Houghton (1994) has recently described ways in which inhibitory processes may indeed be important in explaining human sequential behaviour, and various types of inhibitory links have been important in a number of recent memory models. An important feature of the Estes (1972) perturbation model, mentioned above, is the claim that long-term memory for serial order is encoded in terms of inhibitory links between each item and successive items within a chunk. Recently, it has become clear that inhibitory processes are both ubiquitous in cognitive processing (Dagenbach & Carr 1994) and also a powerful influence on memory performance (Anderson & Bjork 1994). Furthermore, many recent models of memory for serial order (Houghton 1990, Norris 1994) have accorded a central role to inhibitory processes.

In this section, we describe how inhibitory processes can be a useful feature of models for serial order.

The "competitive queueing" approaches of Houghton (1990) and Burgess & Hitch (1992) make use of an inhibitory process acting subsequently to the retrieval of each item during recall of a sequence. In these models, items compete with one another (on the basis of how highly activated they are) to determine which will be the next item to be output at a given point in the sequence. The item that wins the competition then inhibits itself, to avoid perseverative errors; the control signal moves on, and the competition for the next output in the sequence begins.

We describe this model in more detail below. However in this section we consider the functioning of a simple model that relies heavily on inhibitory processes. The mechanism we describe for illustration is like a simplified version of the "primacy gradient" proposed by Norris (1994) and Henson et al. (in press). If the task is to remember a six-item list, then each item can be assigned an "activation value" with items earlier in the list being given higher activations. This is illustrated in Figure 3.9(a), in which each successive item is assigned an activation that is some fraction of the activation of the preceding item in the list. Sequential recall can then be achieved extremely easily, in the following manner. First of all, the most highly activated item is output. If the activations are as in Figure 3.9(a), this will be the first item. After this item is recalled, its activation is suppressed, by a reciprocal inhibition process. Thus, once recalled, this item will have a very low level of activation, and is therefore unlikely to be re-recalled. The activations of all the six items in the list may now look something like those depicted in Figure 3.9(b). There is then another competition, and the most highly activated item (in this case, item two) is output. Thus the first two items have now been correctly recalled. When the second item has been recalled, its activation is suppressed by the reciprocal inhibition process, and so it (like item 1) is unlikely to be recalled again, at least in the near future while its inhibition is still strong.

Page & Norris (1995) describe a more sophisticated form of this scheme, in which small amounts of noise influence the relative activations of the items, and this can lead to errors in recall. They show that, despite its simplicity, this general approach can give a good account of a very wide range of data from the study of short-term memory for serial order.

FIG. 3.9.   Activations of items in an inhibition model, like the primacy gradient model, both (a) before and (b) after recall of the first item in the list.

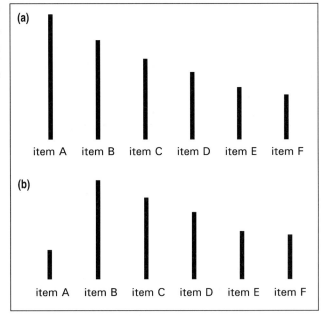

As Houghton (1990, 1994) has demonstrated in a series of publications, the use of this form of what he terms "opponent processes", whereby an item's representation inhibits itself after that item has been output, appears to be ubiquitous in the control of serially ordered behaviour in a wide range of domains. Thus, for example, with this kind of scheme it is difficult to output the same item twice in succession, and there is considerable evidence that this is indeed the case: special mechanisms to overcome the opponent processing seem to be necessary when a repeated letter must be produced twice in succession in spelling, as in words like "accommodate", and this can explain many of the characteristic errors produced in spelling (Houghton et al. 1994). Furthermore, it is indeed difficult to remember separated items that are repeated in a sequence; such items tend to be produced only once. (This is known as the "Ranschburg effect", and is of course exactly what would be expected if the inhibitory processes described above do operate.) Thus there is considerable evidence for the suggestion that inhibitory mechanisms are indeed involved in memory for serial order, although at the time of writing these models are still in the early stages of development.

We now turn to a further class of model, that we refer to as "context association models" or "item-to-context" models. In practice, however, most of these context-association models do also make use of inhibitory processes of the type described above.

Context-based models

The final class of models we wish to describe has, like the group of inhibition-based models described above, only recently seen adequate computational expression. The central idea of these is that successive items in a sequence to be learned become associated with successive states of a time-varying "context signal" or "control signal" (Houghton 1990, 1994, Burgess & Hitch 1992, Glasspool 1995). The precise nature of the associative mechanism employed is not crucial, but is usually simple Hebbian (one-trial) association.

A basic architecture is illustrated in Figure 3.10. In this architecture, a series of context-to-item associations is learned. Here, "context" may be seen as some time-varying representation of the internal state of the

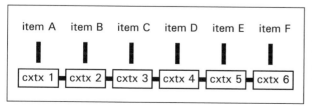

FIG. 3.10. An item-to-context model. Each successive item representation is associated to a different context-of-learning representation.

learning system at the time of learning. Each item, and each successive state of the context, may be represented as a vector as described earlier. Recall of the sequence involves reinstatement of the successive states of the context signal, and these are used as probes with which item representations are retrieved; recall therefore involves reinstatement of the context of learning. Thus, for example, context 1 would be used as a probe to retrieve item **A**, then context 2 would be used to retrieve item **B**, and so on.

A central feature of most such models is that the context or control signal changes only gradually over time. Thus, states of the context of learning that are near to each other in time (e.g. context 3 and context 4 in Figure 3.10) will be more similar to each other than states of the context that are widely separated from each other (e.g. context 3 and context 6 in Figure 3.10). Because nearby states of the control signal are similar to one another, items that were near in the sequence to the target will also be partially retrieved during recall. For example, when context 3 is used as the probe during recall of the third item, the item vector that is retrieved should correspond most closely to item C. However, because the retrieval cue (context 3) is very similar to context 2 and context 4, the item vector that is retrieved will be partially similar to items **B** and **D**. This, if there is any noise in the system, or if it is near to its maximum capacity, there is the possibility that (for example) item **D** will be incorrectly recalled in place of item **C**. This will be particularly likely to occur if items **C** and **D** are themselves similar, and this feature of the general architecture explains why errors in the order in which items are retrieved are more likely to occur when the items are similar to one another (Conrad 1964).

A vector that has been retrieved will tend to be similar to the vectors corresponding to other items in the learned list (as in the above example, where a vector that is most similar to item **C**, but is also somewhat similar to item **B** and item **D**, is retrieved). It is then necessary to choose which actual item is to be output on the basis of the retrieved vector. Competitive inhibitory processes may therefore be used to choose an output from the multiple items that are partially activated. Once an item has been output its representation is inhibited, and the pattern of activation of other nodes is altered (Houghton 1990, 1994, Burgess & Hitch 1992). The next element in the sequence to be output will correspond to the node that has now become most highly activated.

This class of model provides an excellent account of sequence learning and many sequential phenomena of speech production and spelling (see Houghton 1990, 1994, Houghton et al. 1994). A similar architecture has been successfully applied to a wide range of data from the study of human memory for serial order (Burgess & Hitch 1992).

Constructing the context signal

A central question in any context-based model concerns the precise nature of the time-varying signal to which items in an ordered list become associated. It is important that this be independently motivated, for the properties of the context signal give rise to many of the most interesting behaviours of the resulting model. The approach adopted by Houghton in his competitive queueing model, as described above, is to make the contextual signal as simple as possible. Thus the Houghton model uses just two nodes for each sequence, a "start node" and an "end node", and each of these has a level of activation that changes over time according to a simple exponential function. The context vector to which successive items become associated is simply made up of the state of these two control elements at any given time. Thus, the Houghton competitive queueing approach shows how it is possible to get complex sequential behaviour to emerge on the basis of the very simple time-varying context signal in the network.

In some of our own recent work we have adopted a different approach. Rather than try to minimize the complexity of the context signal, we have used a more complex signal that is independently motivated as far as possible. The approach we have adopted is based on the concept of internal oscillators and, like the inhibitory mechanisms discussed above, can be partially motivated in the light of some ecological considerations.

An oscillator based control signal. There is a wide range of independent motivation for the use of oscillators in sequential control of cognitive and other processes (e.g. Wing & Kristofferson 1973, Church & Broadbent 1990, Dehaene 1993, Treisman et al. 1994). There is thus good reason for using oscillators as a basic "dynamic building block" from which a cognitive system can construct internal, dynamic sequences that can be related ("hooked up") to sequences of events (e.g. lists of words in a memory experiment, or phonemes in a word) in the world.

One intuition underlying the approach can be given by a simple example that also serves to illustrate the conviction that human memory for serial order can usefully be examined through functional consideration of the question of what memory is for, especially in the case of simpler organisms. Consider the case of a simple organism, like a wasp, and a source of food that is available at the same time every day (e.g. someone eating marmalade sandwiches at 3.30 p.m. every afternoon). Many animals, including wasps, are good at arriving at the same time of day at a known food location, and the distribution of arrival times peaks at the correct time. How would one design a memory to have the ability to behave in this way? The obvious solution would be to build an internal oscillator, with a period of 24 hours. Thus, at each time of day, this oscillator would output a different vector of neuronal activity. This changing neuronal activity can act as the time-varying context-of-learning signal. The neuronal context vector that corresponds to "3.30 p.m." could become associated, via standard Hebbian association, to the neuronal activity vector corresponding to "marmalade sandwich". Then, every afternoon at 3.30 pm and at no other time, the internal "marmalade sandwich" representation will become active, and can guide the wasp's foraging behaviour (cf. Gallistel 1990). It is easy to see how sequential memory and behaviour can emerge out of such a system; for example: flying to jam sandwiches at 11.30 a.m., to a honey pot at noon, to marmalade sandwiches at 3.30 p.m.

Our model of memory is essentially an extension of the same principle: sequences of item representations are associated to a time-varying control signal, although in our model the context signal is made up of the combined and distributed output of many different oscillators, some of sufficiently low frequency to ensure that states of the control signal never repeat themselves. A rough analogy would be that of an analogue clock face, with many different hands: some rotating fast, like the second hand of a watch, and others rotating arbitrarily slowly, perhaps completing a revolution only once every several years. Such a clock could provide a distinct context-of-learning representation that never repeated itself over an arbitrarily long time period. The clock analogy is imperfect, for in practice it is necessary to give greater weight to the slower oscillators if such a system is to be workable.

In the model we have constructed, each element of the context vector is made up of the output of several different oscillators, with different periodicities. This is illustrated in Figure 3.11.

A time-varying context signal constructed in this way turns out to have important and necessary properties: (a) states of the signal that are near to each other in time are more similar than states separated in time; (b) states of the signal never repeat themselves provided the lowest frequency oscillator is sufficiently slow. This means that states of the signal that are far apart in time are never more similar to one another than states of the signal that are close to one another in time. This is because the context signal that results from a distributed pattern of oscillatory inputs has both "fast" and "slow" underlying components; the "fast" components serve to distinguish states of the context that are nearby in time, and the "slow" underlying components serve to distinguish states of the context that are widely separated in time. This, like Houghton's competitive queueing approach, leads to a dynamic system with many of the right basic properties to account for human

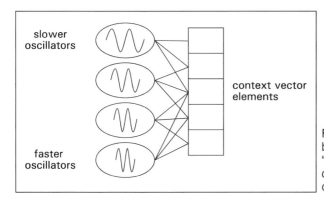

Figure 3.11. An oscillator-based context vector. Both "fast" and "slow" oscillators contribute to each element of the context vector.

memory for serial order. For example: transposition errors arise because context states that are near to each other in time are similar to one another, and hence tend to lead to the erroneous recall of items that were adjacent in the sequence. Thus, as in the human data, there are often transposition errors, especially when items are similar to one another.

We have found that this type of architecture can account for many of the basic phenomena observed in human serial recall: primacy and recency effects; chunking effects; the abolition of recency with a filled delay, and the empirically observed increase in order errors rather than item errors when there is high intra-list similarity.

As in Houghton's competitive queueing model, competitive processes are used to select between different items that are competing to be retrieved, and it is also necessary to inhibit the representations of items when they have been output. However, the need for such processes can be reduced compared with the competitive queueing architecture, because the time-varying context signal is more powerful and hence more able to choose the correct item for output even without the inhibitory processes.

Thus one important difference between our approach and Houghton's competitive queueing model is that the competitive queueing approach minimizes the dimensionality of the time-varying control signal at the cost of increasing the importance of inhibitory competitive processes in sequential control, while our approach, in contrast, allows for a more complex control signal (effectively, this means one with many more time-varying elements) and attempts to minimize the need for inhibitory processes. A combination of these two processes will clearly be needed: more complex time-varying control or context signals will be necessary for more complex tasks and to model the transition to more skilled sequence recall, in which inhibitory and competitive processes could be expected to be reduced as contextual control increases. Second, it will ultimately be necessary to provide some independent motivation for the characteristics of the time-varying control signal, and the oscillator-based approach may provide this.

CONCLUSION

We have reviewed several different architectures that have been used to model human memory for serial order. Early models, such as bin models, failed to give an account of the low-level mechanisms that allow serially ordered behaviour to be produced. Chaining models erroneously predict that transposition errors will be more likely to occur between items that follow similar items; the fact that this prediction is not confirmed experimentally also casts doubt on the widely used connectionist models of sequential behaviour.

Of those that have been implemented at the level of mechanism, both inhibition-based models and models that are based on the idea that items become associated to some representation of a time-varying context signal appear most able to account for key aspects of the human data. Furthermore, some ecological justification can be given for the mechanisms involved. It seems likely that future models will make use of both inhibitory mechanisms and time-varying contextual signals.

NOTES

1. The method is very similar to that used in various types of connectionist model, with the values of the memory trace vector elements that are produced by the convolution algorithm simply being the sum of various connection strengths (in fact, the sum of some of the diagonals of the weight matrix in a simple linear associator).

REFERENCES

Anderson, M. C. & R. A. Bjork 1994. Mechanisms of inhibition in long-term memory: a new taxonomy. In *Inhibition in attention, memory and language*, D. Dagenbach & T. Carr (eds), New York: Academic Press.

Baddeley, A. D. 1986. *Working memory*. Oxford: Oxford University Press.

Baddeley, A. D., C. Papagno, D. Norris 1991. Phonological memory and serial order: a sandwich for TODAM. In *Relating theory and data: essays on human memory in honor of Bennet B. Murdock*, W. E. Hockley & S. Lewandowsky (eds), Hillsdale, New Jersey: Erlbaum.

Bower, G. H. 1971. Adaptation-level coding of stimuli and serial position effects. In *Adaptation-level theory*, M. H. Appley (ed.), 175–201. New York: Academic Press.

Brown, G. D. A. & C. Hulme 1995. Modelling item length effects in memory span: no rehearsal needed? *Journal of Memory and Language* **34**, 594–621.

Brown, G. D. A., P. Dalloz, C. Hulme 1995a. Mathematical and connectionist models of memory: a comparison. *Memory* **3**(2), 113–45.

Brown, G. D. A., C. Hulme, T. Preece, 1995b. The development of associative memory: a connectionist account of learning-to-learn. In *Connectionist models of memory and language*, J. Levy, D. Bairaktaris, J. Bullinaria, D. Cairns (eds), 41–56. London: UCL Press.

Brown, G. D. A., C. Hulme, P. Dalloz 1996. Modelling human memory: connectionism and convolution. *British Journal of Mathematical and Statistical Psychology* **49**, 1–24.

Burgess, N. & G. J. Hitch 1992. Towards a network model of the articulatory loop. *Journal of Memory and Language* **31**(4), 429–60.

Chater, N. & P. Conkey 1994. Sequence processing with recurrent neural networks. In *Neurodynamics and psychology*, M. Oaksford & G. D. A. Brown (eds), 296–94. London: Academic Press.

Church, R. M. & H. Broadbent 1990. Alternative representations of time, number, and rate. *Cognition* **37**, 55–81.

Conrad, R. 1964. Acoustic confusions in immediate memory. *British Journal of Psychology* **55**, 75–84.

Conrad, R. 1965. Order error in immediate recall of sequences. *Journal of Verbal Learning and Verbal Behavior* **4**, 161–9.

Dagenbach, D. & Carr, T. (eds) 1994. *Inhibitory mechanisms in attention, memory and language*. London: Academic Press.

Dehaene, S. 1993. Temporal oscillations in human perception. *Psychological Science* **4**(4), 264–70.

Elman, J. 1988. *Finding structure in time*. CLR Technical Report 8801, Centre for Research in Language, University of California, San Diego.

Estes, W. K. 1972. An associative basis for coding and organization in memory. In *Coding processes in human memory*, A. W. Melton & E. Martin (eds). Washington, DC: Winston.

Gallistel, C. 1990. *The organization of learning*. Cambridge, Mass.: MIT Press/ Bradford Books.

Gillund, G. & R. M. Shiffrin 1984. A retrieval model for both recognition and recall. *Psychological Review* **91**, 1–67.

Glasspool, D. (1995). Competitive queueing and the articulatory loop. In *Connectionist models of memory and language*, J. Levy, D. Bairaktaris, J. Bullinaria, D. Cairns (eds), 5–30. London: UCL Press.

Henson, R. N. A., D. G. Norris, M. P. A. Page, A. D. Baddeley 1996. Unchained memory: error patterns rule out chaining models of immediate serial recall. *Quarterly Journal of Experimental Psychology* **19**, 80–115.

Hintzman, D. L. 1986. "Schema abstraction" in a multiple-trace memory model. *Psychological Review* **93**, 411–28.

Houghton, G. 1990. The problem of serial order: a neural network model of sequence learning and recall. In *Current research in natural language generation*, R. Dale, C. Mellish & M. Zock (eds), 287–319. London: Academic Press.

Houghton, G. 1994. Inhibitory control of neurodynamics: opponent mechanisms in sequencing and selective attention. In *Neurodynamics and psychology*, M. Oaksford & G. D. A. Brown (eds). London: Academic Press.

Houghton, G., G. W. Glasspool, T. Shallice 1994. Spelling and serial recall: insights from a competitive queueing model. In *Handbook of spelling*, G. D. A. Brown & N. C. Ellis (eds). Chichester: Wiley.

Humphreys, M. S., J. D. Bain, R. Pike 1989. Different ways to cue a coherent memory system: a theory for episodic, semantic and procedural tasks. *Psychological Review* **96**(2), 208–33.

Johnson, G. J. 1991. A distinctiveness model of serial learning. *Psychological Review* **98**(2), 204–17.

Jordan, M. I. 1986. Attractor dynamics and parallelism in a connectionist sequential machine. *Proceedings of the Eighth Annual Conference of the Cognitive Science Society*, 531–9. Hillsdale, New Jersey: Lawrence Erlbaum.

Lewandowsky, S. & B. B. Murdock 1989. Memory for serial order. *Psychological Review* **96**, 25–57.

McClelland, J. L., B. L. McNaughton, R. C. O'Reilly 1994. *Why are there complementary learning systems in the hippocampus and neocortex: insights from the successes and failures of connectionist models of learning and memory.* Technical Report PDP.CNS.94.1, Carnegie Mellon University, March.

Metcalfe Eich, J. M. 1982. A composite holographic associative recall model. *Psychological Review* **89**(6), 627–61.

Metcalfe Eich, J. M. 1985. Levels of processing, encoding specificity, elaboration, and CHARM. *Psychological Review* **92**(1), 1–38.

Mewhort, D. J. K., D. Popham, G. James 1994. On serial recall: a critique of chaining in the theory of distributed associative memory. *Psychological Review* **101**(3), 534–38.

Murdock, B. B. 1960. The distinctiveness of stimuli. *Psychological Review* **67**, 16–31.

Murdock, B. B. 1982. A theory for the storage and retrieval of item and associative information. *Psychological Review* **89**, 609–26

Murdock, B. B. 1983. A distributed memory model for serial-order information. *Psychological Review* **90**, 316–38.

Murdock, B. B. 1993. TODAM2: a model for the storage and retrieval of item, associative, and serial-order information. *Psychological Review* **100**, 183–203.

Murdock, B. B. & W. vom Saal 1967. Transpositions in short- term memory. *Journal of Experimental Psychology* **74**, 137–43.

Nairne, J. S. 1990. Similarity and long-term-memory for serial order. *Journal of Memory and Language* **29**(6), 733–46.

Nairne, J. S. 1991. Positional uncertainty in long-term-memory. *Memory and Cognition* **19**(4), 332–40.

Nairne, J. S. & Neath, I. 1994. Critique of the retrieval/deblurring assumptions of the theory of distributed associative memory. *Psychological Review* **101**(3), 528–33.

Norris, D. 1994. Serial order: it's all in the representations. Paper at the International Conference on Working Memory, Cambridge, UK

Oaksford, M. & G. D. A. Brown 1994 (eds), *Neurodynamics and psychology*. London: Academic Press.

Page, M. P. A. & D. Norris 1995. *The primacy model: a new model of immediate serial recall.* Ms submitted for publication.

Pike, R. 1984. Comparison of convolution and matrix distributed memory systems for associative recall and recognition. *Psychological Review* **91**(3), 281–94.

Rumelhart, D. E., G. E. Hinton, R. J. Williams 1986. Learning internal representations by error propagation. In *Parallel Distributed Processing* vol. 1, D. E. Rumelhart and J. L. McClelland (eds) 318–62. Cambridge, Mass.: MIT Press.

Treisman, M., N. Cook, P. L. N. Naish, J. K. MacCrone 1994. The internal clock: electroencephalographic evidence for oscillatory processes underlying time perception. *Quarterly Journal of Experimental Psychology* **47A**, 241–89.

Wickelgren, W. A. 1965. Acoustic similarity and intrusion errors in short-term memory. *Journal of Experimental Psychology* **70**, 102–8.

Wickelgren, W. A. 1966. Associative intrusions in short-term recall. *Journal of Experimental Psychology* **72**, 853–8.

Wing, A. W. & A. B. Kristofferson 1973. The timing of interresponse intervals. *Perception and Psychophysics* **13**, 455–60.

Young, R. K. 1968. Serial learning. In *Verbal behavior and general behavior theory*, T. R. Dixon & D. L. Horton (eds). Englewood Cliffs.: Prentice Hall.

ACKNOWLEDGEMENT

The author gratefully thanks E. Heit, G. V. Jones and M. Oaksford for many helpful discussions.

PART TWO
Conceptual knowledge

CHAPTER FOUR

Psychological representation of concepts

James A. Hampton

This chapter concerns the psychological representation of the concepts that people use to classify, label and understand the surrounding world. As a first step, let us consider what we mean by concepts and conceptual representation. Shanks (this volume) differentiates categorization learning from conceptual knowledge. Categorization itself (the association of particular responses to particular classes of stimuli) is a very broad class of behaviour. At one extreme of complexity it may involve sophisticated judgments requiring lengthy argument and consideration of evidence. For example a juror in a trial must choose to categorize the accused in one of two categories: guilty or not guilty. Similarly an expert in fine art may have to categorize a painting as being a genuine work or a fake. At the other end of the complexity scale, very simple machines regularly perform categorization: a central heating system categorizes the surrounding temperature as above or below the desired level, and responds accordingly. Even simple objects and materials in the world could be said to categorize if they respond differentially to different environmental conditions; for example water categorizes temperatures into those above 0°C (where it is in liquid form) and those below 0°C (where it is solid).

We can see then that categorization *per se* is a behavioural measure that may tell us little about the basis on which that categorization is made. Categorization behaviour does not itself indicate any conceptual understanding. We would not wish to claim that water possesses the concept of its freezing point. Thus a system may be categorizing on the basis of complex thought processes involving deep conceptual knowledge, or it may be categorizing in a simple mechanical fashion. If we have no knowledge of the mechanism itself, then we can only characterize the classification behaviour in terms of the categorization rule that it appears to be following, that is, the categories that it imposes on the stimulus input. Chater & Heyes (1994) develop this point and argue that even in the case of other species of animals, we have no way of determining what kind of concepts they possess, or indeed whether it even makes sense to speak of "concepts" in other species. With other humans, we have the additional source of information that is provided by our ability to speak to each other, and by our common assumption that our thought processes work in the same way. Thus not only can we set people categorization tasks, but we can also instruct them on the basis of categorization to use, and interrogate them on how they believe they are doing the task. We may also introspect and examine our intuitions about how we use our own concepts. We therefore have a far richer set of methods for studying human categorization. The question that has interested many psychologists for the last 40 years or more is how people use concepts as the basis of categorization. The main concern of this chapter will be to consider rival views of how concepts are represented in memory and used to categorize the world.

In 1981, Smith & Medin published an account of the prevailing state of theorizing about concepts, in which they described three main classes of model: the classical, the probabilistic, and the exemplar model (see also Hampton & Dubois 1993). Since that time, two further related "views" of concepts have been developed, namely the theory-based and the essentialist views of concepts. The following sections provide brief accounts of each of these models, and review evidence for and against each one.

THE CLASSICAL VIEW

The view of concepts first developed by cognitive psychologists was one that was borrowed from many sources: analytic philosophy, set logic, lexical semantics, behaviouristic psychology, and the "exact" sciences such as chemistry and biology. In their ground-breaking work, Bruner et al. (1956) set out to explore how people go about discovering the conceptual basis of a given way of classifying a set of stimuli. Presented with an array of stimuli that varied along a number of different dimensions, subjects in their experiments were required to select a particular example stimulus for testing. Having made a selection they would be told whether or not the stimulus fell within the category that had been defined. Subjects were also told what logical form the categorization rule would take; for example a conjunctive rule involving two "necessary" attribute values that were both required for category membership, or a disjunctive rule in which either of two attribute values would be sufficient for category membership. Bruner et al. were therefore interested initially in how subjects would develop search strategies for arriving at a correct hypothesis of the rule in question.

This characterization of concepts as categorization rules was also commonly applied in behaviouristic studies conducted at the time. For example Shepard et al. (1961) devised stimulus sets based on three binary dimensions. The combination of three dimensions, each with two possible values yields eight possible types of stimulus. Shepard et al. investigated a variety of different rules for categorizing the eight stimuli into two classes, including simple unidimensional concepts (based on just one of the dimensions), conjunctive and disjunctive combinations of two dimensions, and more complex rules such as exclusive disjunction (either one or the other of two dimensional values, but not both). Their focus was on the difficulty of learning of these different "concepts", as subjects performed a serial task learning through trial and error to classify the stimuli in the predefined manner.

Smith & Medin (1981) characterized the classical view of concepts as one in which it is assumed that conceptual categorization is based on logical classification rules. More specifically this view of concepts typically assumes that the logical structure of most natural concepts is that of a conjunction of necessary features.

The notion of "feature" had been borrowed from its use in structural linguistics. Early theories of lexical semantics such as that of Katz & Fodor (1963) had proposed that the meaning of nouns could be characterized in terms of a limited set of defining features. Thus the meaning of the word BACHELOR could be represented by the set of features:

>HUMAN +
>ADULT +
>MALE +
>MARRIED –

Note that in this treatment, a semantic feature is normally a dimension with just two values: present (+) or absent (–).

The classical view of concepts thus presented a very "clean" view of semantic representation (and hence of conceptual structure). Conceptual categories are defined in terms of the presence or absence of a conjunction of defining features. Thus all category members have the same set of defining features in common, and any instance that lacks any of the defining features is by definition not in the category. The advantages of this type of conceptual structure are readily apparent in the exact sciences. For example the classical approach to classification of the variety of biological kinds, was to divide the natural world into major divisions, which were each then divided into smaller, mutually exclusive, subclasses in what is known as a "taxonomy". The principle of a classical taxonomy is that each class "inherits" all the defining features of the classes above it—the "superordinate" classes. Thus a SPANIEL will have all the defining features of DOGS, all the defining features of MAMMALS, and all the defining features of all the remaining superordinate classes of ANIMAL, and BIOLOGICAL KINDS. As a model of concepts this taxonomic structure has many advantages: it is a highly efficient system for storage of information, as featural information need only be represented at one level of the taxonomic hierarchy, rather than for all the different classes of which it is true. It also permits rapid semantic decisions to be made simply by reading them off the taxonomic tree. Thus the following kinds of sentences could all be easily verified by a straightforward "look-up" procedure.

> All spaniels are mammals.
> All cats have kidneys.
> No cats are dogs.
> No cats have gills.

The classical view of concepts together with the assumption of a taxonomic storage structure was used by Collins & Quillian (1969, 1972) to develop an early model of "semantic memory". (The latter term was introduced by Tulving (1972) to refer to that part of our memory that stores knowledge of the world and the meaning of words, as opposed to memories of particular episodes or events.) They represented the taxonomy as a "semantic network", involving concepts as nodes, connected by directional links indicating two kinds of semantic relation: "is a type of" and "is a property of". Collins & Quillian showed that the time taken to verify sentences involving superordinate classification ("All cats are animals") or property possession ("All cats breathe") reflected the distance in the taxonomic structure between the head noun term ("cats") and the level at which the information was stored. The advantages of this form of structure were obvious and similar structures are commonly found in artificial intelligence systems for knowledge representation.

Evidence and critique

Beyond its intuitive appeal, there is not a lot of evidence directly supporting the classical view, probably because many researchers took it to be self-evident. For those who still support this view (Osherson & Smith 1981, 1982, Armstrong et al. 1983), the main arguments in its favour are arguments against the other views—in particular the probabilistic view described below (see also Fodor 1994). There are however serious difficulties with maintaining the classical view.

First, it is fair to say that the classical view was heavily dependent on biological kinds as a model for all concepts. However, when applied to the full range of concepts that need to be represented, the suitability of a taxonomic structure becomes highly suspect. How do we categorize the range of objects found in a domestic household for example? There are many cross-classifications that would be possible, for instance in terms of their size and weight, their function, their value or their material. To select any one feature and place it at the head of a taxonomy would be an arbitrary choice. Even the hierarchies explored by Collins & Quillian (1969, 1972) were shown to be problematic. Collins & Quillian took the structure of the taxonomy to be self-evident, and set about exploring times taken to compare concepts at different levels. However when the problem was approached more systematically it was found that categorization times were not always predictable from distance in the taxonomy. For example Smith et al. (1974) showed that in some selected cases, a more distant category relation could be verified faster than a closer one. Subjects were quicker for instance to judge that "A chicken is an animal" is true, than that "A chicken is a bird" is true. It was not therefore possible that subjects were inferring the former by retrieving the two facts "A chicken is a bird" and "A bird is an animal", and then performing a transitive inference. Conrad (1972) found that the associative frequency of properties to nouns was a better predictor of verification time for properties than was distance in the taxonomic tree. Hampton (1982) and Randall (1976) found evidence that even the common assumption that taxonomies represent class inclusion hierarchies could be challenged. Hampton's subjects agreed that CHAIRS are a type of FURNITURE, and that CARSEATS are a type of CHAIR, but were then unwilling to allow that CARSEATS were a type of FURNITURE. It follows that if there is a taxonomy with classes ordered FURNITURE—CHAIR—CARSEAT, there can not be complete inheritance of the defining features of superordinate classes by those below.

The second source of difficulties came from the lack of easily available defining features for many common concepts. Hampton (1979) asked subjects to provide feature information for eight common categories like FRUIT, FISH or FURNITURE. They were interviewed individually and asked to think of features that were important to the definition, features that might make some examples more or less typical, and features that might be relevant at the borderline of the category in determining whether some instance was in or out of the category. From the resulting feature lists, Hampton drew up an inclusive list of features for each category and had another group of subjects judge the extent to which a set of potential category instances possessed each feature. Finally a third set of judges made categorization judgments about the same set of instances. It was clear when comparing the three sets of judgments that for most of the categories there was no conjunctive combination of defining features that would successfully separate category members from category non-members. Most of the features that subjects generated were of one of two kinds; they were either very general features such as "Used by people" or "Living", which were too general to pick out the category from others in the same domain, or they were features such as "Tastes sweet" (of FRUIT) or "Flies" (of BIRD) that were typically true of many category members but not of all. It therefore appears to be the case that people's representation of featural (intensional) information does not contain features that could provide a classical common element definition, but does contain a lot of other information about what kinds of properties are commonly found across category members. It was as an answer to this kind of problem with the classical view that the probabilistic view gained credence.

THE PROBABILISTIC VIEW

The probabilistic view of concepts arose largely from difficulties in applying the classical view to the actual concepts that people possess, as opposed to those that they would possess in some ideal world. Once again, the roots of the view can be traced to a number of other disciplines. In philosophy, Ryle (1951) and Wittgenstein (1958) discovered that many interesting concepts, such as work, or game, or individual identity, were frustratingly difficult to pin down within the classical system of giving definitions. Whenever one proposed an apparently defining feature of such a concept, counterexamples would immediately spring to mind. The reader may like to consider how one would define the essential nature of an activity that would make it count as WORK. Perhaps work always involves some effort, but then a night watchman is working even when simply sitting in a chair drinking coffee. Perhaps payment for one's time may be a required feature, but voluntary and charity workers are presumably still engaged in work. Interestingly, similar problems had arisen within biological classification, where the standard taxonomy developed by Linnaeus was found to create all kinds of anomalies. Disputes arose between different types of taxonomy, and a new form of taxonomy was developed—numerical taxonomy—which used the statistical properties of similarities amongst organisms to derive classes, rather than selecting the major divisions amongst classes *a priori* (Jardine & Sibson 1971).

In cognitive psychology, the probabilistic view of concepts was developed largely through the work of Eleanor Rosch and Carolyn Mervis, who proposed the prototype theory of concepts. Rosch (writing initially under the name of Heider) had spent some time studying the basis of colour and shape concepts in the primitive culture of the Dani in New Guinea (Heider 1972). She had observed that colour concepts like RED and BLUE appeared to be natural "anchor points" or prototypes on the colour spectrum, such that even although the Dani had only two colour words in their language, and no words corresponding to RED or BLUE, they found it much easier to learn to categorize colours around these anchor points than around intermediate colour hues (for which few if any languages in the world have specific colour terms). Rosch & Mervis (1975) went on to develop the notion of prototypes to apply also to common noun categories like BIRD, FRUIT or VEHICLE. These were just those categories which philosophers like Wittgenstein had proposed as examples of concepts with no clear defining features. Wittgenstein (1958) had pointed out that although it was difficult to define the boundary of such categories (that is to find an exact rule for classification), no-one would dispute the classification of clear typical examples. He had suggested that such categories were similar in structure to the way that people in the same family resembled each other; there might be a characteristic family nose, and family eye colour, and family hair type, and different family members would be expected all to have at least some of these characteristics, although not all.

The prototype theory of concepts as developed by Rosch & Mervis (1975) therefore proposed that categorization in many everyday concept categories might follow similar "family resemblance" principles. A particular type of object might be classified as a FRUIT or as a VEHICLE on the basis of a variety of different characteristics (or features), none of which alone need be common to all category members, or sufficient for categorization. In terms of the formal or logical structure of such categories, the prototype view can be seen as involving a set of category features and a categorization rule that states that an instance belongs in the category provided that it possesses a sufficient number of those features. It is therefore still a logical classification rule that can be stated quite explicitly, although it would be inelegant to express it purely in terms of a conjunction and disjunction of features.

An alternative way in which prototype categories have been defined is in terms of similarity. Similarity is commonly assumed to depend on the proportion of common versus distinctive features between two objects (see for example, Tversky 1977). Thus the prototype representation of a concept could be seen also as an "idealized" instance, together with a way of measuring the similarity of other instances to that ideal prototype (that is to say a "similarity metric"). The categorization rule is then specified in terms of whether similarity of an instance to the prototype for the category exceeds some criterion value. While the family resemblance characterization of a prototype as a set of attribute features can be translated into the similarity-based characterization, the reverse is not always the case. For example colour terms like RED are presumed to depend on similarity as measured in terms of psychological distance along the hue spectrum. Other stimuli have also been created for use in psychology experiments that are not easily translated into a featural description. For example Posner & Keele (1968) used a set of dots randomly distributed around a matrix as the "prototype" stimulus, and then defined the categories of stimuli to be learned in terms of the amount of distortion introduced to this random prototype by moving individual dots to neighbouring positions in the matrix. Shanks (this volume) gives more details of this type of prototype stimulus structure. For this kind of stimulus, a prototype concept can be represented as a region within a similarity space, organized around a central "prototype" point, but cannot easily be described in terms of family resemblance.

The "family resemblance" notion of prototype and the "region of similarity space" notion of prototype concepts are not equivalent, and care needs to be exercised not to confuse the two. Osherson & Smith (1981, 1982) provide a formal account of prototypes in which the similarity space figures as a part of the definition, whereas Hampton (1993) prefers to specify prototypes as attribute descriptions. Given that many of the concepts that we are chiefly interested in are complex semantic entities rather than simple unanalyzed visual shapes, the attribute description approach is likely to provide a richer characterization of the information available in conceptual memory. Similarity space representations place severe constraints on what is represented (the prototype is a vector of coordinates on a set of dimensions). There are also many difficulties to be found in mapping similarity directly into metric spaces (Tversky & Gati 1982).

Prototype theory is thus a different way of providing a classification rule for categorization; one that is based on a cluster of attributes, or on a similarity criterion. The advantages of this approach are twofold. First, it fits better with what is known about the kinds of property information that people generate when asked to define concepts. As discussed above, when defining concepts, people do not distinguish between properties that are common to all members of a category and those that are just common to many members. In one unpublished study, Barsalou (personal communication) asked one group of subjects to generate only the most defining attributes of a class, while a second group generated any attributes that they felt were associated with it, however loosely. Barsalou found no reliable difference between the two sets of attributes generated. Second, it provides a ready explanation of why there are many borderline cases of classification. In any similarity-based categorization, there is always the possibility that a particular instance will have a similarity to the prototype (or a number of matching features) that is very close to the criterion for category membership. In such a case, small variations in individuals' concept representations, or small contextual effects on the weight of different features or dimensions, or on the membership criterion itself, will result in instability in categorization. Subjects will feel unsure whether the instance really should be in the category or not. There is plenty of evidence that this kind of borderline instability occurs. McCloskey & Glucksberg (1978) asked a group of subjects to categorize lists of category instances in 17 different categories on two occasions. They found that for items that were judged to be good members of the categories, subjects were quite consistent, but that for items that were atypical, categorization was probabilistic as subjects disagreed with each other, and often changed their decision from one occasion to the next.

Rosch & Mervis also introduced two important new notions in their theory. The first notion has already been referred to, and is the idea that category members differ in their typicality as members of the category. Rosch (1975) asked subjects to consider a list of instances of a category and to judge the "goodness of example" or typicality of each instance as an example of the category. These typicality ratings were made on a seven-point scale, with 1 as "Highly typical" and 7 as "Not a member of the category". The mean typicality ratings were shown to be highly reliable (although as Barsalou 1987, later pointed out, the reliability of the mean ratings was partly just a function of the sample size from which the means were calculated). Furthermore, compared to atypical items, typical category members were shown to have a higher degree of "family resemblance" to other category members and a lower degree of family resemblance to instances from contrasting categories (Rosch & Mervis, 1975). Further research has established category typicality as a major dimension of semantic memory, influencing a wide range of experimental measures and tasks (for example: categorization time, inductive inference, anaphoric reference, and episodic memory).

The second notion introduced by Rosch & Mervis was the idea of a basic level of categorization. In a variety of different tasks, Rosch et al. (1976) were able to show that a particular object was most easily categorized at an intermediate level of categorization that they termed "basic". Thus a particular object might be most naturally or readily categorized as a CAR, and less easily categorized as a VEHICLE (superordinate level) or as a VOLKSWAGEN GOLF (subordinate level). Compared to higher or lower levels, basic level categories were shown to have a higher frequency of single-word names, to be the terms most often used by parents in naming objects for children, to be the most general level at which a generic image of the object class could be formed, and to be the level at which picture-word matching was most rapid.

Subsequent research has suggested that basic level terms are also the most general categories where the kinds and arrangement of parts are the same (Tversky & Hemenway 1984). It has also been shown that the notion of basicness may not be correctly applied to a whole level of categorization, since the term that is basic for an object may vary as a function of typicality, as defined above. For example, when considering SPARROWS, THRUSHES and BLACKBIRDS, Rosch's results suggest that BIRD is the basic level term. It has a higher word frequency, and provided the quickest word-picture matching. However if atypical birds are considered such as OSTRICH or PENGUIN, then it is highly likely that the basic level term is no longer "Bird", but is "Ostrich" or "Penguin" (Hoffman 1982, Jolicoeur et al. 1984). Some caution should therefore be exercised in using the notion of basic level as if it applied generally to all the terms at a particular level of a taxonomic structure.

Evidence and critique

Much of the evidence for the prototype theory of concepts derives from an extensive series of experiments performed by Rosch, and by Rosch & Mervis, and published in 1975 and 1976. They established the importance of typicality as a psychological dimension of natural categories, and the relation of typicality to family resemblance. Hampton (1981) investigated eight abstract categories, like RULE, INSTINCT and SCIENCE, and found that some concepts appeared to have family resemblance structure whereas others did not. Other research showed that prototype concepts were used in a variety of other domains, for example, personality perception (Cantor & Mischel 1977, 1979, Hampson 1982), categorization of everyday situations (Cantor et al. 1982), and psychiatric diagnosis (Cantor et al. 1980).

Criticism of prototype theory and the probabilistic view has come from three main sources. First there is the problem that the simple feature list representations assumed by prototype models are clearly inadequate as full representations of conceptual knowledge. We know and understand a great deal more about a biological kind such as BIRD than a simple list of descriptions about its common appearance, behaviour and habitat. For example we know that it has wings and that it flies, but also that it uses the wings in order to fly. (In fact the reason that we call its upper limbs "wings" has precisely to do with this functional relationship.) As with manufactured objects, we have an understanding about structure–function relationships that involves theoretical notions of cause, and purpose. Our concepts are thus embedded in deeper theoretical domain knowledge (see the theory-based view below). One way to develop this idea is to use a more sophisticated form of knowledge representation, such as the notion, taken from artificial intelligence, of a frame. Barsalou (Barsalou 1992, Barsalou & Hale 1993) developed the argument for a complex system of frame-based representation of concepts, in order to account for our ability to use concepts in planning and achieving goals. Note that more powerful representational forms are not necessarily incompatible with a similarity-based categorization rule involving a "prototype". The central notion of a prototype need not be tied to any one particular form of knowledge representation. A second criticism of feature lists is that they are not only too simplistic, but also appear to involve a degree of circularity: one is "explaining" categorization with respect to one category (Bird) by appeal to a series of other categories (flying, feathers, head, legs, eggs, etc.) many of which probably depend on the category itself for their definition. Birds have heads, but not just any head will do. Whether or not this move is getting us any nearer to our goal of modelling conceptual representation is debatable (Fodor et al. 1980). Future development of the theory will need to move away from purely linguistic descriptions of "features" and replace them with semantic values that are better grounded in a subsymbolic level. Just as a foreigner could never learn a language from a dictionary since the meaning of each word is given using other words in the same dictionary, so the features themselves need to be translatable into nonlinguistic representations related to action and perception, if the representational system is to avoid circularity. Barsalou (1993) has developed a proposal that visual imagery may be able to provide such a prelinguistic representational language for concept representation.

The second critique of prototype theory and the probabilistic approach to concepts comes from a seminal article by Osherson & Smith (1981) that set in train a new research programme on the problem of conceptual combination. Osherson & Smith investigated the claim that probabilistic concepts could be treated formally as fuzzy sets, using the axioms of fuzzy logic developed by Zadeh (1965). Fuzzy logic is a system of logic in which membership of a set, and the truth of a statement can take continuous values intermediate between true (1) and false (0). An example is the truth of the statement "John is tall". In classical logic, this statement must be either true or false (or meaningless). However this would require the fixing of a particular value for height such that everyone above some height is tall, and everyone below that height is not tall. While possibly making life easier for logicians, this kind of fixed criterion does not capture the way that we normally understand the truth of such statements. It is more the case that membership of the set of "tall men" is graded, and increases from a clear false for a 5-foot-tall fully grown individual, to a clear true for a 7-foot-tall basketball player. Zadeh proposed that such intuitions could be captured by assigning a value in the range from zero to one to represent "how true" the statement was. Osherson & Smith (1981) picked up on various suggestions in the prototype literature that membership of natural categories like FRUIT or FISH might also be modelled by fuzzy logic. In particular it had been suggested that typicality gradients and borderline uncertainty were the kind of phenomena that lent themselves well to a fuzzy characterization.

Osherson & Smith considered a number of the axioms of fuzzy logic as applied to natural concepts. The best of their arguments concerned the way in which set conjunction could be applied to prototype concepts. The conjunction of two sets is the class of instances that belong in both sets; thus the conjunction of Pets and Fish is the class of Pet Fish. Without going into the technical details of the argument, fuzzy logic proposes that the degree of membership in a conjunction must always be less than or equal to the degree of membership in either constituent set. It should, after all, be at least as difficult to achieve membership in two sets at once as it is to achieve membership in just one of those sets alone. However people's intuitions of typicality do not fit this stipulation. Common pet fish like a GUPPY or a GOLDFISH are considered to be more typical examples of the conjunction PET FISH than they are either of PETS (cats and dogs being the most typical) or of FISH (salmon and cod are more typical). On the basis of this and other examples, Osherson & Smith argued that the probabilistic approach was not amenable to a logical treatment, and could therefore not be taken seriously as a basis for conceptual thinking. Set logic, they contended, requires that concepts have some kind of classical logical definition as their "core". (Fodor 1994 makes similar claims about the failings of prototypes to provide us with a sufficient basis for a compositional semantics.)

If we are to return to the classical model of concept definitions for the purposes of conceptual thinking, then what are we to make of all the evidence for nondefining properties being represented, and variations in typicality of instances? The answer proposed is that concepts have not only a classically defined core, but also a set of "stereotypical" information that is used to drive typicality judgments. Hampton (1988, 1995) describes this as the "binary view" of concepts. The view makes a distinction between issues of category membership, i.e. what is and what is not an example of the category, and category typicality, i.e. how similar something is to a prototypical or stereotypical example. A version of this distinction was originally proposed by Smith et al. (1974), and it has been supported by several others (Miller & Johnson-Laird 1976, Landau 1982, Armstrong et al. 1983, Rey 1983, 1985). It is also suggested that the category stereotype may be of particular value in the case of real-life situated categorization. We are often unable to tell the "true" nature of something by its external appearance, but the stereotype information allows us to make a good probabilistic guess as to what kind of thing we are dealing with, and hence how to react to it appropriately. Hence the stereotype has sometimes been termed the "identification procedure" for the concept.

The binary view tries to have the best of both models: it can use core definitions to ensure proper set logical relations for conceptual thinking, and it can use the stereotypical information to account for the wide range of typicality effects. It still however suffers from the central problem of the classical model, that is the difficulty of identifying core definitions for more than a handful of concepts. This has led some to postulate that people's representation of these core definitions may actually be empty (see the essentialist view described below). There is also some evidence against the binary view from the literature on conceptual combination (see Rips 1995, Hampton 1997, for reviews). Hampton (1987, 1988) provided evidence that the way people categorize items in conjunctive concepts (like "a sport that is also a game") was not in fact constrained by traditional set logic. People were frequently willing to accord membership in the conjunction to items that they failed to classify as belonging to one of the two sets. Thus CHESS was not considered to be a SPORT, but was considered to be a SPORT WHICH IS A GAME. Membership of conjunctions it appears is also flexible and subject to similarity comparisons; a conclusion that led Hampton (1988) to propose that conjunctions are understood by the formation of a composite prototype constructed from the two prototype representations of the individual constituent concepts.

The third critique of prototype theory came from a paper by Armstrong et al. (1983) in which they demonstrated that typicality gradients were not specifically restricted to prototype concepts. They asked subjects to judge the relative typicality of the members of well-defined categories, like odd or even numbers. They argued that if typicality reflects similarity-based categorization, then where categorization was clearly not based on similarity, there should be no reliable typicality effects. In contrast, they found that typicality differences for odd numbers were just as strong and as reliable as they were for "Roschian" categories like FRUIT or FURNITURE. Hence, they argued, typicality may not be taken as evidence for prototypes.

The critique of Armstrong et al. makes an important point. Typicality gradedness alone is not sufficient evidence for inferring a prototype structure. However it also fails to prove that in the case of Roschian concepts typicality may not also reflect similarity-based categorization. Barsalou (1985) investigated the determinants of typicality in both natural categories and what he called "ad hoc" categories (such as "Birthday presents") using a regression approach. He found that the representativeness of exemplars was of prime importance in predicting typicality ratings for natural categories, but that some other variables were also significantly involved, for example the frequency with which someone encountered a particular example. In the case of well defined categories like "odd number", it will be the case of course that "representativeness" will be constant: all odd numbers are equally good at fitting the rule for determining category membership. In this case, then, other dimensions will take over the determination of typicality, with more frequently used numbers like 3 or 7 being considered more typical than unusual numbers like 831.

THE EXEMPLAR VIEW

The third of the approaches to concept representation is the exemplar view. Described simply, exemplar models propose that conceptual categories are represented by collections of individual exemplar representations. A standard theory of exemplar representation was proposed by Medin & Shaffer (1978), and extended in Nosofsky's generalized context model (1988). Other proponents of the view include Brooks (1978, 1987) who argued for a nonanalytic approach to conceptual structure, meaning that often conceptual tasks depend on the use of actual remembered individual instances situated in a particular context. For example if you were faced with some novel type of exotic fruit, your ability to classify it as a fruit might well depend on processes of comparison of the object along different dimensions of similarity with remembered examples of other common fruits with which you are familiar. According to this view, categorization would not depend on an explicit logical classification rule (as in classical theory) nor on comparison to any generic category representation (as in prototype theory) but rather on a series of comparisons to particular remembered individual exemplars. The classification rule would therefore be stated in terms of the overall similarity of a stimulus to stored exemplars of the category compared to the similarity of the exemplar to stored exemplars of alternative categories.

It is clear that this proposal can readily explain the same evidence that led to the rise of the probabilistic view. When asked to generate concept definitions, subjects would in fact retrieve memories of individual exemplars and offer descriptive properties that they find tend to occur reasonably often across exemplars. The difficulty that subjects have in framing successful definitions is entirely in keeping with an exemplar representation. Similarly the existence of borderline cases is easily explained within the exemplar approach. Some object may turn out to share similarities with the members of two distinct categories, and hence its classification in one or the other may be unstable and subject to individual and contextual variation.

A demonstration of exemplar-based effects comes from a study by Medin & Shoben (1988) in which they asked subjects to judge the typicality of different objects in subclasses of a category. For example, subjects were asked to rate the typicality of a variety of spoons in the two classes SPOON or LARGE SPOON. Medin & Shoben showed that typicality in the two classes varied as a function of another unrelated dimension, namely what the spoon was made from. They showed that while metal spoons were more typical of SPOON, wooden spoons were more typical of LARGE SPOON. The most likely explanation of this effect is that subjects are retrieving familiar instances of large and small spoons and noting the material from which they are made.

Evidence for the exemplar view is reviewed in Shanks' chapter in this volume. Much of the evidence relates to classification learning tasks where subjects learn to classify a set of well controlled, artificially constructed stimuli over many trials. Such experiments frequently show exemplar-based effects, such that similarity to a particular learned exemplar may have a more powerful influence on the speed and probability of a positive classification, than does similarity to the central tendency or prototype of the stimulus set. Exemplar models provide a good fit to many results in the classification learning area. For example, Medin and Schwanenflugel (1981) investigated the learning of two stimulus sets. One could be learned with a prototype-based rule, since the categorization was "linearly discriminable"; a classification rule could be given based on the sum of matching features. The other task could not be learned through forming a prototype, as the categorization structure was not linearly discriminable. (To achieve this, a pair of features would contribute to an item's being in category A if they were both present or both absent, but to category B if either one were present alone). The results showed no advantage for the linearly discriminable stimulus set, from which Medin & Schwanenflugel concluded that subjects were not forming generic prototype representations in this learning task.

Another interesting result was reported by Barsalou et al. (1995). Their subjects viewed a number of exemplars of tropical fish displayed on a computer screen, and learned about the different individuals. They were tested in a transfer task to judge which of various novel exemplars were more likely to come from the same category as those seen previously. The stimuli in the training set involved four very similar fish, and one very atypical-looking one. When the five different fish were presented equally often (and when they were easily differentiated), then transfer to new stimuli was driven by the more common pattern of the four similar fish. However when the atypical fish was presented more frequently than the rest, transfer was affected more by similarity to the frequent atypical exemplar. It therefore appears that subjects are affected by the storage of individual traces, as an exemplar model might predict. In one experiment, however, Barsalou et al. varied the instructions given to subjects. One group were told that all stimuli seen were different individuals, so that the frequency of occurrence reflected the actual frequency of those stimuli in the category at large. The other group were told that there were only five individuals which were seen repeatedly, and that one (the atypical looking one) was less shy of people, and so was more likely to be observed. The results showed a strong effect of this manipulation of instructions: the first group transferred on the basis of the frequency of encounter of the stimuli, whereas the second group were able to discount frequency and base their transfer on the fact that of the five individuals, four were similar to a prototype and one was not. (This result was only obtained under quite particular conditions, notably when the four similar individuals were identical to each other and differed from the atypical individual on eight different dimensions, and when two additional dimensions provided clear individuating information to allow all four similar fish to be clearly differentiated from each other.) The Barsalou et al. study highlights a potential ambiguity, in many exemplar models, in how they define what is to count as an exemplar. It appears that under certain conditions, subjects may be able to choose either to treat each occurrence of an exemplar as an independent exemplar trace, or to treat occurrences of the same individual as contributing to a single exemplar representation.

Exemplar models lend themselves to modelling with neural network models of classification learning. Neural network models in fact tend to blur the distinction between exemplar and prototype representations (see also Barsalou 1990, on the points of similarity and difference between these models). In a simple neural network set up to learn a classification of stimuli, the common structure is for an input layer of nodes in which the full characterization of the stimulus is represented to be connected to an output layer with just two nodes (category A versus category B) via a "hidden layer" of nodes in which the learning itself occurs. Depending on the number of nodes allowed in the hidden layer, the network will show either more or less exemplar learning. With a large number of hidden layer nodes, the network can learn what is effectively a "look-up" table of the classification of each individual stimulus, thus showing completely exemplar-based categorization. With a much smaller number of hidden layer nodes, the network is forced to find general patterns in the stimulus array, and to respond to similarities amongst the stimuli in each set, and the differences between stimuli in the different sets. In fact when the hidden layer has just one node, the network is only able to learn to discriminate stimuli on the basis of a weighted average of the activation from the input nodes (a linearly discriminable classification), which is directly equivalent to a simple prototype model.

Evidence and critique

The topic for the current chapter is the representation of conceptual knowledge rather than classification learning *per se*, and so one has to question the value of exemplar models for the representation of naturally occurring concepts and instances. Evidence from classification learning is not always directly relevant to the question of natural concepts. For example, as described previously Medin & Schwanenflugel (1981) showed that linearly discriminable sets are no easier to learn than nonlinearly discriminable sets. But this doesn't address the question of whether natural concept classes are linearly discriminable in terms of their attributes, and hence whether prototype models are adequate representations of natural concept classes. The learning of new categories through a training procedure has little relation to the evolution of natural concepts during the cultural and linguistic development of a society.

In support of exemplar representations for non-artificial concepts, Brooks (1987) has shown that in the classification of actual objects, there is a processing advantage for objects that have been seen previously over those that are novel, even when the previously categorized objects are wildly atypical. Thus it appears that people can remember the categorization of individuals, and do not need to reconstruct the category decision each time. However as a general model of concepts, exemplar theory appears to leave too much out. It offers no account, for example, of how conceptual categories are formed in the first place. This is also a problem for many other models (see the theory-based account below), but the exemplar model has no account of why people with differing day-to-day experiences do not end up with widely different concepts, or why we end up with categorized experiences at all. The model also needs to assume a similarity metric (otherwise new instances could not be compared with old), which presupposes an underlying semantic structure that is not made explicit. The similarity amongst experimenter-constructed stimuli may be relatively easy to control and its basis understood, but when it comes to categorization of objects in natural categories of biological kinds, or artifacts, or of events or actions in other more general categories, the basis on which similarity to stored instances is judged is far from clear. If this computation of similarity is based on underlying attribute representations of the instances (of the kind used in family resemblance prototypes) then it would appear that the exemplar view needs to specify just what that information is and how it is used to compute similarity. If the computation is not based on attributes, then it remains mysterious how unanalyzed stimuli can be compared in order to compute a sensitive measure of similarity.

Exemplar models are also frequently vague about just what an exemplar is. There is an ambiguity between types and tokens of exemplars that is not always resolved (see, for example, Barsalou et al. 1995). When storing exemplars of spoons to represent the conceptual category of SPOON, do I store every occasion on which I see any individual spoon as a separate "exemplar", or do I keep track of different individuals, but represent each individual only once? Alternatively I might keep track of different indistinguishable subtypes of exemplars; there are, after all, usually many spoons in the kitchen drawer that all look alike. Many exemplar-based effects in natural categories (as opposed to classification learning tasks) may in fact reflect the learning of subcategories of concepts, for example that the category of spoons can be divided into teaspoons, soup spoons, cooking spoons and so forth, rather than a true exemplar representation. The results of Barsalou et al. (1995) suggest that in learning a new category people are heavily influenced by the availability of exemplars in memory (an example of the availability heuristic identified by Tversky & Kahneman 1973). It remains to be seen to what extent conceptual categories in long-term semantic memory are also influenced by such factors.

THE THEORY-BASED AND ESSENTIALIST VIEWS

The last two approaches to conceptual structure will be described together. Although there are different points of view within this approach, they share the major claim that the other views of concepts are too simplistic and reductionist in their approach. The theory-based approach was introduced by Murphy & Medin in a seminal paper in 1985. They posed the important question: why do we have the concepts that we do, and what makes them coherent? The answer, they claimed, was that concepts are not simply arbitrary ways of dividing up the world into similarity-based classes for the convenience of giving things names. Rather, concepts provide a vital function in helping us to understand the world around us. By understanding, we mean that concepts play a central role in allowing us to construct theories of the world. The success of any theory is dependent on the appropriateness of the concepts from which it is constructed. Hence, Murphy & Medin argued, we have developed particular ways of classifying and labelling our world in order to maximize our ability to understand and explain it. Rips (1995) characterizes this approach in terms of "explanation-based" classification. He proposes that we classify an object into a conceptual category that is best able to explain why the object has the attributes that it does. Concepts come with "mini-theories" that are able to provide explanations of the set of properties displayed by an instance. Whichever concept provides the best explanation is the one that the instance is most likely to belong to.

Note that the theory-based view of concepts denies the importance of similarity as an organizing principle in forming categories. There are many classes of object and event that we class together on the basis of deeper aspects, regardless of superficial similarity. This theme has been developed particularly strongly in work with adults by Rips (1989) and in the developmental literature on children's acquisition of concepts (Carey 1985, Gelman 1988, Keil 1989). Rips (1989) developed a number of arguments against similarity as a basis for conceptual categorization. In one set of studies he showed a dissociation between judgments of similarity and judgments of category membership. For example, Rips asked his subjects to tell him in inches the smallest diameter that they thought a pizza could be, and the largest diameter that they thought a quarter (an American coin) could be. Subjects were then asked to imagine an object half way between these two sizes, and asked (a) to judge its similarity to a pizza or a quarter, and (b) to say which it was more likely to be—a pizza or a quarter. Similarity judgments did not follow category membership, in as much as subjects used the inherent variability of the categories in judging membership (pizzas being more variable than quarters), but subjects ignored variability in judging similarity. (Smith & Sloman 1994, have since replicated this study and find that the range of situations in which the dissociation occurs is relatively restricted; in many situations subjects continued to categorize by similarity.)

In another study, Rips (1989) told subjects a story about a creature called a sorp that looked and acted pretty much like a bird, but that lived on a radioactive waste dump. Over the years, the sorp suffered a metamorphosis, losing its feathers, and growing four extra legs until it had an insect-like appearance. Although subjects were happy to say that the sorp was now more similar to an insect than to a bird, they were more likely to categorize it as a bird. These studies make the point that in classification people pay attention to more information than simply the surface appearance of the object being categorized. Its history and ontogeny may be more influential than its current state in determining how it will be classified.

In the developmental field, there have been a number of similar demonstrations of the importance of "deeper", more theoretical knowledge in determining how even quite young children choose to classify. For example, Carey (1985) showed children aged between 4 and 10 a mechanical toy monkey that could move its arms to bang a pair of cymbals. Although they judged the monkey to be more similar to people than any of a range of other animals, all except one group of 4-year-olds nonetheless denied that the toy could breathe, eat or have babies. Gelman & Markman (1986) similarly showed that when told some new fact about a reference object, 4-year-olds were more likely to generalize the fact to an object from the same general category as the reference object, than to another object that was superficially more similar to the reference. Their willingness to induce properties was driven by categorization rather than similarity. Hence it can be argued that categorization cannot be simply based on similarity.

Keil (1986, 1989) showed children a series of pictures of a horse that is painted with stripes until it ends up looking like a zebra. Children then had to say whether it was now a horse or a zebra. While kindergarten children went along with the transformation and accepted that the horse had turned into a zebra, by the age of 8 years most children believed that this kind of transformation would not change what kind of animal it was. In contrast, when an artifact kind, like a coffee pot was similarly transformed until it looked like a bird feeder, the older children (and adults) accepted that the object was no longer a coffee pot. It thus appears that we may have different kinds of definition for natural biological kinds and for artifact kinds, and that our concepts for objects in each domain rely on different underlying theories about what makes something the kind of thing that it is. Keil (1981, 1989) has speculated that there may be a small number of such domain-specific theories, which are available from a very early age and help to determine the path of conceptual development. He argues that, in the same way that Chomsky (1980) has argued for an innate basis for the learning of the deep aspects of linguistic structure, so there must be an innate structure to our conceptual understanding in order to get the inductive process started. The statistically based clustering of "similar" objects, (what Rosch called the "correlational structure of the world"), as exemplified by neural network classification learning models, can only begin to work once a clear domain of input has been selected. The input vector to the network must be of restricted size, and must contain information that is coherent and relevant to the classification of the domain. There is currently no satisfactory proposal as to how such organization could arise through the process of learning alone.

The final view of concepts to be described in this brief overview is the essentialist view. Discussion of the nature of concepts has a long tradition within philosophy, and a rival view of concepts has been developed on the basis of insights arrived at by Putnam (1975) and Kripke (1972), which takes a more radical approach to the rejection of similarity as a basis of concepts. The theory-based view rejects appearance and surface features as being of incidental relevance to the "true nature" of things and their categorization. Instead it proposes that categorization is based on less obvious aspects of the objects. In the case of biological kinds this might be the anatomy and physiology of the organism, while in the case of artifacts it could be the purpose and function for which the object was originally created, and is currently used. According to the essentialist position, even these deeper, more theoretically relevant aspects still do not capture the real definition of a concept. Consider a cat. One of the features in common to all cats may be that they have a liver. But suppose that a mutant creature appeared that was like all other cats in all respects except that the physiological functions normally performed by the liver were somehow performed by other organs in the body; it had no liver. It does not appear likely that we would automatically wish to reject the creature as being a cat. But the same argument could be applied to any other deep "innards"-based aspect of an instance of cat, and so one may not presume that the theory-based definition of the concept is truly capturing the definition of the kind any more than the surface features of fur, ears and purring do.

The doctrine of psychological essentialism as proposed by Medin & Ortony (1989) argues that people have essentialist beliefs for many concepts. That is to say that they believe that both the internal and external properties that we observe in a class of things are present as the result of some common hidden essence, which defines the true nature of the class. A cat is a cat, according to this view, because all cats have some essence in common, but that essence is itself not directly identifiable with any particular set of observable properties. Rather the essence reveals itself through the occurrence of common regularities and similarities amongst the members of the concept category (note the similarity with Rips' account of finding the concept that best explains the instance). Medin & Ortony argue that we understand that there are these essences, even though we may be quite ignorant as to what they are in any particular case.

Psychological essentialism depends for its insights on the related philosophical doctrine of essentialism, as developed by Putnam and Kripke, and more recently by Rey (1983, 1985). The psychological version of the view holds that people subscribe to the existence of essences. The philosophical doctrine is that concepts actually do have essences. It is important to note that the psychological theory is independent of whether or not the philosophical view is correct or not. We may mistakenly believe in essences that don't exist, or similarly we may be mistaken in not believing in essences that actually do exist. It is important therefore that discussions about the nature of psychological representations of concepts, i.e. epistemology do not become confused with discussions about the true nature of the real world, i.e. ontology (see Rey 1983, 1985 and Smith et al. 1984).

How do essentialist beliefs work? According to Putnam, when a particular class of things is given a name, then by the name we mean to refer to whatever is essential to that class—whatever it may be. Hence the word "water" refers to the stuff that we call water, and anything else that has the same essential character. According to Putnam and Kripke, the first naming event "fixes" the reference of the term in a rigid way. We may discover that our current theory that water is H_2O is incorrect, and that in fact water is something else; however water will remain water regardless. Effectively, Putnam argues, we must hand over responsibility for determining the true meaning of many of the words and concepts that we use to the "experts" in society who are in charge of discovering the essential nature of the world. It follows that for many people and for many of their concepts, the concept representation must contain an empty marker for the concept definition. For example if asked what makes petrol petrol rather than anything else (that is, what is its essential nature), most people will admit that they don't know, but that they believe that there is some essence, which some expert chemist could probably define. Our conceptual representation for petrol would therefore contain (along with information about its use, characteristic appearance and smell, combustibility and origin) a "place-holder" for the critical essence, which would say "Ask a chemist!".

Evidence and critique

It is undoubtedly true that our concepts may often form part of wider networks of related conceptual structures, and that in some cases these structures could be described as "theories". The similarity-based theory of concepts (as exemplified by the prototype and exemplar theories) has to rely on the statistical properties of the objects in the environment in order to account for the concepts that we develop. Given that we attend to certain dimensions and attributes of the environment, then statistical clustering on the basis of similarity would provide us with a structure of categories and subcategories with prototype-like properties (in terms of graded typicality, borderline uncertainty, lack of clear-cut definitions and lack of mutually exclusive taxonomically ordered classes). Once a child has developed such a structure, however, why should it change? Work reported in the developmental literature (e.g. Keil & Batterman 1984) shows that children may often start out with apparently similarity-based concepts, but that there is a trend to replace these with deeper, more theoretically relevant concepts as the child grows older. Clearly, therefore, we need an account of the development of deeper understanding, and how conceptual structure has to change to facilitate this understanding.

Sometimes however it appears that psychologists have overestimated the depth of our conceptual understanding. Recent work by Malt (1990, 1991, 1994, Malt & Johnson, 1992) has challenged the theory-based view of artifact and natural kind concepts. Consider for example the case of water (Malt 1994). It is commonly claimed that water is a well defined, scientifically based concept, one with a well known essence, namely H_2O. Malt collected a large number of examples of familiar liquids like coffee, beer, pond water, or swimming pool water. She separated the liquids into those that were called water in the context from which they were taken and those that were "similar to" but not actually water. Malt then asked subjects to estimate what percentage of H_2O was to be found in each one. Surprisingly, the estimates of percentage H_2O varied widely but were of no use for discriminating examples of water from other liquids. It appeared that whether something was called "water" or not, depended not only on its chemical composition, but also on much less scientific aspects, such as its current location, its source and its function for humans.

Malt's work illustrates an important point that is often overlooked in work on concepts: that the way in which we use words to describe the world is not a purely conceptual problem, but also involves the historical development of the language that is being used. There is a tension between the intuition that a word has a meaning that is derived from its semantics in a particular language, and the intuition that word meanings are direct reflections of our conceptual understanding of the world. This tension is frequently unresolved in both the minds of experimenters and in the minds of their subjects.

A recent study of my own (Hampton 1995) further illustrates the difficulty of assuming that the "average person" has well developed theory-based concepts. In this study, subjects were given different scenario instances of a range of concepts. For example they were given different descriptions of objects and asked to say whether the object described was an UMBRELLA. The object descriptions were manipulated with the intention of independently varying a feature that should be part of the core definition of the concept class (for example that the object was designed and used for holding above one's head to keep off the rain), and a set of features that should be incidental to the category definition (for example that the object was a dome made of cloth and wire, as opposed to a flat hexagon made of plastic and wood). Core-defining features were constructed on the basis of the "theory-based" model of concepts: namely, artifacts were defined in terms of intended and actual function, and biological kinds were defined in terms of inheritance of genetic information. The expectation was that the absence of a core-defining feature would bring categorization down from 100% to 0%, whereas manipulation of the incidental features would have no effect on categorization. Surprisingly, it proved extremely difficult to identify sets of features for which this pattern could be obtained. In spite of four recursive attempts to improve the materials for the experiment, weeding out poor examples, and strengthening others, it was impossible to prevent the incidental features from influencing categorization. For example, when told a story about a zebra, the offspring of two normal zebra parents, which was given a special nutritional diet during development that led it to develop into something that looked and behaved just like a horse, two-thirds of the subjects stated that it was no longer a zebra.

A re-examination of Rips' (1989) study with the metamorphosis of a bird into an insect reveals that in his data also there was an effect of the "incidental" information on the likelihood of categorization. Similarity-based effects are thus difficult to eradicate from people's categorization. It may of course be the case that subjects are poor theorists. Many people may well believe that nutritional diet can affect the "essential" nature of some organism. The results of Hampton (1995) may therefore also be taken as supporting the psychological essentialist theory that people do not really know what makes something fall into a certain conceptual class. A rapprochement may indeed be possible between prototype theory and psychological essentialism, if one allows that people believe in essences but, failing to have very much knowledge about them, are inclined to base most of their categorization on similarity to prototype representations. The use of "essences" in people's categorization may be highly restricted in practice.

If most people have "empty slots" for representing concept essences, then what is the value of representing the essence at all? One answer was suggested by Rips (1995) who discusses a problem frequently raised in philosophy concerning the stability of concepts. If the identity of a concept is determined by all the semantic information used to represent it (as for example in the prototype view), then it becomes hard to explain how it is that conceptual differences and development occur for a single concept. This difficulty arises because if two people (or the same person at different times) have two different prototype representations, then it follows that they simply have two different concepts. It is not possible to individuate concepts in terms of the full set of semantic information they contain without coming to the conclusion that everyone has a different set of concepts, and therefore that mutual understanding is impossible. For example if you and I have different conceptual representations of the concept DAISY, then there is in principle no way of showing that they are in fact both representations of the "real" class of daisies, rather than representations of two different concepts, i.e. my concept of DAISY and your concept of DAISY. The "empty essence" slot may then be a way of adding commensurability and stability to concepts. If you and I both acknowledge that there is a real class of daisies that is defined by the daisy "essence", then we can agree that we are talking about the same class of entities, and have discussions and even disagreements about matters of fact pertaining to the class, without the problem arising of knowing whether we are talking about the same thing.

CONCLUSIONS

This chapter has reviewed four major types of model of conceptual representation. What becomes clear as one reviews the evidence for and against each model, is the variety and complexity of human concepts. There is a temptation for theorists to wish to apply their own approach to all conceptual representations. It is however most unlikely that all concepts are defined or represented in the same way. What is needed for the advance of the field is for a principled account to be given of the range of representational powers that people possess, and for a matching up of different kinds of representation with different conceptual domains. Keil (1989) has argued for a two-process view of concept acquisition and representation. On the one hand there are domain-general procedures for recording frequency and correlation information about the co-occurrence of attributes across categories. Such procedures would be good at detecting prototypes, and at storing relevant salient exemplars or subtypes of superordinate classes, and could be easily implemented in neural network learning paradigms. On the other hand, Keil argues that there are domain-specific beliefs about causal relations in different domains. Keil suggests that broad domains such as sentient beings, biological kinds and artifacts are represented with respect to quite different domain theories. These theories, which must presumably have innate origins, drive the child's hypothesis formation about which aspects of the world are relevant for concept formation in different domains. Without constraints on hypothesis formation, it is clear that induction of concepts from raw data is not possible. There are just too many possible ways of categorizing the world for the problem to be soluble without some strong prior constraint. Keil proposes that the child comes equipped with different constraints for different conceptual domains. If this is the case, then we should expect differences to emerge also in adult conceptual representation across different domains. The future for the psychology of concepts may then lie in investigating such differences.

REFERENCES

Armstrong, S. L., L. R. Gleitman, H. Gleitman 1983. What some concepts might not be. *Cognition* **13**, 263–308.

Barsalou, L. W. 1985. Ideals, central tendency, and frequency of instantiation as determinants of graded structure in categories. *Journal of Experimental Psychology: Learning, Memory, and Cognition* **11**, 629–54.

Barsalou, L. W. 1987. The instability of graded structure: implications for the nature of concepts. In *Concepts and conceptual development: ecological and intellectual factors in categorization*, U. Neisser (ed.), 101–40. Cambridge: Cambridge University Press.

Barsalou, L. W. 1990. On the indistinguishability of exemplar memory and abstraction in category representation. In *Advances in social cognition, volume III: content and process specificity in the effects of prior experiences*, T. Skrull & R. S.Wyer (eds), 61–88. Hillsdale, New Jersey: Lawrence Erlbaum Associates.

Barsalou, L. W. 1992. Frames, concepts, and conceptual fields. In *Frames, fields, and contrasts: new essays in semantic and lexical organization*, E. Kittay & A. Lehrer (eds), 21–74. Hillsdale, New Jersey: Lawrence Erlbaum Associates.

Barsalou, L. W. 1993. Structure, flexibility, and linguistic vagary in concepts: Manifestations of a compositional system of perceptual symbols. In *Theories of memory*, A. C. Collins, S. E.Gathercole, M.A.Conway (eds), 29–101. Hove, UK: Lawrence Erlbaum Associates Ltd.

Barsalou, L. W. & C. R. Hale 1993. From feature lists to frames. In *Categories and concepts: theoretical views and inductive data analysis*, I. van Mechelen, J. A. Hampton, R. S. Michalski, P. Theuns (eds), 97–144. London: Academic Press.

Barsalou, L. W., J. Huttenlocher, K. Lamberts 1995. Processing individuals during categorization. (Unpublished manuscript.)

Brooks, L. R. 1978. Nonanalytic concept formation and memory for instances. In *Cognition and categorization*, E. Rosch and B. B. Lloyd (eds), 169–211. Hillsdale, New Jersey: Lawrence Erlbaum Associates.

Brooks, L. R. 1987. Nonanalytic cognition. In *Concepts and conceptual development: ecological and intellectual factors in categorization*, U. Neisser (ed.), 141–74. Cambridge: Cambridge University Press.

Bruner, J. S., J. J. Goodnow, G. A. Austin 1956. *A study of thinking*. New York: Wiley.

Cantor, N. & W. Mischel 1977. Traits as prototypes: effects on recognition memory. *Journal of Personality and Social Psychology* **35**, 38–48.

Cantor, N. & W. Mischel 1979. Prototypes in person perception. In *Advances in Experimental Social Psychology* **12**, L. Berkowitz (ed.), 3–52. New York: Academic Press.

Cantor, N., W. Mischel, J. C. Schwartz 1982. A prototype analysis of psychological situations. *Cognitive Psychology* **14**, 45–77.

Cantor, N., E. E. Smith, R. French, J. Mezzich 1980. Psychiatric diagnosis as prototype categorization. *Journal of Abnormal Psychology* **89**, 181–93.

Carey, S. 1985. *Conceptual change in childhood*. Cambridge, Mass.: MIT Press.

Chater, N. & C. Heyes 1994. Animal concepts: content and discontent. *Mind and Language* **9**, 209–46.

Chomsky, N. 1980. *Rules and representations*. New York: Columbia University Press.

Collins, A. M. & M. R. Quillian 1969. Retrieval time from semantic memory. *Journal of Verbal Learning and Verbal Behavior* **8**, 240–8.

Collins, A. M. & M. R. Quillian 1972. How to make a language user. In *Organization of memory*, E. Tulving and W. Donaldson (eds). London: Academic Press.

Conrad, C. 1972. Cognitive economy in semantic memory. *Journal of Experimental Psychology* **92**, 149–54.

Fodor, J. A., M. F. Garrett, E. T. Walker, C. Parks 1980. Against definitions. *Cognition* **8**, 1–105.

Fodor, J. A. 1994. Concepts—a pot-boiler. *Cognition* **50**, 95–113.

Gelman, S. A. 1988. The development of induction within natural kind and artifact categories. *Cognitive Psychology* **20**, 65–95.

Gelman, S. A. & E. M. Markman 1986. Categories and induction in young children. *Cognition* **23**, 183–208.

Hampson, S. E. 1982. Person memory: a semantic category model of personality traits. *British Journal of Psychology* **73**, 1–11.

Hampton, J. A. 1979. Polymorphous concepts in semantic memory. *Journal of Verbal Learning and Verbal Behavior* **18**, 441–61.

Hampton, J. A. 1981. An investigation into the nature of abstract concepts. *Memory and Cognition* **12**, 151–64.

Hampton, J. A. 1982. A demonstration of intransitivity in natural concepts. *Cognition* **12**, 151–164.

Hampton, J.A. 1987. Inheritance of attributes in natural concept conjunctions. *Memory and Cognition* **16**, 579–91.

Hampton, J. A. 1988. Overextension of conjunctive concepts: evidence for a unitary model of concept typicality and class inclusion. *Journal of Experimental Psychology: Learning, Memory and Cognition* **14**, 12–32.

Hampton, J.A. 1993. Prototype models of concept representation. In *Categories and concepts: theoretical views and inductive data analysis*, I.van Mechelen, J. A. Hampton, R. S. Michalski, P. Theuns (eds), 67–95. London: Academic Press.

Hampton, J. A. 1995. Testing prototype theory of concepts. *Journal of Memory and Language* **34**, 686–708.

Hampton, J.A. 1997. Conceptual combination. In *Knowledge, concepts and categories*, K. Lamberts & D. Shanks (eds), 135–62. London: UCL Press.

Hampton, J. A. & D. Dubois 1993. Psychological models of concepts: introduction. In *Categories and concepts: theoretical views and inductive data analysis*, I.van Mechelen, J. A. Hampton, R. S. Michalski, P. Theuns (eds), 11–33. London: Academic Press.

Heider, E. R. 1972. Universals in color naming and memory. *Journal of Experimental Psychology* **93**, 10–20.

Hoffman, J. 1982. Representations of concepts and the classification of objects. In *Cognitive research in psychology*, F. Klix, J. Hoffman, E. van der Meer (eds). Amsterdam: North-Holland.

Jardine, N. & R. Sibson 1971. *Mathematical taxonomy*. London: Wiley.

Jolicoeur, P., M.A. Gluck, S. M. Kosslyn 1984. Pictures and names: making the connection. *Cognitive Psychology* **16**, 243–75.

Katz, J. J. & J.A. Fodor 1963. The structure of a semantic theory. *Language* **39**, 170–210.

Keil, F. C. 1981. Constraints on knowledge and cognitive development. *Psychological Review* **88**, 197–227.

Keil, F. C. 1986. The acquisition of natural kind and artifact terms. In *Language learning and concept acquisition: foundational issues*, W. Demopoulos & A. Marras (eds), 133–53. Norwood, N. J.: Ablex.

Keil, F. C. 1989. *Concepts, kinds, and cognitive development*, Cambridge, Mass.: MIT Press.

Keil, F. C. & N. Batterman 1984. A characteristic-to-defining shift in the development of word meaning. *Journal of Verbal Learning and Verbal Behavior* **23**, 221–36.

Kripke, S. 1972. Naming and necessity. In *Semantics of Natural Language*, D. Davidson and G. Harman (eds). Dordrecht: Reidel.

Landau, B. 1982. Will the real grandmother please stand up? The psychological reality of dual meaning representation. *Journal of Psycholinguistic Research* **11**, 47–62.

Malt, B. C. 1990. Features and beliefs in the mental representation of categories. *Journal of Memory and Language* **29**, 289–315.

Malt, B. C. 1991. Word meaning and word use. In *The psychology of word meanings*, P. Schwanenflugel (ed.). Hillsdale, N. J.: Erlbaum.

Malt, B. C. 1994. Water is not H_2O. *Cognitive Psychology* **27**, 41–70.

Malt, B. C. & E. C. Johnson, 1992. Do artifact concepts have cores? *Journal of Memory and Language* **31**, 195–217.

McCloskey, M. & S. Glucksberg 1978. Natural categories: well-defined or fuzzy sets? *Memory and Cognition* **6**, 462–72.

Medin, D. L. & A. Ortony 1989. Psychological essentialism. In *Similarity and analogical reasoning*, S.Vosniadou & A.Ortony (eds), 179–95. Cambridge: Cambridge University Press.

Medin. D. L. & P. J. Schwanenflugel 1981. Linear separability in classification learning. *Journal of Experimental Psychology: Human Learning and Memory* **7**, 355–68.

Medin, D. L. & M. M. Shaffer 1978. Context theory of classification learning, *Psychological Review* **85**, 207–38.

Medin, D. L. & E. J. Shoben 1988. Context and structure in conceptual combination, *Cognitive Psychology* **20**, 158–90.

Miller, G.A. & P. N. Johnson-Laird 1976. *Language and perception*. Cambridge, Mass.: Harvard University Press.

Murphy, G. L. & D. L. Medin 1985. The role of theories in conceptual coherence. *Psychological Review* **92**, 289–316.

Nosofsky, R. M. 1988. Exemplar-based accounts of relations between classification, recognition, and typicality. *Journal of Experimental Psychology: Learning, Memory and Cognition* **14**, 700–8.

Osherson, D. & E. E. Smith 1981. On the adequacy of prototype theory as a theory of concepts. *Cognition* **9**, 35–58.

Osherson, D. & E. E. Smith 1982. Gradedness and conceptual conjunction. *Cognition* **12**, 299–318.

Posner, M. I. & S. W. Keele 1968. On the genesis of abstract ideas. *Journal of Experimental Psychology* **77**, 353–63.

Putnam, H. 1975. The meaning of "meaning". In *Philosophical papers. vol 2: Mind, language and reality*. Cambridge: Cambridge University Press.

Randall, R. A. 1976. How tall is a taxonomic tree? Some evidence for dwarfism. *American Ethnologist* **3**, 543–53.

Rey, G. 1983. Concepts and stereotypes. *Cognition* **15**, 237–262.

Rey, G. 1985. Concepts and conceptions: a reply to Smith, Medin & Rips. *Cognition* **19**, 297–303.

Rips, L. J. 1989. Similarity, typicality and categorization. In *Similarity and analogical reasoning*, S.Vosniadou & A.Ortony (eds), 21–59. Cambridge: Cambridge University Press.

Rips, L. J. 1995. The current status of research on concept combination. *Mind and Language*,**10**, 72–104.

Rosch, E. 1975. Cognitive representations of semantic categories. *Journal of Experimental Psychology: General* **104**, 192–232.

Rosch, E. & C. B. Mervis 1975. Family resemblances: studies in the internal structure of categories. *Cognitive Psychology* **7**, 573–605.

Rosch, E., C. B. Mervis, W. D. Gray, D. M. Johnson, P. Boyes-Braem 1976. Basic objects in natural categories. *Cognitive Psychology* **8**, 382–439.

Ryle, G. 1951. Thinking and language. *Proceedings of the Aristotelian Society* (supplementary series), **25**, 65–82.

Shepard, R. N., C. I. Hovland, H. M. Jenkins 1961. Learning and memorization of classifications. *Psychological Monographs* **75**, 1–42.

Smith, E. E. & D. L. Medin 1981. *Concepts and categories*. Cambridge, Mass.: Harvard University Press.

Smith, E. E., D. L. Medin, L. J. Rips 1984. A psychological approach to concepts: comments on Rey's "Concepts and stereotypes". *Cognition* **17**, 265–74.

Smith, E. E., E. J. Shoben L. J. Rips 1974. Structure and process in semantic memory: a featural model for semantic decisions, *Psychological Review* **81**, 214–41.

Smith, E. E. & S. Sloman 1994. Rule-based and similarity-based categorization. *Memory and Cognition* **22**, 377–86.

Tulving, E. 1972. Episodic and semantic memory. In *Organization of memory*, E. Tulving & W. Donaldson (eds). London: Academic Press.

Tversky, A. 1977. Features of similarity. *Psychological Review* **84**, 327–52.

Tversky, A. & I. Gati 1982. Similarity, separability, and the triangle inequality. *Psychological Review* **89**, 123–54.

Tversky, A. & D. Kahneman 1973. Availability: a heuristic for judging frequency and probability. *Cognitive Psychology* **5**, 207–32.

Tversky, B. & K. Hemenway 1984. Objects, parts, and categories. *Journal of Experimental Psychology: General* **113**, 169–93.

Wittgenstein, L. 1958. *Philosophical investigations*. New York: Macmillan.

Zadeh, L. 1965. Fuzzy sets. *Information and Control* **8**, 338–53.

CHAPTER FIVE

Representation of categories and concepts in memory

David R. Shanks

INTRODUCTION

In this chapter, I shall be concerned with the topic of how two closely related sorts of information, namely categorical and conceptual knowledge, are stored in the human memory system. Categorical knowledge allows an organism to generalize what it has learned about one object or event to another similar object or event; while a concept is a representation of a class of objects. Together, much of the information stored in memory is of these two sorts.

To clarify exactly what issues this chapter addresses, let us start by considering the process of categorization, and its opposite, discrimination. These processes have been central to an enormous amount of work in human cognition (see Pearce 1994, for a recent review). Every organism, from the lowly mollusc *Hermissenda* to an adult human being, is capable both of discriminating between objects and of treating distinct objects as similar (categorization). For instance, as a result of learning that a particular plant is toxic, an organism will be able to avoid that type of plant while continuing to eat others. The organism not only discriminates between toxic and nontoxic plants, but also treats a number of perceptually distinguishable objects as alike: specifically, all toxic plants are avoided. Similarly, as a result of exposure to a large number of people, a child is able to say "man" to all men that it encounters and "woman" to all women. The child has the ability to discriminate between men and women and also to categorize a person as a man or woman.

Plainly, the ability to categorize objects is of great advantage, in that it lies at the heart of an organism's ability to adapt its behaviour to the environment, and equally plainly, this ability is underpinned by some form of information that has been acquired and mentally represented by the organism as a result of prior learning. Thus, one goal of the present chapter is to consider what form this knowledge takes. However, categorization is limited in an important way, and in addition to categorical knowledge, people (and some other organisms) are capable of acquiring and using conceptual knowledge. The second goal of the chapter is therefore to analyze the relationship between these two forms of knowledge and to say something about how conceptual knowledge is represented in memory.

In what way is categorical knowledge limited in its usefulness? The answer is that it relies intimately on the perceptual similarity of the to-be-classified object with previous objects that have been encountered. A child says "woman" because the person in front of it resembles previous women it has encountered, and when it sees a robot-woman, or a cartoon character from another planet, it will continue to make a "woman" classification so long as the character sufficiently resembles women it has seen, and although this generalization will often be useful, it can serve to highlight the limitations of categorical knowledge. For instance, a child who has seen examples of circles will be mistaken if it calls an ellipse a circle, no matter how circle-like the ellipse is. Of even greater usefulness than categorization, therefore, is the ability to form conceptual representations of objects or events. In its simplest terms, a concept is a *representation of a class of objects*, such as the class of circles. This representation serves to demarcate circles from members of other categories (such as ellipses) by a principle rather than just on the basis of perceptual similarity.

There are two benefits obtained from being able to construct such a representation. The first is that perceptual similarity can be transcended. For example, human adults who possess the concept woman will not classify robots or cartoon characters as women, because they do not fall into the true class designated by this term. Conceptual knowledge means that people are not forever constrained by perceptual similarity but can instead base their decisions on deeper and more abstract properties of objects (Gelman & Markman 1986, Goldstone 1994). My conceptualization of women tells me that they are human beings made of cells possessing two X chromosomes, and this knowledge allows me to judge that robot women are not true women, no matter how superficially similar to real women. Likewise, a liquid is not water no matter how similar it is in appearance, taste, and so on to water unless it is H_2O (Malt 1994, Putnam 1975). The second benefit is that by possessing a concept, inferences can be automatically be drawn about entities covered by the concept. By possessing the concept *woman*, for instance, I partition this class off as a separate mental representation, and this means that if I learn something new about the class, that property extends to all of the members of the class. For example, if I learn that women have ovaries, I can extend that knowledge equally to all of the individual women I know about (but not to any of the members of other classes, such as robot women). This would be very difficult to achieve without a mental representation of the class.

It should be apparent that categorical and conceptual representations have immense significance in the operations of the mind. Not only is it of great benefit to be able to classify distinct objects as being in some way similar, but the processes of inference and decision-making would be impossible without appropriate mental representations, i.e. concepts, on which to operate. For a thorough discussion of the utility of these representations, see Lakoff 1987. In this chapter, I concentrate initially on the process of categorization, and then consider some of the evidence concerning the representation of concepts. Hampton's chapter in this volume considers conceptual representation in greater depth and from a more linguistic viewpoint than that adopted here.

Before starting to consider how concepts and categories are mentally represented, which is the main goal of this chapter, it may be worth commenting on the relationship between conceptual knowledge and "memory", because at first glance these two appear to be only tenuously related. If one thinks of memory in terms of knowledge about the past—remembering where one went on holiday last year, for instance—then it is clear that this is a very different capacity from the ability to classify objects and conceptualize the world. But it is important to realize that remembering the past is only one form of memory. This type of memory is commonly called *explicit* (or *declarative*) memory and is to be contrasted with *implicit* memory, that is skills, procedures and other sorts of *nondeclarative* memory that are expressed in the absence of conscious recollection of their origins (for reviews, see Richardson-Klavehn & Bjork 1988, Roediger & McDermott 1993, Squire et al. 1993). Thus, for instance, a person with spider phobia may recoil in fear at the sight of a spider without remembering the episode in which their phobia originated. Nevertheless, there is clearly a sense in which their memory does contain information derived from the original episode. Within this taxonomy, categorical and conceptual knowledge are forms of implicit memory.

In this chapter, I shall suggest that categorization is mediated (to a first approximation) by reference to the memorization of instances, with stimuli being represented in a multidimensional psychological space and with inter-stimulus similarities being computed in the course of categorization. Furthermore, current connectionist models provide an excellent description of the specific mechanism by which instances are encoded and represented. Conceptual knowledge, I shall argue, is quite different. I shall review evidence indicating that this form of knowledge is mediated by rules that are abstracted across the objects that fall under the concept. I begin with an extended consideration of the mental representations underlying categorization.

PROTOTYPE ABSTRACTION

Two quite different views of the form of information underlying categorization have been embodied in prototype and instance theories, and for these theories generalization is a central issue. They attempt to describe how learning takes place in situations where there is considerable stimulus variation from trial to trial, and where the ability to generalize to new stimuli perceptibly different from ones already encountered is essential.

In order to understand how prototype and instance theories construe the learning process, and how they explain generalization, it is necessary first to consider the concept of *similarity*. Essentially, prototype and instance theories assume that some mental representation is formed as a result of exposure to a set of training stimuli, with responses to further stimuli being a function of their similarity to the represented stimuli. Although similarity is a common everyday term, psychologists have developed a number of tools for measuring and analyzing it; in particular, it has become commonplace to interpret similarity in terms of distance in a psychological space. As Nosofsky (1992) has noted in a recent review, the idea of a psychological space and the development of accompanying techniques for analyzing such spaces have proven to be amongst the most significant advances made in cognitive psychology in the last 40 years, since they allow us to discover regularities about that space that are distinct from regularities holding in physical space.

One approach to the question of categorical representation, first advocated by Eleanor Rosch (1973), is to say that categories of stimuli are represented by mental prototypes and that learning involves abstracting the appropriate prototype. The category *bird*, for example, might be represented by a typical bird that has been mentally abstracted from our experience of a large number of actual birds. On this account, responding to a new stimulus is a function of its similarity to the prototype. As test stimuli get closer to the prototype, they should therefore become easier to categorize, an effect that is readily demonstrated in the laboratory. For instance, Rosch et al. (1976) asked subjects to categorize artificial stimuli such as random dot patterns. A pattern from one of four categories was presented on each trial and the subject made a classification decision, with corrective feedback for incorrect responses. For each category, the patterns were the category prototype plus one pattern at each of five levels of distortion. After learning the category assignments, subjects were instructed to continue classifying the patterns as rapidly as possible and their response times were recorded. Finally, subjects rated each of the patterns in terms of how typical it was of its category.

On the basis that typical items are closer to the category prototype, the prototype view predicts that differences should be observable in responding to the stimuli as a function of their distance from the prototype, and this is exactly what Rosch et al. observed. Items judged highly typical were classified more rapidly in the test stage than ones judged less typical.

Perhaps the most compelling reason to believe that abstraction of the prototype underlies categorization is the abundant evidence that the prototype stimulus itself will be accurately classified even when it has never been presented in the training stage of an experiment. For instance, Homa et al. (1981) trained subjects to classify geometrical patterns into three categories that varied in size. Three prototype patterns were defined, and training patterns were constructed by distorting these prototypes. In each block of the study phase, subjects saw 20 different patterns from category A, 10 from category B, and 5 from category C. One of these patterns was presented with corrective feedback on each trial, and subjects continued until they had achieved two errorless blocks. In the transfer phase, which occurred either immediately or after 1 week, the original training patterns plus the unseen prototypes were presented for classification.

Homa et al. found that subjects were in some cases more likely to correctly classify the prototype (which they had never seen) than any of the specific training instances, and this was particularly the case when the category contained a large number of instances (20). Figure 5.1 shows that the benefit for the prototype over the original training items was enhanced when a long interval (1 week) intervened between training and testing. Here, the prototype was correctly classified on 96% of trials, while the original patterns were only classified correctly on 85% of trials. Such results seem to imply that the prototype, at least in some

FIG. 5.1.   Mean probability of correct classification responses for original training patterns and novel prototypes. Subjects were trained to classify geometrical patterns into 3 categories. Either immediately or after 1 week, the training items and prototypes were presented as test stimuli. When tested after a week, subjects were more accurate in classifying the prototype than the original training stimuli. Also, the old training items were more susceptible to being forgotten than the prototypes. (After Homa et al. 1981.)

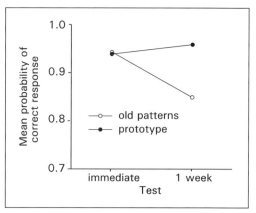

instances, is mentally represented, with categorization being determined by similarity to the prototype.

Homa et al. observed a further interesting result. When classification performance was tested after a delay of a week, considerable forgetting was evident for the original training items: for the 20-item category, performance fell by about 10%. In itself this result is not surprising, but as Figure 5.1 illustrates, Homa et al. found no such forgetting with regard to the prototype patterns. For these, performance if anything slightly improved across the delay. Thus prototype classification may continue to be highly accurate even when memory for the training instances has deteriorated, a result that is consistent with the notion that it is the abstracted prototype that is mediating classification.

These findings support the idea that categorization is guided by prototype representations that are abstracted from the specific training stimuli, and such a view obviously has the attraction of great cognitive parsimony in that only a single representation needs to be maintained for each category of objects. But despite these findings, there are some well known problems with the notion that concepts are represented by prototypes, so much so that it is now generally doubted whether prototype abstraction actually takes place in classification experiments. In the formation of a prototype, a large amount of information is discarded, yet this is information to which people can in fact be shown to be sensitive. For example, abstraction of the prototype means that information about the variance of the studied items, the number of such items, and correlations between values on different dimensions is lost. With regard to the last of these, consider the category of *birds*, for example. Within this category, there is a modal value on the *size* dimension, and a modal value on the *singing* dimension, and an abstracted prototype would encode these values. However, it is also the case that small birds are more likely to sing than large ones, a correlation between the dimensions that could not be recovered from the prototype. The evidence suggests that people are sensitive to such correlations, and therefore the notion that classification depends on distance to an abstracted prototype is at the very least inadequate.

As an illustration, consider an experiment by Medin et al. (1982). In the study phase, subjects were shown 4-dimensional stimuli that represented instances of two categories, where the dimensions encoded two values of each of four symptoms (e.g. 1 = muscle stiffness, 0 = muscle spasms) and the categories were fictitious diseases. The prototype of category A had a value of 1 on dimensions 1 and 2, while the prototype of category B had values of 0 on these dimensions. The remaining dimensions were not individually diagnostic, but instead had correlated values in the two categories. Thus all category A exemplars had the same values on dimensions 3 and 4, while all category B exemplars had different values on these dimensions. By the end of the training stage, the category 1 items were all being assigned to category 1 with probabilities greater than 0.5, while the category 2 items were being assigned to category 1 with probabilities less than 0.5 (which means they were being assigned to category 2).

Medin et al. found that classification of test patterns was strongly affected by whether the values on dimensions 3 and 4 were the same or different. All test stimuli in which these values were the same were more likely to be assigned to category A, while all those in which the values differed tended to be assigned to category B, in accordance with the correlations of the study items. Pattern 1101, for instance, was classified in category B despite the fact that its values on the first two dimensions were diagnostic of category A. Responding must therefore have been affected by the correlation between dimensions 3 and 4.

EVIDENCE FOR INSTANCE MEMORIZATION

Perhaps the strongest motivation for doubting the adequacy of prototype abstraction as the basis of category learning comes from experiments showing that information retained about specific training items influences classification. According to the logic of prototype theories, if the prototype is the only representation in memory that plays a role in the classification process, then specific training items that may have been studied should not affect classification performance. However, such "exemplar" effects can be demonstrated in a number of ways. The simplest is to compare classification performance on old and new patterns equated for distance to the prototype. If classification is based purely on an abstracted prototype, then in experiments such as those of Rosch et al. (1976) and Homa (1981), we should expect the original training items to be classified no better than new test items equidistant from the prototype. Instead, numerous experiments have found that old items are responded to better or faster than new items even when equated for similarity to the prototype.

To illustrate, the original patterns in the experiment of Homa et al. (where subjects were trained to classify simple geometrical shapes into three categories of different sizes) were classified better than new ones equidistant from the prototype. Subjects were tested on new patterns that were distorted from the prototype as much as the original patterns, but which were systematically varied in terms of their similarity to specific old patterns. As Figure 5.2 shows, increased similarity to an old training item went with increased classification accuracy. If information about the specific training items is discarded in the formation of the prototype, it is difficult to see why such a result should emerge.

Another example of the importance of instance memory in categorization comes from an ingenious study by Whittlesea (1987). He constructed the stimulus set shown in Table 5.1. A pseudoword (FURIG) was defined as the prototype, and various distortions around this prototype were constructed. Thus the type I words each differed from the prototype by one letter, the type II words by two letters, and the type III words by 3 letters. However, note that FURIG is the objective prototype for each set of words, in that it contains the modal letter in each position. For the Ia set, for instance, 4 of the 5 items begin with F, 4 have U as their second letter, and so on. Note also that while the IIa, b, and c items each differed from the prototype by two letters, the IIb items differ from the IIa items by one letter while the IIc items differ from the IIa items by two letters.

FIG. 5.2. Percentage of correct classifications for new stimuli varying in their distance from old training items. The experiment is the same one that generated the results shown in Figure 5.1. After learning to classify stimuli into one of 3 categories, which contained either 5, 10, or 20 stimuli, subjects were tested with new stimuli equated in their distance from the category prototypes but differing in their similarity to old training items. Stimuli similar to training items were classified much more accurately then those further away. (After Homa et al. 1981.)

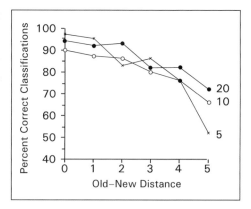

TABLE 5.1
Stimuli used by Whittlesea (1987).

Prototype	Ia	Ib	IIa	IIb	IIc	III
FURIG	FUKIG	FUTIG	FEKIG	FYKIG	FUKIP	PEKIG
	FUREG	FURYG	FUTEG	FUTYG	PUTIG	FYTEG
	PURIG	KURIG	PURYG	PUREG	FURYT	PURYT
	FYRIG	FERIG	FYRIP	FERIP	FYREG	FYKIP
	FURIT	FURIP	KURIT	PURIT	KERIG	KURET

The I stimuli differ from the prototype by 1 letter, the II items by 2 letters, and the III items by 3 letters. FURIG is the prototype of each letter set. Relative to the IIa items, the IIb items differ by one letter, the IIc items by two letters, and the III items by one letter.

Whittlesea examined the way these letter strings were mentally represented using a speeded letter identification task. In the preliminary stage, the IIa, IIb, and IIc words were presented for 30 ms followed by a pattern mask that made identification very difficult, and subjects had to write down in their correct positions as many of the letters as they were able to read. This established a baseline against which later performance could be compared. In the study phase, the IIa words were presented for unlimited time and the subject merely had to write down each word. Then in the test phase the IIa, IIb, and IIc words were again presented for speeded classification as in the preliminary phase.

Since the IIa items presented in the study phase are derived from the FURIG prototype, it is reasonable to imagine that subjects would abstract this prototype during exposure to the study items. But if that were the case, then the encoded prototype should facilitate the subsequent speeded identification of test words to the extent that they share letters with the prototype. Since the IIa, IIb, and IIc test words all differ from the prototype by 2 changed letters, they should therefore receive equal amounts of facilitation. Note also that the test sets are equated for the numbers of times specific letters appear in specific positions.

In contrast to this prediction, if the subjects have memorized the actual IIa study items and respond on the basis of similarity to those separate memorized exemplars then we would expect a greater degree of facilitation on the IIa test items than the IIb items, which in turn should show more facilitation than the IIc words. The IIa items should receive maximal facilitation, since they have themselves been memorized, the IIb items should receive less facilitation because they each differ from the IIa items by one letter, and the IIc items should receive least facilitation since they differ by two letters from the memorized exemplars. This result is exactly what Whittlesea observed. The top portion of Table 5.2 shows the degree of facilitation for each test type in this experiment. The figures in the table give the mean increase in

TABLE 5.2
Results of Whittlesea's (1987) experiments.

Training stimuli	Transfer scores	
IIa	IIa	1.07
	IIb	0.80
	IIc	0.51
IIa	IIa	1.22
	IIc	0.65
	III	0.86

Data are the mean increase in the number of letters correctly identified, relative to the preliminary baseline stage.

numbers of letters correctly identified in position compared to the score from the preliminary phase. Since the maximum score on a test word is 5 letters correct in position, a facilitation of 0.5 represents a 10% increase in letter identification. The critical result was that there was a progressive decrease in facilitation from the IIa to the IIb to the IIc items, despite the fact that these were all the same distance from the FURIG prototype.

Whittlesea's stimulus set allows a further and even more damaging test of the notion of prototype abstraction. Suppose subjects are trained on the IIa items and then tested on the IIa, IIc, and III items at test. The new aspect is the inclusion of the type III test items, and for these, we would have to predict poorer performance than for the other items if similarity to the prototype underlies facilitation, since the type III items differ from the prototype by three letters while the IIa and IIc items differ by only two. The results of this second experiment, also shown in Table 5.2, show the direct opposite of this in that the type III items receive significantly more facilitation than the type IIc items. Why should this be? Inspection of the stimuli reveals that each of the type III items is constructed so as to differ from a IIa study item by at most one letter, while the IIc items differ by two letters. If facilitation is a function of the similarity of a test item to a memorized study item, then this is exactly the outcome that would be expected. Whittlesea's results therefore not only provide a further illustration of instance memorization, but also demonstrate that increasing the proximity of an item to the prototype can have a detrimental effect if the item becomes less similar to the study items, as in the comparison between the IIc and III items.

One final point is worth making concerning the nature of the entity that, according to instance theories, is memorized. Whittlesea & Dorken (1993) have provided evidence that what is encoded in memory is not just a representation of the stimulus itself, but instead is a highly specific entity that retains all sorts of detailed information about the item and about how it was treated at study. Thus the stored instance representation is different if an item is read than if it is spelled. From the point of view of categorization, the inference is that when an item is presented that contains structural relationships between a set of experimenter-defined elements, what is stored in memory is a "snapshot". This snapshot not only preserves those structural relationships, but also many of the relationships pertaining at that moment between the elements of the stimulus and the mental operations performed upon them, as well as such things, perhaps, as the experimental context and mood state of the subject.

THE CONTEXT MODEL

On the basis of the evidence that instance memorization plays an important role in category learning, Medin & Schaffer (1978) proposed that a significant component of the mental representation of a category is simply a set of stored exemplars or instances. The mental representation of a category such as *bird* includes representations of the specific instances belonging to that category, each presumably connected to the label *bird*. In a concept-learning experiment, the training instances are encoded along with their category assignment.

Medin & Schaffer assumed that both instance storage and prototype abstraction could occur during the learning of a concept, and of course any combination of these two processes is possible. However, subsequent studies have shown that performance in a great many category learning studies can be understood in terms of instance storage alone and that the notion of prototype abstraction may be unnecessary. For example, it is not necessary to cite prototype abstraction in order to explain the accurate and rapid classification of prototype stimuli: as originally noted by Hintzman & Ludlam (1980), instance theories can account for prototype effects, because as a test item gets closer to where the prototype would be, its summed similarity to the training instances also increases. Thus classification decisions based on summed similarity will be maximally accurate for the prototype pattern. If instance storage is known to take place, and if instance storage models are able to explain a broad range of empirical phenomena, then adding a prototype abstraction process adds little in terms of explanatory power while reducing the parsimony of the theory.

Although there remain advocates of prototype extraction (e.g. Homa et al. 1991) as well as sceptics about the distinguishability of prototype and instance theories (e.g. Barsalou 1990), the evidence seems to go against the notion that categorization is based on prototype abstraction, and instead supports instance memorization. The instance view proposes that subjects encode the actual instances during training and base their classifications on the similarity between a test item and stored instances. When a test item is presented, it is as if a chorus of stored instances shout out how similar they are to the test item. At the formal level, the best developed such theory is the *context model* of Medin & Schaffer (1978) and Nosofsky (1986). The basic idea is simple: the probability of assigning a stimulus i to category J is a function of the summed similarity of i to each of the j members of category J that have been stored in memory, divided by the summed similarity of stimulus i to all k exemplars of all K categories:

$$P(J/i) = \frac{\sum_j s_{ij}}{\sum_K \sum_k s_{ik}}. \tag{5.1}$$

In this equation, s_{ij} is the similarity of stimulus i to stimulus j. The name "context model" denotes the fact that an instance is a complex conjunction of the target item together with the current context.

We can illustrate the power of instance-storage theories by considering the results of a category learning study by Nosofsky (1987). With one group of subjects, Nosofsky was able to obtain the psychological co-ordinates of each of a set of 12 colour patches by use of a procedure known as multidimensional scaling (MDS). By requiring subjects to learn to respond differently to each of the 12 stimuli, Nosofsky obtained information about the pairwise confusability of these items. MDS is a procedure that recovers the relative psychological co-ordinates of the stimuli from such confusability information (Shepard 1980). With other groups of subjects, Nosofsky then examined category learning. These subjects were trained to classify the stimuli across 240 trials into two categories with appropriate feedback, and the relevant data are from the last 120 trials. Three of the classifications are shown in Figure 5.3. In the pink–brown problem (so-called because the members of the one category are shades of pink and those of the other category shades of brown) the members of the two categories are discriminable by a boundary going from top-left to bottom-right. In the diagonal classification, four stimuli on the diagonal are in category 2 and the rest in category 1. Note that this classification cannot be solved by a single linear boundary. Finally, in the brightness problem the members can be classified on the basis of a horizontal boundary. In this latter problem, stimuli 1, 3,

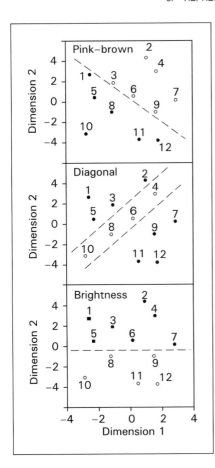

FIG. 5.3.   Three classification problems used by Nosofsky (1987). In each case, the same set of 12 stimuli (Munsell colour patches) was used. The locations of these stimuli in psychological space come from a separate multidimensional scaling analysis. Subjects were trained to classify some stimuli (filled circles) into category 1 and others (open circles) into category 2. In the brightness problem, filled squares represent transfer stimuli. Note that the diagonal classification cannot be solved by a single linear boundary. Copyright © 1987 by the American Psychological Association. Reprinted with permission.

and 5 were presented without explicit feedback and therefore represent transfer stimuli.

Since Nosofsky knew the psychological locations of each stimulus, he was therefore able to compare subjects' classification decisions with the predictions of the context theory. For each stimulus, its similarity to each other stimulus was computed from the appropriate distances obtained in the MDS analysis. Then, the probability of assigning the stimulus to category 1 was determined by Equation 5.1. Nosofsky found a remarkable degree of concordance between predicted and observed classifications, with over 99%, 97%, and 99% of the variance in the observed classifications in the pink–brown, diagonal, and brightness classifications being accounted for, respectively. Clearly, the concordance between the subjects' responses and the predictions of the model are exceptional.

Nosofsky obtained one additional important result. The psychological co-ordinates of the stimuli were obtained from subjects performing an identification learning experiment, and from these co-ordinates can be computed the distances, and hence classification probabilities, of the subjects who performed the categorization part of the study. However, except in the pink–brown problem, these distances did not on their own provide a very good fit to the data. Instead, Nosofsky had to assume that for the categorization subjects, the psychological space in which the stimuli fell was stretched and shrunk along its component dimensions relative to the space for the identification subjects. That is to say, Nosofsky had to assume that selective attention was operating when subjects were classifying the stimuli.

To illustrate, Nosofsky found that no stretching of the space was required for the pink–brown problem in order to predict classification responses, whereas a considerable amount of distortion was required in the diagonal and brightness problems: in both of these, the space had to be stretched vertically and shrunk horizontally. This makes good sense. In the brightness condition, especially, it is clear that subjects can solve the classification by ignoring the saturation dimension (dimension 1) and by attending instead to the brightness dimension (dimension 2). Variations in saturation are irrelevant for the purposes of classification, while variations in brightness, especially in the vicinity of the category boundary, are highly significant. By ignoring the saturation dimension, subjects are effectively shrinking the space horizontally such that stimuli differing only in saturation become more similar. Conversely, stretching the space vertically makes stimuli differing in brightness appear more distinct and hence less confusable.

It is clear that subjects could solve some of these classifications by abstracting a prototype, and so to test this, Nosofsky compared the fits of the context model with those of a prototype theory, assuming that the training instances formed the basis for an abstracted prototype. For the brightness condition, an excellent 99% of the variance in the category responses was accounted for, indicating that this categorization problem is unable to distinguish between the prototype and instance theories. For the pink–brown condition, 95% of the variance was accounted for, and although this is again quite good, it is statistically much worse than the fit of the context model. For the diagonal problem, on the other hand, only 33% of the variance was accounted for. Clearly, the formation of a single category 1 prototype would not allow that problem to be solved. In fact, the fit in this condition was still poor (82%), relative to that of the context model, when it was assumed that two category 1 prototypes were abstracted, one for stimuli 1, 2, 3, and 5, the other for stimuli 7, 9, 11, and 12.

These results suggest, then, that categorization can be well under-stood on the basis of instance memorization. But despite these success-ful predictions, I shall argue that instance memorization theories such as the context model have an important limitation. Essentially, such theories assume that every element of the stimulus is coded as part of the memory trace and is associated with the outcome. But it is rela-tively straightforward to show that this is not necessarily the case.

Table 5.3 shows the design of a very simple experiment that used a medical diagnosis learning procedure to test this assumption. On each trial, the subject saw the case history of a hypothetical medical patient that gave a list of the symptoms that patient had. The subject's task was to diagnose the disease they thought each patient had, and feedback was provided on each trial to tell them whether they were correct or not. On 16 trials symptoms A and B occurred together and predicted disease 1, while on 16 other trials these symptoms were paired with disease 2. On another 16 trials, symptom B occurred on its own and predicted disease 1 (other filler trial types were included in the experiment). The trials were presented in a random order, and 16 undergraduates participated in the experiment. Subjects were tested individually with all events being presented on a computer, and the general procedure was the same as that used in previous similar experiments (e.g. Shanks 1991).

The learning phase of the experiment gave subjects the opportunity to learn about the category structures of diseases 1 and 2. What would we predict will be subjects' judgments of the relationship between symptom A and diseases 1 and 2 at the end of the learning stage? According to instance theories, subjects should store a number of memory traces that assign AB to disease 1 and an equal number that assign it to disease 2, as well as traces of B assigned to disease 1. When making a judgment about A, its similarity to these traces will be com-puted. Schematically, the design of the experiment can be understood by reference to Figure 5.4 which represents a psychological space with two dimensions corresponding to the presence and absence of A and B and with the AB combination falling at the top right-hand corner. As the

TABLE 5.3
Experimental test of exemplar theory.

Trial type	Number
AB→1	16
AB→2	16
B→1	16

A and B are symptoms and 1 and 2 are fictitious diseases.

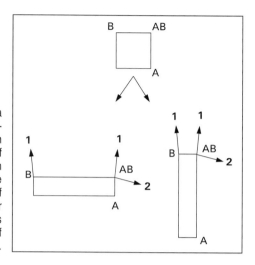

FIG. 5.4. Schematic illustration of a medical diagnosis categorization experiment. Cue compound AB is paired with categories 1 and 2 on equal numbers of trials, while B is paired with outcome 1 on other trials. Possible ways in which the space might be distorted as a result of selective attention are shown in the lower left and right panels. Note that A is always at least as similar to the instances of category 1 as it is to those of category 2.

lower two panels of the figure show, stimulus A is at least as similar to the traces of category 1 as it is to those of category 2. Indeed, if there is some degree of similarity between A and the B→1 traces, then A will be more similar overall to the category 1 traces. Moreover, this will not alter if selective attention leads to one or other dimension being stretched or shrunk.

In contrast to this prediction, subjects rated the A→2 relationship (mean = 93.75 on a scale from 0 to 100) as much stronger than the A→1 relationship (mean = 72.19), Wilcoxon W(9)=1, $p<0.01$. The context model has no explanation for this result, because A's similarity to the members of category 1 should have been at least as great as its similarity to the traces of category 2. So why did the effect occur? We will see in the next section that contemporary connectionist models of categorization, which operate in most situations like instance-memorization devices, can explain this sort of effect straightforwardly. The reason why the effect occurs is a reflection of a well-known phenomenon in animal learning that we shall explore much further in the next section, namely that cue A is a better predictor of category 2 than of category 1. Because of the B→1 trials, cue B is a very good predictor of category 1, and hence on the AB→1 trials A fails to be associated with category 1. At the same time, the occurrence of category 2 on some of the AB trials contradicts the expectation that cue B predicts category 1: therefore, A is a useful predictive event (for category 2) on AB trials. But whatever the precise explanation, the results show that it is mistaken to assume, as the context model does, that all of the elements of a stimulus are equally encoded as part of the memory trace and equally associated with the category.

CONNECTIONIST MODELS

The connectionist approach to memory, which has achieved huge prominence in the last decade (see Quinlan 1991) has its roots in the work of researchers like Rosenblatt (1962), Anderson (1968), and Willshaw et al. (1969) who were interested in how the human brain manages to store large amounts of information. These researchers noted that the brain is essentially an associationist system in that its basic computing element, the neuron, simply transmits electrical excitation or inhibition from its dendrites to its axon. Clearly, networks of highly interconnected neurons do manage to store large numbers of separate memories. But how is this achieved?

The answer that has emerged from this expanding field of research is that information is stored in a distributed fashion in weighted connections between neurons. At the psychological level, this viewpoint proposes that categories are represented in the form of mental associations between the elements of the stimuli and the categories, and that these associations are incremented or decremented on a trial-by-trial basis according to a "connectionist" or "adaptive" learning rule. It might seem that this approach offers nothing beyond the sorts of associative theories that were present 30 or 40 years ago (e.g. Hebb 1949), and therefore would suffer from the same limitations, but two important steps have been taken. One is that the specific rules determining the amount by which an association is changed at a particular moment are vastly more sophisticated than earlier ones, and the other is that contemporary connectionist models are able to learn internal representations that boost to a great extent their learning capabilities. Such internal representations will be considered later in the chapter.

Connectionist models containing very many highly interconnected units have a number of attractive characteristics. First, the only ways in which information is transmitted in an adaptive network are via the excitatory or inhibitory influence of one unit on another, and of course these are precisely the processes by which neural activity is propagated in the brain. Plainly, it is a powerful feature of any psychological model that it appeals only to processes known to operate in the brain.

Secondly, connectionist networks are by their nature parallel processing devices, in that the connectivity of individual units allows parallel sources of information from other units simultaneously to influence the state of activation of any given unit. The appeal of such parallel processing comes from the following observation. People are extremely good at retrieving stored knowledge from partial cues, even when some of the cues are inappropriate. For instance, a friend can often be recognized even if part of their face is occluded or if they are wearing an unfamiliar pair of glasses, a word can be made out even if poorly enunciated, and so on. This kind of memory is called *content-addressable*, because part of the content of the memory is used as the cue for retrieving the whole item. Content-addressable memory is particularly easy to achieve in parallel systems (and correspondingly difficult to achieve in conventional nonparallel ones). Imagine that memories are stored as patterns of activation across a large number of units. When at a later point some subset of those units is reactivated in parallel to represent the retrieval situation, the connections between the units will allow excitation and inhibition to spread such that the entire original pattern of activation is recreated. Even if some units are inappropriately activated, the original pattern may still be recreated if it represents the best "solution" to the current set of input features. Essentially, connections can be seen as constraints that exist on the spread of excitation and inhibition through the system.

A third attractive feature of adaptive connectionist networks is that knowledge is distributed across very many connections. Each connection represents a relationship between a pair of what we might best call microfeatures, and hence it requires a large number of connections to represent memory for a complex object such as a face. At the same time, any given connection can contribute to many different memories. In short, a network can store a large number of superimposed patterns with each one being distributed across the network and with each connection contributing in a small way to very many memories. As a consequence, networks tend to demonstrate considerable resilience in the face of degradation. If some connections are removed or if noise is added to them, there is still a possibility that useful information may be retrieved from the system—again, a characteristic shared by real brains.

Connectionism has had an enormous impact in the last decade across the whole field of cognitive psychology, from perceptual-motor learning to language acquisition. In this section we will consider in detail how connectionist models operate and learn, and ask how successful they are at explaining the basic phenomena of category learning.

The delta rule

While there exist a number of connectionist learning rules, in this chapter I shall focus on one of the simplest, called the "delta rule". This rule has played a major role in several recent connectionist models of human learning. It was first described by Widrow & Hoff (1960), and is formally equivalent, given certain assumptions (Sutton & Barto 1981), to the theory Rescorla & Wagner (1972) developed to account for data from animal conditioning experiments.

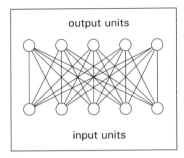

output units

input units

FIG. 5.5. A single-layer feedforward network. A homogeneous layer of input units is connected in parallel to a layer of output units. The connections between the units have modifiable weights. When a pattern of activation (representing the input stimulus) is applied to the input units, activation spreads to the output units via the weighted links between the units. A learning algorithm adjusts the weights on a trial-by-trial basis until the correct pattern of activation is obtained on the output units.

Suppose we have a large set of potential stimulus features and an equally large number of possible categories. We assume that each of the features is represented by a unit in a homogeneous input layer of a large, highly interconnected network such as that shown in Figure 5.5. Each category is also represented by a unit in a separate output layer, and each input unit is connected to each output unit with a modifiable connection (for the moment, we ignore possible hidden units). Networks of this form are called *feedforward* networks or *pattern associators*.

On every trial, some set of features is present and some category is correct. We calculate the activation a_o of each output unit:

$$a_o = \sum_i a_i w_{io}, \qquad (5.2)$$

where a_i is the activation of input unit i and w_{io} is the current weight from feature unit i to category unit o. For a binary-valued feature, a_i will be 1 if that feature is present and 0 if it is not, whereas for a continuous-dimension feature, a_i will take on a value corresponding to the value of the feature on that dimension. Next, we calculate the "error", d_o, on the category unit between the obtained output, a_o, and the desired output, t_o:

$$d_o = t_o - a_o. \qquad (5.3)$$

Values of t_o for binary and continuous dimensions are determined in a similar way to values of a_i, and represent the feedback provided to the learner. Finally, we change each of the weights in proportion to the error:

$$\Delta w_{io} = \alpha a_i d_o, \qquad (5.4)$$

where Δw_{io} is the weight change and α is a learning rate parameter for the feature.

At the end of a series of training trials, we can assume that the probability of classifying the stimulus as a member of category J will simply be the output a_j produced on the category j output node given feature f divided by the total output across all n output units:

$$P(j/f) = \frac{a_j}{\sum_n a_n}.$$ (5.5)

As described above, the procedure for training a connectionist network is to provide a set of input patterns together with their associated target patterns. As a result of incremental weight changes dictated by the delta rule, the network will come to produce the correct output pattern for each input pattern. It is important to note that the delta rule is guaranteed (given enough trials) to produce a set of weights that is optimal for the training stimuli (see Kohonen 1977). That is to say, the rule will find a set of weights that minimizes the squared error between actual and desired output patterns. Often, this squared error will be zero, meaning that the network produces exactly the desired output for each input pattern. We will discuss below some cases where this is impossible unless extra units are included between the input and output units, but even without such units, the delta rule will minimize the squared prediction error. The ability to prove that a learning rule will *converge* in this way towards an acceptable solution is of great benefit.

The connectionist theory outlined above has been applied in various forms to a very large number of category learning tasks, ranging from the very simple to the very complex.

Representation in connectionist networks

Earlier in the chapter we saw that an instance theory like the context model can account for much of the data obtained in concept learning tasks. Recall that there are two principal phenomena which a categorization model must account for, (a) accurate responding to an unseen prototype, and (b) evidence that categorization is mediated at least to some degree by comparison to memorized instances. How do connectionist models fare with these phenomena? In particular, to what extent can it be said that connectionist systems memorize training stimuli?

Beginning with prototype effects, it has been known since the seminal articles by Knapp & Anderson (1984) and McClelland & Rumelhart (1985) that connectionist networks are able to reproduce these effects. This comes about simply because the prototypical pattern activates all of the input units that are most strongly associated with the target category, and few of the units that are strongly associated with other categories. The matrix of weights the network acquires during training represents an abstraction from the training exemplars corresponding (in a very loose way) to a prototype.

What about instance effects? On the face of it, such effects should be difficult to reproduce since each weight in the network is the result of experience of a very large number of different exemplars. McClelland & Rumelhart (1985) showed that a connectionist network can reproduce the instance results obtained by Whittlesea (1987). Remember that Whittlesea's subjects saw letter strings (see Table 5.1) such as FUKIP and attempted to learn something about the internal structure of the strings. In one experiment, subjects were trained on the IIa items and tested on the IIa, IIb, and IIc items. Despite the fact that these test items are equidistant from the prototype, they received different degrees of facilitation as shown in Table 5.2. In another experiment subjects were again trained on the IIa items and tested on the IIa, IIc, and III items. Although the IIc items are closer to the prototype than the III items, it was the latter that received more facilitation, a finding that Whittlesea attributed to the fact that the III items were more similar to the studied IIa items than were the IIc items.

McClelland & Rumelhart (1985) simulated these results by presenting a network with exactly the same events as the subjects received. Each unit coded a letter occurring in a given position. In the learning stage, a stimulus was presented on each trial and weights adjusted according to the delta rule, and then in the test stage the relevant test items were presented to the network (with learning switched off). Table 5.4 shows that both of the key results were reproduced by McClelland &

TABLE 5.4
McClelland and Rumelhart's (1985) simulation of Whittlesea's (1987) results.

Training stimuli	Test stimuli	Observed transfer	Predicted transfer
	IIa	1.07	1.45
IIa	IIb	0.80	0.70
	IIc	0.51	0.60
	IIa	1.22	1.45
IIa	IIc	0.65	0.60
	III	0.86	0.75
	P	—	1.40
Ia	Ia	—	1.20
	IIa	—	0.60

Observed transfer = mean increase in the number of letters correctly identified, relative to the baseline stage. Predicted transfer = increase in dot product between input and output vectors. P = prototype.

Rumelhart's model, where the figures represent the increase in the dot product between the input and output vectors. In showing a greater degree of facilitation to the IIa than to the IIc items the model is clearly demonstrating its ability to maintain information about the specific instances that it was trained with. The benefit of the III items over the IIc items shows that the network can respond to new test items as a function of their similarity to studied items.

Despite this ability to encode instances, in further simulations McClelland & Rumelhart established that their model can also show the superior responding to an unseen prototype that, as we saw in the Homa et al. (1981) experiment, is a feature of human classification. McClelland & Rumelhart trained their network on the Ia items that are similar to the prototype, and then tested it on the prototype, the Ia items, and the IIa items. The results, shown in the bottom part of Table 5.4, reveal a clear benefit for the unseen prototype over the studied Ia items. Although Whittlesea did not conduct the equivalent of this experiment with his subjects, the simulation results correspond to those obtained in other circumstances (such as the experiment of Homa et al.) where the prototype is more accurately or rapidly classified than the training items. In sum, McClelland & Rumelhart (1985) demonstrated an extremely impressive correspondence between data obtained in categorization tasks and the behaviour of their connectionist model.

Internal representations

In the models we have been considering thus far, knowledge is represented in weighted connections. While the learning mechanism discussed in this section, the delta rule, has been successfully applied to many tasks, there is evidence to suggest that the "elemental" representational assumption (that features are directly associated with the category) is inadequate. In learning to associate a stimulus with a category, for instance, it appears that in addition to learning direct associations between the features of the stimulus and the category, intermediate representations of the stimulus can also be involved in associations with the category.

The inadequacy of the elemental assumption comes from the fact that humans can learn nonlinearly separable classifications. In single-layer networks, in which just one layer of modifiable connections exists between the input and output units, it is easy to see that the predicted outcome a_o must be a linear sum of the inputs. Consider a network consisting of two input units (denoted x and y) connected to one output unit, where the inputs and correct output, t_o, can take on values between 0.0 and 1.0, and where the network is trained to classify input patterns into one of two categories. Regardless of the weights, Equation

5.6 tells us that the output a_o must always be a simple linear sum of the activations (a_x and a_y) of input units x and y:

$$a_o = a_x w_{xo} + a_y w_{yo}. \tag{5.6}$$

It follows that the only types of classification such a system can learn are *linearly separable* ones in which the members of the two categories can be distinguished by a simple linear boundary. Specifically, for the delta rule model to learn a classification, it must be possible to construct a straight line in the x, y input space that exactly divides the stimuli into their correct categories. If such a line can be drawn, then there exist weights that will allow the model to produce greater outputs for members of one category than for members of the other category. The classification is solved by making one category response whenever the output is greater than a threshold and the other response whenever it is less.

However, people have no difficulty learning nonlinearly separable classifications which the delta rule model we have been considering would be unable to master. For instance, humans and animals can readily learn discriminations in which two red stimuli are shown on some trials and reward depends on choosing the right-hand one, while on other trials, a pair of green stimuli is presented and reward is given for choosing the left-hand stimulus (Bitterman et al. 1955). Such a discrimination cannot be solved by networks of the sort considered thus far, because each element (red, green, left, right) should be equally associated with reward. A second example comes from Nosofsky's (1987) categorization data. In one of Nosofsky's classification tasks (the diagonal problem shown in Figure 5.3) the two categories cannot be separated by a linear discrimination, yet subjects had no obvious difficulty learning to solve that problem.

It is for this reason that many feedforward connectionist models incorporate a layer of "hidden" units that intervene between the input and output units, as shown in Figure 5.6. Such a network can operate exactly like a single-layer pattern associator if we continue to use the delta rule as the learning algorithm. One particular type of hidden-unit network has been extremely widely investigated and has been shown to have some very powerful properties. In such a "backpropagation-of-error" network, the delta rule applies exactly as before except that it is refined in order to determine how much the input–hidden weights and the hidden–output weights should be changed on a given trial.

The development of multilayer networks using this generalized version of the delta rule has provided a major contribution to recent connectionist modelling, since phenomena such as the learning of

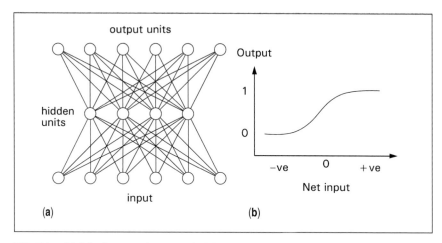

FIG. 5.6.   (a) A backpropagation network. A homogeneous layer of input units is connected in parallel to a layer of hidden units which are in turn connected to a layer of output units. The connections between the units have modifiable weights. The backpropagation algorithm adjusts the input–hidden and hidden–output weights on a trial-by-trial basis until the correct pattern of activation is obtained on the output units. (b) The logistic activation function. The graph shows the sigmoidal relationship between the net input to a hidden or output unit in a backpropagation network and the unit's output.

nonlinear classifications that are impossible for single-layer networks can be easily dealt with by multilayer networks. Although Minsky & Papert (1969) in their famous critique of connectionism were quite correct in highlighting the many weaknesses of single-layer networks, it is regrettable that their critique led so many researchers to lose interest in associationist learning devices. The development of usable training procedures for multilayer networks might otherwise have occurred somewhat earlier.

Be that as it may, even more impressive than their ability to learn nonlinear classifications is the fact, proved by Hornik et al. (1989), that backpropagation networks can learn essentially any mapping between a set of input and output patterns that one cares to construct. Thus, for any set of mappings from arbitrary input patterns to arbitrary output patterns ($I_1 \rightarrow O_1$, $I_2 \rightarrow O_2$, $I_3 \rightarrow O_3$,...), a backpropagation network with sufficient hidden units will construct a set of weights to learn the mapping to any desired degree of approximation. Hence there is no question about the power of this sort of connectionist network for learning associative relationships. But the question remains, does it learn in the same way as humans?

There is undoubtedly evidence of persuasive correspondences between human behaviour and the predictions of backpropagation networks. Some of the best evidence concerns child language acquisition, where it is possible to provide a network with approximately the same sort of input that children receive and see whether characteristics of the network's learning match those seen in children. One much debated example concerns the learning of the past tense in English. While most verbs are regular in adding -ed to produce the past tense (e.g. walk–walked), a number of very common verbs are irregular (e.g. go–went, send–sent, have–had, etc.). Children, of course, are able eventually to learn the correct past tenses, but they also produce some interesting errors in that they occasionally "over-regularize" irregular verbs: they say "goed", "sended", and so on. It turns out that backpropagation networks are also able to produce such errors (Plunkett & Marchman 1991). Because they encounter many more regular than irregular verbs, early on in training, the network may inappropriately generalize the contingency between verb stems and the -ed past tense and apply it to irregular verbs.

From the more general perspective of human categorization, however, the basic backpropagation system is inadequate. The main problem is that backpropagation networks are extremely prone to unlearning; indeed, they seem to suffer from an effect known as "catastrophic interference", whereby target information is almost entirely overwritten or unlearned by later interfering information in a way quite uncharacteristic of human performance. McCloskey & Cohen (1989) observed that a multilayer network using the backpropagation algorithm will perform extremely poorly at reproducing a set of associative A–B relations if it is taught some other information following these pairings. It is very difficult for such a network to maintain a record of a set of information in the face of some new information that has to be learned. In the extreme case, McCloskey & Cohen found that one set of input–output pairings (A–B) was entirely abolished in a backpropagation network by a new set of A–C pairs involving the same input features. Kruschke (1993) has conducted a more systematic demonstration of this effect. Why does the backpropagation learning algorithm lead to this inappropriate behaviour? The reason is that each of the hidden units in such a network is activated by a very high proportion of input patterns, which means that new patterns are very likely to lead to adjustments in the weights connected to a given hidden unit. Such weight changes, of course, almost inevitably entail unlearning. The large receptive fields of the hidden units mean that it is very difficult for a backpropagation network to isolate a particular item of knowledge and protect it from interference.

The above results all suggest that there is a serious problem with the way in which hidden units in a backpropagation network represent stimuli. While there can be little doubt that internal representations are required in some situations, the way in which the generalized version of the delta rule changes weights, coupled with the logistic activation functions of the hidden units, means that it does not provide a good model of human behaviour. In response to this, alternative models have been developed that retain the hidden layer of units, but that use different coding schemes for these units. Space does not allow a detailed review, but the models described by Kruschke (1992) and Shanks & Gluck (1994) have been successfully applied to many human category learning-tasks.

CONCEPT LEARNING

At the beginning of this chapter I drew a distinction between categorization and conceptualization, pointing out that the former refers to the practical ability to respond in a similar way to similar stimuli while the latter refers to the ability to represent a class of stimuli as a whole. The discussion up to this point has focused on categorization and has had little to say about the formation of concepts. Theories like the context model concern themselves solely with the process of categorization. We must turn now, therefore, to consider some of the evidence concerning the formation of genuine concepts.

It is necessary first to consider what exactly we mean by a "concept". This term has, to put it mildly, been a source of some debate and confusion amongst psychologists and philosophers. On the surface, the definition of a concept seems unproblematic: we simply say that a concept is a representation of a class of objects, or (to put it another way) a principle that specifies definitively whether an object or event is a member of that class. For instance, if an object has four sides of equal length lying in a plane and with right-angles between them, then it is a square. Any object conforming to this principle is a square, and any object that violates the principle is not a square. Psychologists and philosophers have been divided on what sort of behaviour is characteristic of conceptual rather than categorical knowledge (see Chater & Heyes 1994), but in this chapter I shall follow Herrnstein (1990) and Smith et al. (1992) in adopting the instrumental definition that behaviour is based on conceptual knowledge if no difference is observable between performance to trained (old) and untrained (new) stimuli that fall into the same category.

To see why this definition is adopted, we must first remind ourselves of what the characteristics are of behaviour based on category representations. Let us suppose that subjects in some category learning task improve their classification performance in the study phase either by memorizing the training stimuli just in the way the context model proposes, or by abstracting the underlying prototype. Thus if the stimuli fall into two categories, subjects respond "category 1" if a stimulus is more similar to the exemplars or prototype of category 1 than to the exemplars or prototype of category 2. Clearly, on this account, responding to test stimuli is going to be graded: some new test stimuli will be highly similar to training stimuli from one category, and hence will evoke rapid and accurate responses, whereas others will be more equally similar to training stimuli from the two categories and hence will be classified more slowly and less accurately. Of course, this is just the behaviour we saw in the experiment of Homa et al. (1981).

In contrast to the behaviour expected if subjects abstract a prototype or memorize the training instances, we would expect to observe none of these differences if subjects learn and respond on the basis of a concept. Imagine a hypothetical boundary dividing the two categories. If this boundary perfectly divides members of one category from those of the other, then it constitutes a rule for classifying the stimuli: a stimulus on one side of the boundary is in category 1, one on the other side is in category 2. We would be strongly motivated to conclude that subjects have learned and are responding on the basis of this rule if the probability and latency of making a correct response is the same for all stimuli (whether old or new) falling on one side of the boundary, for such a result would suggest that the subject is merely analyzing the stimulus to decide on which side of the boundary it falls and is not concerned in the least to compare it to previously seen stimuli.

Thus, suppose the stimuli are rectangles varying in width and height, and suppose the two categories are defined by a rule that unequivocally assigns a stimulus to category 1 if its width is greater than its height and to category 2 if its height is greater than its width. If subjects are able to learn this rule from exposure to some training examples, and if they respond according to the rule, then when they make a classification decision they should merely be interested in whether the stimulus is wider or not than it is high; its similarity to training items should be immaterial. And if responding is based on a decision as to whether the stimulus is wider or not than it is high, that decision (ignoring what happens when width and height are perceptually difficult to discriminate) should be performed equally rapidly and accurately for all stimuli, regardless of how similar they are to stimuli seen in the training phase.

Of course, not all categories can be accurately described by an objective rule or boundary. For instance, the random dot stimuli used in many laboratory experiments are generated by adding noise to each of two or three prototype patterns. Unless the prototypes are highly dissimilar or the amount of added noise is quite small, it is always a possibility that a given pattern could have been generated from more than one category. Unless there is only one correct response for each stimulus, it cannot be said that there is an objective rule for classifying the stimuli. But this does not mean that subjects do not still try to learn a concept by imposing a rule-based classification on the stimulus set: they may incorrectly come to believe that there does exist a classification rule.

The notion that concept-based learning is characterized by an absence of any detectable difference between performance to trained and untrained stimuli is intimately connected to the idea that people are able to form abstractions that go beyond the specific items they experience. Equivalent responding to new and old stimuli implies that an induction has been formed that governs responding to all stimuli. As we shall see below, it is relatively straightforward to obtain evidence for the formation of abstract representations capable of playing a role in categorization.

EVIDENCE FOR CONCEPT-BASED BEHAVIOUR

Laboratory demonstrations of contrasts between concept- and instance-based learning have been provided in a number of studies, and in this section we will consider some examples (see Shanks 1995, for a more detailed review). We begin with compelling evidence obtained by Lee Brooks and his colleagues (Allen & Brooks 1991, Regehr & Brooks 1993). The rationale of the experiments was as follows: suppose that subjects learn to classify stimuli in a situation where a simple, perfectly predictive classification rule exists, and are then tested on transfer items that vary in similarity to the training stimuli. Observed behaviour to the transfer items can be of two contrasting types. On the one hand, "bad" transfer stimuli similar to training items that the rule assigns to the *opposite* category may be classified as quickly and as accurately as "good" items similar to training items the rule assigns to the same category. This would be consistent with classification being determined by the speeded application of a concept, where all that matters is whether the concept assigns the transfer item to one category or the other; whether the item is similar or not to a training instance, and whether that instance was in the same or a different category, should be immaterial. On the other hand, bad transfer items may be classified much less rapidly and accurately than good items, which would be consistent with categorization on the basis of similarity to training instances; there would be no need to cite a concept as being part of the classification process.

Of course, we have already seen in studies like that of Homa et al. (Figure 5.2) that categorization in some circumstances may be influenced by similarity to training items and hence is not concept-based, but Allen & Brooks (1991) and Regehr & Brooks (1993) obtained evidence that both types of outcome can occur, depending on the type of stimuli used and the precise nature of the task. They trained subjects to classify animals into two categories ("builders" or "diggers"). The animals varied in terms of five binary-valued dimensions: body shape, spots, leg length, neck length and number of legs, but only three of the dimensions were relevant. The classification rule stated that category 1 was defined by the conjunction of long legs, angular body, and spots.

In one of Regehr & Brooks' experiments, subjects received 40 trials in the study phase in each of which one animal was presented and feedback was provided for the category decision. Then in the test phase old items were intermixed with new items that were either "good" or "bad". Subjects were encouraged to respond quickly and accurately. Both good and bad items were highly similar to training stimuli, in that they differed on only one dimension, but the good items were in the same category as the study items to which they were similar while the bad items were in the opposite category.

There was one further manipulation in the experiment. For some subjects, the cartoon animals were highly distinctive in that the dimensions of variation of the stimuli were not interchangeable across stimuli. Thus half the animals had spots and half did not, but one animal's spots were different from another's. Similarly, half the animals had long legs and half short, but each set of long legs was slightly different. In contrast, for other subjects the stimuli were much more uniform, with the dimensions being interchangeable: spots for one animal were identical to those for another.

Figure 5.7 shows the key results from the experiment. Although not performing perfectly, subjects had clearly learned something about the category assignments of the training stimuli since at test the percentage of errors for old items was considerably less than 50%, which represents chance responding. For subjects shown distinctive stimuli, the original training items were classified best, the good test items somewhat worse, and the bad items were classified incorrectly on nearly 80% of occasions. This suggests that bad items were classified into the category of their nearest neighbour (which was, of course, in the alternative category). However, for subjects shown uniform stimuli, the pattern of results was quite different: There were no differences between the three types of test item, with the bad items in fact being classified slightly better than the good ones.

FIG. 5.7. Percentage classification errors for distinctive and uniform stimuli. Subjects learned to classify cartoon animals in a situation where a three-dimensional rule perfectly divided the two categories, and then were tested with training (old) items and "good" and "bad" transfer stimuli. Good and bad transfer items were highly similar to training items, but the good items were in the same category as the study items to which they were similar while the bad items were in the alternative category. For distinctive stimuli, bad items were classified much less accurately than good items, suggesting that classification was instance-based. For the uniform stimuli, good and bad items were classified with equal accuracy, suggesting that classification was rule-based. (After Regehr & Brooks 1993.)

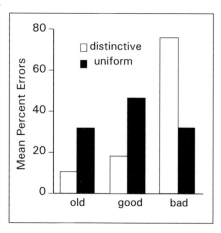

The implication of these results is that the specific dimensional structure of the stimuli controls whether they will be analyzed into their component parts, which in turn determines whether concept- or instance-based classification will occur. While the decomposable uniform stimuli can readily be described and classified on the basis of a concept, the distinctive stimuli lend themselves less well to description in terms of a rule. Taken together, the results suggest that under some circumstances concept-based classification is possible.

An even more compelling example comes from experiments demonstrating the formation of so-called "equivalence sets". Suppose subjects are taught that some stimuli (the A set) are paired with a reward such as food while other stimuli (the B set) are nonreinforced. The subjects then see a reversal in which the B stimuli are reinforced and the A ones not, then a reversal back to the original contingency, and so on for many reversals. At the end of one reversal phase, the subject has learned, say, that the A stimuli are rewarded and the B ones not. Then at the beginning of the next reversal, to the subject's surprise one of the B stimuli is reinforced. Will the subject be able to infer that the reward contingency has now changed across the whole set? That is, will it now expect reward following the remaining B stimuli and not following the A stimuli?

The answer appears to be yes. In appropriate circumstances, a whole set of stimuli can come to be treated as equivalent, such that when something new is learned about one of the stimuli, that knowledge automatically transfers to the remaining ones. This can occur not only in humans but in other animals too. To digress for a moment onto the subject of conceptual representation in pigeons, consider an experiment by Vaughan (1988). He took a collection of 40 photographs of outdoor scenes and divided them at random into two sets such that there was no obvious feature or set of features that distinguished the sets. A slide was presented on each trial, with half of the slides being followed by food and half being nonreinforced. Since the pigeons were hungry, it is reasonable to assume that they would try to work out what it was that characterized the reinforced slides. Over many trials, pigeons learned to respond to members of one set but not to members of the other. When stable responding had been established, a series of reversals occurred, each lasting long enough for the pigeons to learn the new reinforcement arrangement. In each reversal, all of the stimuli that had previously been paired with food were now presented without food and *vice versa*. After many such reversals, the pigeons only had to see one or two slides at the beginning of a reversal to be able to work out the reward contingencies for all of the remaining stimuli. Thus members of the two sets were treated as equivalent, which fulfils our requirement for concept-based responding. Presumably, this equivalence derives from the fact that the different stimuli in a set all had a common consequence. In situations of this sort, groups of arbitrary stimuli are mentally represented as sets or classes, such that a property that comes to be associated with one member of the set is immediately inherited by all of the other members. Evidence concerning the formation of equivalence sets and its relevance to the study of concepts has recently been reviewed by Wasserman & Astley (1994).

Relational concepts

In the cases we have considered thus far, rule induction requires the existence of relational concepts. To see what I mean by this, let us return again to the example of rectangles varying in height and width. In order to decide whether a sample stimulus falls into the target category or not, we need to be able to judge whether its height is greater or less than its width. But there is no simple perceptual feature, or set of features, whose presence or absence will tell us the answer to this question. Instead, we need to make a comparison between two features (height and width). This may seem trivially obvious, but it is important to note that the ability to make this judgment presupposes the possession of relational concepts such as "greater than."

We tend to take the possession of such concepts for granted, but their importance can be illustrated by considering a task that is trivially easy for humans to learn but which would be beyond the capabilities of an organism lacking the simplest of relational concepts. Herrnstein et al. (1989) conducted a well-known categorization experiment with pigeons in which a slide was presented on each trial, with half of the slides being followed by food and half being nonreinforced. The essential property was not any single perceptual feature or set of features, but rather the presence or absence of the abstract relation of "insideness". Specifically, each slide consisted of a dot that was either inside or outside a closed figure, and food accompanied all of the "inside" stimuli. Because of the way the stimuli were constructed, there were no particular perceptual features or sets of features that correlated with food; for example, the "outside" stimuli did not occupy a larger region of the slide than the "inside" stimuli. Rather, the discrimination could only be learned by judging whether or not the dot was inside the figure.

The key question is whether the pigeons were able to master this classification problem. It is obvious that it would be trivial for humans. Children as young as four are known to have relational concepts such as insideness, sameness, and so on (e.g. Smith 1989). In fact, in the experiment of Herrnstein et al. the pigeons showed only very weak evidence of being able to learn the classification, suggesting that "insideness" is beyond their conceptual capability. What is it that allows humans but not pigeons to master this sort of problem? Clearly, the simplest answer is that possession of genuine relational concepts like "insideness" is the critical factor. It must be possible, given a stimulus array, to extract from it certain abstract features such as that one part is inside another, one element is different from another, and so on. The associative learning capabilities of humans are plainly boosted by the ability to interpret stimuli in terms of such concepts.

We are naturally led to wonder where such concepts come from. This chapter is not the place to consider this topic in any detail, but it is worth noting that possession of such concepts represents a considerable challenge to empiricism, since it is hard to see how exposure to positive and negative examples of a concept like "insideness" could ever be sufficient for that concept to be acquired, no matter how powerful the learning mechanism. To learn such a concept seems to require the ability to represent the stimulus on a dimension (inside–outside) that presupposes the very concept that we are trying to explain.

CONCLUSIONS

This chapter has been concerned with the question of how categorical and conceptual knowledge is stored in memory. To a first approximation, category information can be understood in terms of the memorization of training instances, with classification decisions being guided by similarity to stored instances. This first approximation can be refined by moving down to a more mechanistic level of explanation.

Connectionist networks behave very much like instance memorizers, although in truth memories are superimposed on top of one another in a distributed fashion. By using a learning algorithm such as the delta rule, and by allowing internal units to mediate between the input features and the category, an impressive amount of categorization data can be understood.

Humans can go beyond simple categorization, however, insofar as they can form representations of classes of objects (i.e. concepts). Conceptual knowledge means that people are not forever constrained by perceptual similarity but can instead base their decisions on deeper and more abstract properties of objects, and also that new knowledge about the class can be extended to each of its members. A number of experiments have been reviewed that illustrate the application of such abstract properties.

Although connectionist models may be able to construct genuinely conceptual representations, current research has not established how this might be achieved. One of the main goals for future research into the representation of concepts in memory is to understand at the computational or mechanistic level how such representations are formed.

REFERENCES

Allen, S. W. & L. R. Brooks 1991. Specializing the operation of an explicit rule. *Journal of Experimental Psychology: General* **120**, 3–19.

Anderson, J. A. 1968. A memory storage model utilizing spatial correlation functions. *Kybernetik* **5**, 113–19.

Barsalou, L. W. 1990. On the indistinguishability of exemplar memory and abstraction in category representation. In *Advances in social cognition*, T. K. Srull & R. S. Wyer (eds), vol.3, 61–88. Hillsdale, New Jersey: Lawrence Erlbaum Associates.

Bitterman, M. E., D. W. Tyler, C. B. Elam 1955. Simultaneous and successive discrimination under identical stimulating conditions. *American Journal of Psychology* **68**, 237–48.

Chater, N. & C. Heyes 1994. Animal concepts: content and discontent. *Mind and Language* **9**, 209–46.

Gelman, S. A. & E. M. Markman 1986. Categories and induction in young children. *Cognition* **23**, 183–209.

Goldstone, R. L. 1994. The role of similarity in categorization: providing a groundwork. *Cognition* **52**, 125–57.

Hebb, D. O. 1949. *Organization of behavior*. New York: Wiley.

Herrnstein, R. J. 1990. Levels of stimulus control: a functional approach. *Cognition* **37**, 133–66.

Herrnstein, R. J., W. Vaughan, D. B. Mumford, S. M. Kosslyn 1989. Teaching pigeons an abstract relational rule: insideness. *Perception and Psychophysics* **46**, 56–64.

Hintzman, D. L. & G. Ludlam 1980. Differential forgetting of prototypes and old instances: simulation by an exemplar-based classification model. *Memory and Cognition* **8**, 378–82.

Homa, D., S. Dunbar, L. Nohre 1991. Instance frequency, categorization, and the modulating effect of experience. *Journal of Experimental Psychology: Learning, Memory, and Cognition* **17**, 444–58.

Homa, D., S. Sterling, L. Trepel 1981. Limitations of exemplar-based generalization and the abstraction of categorical information. *Journal of Experimental Psychology: Human Learning and Memory* **7**, 418–39.

Hornik, K., M. Stinchcombe, H. White 1989. Multilayer feedforward networks are universal approximators. *Neural Networks* **2**, 359–68.

Knapp, A. G. & J. A. Anderson 1984. Theory of categorization based on distributed memory storage. *Journal of Experimental Psychology: Learning, Memory, and Cognition* **10**, 616–37.

Kohonen, T. 1977. *Associative memory: a system theoretical approach*. New York: Springer-Verlag.

Kruschke, J. K. 1992. ALCOVE: an exemplar-based connectionist model of category learning. *Psychological Review* **99**, 22–44.

Kruschke, J. K. 1993. Human category learning: implications for backpropagation models. *Connection Science* **5**, 3–36.

Lakoff, G. 1987. *Women, fire, and dangerous things: what categories reveal about the mind*. Chicago: University of Chicago Press.

McClelland, J. L. & D. E. Rumelhart 1985. Distributed memory and the representation of general and specific information. *Journal of Experimental Psychology: General* **114**, 159–88.

McCloskey, M. & N. J. Cohen 1989. Catastrophic interference in connectionist networks: the sequential learning problem. In *The psychology of learning and motivation*, G. H. Bower (ed.), vol. 24, 109–65. San Diego: Academic Press.

Malt, B. C. 1994. Water is not H_2O. *Cognitive Psychology* **27**, 41–70.

Medin, D. L. & M. M. Schaffer 1978. A context theory of classification learning. *Psychological Review* **85**, 207–38.

Medin, D. L., M. W. Altom, S. M. Edelson, D. Freko 1982. Correlated symptoms and simulated medical classification. *Journal of Experimental Psychology: Learning, Memory, and Cognition* **8**, 37–50.

Minsky, M. L. & S. A. Papert 1969. *Perceptrons: an introduction to computational geometry*. Cambridge, Mass.: MIT Press.

Nosofsky, R. M. 1986. Attention, similarity and the identification–categorization relationship. *Journal of Experimental Psychology: General* **115**, 39–57.

Nosofsky, R. M. 1987. Attention and learning processes in the identification and categorization of integral stimuli. *Journal of Experimental Psychology: Learning, Memory, and Cognition* **13**, 87–108.

Nosofsky, R. M. 1992. Similarity scaling and cognitive process models. *Annual Review of Psychology* **43**, 25–53.

Pearce, J. M. 1994. Similarity and discrimination: a selective review and a connectionist model. *Psychological Review* **101**, 587–607.

Plunkett, K. & V. Marchman 1991. U-shaped learning and frequency effects in a multi-layered perceptron: implications for child language acquisition. *Cognition* **38**, 43–102.

Putnam, H. 1975. The meaning of "meaning". In *Minnesota studies in the philosophy of science, vol. VII: language, mind, and knowledge*, K. Gunderson (ed.), 131–93. Minneapolis: University of Minnesota Press.

Quinlan, P. T. 1991. *Connectionism and psychology: a psychological perspective on new connectionist research*. London: Harvester Wheatsheaf.

Regehr, G. & L. R. Brooks 1993. Perceptual manifestations of an analytic structure: the priority of holistic individuation. *Journal of Experimental Psychology: General* **122**, 92–114.

Rescorla, R. A. & A. R. Wagner 1972. A theory of Pavlovian conditioning: Variations in the effectiveness of reinforcement and nonreinforcement. In *Classical conditioning II: current theory and research*, A. H. Black & W. F. Prokasy (eds), 64–99. New York: Appleton-Century-Crofts.

Richardson-Klavehn, A. & R. A. Bjork 1988. Measures of memory. *Annual Review of Psychology* **39**, 475–543.

Roediger, H. L. & K. B. McDermott 1993. Implicit memory in normal human subjects. In *Handbook of neuropsychology*, F. Boller & J. Grafman (eds), vol. 8, 63–131. Amsterdam: Elsevier.

Rosch, E. 1973. On the internal structure of perceptual and semantic categories. In *Cognitive development and the acquisition of language*, T. E. Moore (ed.), 111–44. New York: Academic Press.

Rosch, E., C. Simpson, R. S. Miller 1976. Structural bases of typicality effects. *Journal of Experimental Psychology: Human Learning and Memory* **2**, 491–502.

Rosenblatt, F. 1962. *Principles of neurodynamics*. New York: Spartan.

Shanks, D. R. 1991. Categorization by a connectionist network. *Journal of Experimental Psychology: Learning, Memory, and Cognition* **17**, 433–43.

Shanks, D. R. 1995. *The psychology of associative learning*. Cambridge: Cambridge University Press.

Shanks, D. R. & M. A. Gluck 1994. Tests of an adaptive network model for the identification and categorization of continuous-dimension stimuli. *Connection Science* **6**, 59–89.

Shepard, R. N. 1980. Multidimensional scaling, tree-fitting, and clustering. *Science* **210**, 390–98.

Smith, E. E., C. Langston, R. Nisbett 1992. The case for rules in reasoning. *Cognitive Science* **16**, 1–40.

Smith, L. B. 1989. From global similarities to kinds of similarities: the construction of dimensions in development. In *Similarity and analogical reasoning*, S. Vosniadou & A. Ortony (eds), 146–78. New York: Cambridge University Press.

Squire, L. R., B. Knowlton, G. Musen 1993. The structure and organization of memory. *Annual Review of Psychology* **44**, 453–95.

Sutton, R. S. & A. G. Barto 1981. Toward a modern theory of adaptive networks: expectation and prediction. *Psychological Review* **88**, 135–70.

Vaughan, W. 1988. Formation of equivalence sets in pigeons. *Journal of Experimental Psychology: Animal Behavior Processes* **14**, 36–42.

Wasserman, E. A. & S. L. Astley 1994. A behavioral analysis of concepts: its application to pigeons and children. In *The psychology of learning and motivation*, D. L. Medin (ed.), vol. 31, 73–132. San Diego: Academic Press.

Whittlesea, B. W. A. 1987. Preservation of specific experiences in the representation of general knowledge. *Journal of Experimental Psychology: Learning, Memory, and Cognition* **13**, 3–17.

Whittlesea, B. W. A. & M. D. Dorken 1993. Incidentally, things in general are particularly determined: an episodic-processing account of implicit learning. *Journal of Experimental Psychology: General* **122**, 227–48.

Widrow, B. & M. E. Hoff 1960. Adaptive switching circuits. *1960 IRE WESCON Convention Record* (Part 4), 96–104.

Willshaw, D. J., O. P. Buneman, H. C. Longuet-Higgins 1969. Non-holographic associative memory. *Nature* **222**, 960–2.

ACKNOWLEDGEMENTS

I am very grateful to Shivani Gore for running the medical diagnosis experiment, and to Theresa Johnstone for helpful comments on this chapter. Preparation of the chapter was supported by a project grant from the Biotechnology and Biological Sciences Research Council. The support of the Economic and Social Research Council is also gratefully acknowledged. The work is part of the programme of the ESRC Centre for Economic Learning and Social Evolution.

PART THREE
Mental models

CHAPTER SIX

Representing information in mental models

Alan Garnham

INTRODUCTION

In a recent paper Art Glenberg (in press) tried to answer the question: what is memory for? He concluded that its primary function is to act "in the service of perception and action in a three-dimensional environment". The other side of this conclusion is that the primary function of memory is, in fact, not memorizing. What is the relevance of these ideas to theories of memory? Psychologists may have used memorizing as a tool for studying memory, but surely few have been lured into the belief that the most important thing about memory is that it allows people to learn lists of words. And surely memory theorists do not believe that the way we use memory in everyday life is a by-product of our ability to learn lists. However, Glenberg's point is not that psychologists necessarily have these beliefs about memory. What he claims is that theories of memory embody the assumption that memory is for memorizing. An obvious reason for this assumption is that the data that most of these theories try to explain are data from memorization experiments, and people get wrapped up in their theories and their experiments, and "forget" about everyday uses of memory.

One reaction to this neglect of the everyday functions of memory was the demand for ecologically valid studies of memory; studies of memory in its natural habitat, as it were. I have argued elsewhere (Garnham 1991: 47–8) that scientists do not necessarily need to study things in their natural environments. Physiologists, for example, might find it inconvenient! However, if they do not, they have an obligation to show, at least in principle, how the gap between the laboratory and the real world can be bridged.

In my view the faults of what might be dubbed "memorization" research are best avoided by a different strategy; the one adopted, at least in part, by Glenberg. David Marr (1982) suggested that, to understand a cognitive system, it is first necessary to perform a *task analysis* to determine what the system does. As Marr's own analysis of human vision shows, a task analysis sets out the function that the system performs in the real world, and the constraints under which it operates. So, by task analysis, Marr did not mean the analysis of specific experimental tasks, such as free recall in the domain of memory. But neither did he believe that task analysis should be undertaken by performing ecologically valid experiments. Task analysis requires *thinking*, or analysis in the philosophical sense. And it leads to what Marr, perhaps misleadingly, called a *computational theory*. A computational theory of a cognitive system specifies the input–output mapping that the system computes, and it tries to say something about why the system performs that mapping. So, in the case of human vision, the input is light of varying intensity and wavelength falling on a complex array of receptors (the retina). The output is less tangible, but Marr characterized it as an object-centred internal representation of the three-dimensional structure of the part of the world that is visible. The purpose of constructing this representation, according to Marr, is to enable us to navigate the world successfully.

Marr's ideas gain much of their power from the fact that he was able to base a detailed theory of visual processing on them. Furthermore, they are made more plausible by the way that Marr explains the shortcomings and failings of approaches that focused on the detailed computational mechanisms (artificial intelligence) or neural mechanisms (neurophysiology) without considering the more abstract computational theory. Similarly, a proper theory of memory should show that focusing on lists of words diverts attention from the structure and content of what is usually in memory, and why it is there, and leads instead to potentially misleading talk of such things as memory traces.

This chapter will begin by considering the kinds of information that people need to represent in memory. It will show that such considerations naturally lead to the notion of a mental model, that is, the representation of part of the real or an imaginary world, as a crucial component of both long- and short-term memory. This introduction will be followed by a detailed account of the components of mental models, what they represent, and why they are postulated in the theory. The remaining part of the chapter will consider the two main areas of application of the mental models theory: language processing and reasoning. In each of these domains, mental model accounts will be illustrated with concrete examples, and the strengths and limitations of the theory will be considered.

In discussing these two areas of research, attention will focus on two questions: (a) what information do people represent in memory when they use language, or when they reason, and (b) how is that information assembled and manipulated, on-line, to carry out those tasks? In answering these questions, ideas from mental models theory will be related to more general ideas about long- and short-term memory.

MENTAL MODELS

One important insight of the mental models theory is that our memories are, for the most part, memories of things that happened in the world (or that are portrayed as having happened in some fictional world). Such models can be created when we perceive things happening around us, though we do not commit everything we perceive to memory. They can also be created when we are told about things that happened, or when we read about them. As Miller & Johnson-Laird (1976) pointed out, psychologists need to explain how we put together information derived from language and information derived from perception. The mental models theory solves this problem by claiming that representations derived from language and from perception are of the same kind. They are representations of situations in the real or an imaginary world. The question that the theory prompts is: how are these representations computed from perceptual and linguistic input, and what memory resources are needed for their computation?

The notion of a mental model has the additional advantage that it explains how information that is explicitly presented in a text can be combined with background knowledge. Since background knowledge also takes the form of knowledge about the world, abstracted, in the case of general knowledge, from information about particular situations, it will automatically fit together with information about situations derived from the explicit content of the text.

The mental models theory holds that these representations created from perceptual and linguistic input are also used in much of our high level thinking. Thinking is typically thinking about situations in the real word, as it is, was, might have been, will be, or might be, or about situations in imaginary worlds. It requires the setting up of models of particular situations, and the manipulation of those models to determine the consequences of different events happening in those situations. These manipulations use constraints derived from knowledge about how the world works. As for language, this mental models account explains how background knowledge can be brought to bear on thinking about specific situations.

MENTAL MODELS AND LANGUAGE PROCESSING

Language processing is one of the two major domains of application of mental models theory. The primary focus of attention has been on how mental models are constructed when people understand what they read or what is said to them. Specifically in relation to memory, research on language processing in the mental models framework raises two main questions. The first is about the use of short-term memory resources in the construction of mental models. This question has been addressed only in general terms in this domain. It has been considered in more detail in the domain of reasoning. The second question, and the one I will focus on, is about what is represented. I will begin with some historical considerations, which explain why this question was not originally at the forefront of psycholinguistic research, and how it came to be. I will then turn to detailed issues about what information is represented in mental models, and how it is represented.

From a common sense point of view, it is indisputable that people derive information about situations in the real or an imaginary world from what they read and hear. However, for historical reasons, psycholinguists have had their attention diverted from this aspect of language processing, and onto the use of linguistic structure. Linguistic structure plays a crucial role in the encoding and decoding of the information that is conveyed by a text. However, the point of comprehension is not to compute that structure, but to use it to encode information (in language production), and to help extract the information conveyed (in language comprehension).

The historical reasons for the focus on linguistic structure can be traced to the beginnings of modern psycholinguistics. Chomsky (1957) pointed out the potential relevance of linguistic theory, and in particular his theory of transformational grammar, to psychological theories of language processing. George Miller produced a theory of language comprehension, the *derivational theory of complexity* (DTC), that was based on Chomsky's linguistic insights. Chomsky placed syntax at the heart of linguistic theory. The derivational theory of complexity attempted to explain how difficult a sentence was to understand in terms of the syntactic operations (called *reverse transformations*) required to reduce the sentence to corresponding simple sentences. For example, a sentence such as "The girl he loved was seen by John" would be reduced to (something roughly equivalent to) "John loved the girl" and "John saw the girl", together with the information that the second clause was expressed in the passive voice, and that the first was embedded as a relative clause with the second.

DTC is a theory of the process of understanding, and not a theory of the product of understanding. It focuses on operations that help to derive the meaning of a sentence, but it says little about what that meaning might be. Its claim about meaning is the implicit one that the meaning of a complex sentence, or of a derived sentence, is roughly equivalent to the meaning of the simple sentences to which it can be reduced, plus a record of what operations convert the simple sentences into the complex or derived one. The derivational theory was, in the end, unsatisfactory in many respects (see, Garnham 1983, for some of the reasons). Historically, the first set of arguments against the derivational theory was based on the fact that semantic and pragmatic contributions to comprehension difficulty often mask syntactic contributions. Hence, derivational complexity cannot be the only explanation for difficulties in understanding (see Fodor et al. 1974, for a detailed account). So, although modern theories of sentence processing (see, e.g. Clifton et al. 1994) are more sophisticated in their accounts of syntactic analysis, they may, nonetheless predict that syntactic effects are difficult to isolate.

The second set of reasons for rejecting DTC, which was not entirely separate from the first set, was part of a reaction to DTC's focus on the sentence as the unit of processing, and its implicit claim that the mental representation of a text or discourse was a concatenation of the mental representations of its sentences. A consideration of the comprehension of even short texts led John Bransford (e.g. Bransford 1971, Bransford et al. 1972) to a different type of psycholinguistic theory: the precursor of the mental models theory. Bransford made three interrelated claims about language comprehension. The first was that the mental representation of the content of a text is not a representation of its linguistic structure at any level: phonological, syntactic, semantic, or pragmatic. It is a representation of what the text is about. A narrative text is about a situation in the real or an imaginary world. The mental representation of its context is a representation of that situation. In modern parlance, what is encoded into memory from a text is a mental model.

Bransford's second claim was that comprehension is an integrative process. Understanding text is not just a matter of stringing together representations of individual clauses. Complex processes of integration are necessary to put together the information from different parts of the text. One kind of integrative process is knowledge-based inference. Bransford pointed out, and indeed probably overemphasized, the role of inference in comprehension. His ideas resonated with suggestions from artificial intelligence: it had proved impossible to write programs for understanding texts that did not have, and make direct use of, knowledge about the subject matter of the texts. Another kind of integrative processing, one that Bransford did not study in so much detail, is the processing that establishes the local coherence of a text by creating, for example, referential links between a pronoun (e.g. "it") and an antecedent noun phrase (e.g. "the table"). Some such links can only be made by using background knowledge.

Bransford's third claim was that comprehension is a constructive process. It is not based merely on what is explicit in the text, but on a combination of information from the text and information stored in memory. The meaning of the text must, therefore, be constructed from these two sources of information, and not merely read off from the text using what Bransford referred to as interpretive processes. When inferences are needed to make links between the parts of a text, the integrative and constructive aspects of comprehension are inextricably intertwined (see Garnham 1992). However, construction can be separated from integration, particularly when the inferences are merely elaborative (Garnham 1981, 1989). Bransford overestimated the number of elaborative inferences that people make during comprehension. In memory tests people could not distinguish between a text they had read, and a text that made explicit an obvious inference from that text. For example, he found (Johnson et al. 1973) that subjects claimed they read: "He slipped on a wet spot and broke the delicate glass pitcher when it fell on the floor," when they had seen: "He slipped on a wet spot and dropped the delicate glass pitcher on the floor".

However, later experimental work (see especially Corbett & Dosher 1978) showed that the confusions resulted from the structure of the memory tests, and that the inferences were not made on-line.

Bransford's work brought important aspects of the process and the products of comprehension to the attention of psycholinguists. However, he did not develop a detailed account of mental representations of the content of texts. Nor did he provide a detailed proposal about how those representations were modified during comprehension, as each new part of the text was processed. The mental models theory attempts to flesh out Bransford's account in this respect, and hence to provide an account of the memory structures that result from language comprehension, and of how they are constructed.

A basic tenet of mental models theory is that mental representations of the content of texts are similar in form to representations derived from perceiving the world, and to representations used in thinking about the world. Therefore, to answer the question of what the components of mental models are, we need an account of the ontology, or theory of the kinds of thing that exist, that underlies our mental representations of the world. This ontology is a *folk ontology*, at least in one sense of that term. It is the ontology that underlies our everyday thinking about the world, rather than, for example, our scientific thinking. However, there is no need for psycholinguists to develop an account of this ontology from scratch. Formal semanticists have been working in earnest on the semantics of natural languages since the late 1960s. The work of Richard Montague (see Thomason 1974) was the starting point for this research programme. Later work has become more "linguistic" in flavour. That is to say, particular pieces of research now typically start from (semantic) facts about a particular natural language, or about natural languages in general, rather than general principles derived from the consideration of logical languages (see, e.g. Parsons 1990: Ch. 1).

Not surprisingly, Montague identified *entities* as one of the basic *semantic types* in his system. The only other basic type he recognized was truth values, so his ontological claims were simple, if incorrect (see below). Montague himself was primarily interested in the semantics of individual sentences. His theory specifies the situations that each sentence correctly describes (the possible worlds in which it is true). So, even an expression that we would naturally take as referring to an entity, for example a noun phrase such as "the man", has as its interpretation in Montague's system a function from possible worlds to entities; for each situation, it says which entity, if any, the expression refers to in that situation. (Each syntactic category is associated with a semantic type, which specifies the kind of semantic interpretation that an expression of that category will have.) However, when an expression occurs in a text, the reader typically knows what world, or part of the world, the text is about. In such a context, the expression effectively refers to a single entity. Thus, in a mental model of the situation described by the text, we would expect to find a representation of that entity (in this case a particular man).

In Montague's system all semantic types except those of entity and truth value are derived. For example, ignoring the question of relativization to possible worlds (which is usually called *intensionality*), Montague gives the category of intransitive verbs (which includes composite verb phrases, such as "sees a sparrow") the semantic type <e,t>. This notation means that intransitive verbs denote functions from entities to truth values. Intuitively, an intransitive verb (e.g. "sleeps", "eats a biscuit") needs a subject noun phrase to make a sentence. Thus, an intransitive verb combines with something that has the semantic type of a noun phrase and produces something that has the semantic type of a sentence. Simplifying somewhat, a noun phrase denotes an entity and a sentence denotes a truth value. Hence an intransitive verb is a function from entities to truth values.

A mental models theory of the representation of the content of sentences, based on Montague's ideas, would claim that representations of individual people and things (entities) are one basic component of mental models. It would not, however, claim that representations of events, states, and processes are a basic component of such representations, nor would it claim that representations of properties (or qualities) of individuals are. This is not to say that events, states, processes, and properties would not be represented, but simply that they would not be basic components of the representation.

There are, however, reasons for thinking that events, states, processes, and properties are part of our folk ontology and should be directly represented, but these reasons emerge only from a consideration of the temporal relations between the different events in a text. Montague concerned himself primarily with single-clause sentences (and primarily with sentences in the present tense). He would, nevertheless, have been aware that formal logicians (e.g. Prior 1968) had already begun to think about the problems of formalizing the semantics of tense and temporal reference in natural languages. One crucial idea was put forward by Reichenbach (1947). Reichenbach argued that a proper account of tenses required the identification of three different times, though for simple tenses two or more of these times might be identical. The three times are the utterance time, the reference time, and the event time. Consider a so-called pluperfect sentence in English, for example "John had been eating". If someone utters this sentence, it must be understood as referring to a time in the past (the reference time) before which an event of John's eating was taking place (at the event time). Furthermore, the reference time must be before the time that the sentence was uttered, if the sentence is true.

Reichenbach's ideas apply to single clauses. Thus, to interpret each clause in a text or dialogue, it may be necessary to identify three separate times. In addition, the utterance time necessarily moves forward as a dialogue progresses, and the reference and events times may also change. Not only do the events in a narrative have a complex temporal structure, the extraction of that structure from the linguistic description of those events is not straightforward.

From what has been said so far, moments of time could simply be a special type of entity (or individual), and represented as such in mental models. Indeed, many attempts to provide a formal account of the meaning of tenses of verbs (so-called tense logics) were based on the idea of a *time line* made up of indefinitely many moments in a linear sequence. In most such tense logics, a past tense sentence is true if the corresponding present tense sentence was true at a moment before the present. Although this idea seems initially plausible, it has a fatal flaw when it is applied to text and discourse. A sequence of past tense sentences in a text typically denotes a sequence of events in the order in which they are related ("John came into the room. He sat down. He started to read a newspaper."). However, the (standard) kind of tense logic mentioned above simply says that each of these sentences should be true at some time prior to the utterance time, and says nothing about the relations between these earlier times.

In an attempt to solve this problem Hans Kamp (1979, Kamp & Rohrer 1983) proposed a different approach to temporal reference in which events (in a broad sense that includes events, states, and processes) were basic components in the interpretation of sentences. Thus a sequence of past tense sentences denotes a set of events in the order they are introduced. Events have finite durations. However, on Kamp's view, an event is regarded as temporally undivided when it is first introduced, though it may be divided later, for example if following text or discourse introduces subevents of a main event. States, on the other hand, need not have a finite duration. In French, the language that Kamp analyzes, past states are typically introduced by sentences in the imperfect tense. And whereas two sentences in the simple past denote two events, one following the other, an imperfect followed by a simple past denotes an event (second sentence) that took place while the state (first sentence) held (e.g. "It was raining. Sue put up her umbrella.").

Kamp's theory is a formal semantic theory, and he takes the standard formal semantic view that a semantic analysis should state the conditions under which a text or discourse is true. His theory formalizes a simple idea: a discourse is true if the relations between the events, states, and processes it denotes map in a simple way onto the relations between events, states, and processes in the real world. A description of the world itself will be more complex than what is presented in a text. An event that is effectively treated as undivided in a text will be subdivided in a richer representation. Nevertheless it is a simple matter to stipulate formally what is meant by saying that the relations in the text map onto relations in the world.

We have already seen that Montague treated properties as having a nonbasic semantic type. A property is a function from entities to truth values: it tells us which individuals have the property. Properties have the same semantic type as intransitive verbs ($<e,t>$, see above), since they are often expressed by expressions of this kind. Psychologically, this idea is somewhat implausible. For example, many theories of semantic representation based on semantic networks contain nodes representing properties (e.g. red, feathered, animate) that are regarded as primitives, and that are connected to nodes standing for individuals by HASA or HASPROP links. Similarly, many linguistic semanticists have recognized properties as a fundamental semantic type (see Frawley 1992). In mental models theories of reasoning (see below) salient properties of individuals are often represented directly in the way those individuals themselves are represented. An element, a, of a model might represent an individual with the property a.

Another set of issues that have been important in formal semantics are those about modality (the ideas of possibility and necessity), and related notions such as permission and obligation. Modal logics, which give a formal account of the meaning of such notions, have been the subject of intensive study (e.g. Hughes & Cresswell 1984), as has their relation to the modal adverbs and auxiliary verbs of natural languages (e.g. "necessarily", "possibly", "may", "might", "must"). In this work, the notion of a possible world assumes an important place. Necessarily true statements are said to be true in all possible worlds, for example, and sentences qualified by a "might" are true in at least one possible world. Similar ideas have been used to analyze notions such as belief, desire and obligation. So, for example, there is a possible world, or more strictly a set of possible worlds, in which a particular person's beliefs are true (discounting, for the moment, the question of whether people can have inconsistent beliefs that cannot be true in the same possible world), and a set of possible worlds in which a particular person's desires are fulfilled.

Sets of possible worlds are typically infinite. However, a single mental model can stand for an infinite set of possibilities, and hence can be used to represent, for example, a person's beliefs. It does so by specifying just the actual content of those beliefs. There are many things (in fact indefinitely many things) that a particular person has no beliefs about. Thus my model of what Heathcliff believes the world to be like, which I might derive from a reading of *Wuthering Heights*, can be thought of as a representation of all those (presumably fictitious) worlds in which those beliefs are true, and in which other facts about which Heathcliff has no beliefs, or has beliefs that I do not remember, come out in different ways. For example, if I have no reason to think that Heathcliff remembers what colour dress Nelly Dean was wearing when he was first brought to Wuthering Heights by Mr Earnshaw, my mental model of his beliefs is compatible with a world in which it was brown and a world in which it was grey. By not encoding information about the colour of the dress, the mental model can be compatible with (or represent) both those worlds (and many more).

So far we have been considering the components of mental models. A psychological theory of comprehension must, in addition, specify how these models are constructed during language processing. Crucially, it must show how *linguistic expressions* in discourse or text lead to the introduction of elements into mental models. The general outline of this account is clear, though the details will depend on painstaking analysis of natural languages: psycholinguists ignore the subtleties of linguistics at their peril! Individuals are typically introduced into models by noun phrases, and noun phrases are also used for later references to them. Verbs carry the primary information about events, states, and processes. Adjectives typically denote properties.

Linguists have long recognized the central role that main verbs play in their clauses. Thus, the interpretation of a clause typically involves the identification of the event, state or process denoted by its main verb, and of the participants in that event, state or process. Those participants play certain *thematic* roles in the event, state or process, though whether it is useful to identify a set of recurring roles, such as agent, instrument, source and goal, is a much debated question. Some, at least, of the participants in an event are referred to by noun phrases within the clause. However, an important part of discourse interpretation is to determine which, if any, of these individuals are individuals that have already been mentioned in the preceding discourse, or whose existence has been implied, or which exist in the nonlinguistic context of the discourse. Markers of tense and aspect, and other auxiliary verbs, help to locate the event, state or process in the time frame of the discourse, and conjunctions provide explicit information about the relation between the current clause and other clauses of the same discourse.

Not every collection of true sentences forms a coherent discourse. Coherence is a difficult notion to define, but it is a property of texts and discourse, and not of the world. It has to do with presenting information systematically, and in a way that relates, roughly speaking, to human concerns. *Referential coherence* is one important aspect of coherence: coherent discourse refers to the same individuals over again. Referential coherence cannot be identified with lexical cohesion (see e.g. Sanford & Moxey 1995). Nor can it be identified with *referential continuity* (as studied by, for example, Garnham et al. 1982), which is merely a special case of referential coherence (Stenning et al. 1988). A considerable complication in describing how the referential coherence of a discourse is established, is that second and following (anaphoric) references to an individual typically involve different linguistic expressions.

For example, a full noun phrase (e.g. "the lamp") might be followed by an anaphoric definite pronoun (e.g. "it"). In standard cases in English, the pronoun will match the (antecedent) noun phrase in number and gender. But even in simple texts, there may be other noun phrases that match the pronoun, even if the text is unambiguous (e.g. "The lamp stood on the table. It threw light on the book.").

In such cases, additional information must be used to *resolve* the reference of the pronoun. Here, the final arbiter, though not necessarily the first information used in on-line processing, is knowledge about the world. In this case, the knowledge is about the relation between lamps and throwing light, and the lack of a relation between tables and throwing light. This combination of information from the text and background knowledge is what Bransford referred to as the constructive aspect of comprehension. Phenomenologically, references of this type are not difficult to resolve. However, they take longer to resolve than references in which the morphological information on the pronoun is sufficient to resolve it (e.g. Garnham & Oakhill 1985, Garnham et al. 1995).

In the case just described, the referent of the pronoun is an individual that is already represented in the model. Deciding which entity it is may be a complicated process, and it may be mediated by short-lived representations of the superficial form of the text (Garnham et al. 1995). Nevertheless it does not require the introduction of new elements into the model. Other cases of pronoun interpretation do appear to require such elaboration of the existing model. Garnham & Oakhill (1988) investigated the interpretation of references into so-called anaphoric islands (Postal 1969). For example, in "Tom dreams a lot, but he never remembers them" *them* refers to the dreams that Tom has but does not remember. However, the dreams have only been introduced into the discourse indirectly via the use of the verb *dreams*, not by explicit mention of a set of individuals (the dreams themselves), which would have required the use of the noun phrase *the dreams*. Although such references into anaphoric islands are not as stylistically correct as pronominal references with noun phrase antecedents, they are common in both spoken and written language (Garnham & Oakhill 1988). However, we found that even when they were judged acceptable, they took longer to understand than comparable standard uses, such as "Tom has a lot of dreams, but he never remembers them". This finding suggests that, in the anaphoric island cases, the set of dreams is only introduced into the model when the pronoun is encountered, and has to be interpreted. It is constructed by inference from the representation of the activity of dreaming that is introduced into the model by the verb phrase "dreams a lot". A similar complication arises in the interpretation of so-called conceptual pronouns (Gernsbacher 1991, Oakhill et al. 1992). For example, in "I need a plate. Where do you keep them?", there is no plural noun phrase that introduces into the mental model the set of plates that *them* in the second sentence refers to. In fact, *them* refers to a set of plates that are assumed to exist, presumably in the inferred context i.e. the home of the addressee. The name "conceptual anaphora" reflects the fact that the antecedent is a "concept" that is related to something mentioned in the previous text, but not identical to it. Again, it appears that at least some of the work of establishing the appropriate set in the mental model occurs only when the pronoun is read (Oakhill et al. 1992).

Given that world knowledge is so important in resolving nominal anaphora, it is not surprising that it is also important in resolving the often anaphoric temporal relations between parts of a text. For example, if one event is described as occurring "shortly before" another, the likely time between them depends on the particular events (compare "shortly before setting off on the Everest expedition, ..." and "shortly before opening the can of beans, ...". Furthermore, Kamp's account of the way tenses determine the relation between two events (see above) is oversimplified. Two events presented in the past tense need not follow one another. Other temporal relations, such as part–whole, may hold between them, depending on events described (e.g. "We prepared the picnic. We started by buttering some bread.").

Anaphora is one device that creates links between the parts of a text, and hence contributes to the coherence of the text as a whole. Another is conjunction, both co-ordinating and subordinating. Conjunctions signal relations between parts of a text. *But*, for example, signals a contrastive relation, and *because* signals a relation based on cause, reason, or evidence. Such relations are almost always underpinned by knowledge about the world. Indeed, it is often unnecessary to include explicit conjunctions, as in "A stone hit the window. It broke." However, when the relevant knowledge is unavailable, the presence of an explicit conjunction can, in principle, allow the knowledge to be inferred. For example, assuming that the statement "Connors used Kevlar sails, because there was little wind" is true, it suggests, to someone who does not already know, that Kevlar sails are good in low wind. Nevertheless, from experiments in which they measured processing time for both sentences of this kind, and for following questions probing the causal links, Noordman & Vonk (1992) suggest that such inferences are not typically made in casual reading, but that they are computed when specific questions are asked.

MENTAL MODELS AND REASONING

The second domain of application of mental models theory is thinking and reasoning. In this domain, attention has focused not only on the representations that underlie these activities, but also on the processes that manipulate these representations in short-term memory. Indeed, the amount of short-term storage and processing required has been used to explain the relative difficulty of apparently similar problems. This section reviews mental models research in this domain.

The mental models theory provides a framework for a unified approach to thinking, reasoning and problem solving. Detailed accounts of specific aspects of reasoning within the mental models framework have been under development since the late 1970s (Johnson-Laird & Steedman 1978), and it is these accounts that give the mental models theory much of its credibility. Model theories conceptualize the process of reasoning as mediating between premises and conclusions that are (usually) expressed in a natural language such as English. Reasoning proceeds, however, not by manipulating English sentences, but by constructing abstract models of (parts of) the world as it would be if the premises were true, and manipulating those models. More specifically, each premise or piece of information that contributes to a line of thought must be mentally modelled. The models must then be integrated. If they cannot be, the bits of information are unrelated and nothing of interest follows from them. Many of the integration processes are similar to those required for language comprehension, for example identifying people or things referred to in different premises as the same. The process of integration, which presumably takes place in short-term working memory, produces an *initial model* of the premises. This model will suggest one or more conclusions, but they may not be the correct (or desired) ones. Further processes are required to derive a final conclusion, and these depend on the type of reasoning. In deductive reasoning the correct procedure is to consider all possible models that integrate information from the premises, and to find a conclusion, if there is one, that is consistent with all the models. In inductive reasoning, according to Johnson-Laird (1993, 1994a), when the set of possible models has been constructed, some of them are systematically eliminated before a conclusion is drawn. In some kinds of everyday reasoning, where a previous conclusion is to be overturned, it may be necessary only to check that the negation of that conclusion can be incorporated into the current model without producing a contradiction (Johnson-Laird & Byrne 1991: 183, Garnham 1993a).

The models postulated in mental models theories of reasoning tend to be abstract in nature. For example, in modelling the kinds of reasoning that logicians have formalized in the propositional calculus (which, roughly speaking, captures inferences based on the English words "and", "or", "not", and "if...then"), all the information that would be carried by a sentence of English is represented by a single letter. So, in the form of argument known as *modus ponens* ("if p then q", "p", so "q") p and q can stand for any two sentences. Similarly, in the models theory of conditional reasoning (Johnson-Laird & Byrne 1991: Ch. 4), a conditional premise of the form "if p then q" is represented as follows:

> [p]   q
> ....

Each line is a model, though the second line (the dots) has no explicit content, and merely indicates that other states of affairs are possible. The first line is a model of a situation in which both p and q are true. The square brackets around the p indicate that, in this set of models, situations in which p is true are exhaustively represented with respect to situations in which q is true. So, according to this set of models, there can be no situations in which p is true, but q is not. This aspect of the representation is intended to capture the meaning of "if p then q". The lack of square brackets on the q means that the converse is not true. There can be situations in which q is true, but p is not. When the implicit model (the dots) is fleshed out, two types of situation are, therefore, possible.

> ¬p   q
> ¬p   ¬q

where "¬p" means "not p"

The models theory of conditional reasoning holds that the initial representation of a conditional statement is the first pair of models above. This theory explains why modus ponens is easy, and why *modus tollens* ("if p then q", "not q", so "not p") is harder. The second premise of modus ponens rules out models in which p is not true, and hence eliminates the implicit model. In the only remaining model:

> [p]   q

q is true, and so "q" is a valid conclusion. Modus tollens, on the other hand, requires the fleshing out of the implicit model to give

> p   q
> ¬p   q
> ¬p   ¬q

and the elimination of the first and second of these models, given the information in the second premise. The only remaining model supports the conclusion "not p". The theory also explains why modus tollens is easier if the "not q" premise is presented first (Girotto 1993). This premise forces the explicit representation of a situation in which q is not true, and helps people to avoid mistakes in fleshing out the implicit model of the conditional premise, and in eliminating models produced by this fleshing out.

In moving from the propositional to the predicate calculus (which includes all the inferences of the propositional calculus, plus those based on "all" and "some"), logicians are forced to consider the internal structure of sentences. A simple sentence comprises a predicate (generally expressed by the verb or a predicative adjective) and one or more arguments. So, in "John loves Mary", loves is the predicate and John and Mary the arguments. Specific arguments, such as John and Mary, can be replaced by variables, to allow for quantification (e.g. "Someone loves Mary", "John loves everyone"). A restricted form of quantification (with one quantifier per sentence) is found in the premises and conclusions of syllogistic arguments: the domain in which the mental models theory of reasoning was first elaborated (Johnson-Laird & Steedman 1978).

Syllogisms have two premises, each of which can take four forms (traditionally called moods).

All A are B	(mood A)
Some A are B	(I)
No A are B	(E)
Some A are not B	(O)

One premise relates A and B, the second relates B and C. The conclusion, if there is one, relates A and C and must also be in one of the four moods.

The premises and conclusions of syllogisms are about the relations between people or things belonging to two classes. The mental models theory of syllogistic reasoning represents these classes by arbitrarily selected members from those classes. Recent versions (Johnson-Laird & Byrne 1991: Ch. 6) also use the square bracket and dot notations from the theory of conditional reasoning. Indeed, since "all A are B" is equivalent to "if something is A then it is B", the representation of a premise in mood A parallels that of "if p then q":

[a]   b
    ....

where a is an arbitrary member of the set of things that are A, and b is an arbitrary member of the set of things that are B, and is equated with the a. The representations of premises in the other three moods suggested by Johnson-Laird & Byrne (1991) are:

Some a are b		No a are b		Some a are not b	
a	b	[a]		a	
....			.... [b]	a	[b]
					[b]
				....	

In Johnson-Laird & Byrne's scheme, the explicit content of the models is always of people or things that have the property A (or B or C), and never of people or things that do not have that property. However, although a theory of syllogistic reasoning can be developed on the assumption that the representations of the different premises take this form, there are reasons to believe that this assumption is incorrect.

Moxey & Sanford (1993) considered the mental representation of statements containing quantifiers more generally, and suggested that quantifiers can be divided into those that focus attention on the set of people or things referenced by the material following the quantifier (e.g. dogs that bite postmen in "some dogs bite postmen"), which they call *refset* quantifiers, and those that focus attention on the complement of that set (e.g. dogs that don't bite postmen), which they call *compset* quantifiers. With a refset quantifier, a following pronominal reference will be taken to refer to the referenced set, for example in:

Some dogs bite postmen. They should be tethered.

They refers to dogs that bite postmen. An attempt to make it refer to dogs that do not bite postmen inevitably fails, and results in a highly implausible or uninterpretable sentence:

Some dogs bite postmen. They are the only ones postmen like.

With compset quantifiers, however, a pronominal reference is naturally taken as referring to the complement set.

Few dogs bite postmen. They are generally well behaved.

That is, the dogs that do *not* bite postmen are generally well behaved, and attempts to refer to the referenced set produce implausible sentences:

Few dogs bite postmen. They should be tethered.

Within this scheme *some* is clearly a refset quantifier, as the examples above demonstrate. So, a syllogistic premise in mood O, such as:

Some dogs do not bite postmen

focuses attention on the set of dogs that do not bite postmen, since the word "not" is part of the predicate that specifies the referenced set. The sentence, therefore, makes that set available as the referent of an anaphoric *they* in a following sentence. Since things that are available for anaphoric reference are generally thought to be explicitly represented (see, e.g. Sanford & Garrod 1981), dogs that do not bite postmen should be explicitly represented in the models of *some dogs do not bite postmen*. The representation of "some A are not B" should, therefore, be of the form:

a   ¬b
....

An additional advantage of this representation is that it is parallel in form to the proposed representation of "some A are B".

In Johnson-Laird & Byrne's (1991) theory of syllogistic reasoning, as in its predecessors, syllogisms can have either one, two, or three effectively different models, where effective different models are ones that support different conclusions (see Garnham 1993b). The check on whether there are genuine alternatives to an initial model takes place in working memory. If there are alternative models, they must be held in memory to see if they support a single conclusion. The theory, therefore, predicts that the more models a syllogism has, the more difficult it will be, and this prediction has been supported empirically.

Another set of findings predicted by the models theory are the so-called figural effects. The figure of a syllogism is determined by the relative positions of the terms A, B, and C in the premises, regardless of their mood. There are four figures:

A – B	B – A	A – B	B – A
B – C	C – B	C – B	B – C

The difficulty of these figures increases from left to right. In addition, the first figure favours conclusions of the form A – C, and the second favours conclusions of the form C – A, independently of whether the conclusions are valid. These figural effects are explained by the working memory operations needed to combine the premises. It is assumed that the premises are read into memory in the order in which they are presented, and that conclusions are read out in the same way. Thus, in the first figure, the initial working memory configuration is:

A – B   B – C

which allows for straightforward identification of the Bs, and the generation of an A– C conclusion. In the other figures, additional operations have to be performed to bring the Bs together, to effect integration: either reversal of the order of the two premises or reversal of the model of a single premise. The harder figures require more of these operations to be performed. These ideas derive from Ian Hunter's (1957) theory of performance on three-term series problems (John is older than Bill, Bill is older than Sam, so John is older than Sam).

Mental models accounts of deductive reasoning (including syllogistic reasoning) were the first parts of the theory to be developed in detail. However, the theory was always intended to account for reasoning in general, including inference in language understanding. Johnson-Laird (1993, 1994a) has proposed an account of inductive reasoning within the mental models framework. According to this account, an inductive inference has a conclusion that is compatible with only a subset of the models that are consistent with the premises. A potential problem with this view is that, as the number of models consistent with a set of premises increases, the number of subsets of those models that might be eliminated increases exponentially, and the decision about which subset to eliminate becomes more difficult. Some principles are, therefore, required to constrain the process of induction. Johnson-Laird proposes four such principles: specificity, parsimony, use of existing knowledge, and availability of information from memory (in the sense of Tversky & Kahneman 1973).

Other kinds of reasoning that have been described within the mental models framework are probabilistic reasoning (Johnson-Laird 1994b) and everyday reasoning (Garnham 1993a). Johnson-Laird's account of probabilistic reasoning is based on the notion of the strength of an argument, which he defines as "the proportion of possible states of affairs consistent with the premises in which the conclusion is true" (1994b: 189). This proportion can be estimated from a set of mental models, though not entirely straightforwardly. Complications arise from the fact that a single model may stand for an infinite set of possibilities, as in the representations of syllogistic premises. Probability estimates are likely to be influenced by such factors as how readily different types of models come to mind, and are therefore subject to the biases described by Tversky & Kahneman (1974).

Everyday reasoning is obviously about situations in the world, and hence amenable to an analysis in terms of the manipulation of mental models. However, it is problematic because conclusions that have already been reached can be overthrown by new information. In this respect it contrasts with deductive reasoning. Mental models can be revised, but what is problematic for a mental models theory of everyday reasoning is the idea that a conclusion is valid if it is supported by every model that is consistent with the premises. If a conclusion can be overthrown by new information, this definition of validity is of no use, and everyday reasoning cannot be reasoning to valid conclusions, in this sense. In fact, people find it difficult to keep track of alternative projections from the current situation, which is presumably why they find multiple model syllogisms difficult. They prefer to construct a single model. Thus it has been suggested (Johnson-Laird & Byrne 1991, Garnham 1993a) that in everyday reasoning people usually develop only a single model. They incorporate new information into that model, and check to see if it is consistent with what is already present in it. If it is not, they have to decide what revisions to make. However, even this process can be complicated, and may require further revisions to produce a consistent outcome. So, people sometimes get into difficulties in everyday reasoning.

Finally, mental models theory has an obvious application to problem solving. The primary issue in describing how people solve problems is to explain how they search for a solution to a problem in a space that may contain indefinitely many possible solutions (see Newell & Simon 1972, for the standard account). The usual conceptualization of the space that must be searched uses the notion of a state–action representation. On this view, the problem solver is faced with states of the world and actions that can transform one state into another, and has to find a path from the starting state to the goal state. When applied to chess, for example, the states of the world are configurations of pieces on the chess board, and the actions are the moves permitted by the rules of the game. But a representation of the state of (part of) the world is a mental model! So, the notion of a mental model has a central place in the description of how people solve problems.

More recent approaches to problem solving (see Garnham & Oakhill 1994: Ch. 12, for a summary) emphasize the use of background knowledge, rather than extensive search through a space of possibilities. On this view, problem solving still requires the transformation of one state of the world into another, and the notion of a mental model remains important. Indeed, much of this research makes use of a related concept of a mental model (that presented, for example, in the papers in Gentner & Stevens 1983). Mental models, in this sense, capture general information about objects such as calculators, or phenomena such as electricity. However, these models guide specific interactions with specific objects (calculators or electrical devices) in the world, and an account of how they are used will inevitably appeal to the similarity in format between models of specific situations and background knowledge.

CONCLUDING REMARKS

The notion of a unified theory of cognition was suggested by Allen Newell in his 1987 William James Lectures (Newell 1990). Newell identified John Anderson's ACT[*] (adaptive character of thought; see, e.g. Anderson 1990) and his own SOAR (e.g. Laird et al. 1987) as possible contenders for a unified theory of cognition. In a more modest way, the mental models theory provides a step toward a more unified theory of certain cognitive processes, in particular those of language, high level perception, and thinking. All three of these aspects of cognition depend on memory of various types, and the mental models theory also embodies a number of assumptions about memory. Mental models are models of situations in the real or an imaginary world, and much of what we store in our long-term memories is information about situations. When these memories are memories of situations that we have ourselves experienced they are part of episodic memory. Situations have complex structures, and different situations may have structures in common. This idea lies behind, for example, the Schankian notion of a script (Schank & Abelson 1977). It is compatible with the notion of a mental model, though the theory of mental models is not committed to a Schankian view of how information is structured in memory. Long-term memory also contains information about individuals, which may be abstracted from memories for particular situations in which those individuals participated (as part of semantic memory). Those representations, or at least pointers to them, are incorporated into particular mental models. How much of the information about a familiar individual is directly incorporated into a model is a question that must be answered empirically. In any case, information in memory and structures created for the task in hand (language processing, problem solving, or whatever) have a similar format, and can be readily integrated.

The process of building mental models, and of integrating information from long-term memory into them, takes place in a mental workspace that can conveniently be referred to as working memory. However, the mental models theory is not committed to any particular view of working memory. As we have seen in this chapter, the number of operations that need to be performed on mental models in this workspace can explain the relative difficulties of certain types of problem, or certain types of text.

Clearly, the mental models theory is far removed from traditional approaches to memory. It does, however, make claims both about the information that is stored in memory and the operations that are performed on that information. It links everyday concerns and memory, and in that sense provides at least a partial answer to Glenberg's (in press) question about what memory is for.

REFERENCES

Anderson, J. R. 1990. *The adaptive character of thought*. Hillsdale, N.J.: Lawrence Erlbaum Associates.

Bransford, J. D., J. R. Barclay, J. J. Franks 1972. Sentence memory: a constructive vs interpretive approach. *Cognitive Psychology* **3**, 193–209.

Bransford, J. D. & J. J. Franks 1972. The abstraction of linguistic ideas. *Cognitive Psychology* **2**, 331–50.

Chomsky. N. 1957. *Syntactic structures*. The Hague: Mouton.

Clifton, C. Jr., L. Frazier, K. Rayner (eds) 1994. *Perspectives on sentence processing*. Hillsdale, N.J.: Lawrence Erlbaum Associates.

Corbett, A. T. & B. A. Dosher 1978. Instrument inferences in sentence encoding. *Journal of Verbal Learning and Verbal Behavior* **17**, 479–91.

Fodor, J. A., T. G. Bever, M. F. Garrett 1974. *The psychology of language: an introduction to psycholinguistics and generative grammar*. New York: McGraw-Hill.

Frawley, W. 1992. *Linguistic semantics*. Hillsdale, N. J.: Lawrence Erlbaum Associates.

Garnham, A. 1981. Mental models as representations of text. *Memory and Cognition* **9**, 560–65.

Garnham, A. 1983. Why psycholinguists don't care about DTC: a reply to Berwick and Weinberg. *Cognition* **15**, 263–9.

Garnham, A. 1989. Inference in language understanding: What, when, why and how. In *Language processing in social context*, R. Dietrich & C. F. Graumann (eds), 153–72. Amsterdam: North Holland.

Garnham, A. 1991. *The mind in action*. London: Routledge.

Garnham, A. 1992. Minimalism versus constructionism: a false dichotomy in theories of inference during reading. PSYCOLOQUY **3**(63) reading-inference.1.1.

Garnham, A. 1993a. Is logicist cognitive science possible? *Mind and Language* **8**, 49–71.

Garnham, A. 1993b. A number of questions about a question of number: commentary on *Deduction* by P. N. Johnson-Laird & R. M. J. Byrne. *Behavioral and Brain Sciences* **16**, 350–1.

Garnham, A. & J. V. Oakhill 1985. On-line resolution of anaphoric pronouns: effects of inference making and verb semantics. *British Journal of Psychology* **76**, 385–93.

Garnham, A. & J. V. Oakhill 1989. The everyday use of anaphoric expressions: Implications for the "mental models" theory of text comprehension. In *Models of cognition: a review of cognitive science*, N. E. Sharkey (ed.), vol. 1, 78–112. Norwood, N. J.: Ablex.

Garnham, A. & J. V. Oakhill 1988. "Anaphoric islands" revisited. *Quarterly Journal of Experimental Psychology* **40A**, 719–35.

Garnham, A. & J. V. Oakhill 1994. *Thinking and reasoning*. Oxford: Blackwell.

Garnham, A., J. V. Oakhill, M-F. Ehrlich, M. Carreiras 1995. Representations and processes in the interpretation of pronouns: new evidence from Spanish and French. *Journal of Memory and Language* **34**, 41–62.

Garnham, A., J. V. Oakhill, P. N. Johnson-Laird 1982. Referential continuity and the coherence of discourse. *Cognition* **11**, 29–46.

Gentner, D. & A. L. Stevens 1983. *Mental models*. Hillsdale, N. J.: Lawrence Erlbaum Associates.

Gernsbacher, M. A. 1991. Comprehending conceptual anaphors. *Language and Cognitive Processes* **6**, 81–105.

Girotto, V. 1993. Modèles mentaux et raisonnement. In *Les Modèles mentaux: approche cognitive des représentations*, M-F. Ehrlich, H. Tardieu & M. Cavazza (eds), 101–19. Paris: Masson.

Glenberg, A. M. What memory is for. *Behavioral and Brain Sciences*, in press.

Hughes, G. E. & M. J. Cresswell 1984. *A companion to modal logic*. London: Methuen.

Hunter, I. M. L. 1957. The solving of three-term series problems. *British Journal of Psychology* **48**, 286–98.

Johnson, M. K., J. D. Bransford, S. Solomon 1973. Memory for tacit implications of sentences. *Journal of Experimental Psychology* **98**, 203–5.

Johnson-Laird, P. N. 1993. *Human and machine thinking*. Hillsdale, N. J.: Lawrence Erlbaum Associates.

Johnson-Laird, P. N. 1994a. A model theory of induction. *International Studies in the Philosophy of Science* **8**, 5–29.

Johnson-Laird, P. N. 1994b. Mental models and probabilistic thinking. *Cognition* **50**, 189–209.

Johnson-Laird, P. N. & R. M. J. Byrne 1991. *Deduction*. Hove, UK: Lawrence Erlbaum Associates Ltd.

Johnson-Laird, P. N. & M. Steedman 1978. The psychology of syllogisms. *Cognitive Psychology* **10**, 64–99.

Kamp, H. 1979. Events, instants and temporal reference. In *Semantics from different points of view*, R. Bauerle, U. Egli & A. von Stechow (eds) 376–417. Berlin: Springer Verlag.

Kamp, H. & C. Rohrer 1983. Tense in texts. In *Meaning, use, and interpretation of language*, R. Bauerle, C. Schwarze & A. von Stechow (eds), 250–69. Berlin: Walter de Gruyter.

Laird, J. E., A. Newell, P. S. Rosenbloom 1987. SOAR: an architecture for general intelligence. *Artificial Intelligence* **33**, 1–64.

Marr, D. 1982. *Vision: a computational investigation into the human representation and processing of visual information*. San Francisco: Freeman.

Miller, G. A. & P. N. Johnson-Laird 1976. *Language and perception*. Cambridge: Cambridge University Press.

Moxey, L. M. & A. J. Sanford 1993. *Communicating quantities: a psychological perspective*. Hove, UK: Lawrence Erlbaum Associates Ltd.

Newell, A. 1990. *Unified theories of cognition: the 1987 William James lectures*. Cambridge, Mass.: Harvard University Press.

Newell, A. & H. A. Simon 1972. *Human problem solving*. Englewood Cliffs, N. J.: Prentice-Hall.

Noordman, L. G. M. & W. Vonk 1992. Readers' knowledge and the control of inferences in reading. *Language and Cognitive Processes* **7**, 373–91.

Oakhill, J. V., A. Garnham, M. A. Gernsbacher, K. Cain 1992. How natural are conceptual anaphors? *Language and Cognitive Processes* **7**, 257–80.

Parsons, T. 1990. *Events in the semantics of English*. Cambridge, Mass.: MIT Press.

Postal, P. 1969. Anaphoric islands. *Chicago Linguistics Society* **5**, 205–39.

Prior, A. N. 1968. *Papers on time and tense*. Oxford: Clarendon Press.

Reichenbach, H. 1947. *Elements of symbolic logic*. New York: Macmillan

Sanford, A. J. & S. C. Garrod 1981. *Understanding written language: explorations in comprehension beyond the sentence*. Chichester, West Sussex: John Wiley.

Sanford, A. J. & L. Moxey 1995. Aspects of coherence in written language: a psychological perspective. In *Coherence in spontaneous text*, M. A. Gernsbacher & T. Givón (eds), 161–87. Philadelphia, Penn: John Benjamins.

Schank, R. C. & R. P. Abelson 1977. *Scripts, goals, plans and understanding*. Hillsdale, N. J.: Lawrence Erlbaum Associates.

Stenning, K., M. Shepherd, J. Levy 1988. On the construction of representations for individuals from descriptions of texts. *Language and Cognitive Processes* **3**, 129–64.

Thomason, R. 1974. *Formal philosophy: selected papers of Richard Montague*. New Haven, Co.: Yale University Press.

Tversky, A. & D. Kahneman 1973. Availability: a heuristic for judging frequency and probability. *Cognitive Psychology* **5**, 207–32.

Tversky, A. & D. Kahneman 1974. Judgement under uncertainty: heuristics and biases. *Science* **125**, 1124–31.

CHAPTER SEVEN

The retrieval of situation-specific information

Gabriel A. Radvansky & Rose T. Zacks

Imagine that you are reading a particularly engaging whodunnit where you are trying to solve the mystery before the author hands the solution to you at the end of the book. One of the basic elements of this task is to try to reconstruct the circumstances under which the murder took place. This may include the location of the important objects at the crime scene, the location of the other people at the time of the murder, the relation of the different characters to one another and the victim, and other pieces of information. To make the task more difficult, those aspects of the crime scene that you are allowed to learn about are revealed at different points in time and usually not in the order of their importance. To be successful, you must mentally retrieve and integrate this information to create a mental representation of the situation in which the murder took place. Furthermore, you must be able to success-fully retrieve this representation when there are later references to the crime situation, including avoiding retrieving similar but different situations you have experienced or read about.

Mental representations of situations, such as a murder scene, are referred to as mental models or situation models (although they are typically discussed in reference to less dramatic circumstances). Although these two terms are used by different theorists in somewhat different ways, for the present we consider them to be synonymous and use only the term situation model. *Situation models* (Johnson-Laird 1983, 1989) are representations of specific situations, such as a situation described by a text[1] (e.g. Glenberg et al. 1987, Graesser et al. 1994). In general, the structure of a situation model is a functional analogue of a situation in a real or imaginary world. A situation model acts as a simulation of a unique set of circumstances in the world. In other words, a situation model is a second-order isomorph of the represented situation (Shepard & Chipman 1970), in much the same way that a wrist-watch is a functional representation of the daily rotation of the Earth. This chapter discusses issues and findings related to how memory retrieval is affected by the structure of situation models.

A substantial difficulty in dealing with the concept of situation models is that there is no single accepted view. As a step toward alleviating this confusion and as background for reviewing the literature in the area, we present here our own view of a situation model theory. Some of the ideas of this theory are shared with other researchers, whereas others are unique to our own perspective.

We will first outline some characteristics that compose our situation model view, along with some evidence to support these characteristics. These characteristics are divided into three classes: (a) descriptions of situation model structure; (b) descriptions of how situation models are constructed, and (c) descriptions of the processes involved in retrieving information from situation models. Following this exposition, we address some findings that relate to memory retrieval by considering how different aspects of situation models can influence retrieval. At the end of the chapter, we will discuss some aspects of our view that await further development, pending the outcomes of future research.

A SITUATION MODEL THEORY

The structure of situation models

This first section provides an outline of how we conceive of the structure of a situation model. Later we will show how our notions about situation model structure relates to our conception of how information is retrieved from these representations.

At the heart of the view presented here is the notion that situation models represent specific situations as they might occur in a real or possible world. That is, a situation model is not directly concerned with the representation and organization of general knowledge, such as categorical information. Instead, each model represents a unique situation or event. When aspects of a situation refer to general knowledge, the situation model may contain pointers to information stored in long-term memory. For example, a situation model of a potted palm in a hotel would contain pointers that refer to general information about potted palms and hotels, such as knowledge that potted foliage needs watering and that hotels can overcharge customers. This information would not be stored directly in the situation model.

Situation models contain tokens representing the entities in a situation. Associated with these tokens are the relevant properties of the entities, and the functional relations among those entities. All of this information is represented with a single spatial–temporal framework. In order to use the notion of situation-specificity effectively, we need to define what a situation is. We borrow from Barwise & Perry (1983, Barwise 1989) the idea that a situation is composed of a collection of entities. Each entity may have a set of properties associated with it. Furthermore, there is some specified relation of the entities to one another in the situation. Typically, these can be described as functional relations in the sense that they support a person's understanding of the situation in terms of how the entities interact with one another.

The *entities* of a situation can be any meaningful object, such as a person, inanimate object, or abstract idea (e.g. "George got the idea in the garage"). Each entity is represented by a token in the situation model. For abstract ideas, this tokenization would amount to a process of making the ideas concrete. The *properties* of an entity are its characteristics, such as its being blue, angry, heavy, the leader, or dead (Gernsbacher et al. 1992). The *relations* of a situation are the meaningful associations among objects that provide structure to the situation. These include, but are not limited to, spatial, temporal, or ownership relations. The *spatial temporal location* provides the framework for the situation. While some sort of spatial temporal location needs to be specified, a particular identity does not need to be assigned. In other words, it is not the case that each situation model has a tag that specifies a particular location and time, such as "in Grant Park at 12.30 pm on Thursday the 2nd". Instead, the model refers to a situation that would occur at a particular time in a particular place, although just where and when may be left unspecified.

Situation models may represent either novel or commonplace situations. Although a situation model is not a representation of general knowledge, if the situation is a common one, the model's construction may be heavily influenced by the structure of general knowledge representations, such as schemas (and their ilk, scripts (Schank & Abelson 1977) and frames (Minsky 1986)). In extreme cases, the situation model itself may be little more than an instantiated schema. Unlike a schema, however, a situation model can represent more novel sets of circumstances. For instance, our ability to understand a new narrative with little difficulty suggests that people form a representation of the situations described in the narrative rather than creating a representation based strictly on previous knowledge, as would be the case if only a schema were being instantiated.

In our view, situation models are *abstract* representations, meaning that a situation model need not rely on a perceptual code and need not be constrained by properties of perceptual codes. In support of this view is evidence that situation models are able to convey aspects of a situation, such as ownership (Radvansky et al., in press) or logical relations (Johnson-Laird 1992) that are not concrete or perceptual in nature. In contrast to a perceptual code, such as a visual mental image of a scene, a situation model of a scene would capture the relevant functional relations among the objects in the scene without being limited to a particular perspective or viewpoint. Another way to state this is that situation models represent the gist of a situation. Because a situation model is abstract, it can map onto a number of different possible actual situations. For example, a situation model for "the pay phone is in the city hall" may be able to map onto any number of city halls with any type of pay phone (connected or not), placed anywhere in the building.

It should be noted, however, that the availability of information from within a situation model may be mediated by the perspective of an observer from within that situation (Franklin & Tversky 1990). However, this only occurs when the person uses their imagination to place themselves within the situation as an observer or participant. In these cases, the relations among the entities in the situation (such as the entities a person is interacting with) guide the structure of the situation model. (A more detailed comparison of situation models and mental images will be presented later in the chapter.)

A situation model is also an *analogue* representation in the sense that its structure directly models the structure of the situation that it represents. This is in contrast to other types of memory representations, such as propositional or text-based codes, where the information is coded in a verbal-linguistic format. In this sense, situation models are more similar to mental images. For example, in a situation model of the spatial arrangement of objects, objects that are close in space are coded close to one another in the model (e.g. Glenberg et al. 1987). We would also like to make clear that, by claiming that a situation model directly models the situation it represents, we do not intend that the representation itself is a veridical copy of the situation in the world. Instead, it is a representation of the situation as it is comprehended by the individual. For example, a spatial situation model is not a direct copy of the actual Euclidean space. Instead, the situation model structure may be a mixture of a hierarchical and Euclidean structure in much the same way that people perceive spaces in the world (e.g. McNamara 1989).

Situation models can represent either dynamic or static situations. Following Barwise & Perry (1983), we make a distinction between at least two different types of situations: states-of-affairs and courses-of-events. A state-of-affairs is a static situation in which the major components of the situation do not change. It involves the same collection of entities, in the same relations to one another within a common, continuous spatial–temporal location. A course-of-events, in contrast, is a dynamic situation composed of a series of related event frames that are linked through some common entity or thematic relation.

To make this distinction clearer, consider the following. A mail carrier making a phone call is a state-of-affairs situation. There is only a single spatial–temporal location involved. The entities, their properties, and their interrelations remain the same throughout the situation. In contrast, the situation of the mail carrier delivering the mail on her route is a course-of-events situation. Unlike the other situation type, there are several spatial–temporal locations involved, with different entities at each (e.g. different houses, streets, and obstacles such as dogs). The mail carrier and her constant purpose across the locations serve to unify those separate scenes into a single situation. Static and dynamic situation models have been observed to have different effects on mental processing (e.g. Radvansky et al. 1993).

We consider situation models that involve some sort of causal goal structure, such as those that are constructed from reading a narrative (e.g. Graesser et al. 1994), to be course-of-event types of situations. This is because a causal structure is generated over a series of different time frames, and possibly different locations. In these cases, a causal structure can serve to unite the collection of event frames into a single situation model.

The creation of situation models

This section outlines those aspects of our view which relate to the initial creation and updating of situation models in memory. These notions are constrained to circumstances where a person is representing new information.

The notion of situation specificity that guides our model implies certain constraints on the information integrated into a single situation model. In particular, a model contains only information that can be interpreted as referring to a single situation in the world. For example, if you were told that "Jim bought some hot dogs from a vendor" and "Tom read about Randy in the programme", it is unlikely that these two pieces of information would be stored into a single situation model. Instead, the information would be stored in separate models. In contrast, several pieces of situation-specific information that refer to the same situation will be integrated into a common situation model. For example, if you knew that Jim and Tom went to a ball game together, you could integrate the two pieces of information mentioned above into a single model. Information will continue to be integrated into a previously existing situation model until it becomes clear that a new situation is present (e.g. Anderson et al. 1983).

Once a situation model has been created, it can be updated to include new information that is relevant to the situation. This updating includes the addition of new information not previously available, the removal of erroneous information, and the adjustment of components of the model for a more accurate understanding of the situation.

Another important point is that situation models are not created automatically, as some researchers have argued (McKoon & Ratcliff 1992). Instead, people create a situation model only when they have the goal of understanding a situation that is being presented to them (Graesser et al. 1994, Zwaan 1994). For example, in a study by Zwaan, subjects created a situation model of a text that they were reading only when it was described as an account from a newspaper (encouraging the development of a situation model) rather than when it was described as a literary text (where the emphasis is more on the language used than on the described situation). If a person does not have the goal of understanding a situation as a whole (such as when editing a manuscript for typos), they may store the information in a different form, such as a propositional code. Much of the research supporting this idea comes from the area of discourse comprehension.

Consistently with other situation model researchers, we think that when people encode situation-specific knowledge, the situation model is not the only representation that can be created. In addition to the situation model, people may also create propositional and mental image codes (e.g. Johnson-Laird 1983). Propositional codes capture verbal-linguistic aspects of a situation, such as the characteristics of language that was originally used to describe a situation or the verbal labels associated with the components of a situation. Mental images can be thought of as individual perspectives on a situation model. When a person takes the perspective of an observer within a situation, a mental image may be created. For example, a situation model of a house could be viewed from many different angles, thus producing many different mental images. This does not mean that the mental image will be the representational code used to extract information from that perspective. The situation model may still be used. We will discuss the relevance and influence of other representational codes later in the chapter.

A common assumption of theorists concerned with situation models is that they are created in working memory. We make the additional assumption (which some dispute, e.g. Glenberg & Langston 1992, Payne 1993) that situation models can also be stored in long-term memory. In long-term memory, each situation model is stored as a separate memory trace. Although two or more situation models cannot be part of the same memory trace, connections between situation models, including hierarchical nesting, can be encoded through the use of pointers. With respect to hierarchical nesting, for example, a situation model of a house may contain a pointer referring to a situation model of the dining room. In this way a person can represent subcomponents of a situation without creating an overly complex situation model.

Memory retrieval

The previous sections outlined characteristics of situation models that were important for providing an understanding of what situation models are, and how and when these representations are initially created. In this section, we consider those points that are more important for this chapter, namely, those factors that influence the retrieval of information stored in situation models.

First, only one situation model can be active in working memory at one time. There is a limit on a person's working memory capacity. She is able to directly consider only one situation at a time. Any mental processing that requires the consideration of more than one model will be made more difficult by this constraint. This limitation is observed most prominently in research on logical reasoning (e.g. Johnson-Laird 1992). However, this does not mean that a person cannot keep track of multiple situations. In order to do this, she must keep pointers active in working memory that allow her to call up a particular situation model from long-term memory when she needs it. Nonetheless, it is important to keep in mind the point that the retrieval process is limited to bringing only a single situation model into working memory from long-term memory at one time.

Information pertaining to the entities, properties, relations, and locations that compose a situation is potentially available when the relevant situation model is active in working memory. The ease of accessing these different types of information is dependent on the organizational structure of the situation model itself. For example, in a spatial situation model, those aspects of the spatial framework that have been made more salient by a person's interactions with the situation will be more accessible (Franklin & Tversky 1990).

In addition to the actual structure of the situation model, the availability of information can also be mediated, being dependent on which portion of the model is currently foregrounded or at the focus of attention (e.g. Glenberg et al. 1987). Information is more accessible from foregrounded portions of a model than other portions of the structure. For example, when describing the layout of a room, if the current focus is on the bookcases, information stored at that portion of the situation model will be more accessible than other portions, such as information concerning the windows at the opposite end of the room.

People retrieve information from situation models only when motivated to do so. This idea is similar to the idea that situation models are only created when a person is motivated to do so. Likewise, people retrieve information from a situation model that they have stored only when the circumstances favours the use of these representations. This may occur when the encoding context involved an emphasis on the creation of situation models, and this emphasis is carried over to or reintroduced at the retrieval stage. It is possible for a person to create a situation model and store it in long-term memory, and then use an alternative representation code during later retrieval. For example, people may disregard a situation model when they suspect it may be faulty (Hasher & Griffin 1978).

Situation models are accessed from memory through a parallel, content-addressable search. During a search, the memory probe activates all of the situation models stored in long-term memory that contain features (i.e. entities, properties, relations, and/or locations) that are contained in the retrieval probe. The more features a probe and a model have in common, the greater the activation of that model. This is similar to several feature-matching models of memory retrieval (e.g. Hintzman 1986). In this way, a person can access the appropriate memory for a situation by knowing who or what was involved (e.g. the situation about the banker), what properties these entities had (e.g. it involved something that was green), what relations were involved (e.g. it was the situation where someone bought something), and/or where or when it occurred (e.g. in the hotel).

Following the parallel access of all of the situation models that contain features present in the retrieval probe, a single model is selected to be retrieved into working memory. The model that is first fully activated is the one that can be clearly discriminated from the others by the strength of its level of activation. We do not have the final word on how this selection of one situation model from among those that receive some activation takes place, but some speculations are presented later.

Although situation models are activated in parallel in long-term memory, and this activation is mediated by the feature resemblance of the probe to the model, the internal structure of the model is not available until it is brought into working memory. In other words, the retrieval process is able to access those models that contain certain elements, but it is unable to determine how these elements are connected to one another. For example, a person may know that a situation model may contain a banker, a lawyer, a chair, a pen, and an ownership relation, but will not be able to know that it is the lawyer that owns the chair until a search of the situation model is made in working memory. This notion is supported by research showing that item information is available before relational information (Ratcliff & McKoon 1989).

Having provided an outline of our situation model view, we would now like to turn to the research that is relevant to it. In the next part of the chapter we hope to show how the retrieval of situation-specific information is influenced by: (a) the organizational structure of situation models; (b) foregrounding; (c) memory for the gist of a description, and (d) whether information is stored in a single model or is stored across multiple models.

EFFECTS OF SITUATION MODEL STRUCTURE ON RETRIEVAL

In this section we address how the structure of a situation model influences the retrieval of information. As stated above, our position claims that people do not have the ability to evaluate the internal structure of a situation model while it is in long-term memory. Therefore, any influence of the internal structure of a situation model should be observed only when the model is currently active in working memory. In most cases, this has been studied under conditions where a subject is initially creating and updating the situation model. For example, memory for information may be probed when the subject is currently reading a passage of text.

Model structure

A situation model should have a structure that is analogous to the situation in a real or imaginary world that it represents. This structure should influence the availability of stored information. One of the more common ways to test these claims has been to assess the retrieval of spatial information. This is because there seems to be general agreement about important dimensions of spatial representations. That is, it is expected that a spatial representation would encode relations such as above, below, near, far, etc. If spatial information is needed to understand a situation, then the situation model would contain those spatial relations as part of its structure. Therefore, during the retrieval of information from a situation model, evidence of this spatial structure should be observed in the data.

Spatial reference frames

When a person takes the perspective of a viewer within a situation, the availability of information is mediated by a spatial framework oriented around that observer. This spatial framework is defined by an interaction of the observer and the environment (Bryant et al. 1992, Carlson-Radvansky & Radvansky 1996, Franklin & Tversky 1990). For example, for an upright observer, the above–below dimension is the most salient, followed by the front–back, and left–right dimensions. This arrangement of information availability is presumably dictated by the functional relation of the observer with the world around her. The above–below dimension is the most prominent because of the ever-present effects of gravity. The front–back dimension is also prominent, particularly because humans preferentially interact with the world through what is in front of them.

These notions about effects of spatial frameworks on information ability were tested by Franklin & Tversky (1990). In their study, subjects read a passage that described a spatial environment. During their reading, subjects were encouraged to imagine themselves within that space. The passage provided a general description of the environment as well as the location of various objects within that space in relation to the person. An example of one such passage is provided in Box 7.1.

During the reading of the passage, subjects were interrupted with probes that asked them to identify objects located at various directions from themselves. For example, a subject would be given the probe RIGHT, and have to say which object was in that direction. Response times for these retrievals were recorded. As can be seen in Figure 7.1, the results were consistent with the hypothesis that the internal struc-

---

BOX 7.1   Example passage used by Franklin & Tversky (1990).

You are hob-nobbing at the opera. You came tonight to meet and chat with interesting members of the upper class. At the moment, you are standing next to the railing of a wide, elegant balcony overlooking the first floor. Directly behind you, at your eye level, is an ornate lamp attached to the balcony wall. The base of the lamp, which is attached to the wall, is gilded in gold. Straight ahead of you, mounted on a nearby wall beyond the balcony, you see a large bronze plaque dedicated to the architect who designed the theatre. A simple likeness of the architect, as well as a few sentences about him, are raised slightly against the bronze background. Sitting on a shelf directly to your right is a beautiful bouquet of flowers. You see that the arrangement is largely composed of red roses and white carnations. Looking up, you see that a large loudspeaker is mounted on the theatre's ceiling about 20 feet directly above you. From its orientation, you suppose that it is a private speaker for the patrons who sit in this balcony. Leaning over the balcony's railing and looking down, you see that a marble sculpture stands on the first floor directly below you. As you peer down toward it, you see that it is a young man and wonder if it is a reproduction of Michelangelo's David.

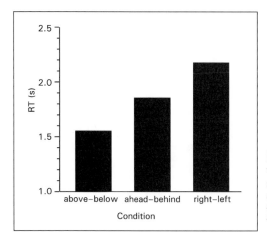

FIG. 7.1.   Response Time (RT) for verifying that a target object is in a specified direction from an upright observer in a situation model. Derived from data presented in Franklin & Tversky (1990).

ture of a situation model reflects the functional relations among objects, in this case a spatial framework. Subjects responded fastest to items located along the above–below dimension, more slowly to items located along the ahead–behind dimension, and slowest to items located along the right–left dimension. This pattern parallels data on the availability of information when subjects are presented with location tasks for perceptually available stimuli (e.g. Bryant et al. 1993, Logan 1995).

Furthermore, the spatial framework changes as the orientation of the viewer changes. In a second experiment, Franklin & Tversky (1990) had subjects imagine that they were reclined in the situation. Under such conditions, the relative accessibility of object identities changed. As can be seen in Figure 7.2, the objects located along the front–back dimension were as accessible as objects along the head–feet dimension, with objects along the right–left dimension being the least accessible. This change in availability is consistent with the notion that the functional relation of the observer within the described situation affects the relative salience of objects within the situation model.

Spatial frameworks are not limited to being defined by the environment or an observer's orientation. There is some evidence that the functional relation between objects can influence the orientation of a reference frame (Carlson-Radvansky & Radvansky 1996). For example, a hammer is typically considered to be above a nail if it is being used to pound it, no matter what the orientation of the nail itself may be. This evidence would seem to indicate that it is the functional relations among entities that people are encoding into their representations of a situation.

Overall these findings support the notion that situation models reflect the functional relations among entities that interact in an

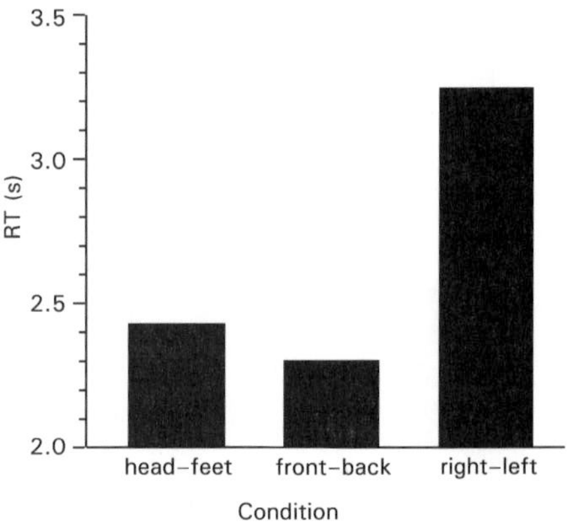

FIG. 7.2.   Response Time (RT) for verifying that a target object is in a specified direction from a reclining observer in a situation model. Derived from data presented in Franklin & Tversky (1990).

environment. Furthermore, these functional relations mediate the availability of information from within the situation model.

Foregrounding

As stated earlier, foregrounded parts of situation models held in working memory show increased availability. One factor determining foregrounding is a strong association with a story protagonist. One means of manipulating whether entities are associated with a protagonist is by varying the relative spatial distance between the two. If the target entity is a lamp, it is more likely that it would be included in the foreground of the situation model when the protagonist is in the living room with the lamp than if she is in the garage. Simply put, if the situation model successfully models the functional relations of entities in the world, then items that are further away from the current focus should be less available than near items.

Such an effect was demonstrated by Glenberg et al. (1987; see also Singer et al. 1994). In the study of Glenberg et al. people read passages in which a critical object was embedded. The story presented in Box 7.2 is an example of one such passage. Subjects were asked to visualize the described scenes while reading, to encourage the creation of a situation model. In half the passages, the critical object was spatially associated with the protagonist ("Warren picked up his bag before going shopping"), whereas in the other half, the critical object was spatially dissociated from the protagonist ("Warren put down his bag before going shopping"). At a later point during the passage, a sentence appeared that anaphorically referred back to the critical object (the bag). Reading times for that sentence were recorded.

BOX 7.2. Example text from a study by Glenberg et al. (1987).

Warren spent the afternoon shopping at the store.
He picked up/set down his *bag* and went over to look at some scarves.
He had been shopping all day.
He thought it was getting too heavy to carry.

As can be seen in Figure 7.3, Glenberg et al. (1987) found that information spatially close to the protagonist, and hence more likely to be foregrounded in the situation model, led to faster reading times than information that was spatially separated. This suggests that situation models embody functional relations of the situation, in this case, spatial distance, and that this factor determines item accessibility. (For a related account, see Anderson et al. 1983, Garrod & Sanford 1983.)

This notion of spatial foregrounding was extended in an interesting set of experiments by Morrow et al. (1987, 1989). There were two ideas behind these studies. The first was that not only should items spatially close to a protagonist be more available than spatially far items, but that the absolute distance between the protagonist and the item should mediate the degree to which items were available. The second idea was that as the foreground of a situation model shifts, there should be residual activation in those portions of the model that had been just previously activated, as well as, those portions that the person was

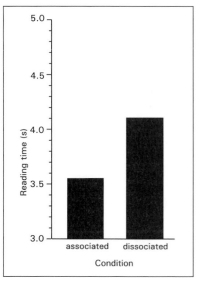

FIG. 7.3.   Reading time for sentences containing a reference to an object mentioned earlier. Associated objects were spatially associated with a story protagonist and were therefore in the foreground of the situation model. In contrast, dissociated objects were spatially dissociated from the protagonist and therefore not in the foreground of the situation model. Derived from data presented in Glenberg et al. (1987).

required to pass through on their way in from one location to the next. As a result, information from these parts of a situation model should be more accessible than parts that had not recently been foregrounded, although to a lesser degree than those parts that were currently in the foreground.

In the experiments of Morrow et al. (1987, 1989), subjects memorized a layout of a building, such as a laboratory or a warehouse, along with the locations of several objects within that building. An example of one such building layout is presented in Figure 7.4. This memorization served to allow subjects to create a relatively complex spatial model of the environment that they could use for reference when later reading stories about events that took place in that location. Afterward, subjects read a narrative in which the protagonist moved about from room to room within the building. During the course of reading the narrative, subjects were probed with pairs of object names (including the name of the protagonist, such as: desk–Bill). The subjects' task was to indicate whether the objects were in the same room in the building.

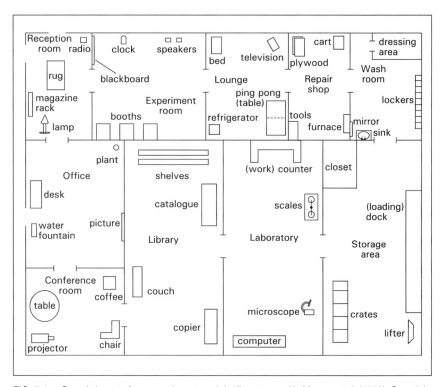

FIG. 7.4.   Sample layout of a research centre originally presented in Morrow et al. (1989). Copyright © 1987 by Academic Press, Inc. Reprinted with permission.

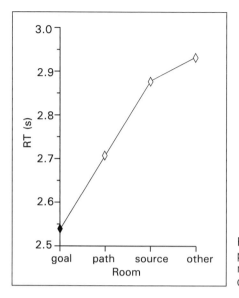

FIG. 7.5.   RT for verifying that target object pairs are in the same room, relative to the room where the protagonist is. Derived from data presented in Morrow et al. (1989).

The result of one experiment is shown in Figure 7.5. The protagonist had started from the source room, passed through the "path" room and arrived in the "goal" room. "Other" refers to some other room in the building. Probe identification was fastest when the objects were in the same room as the story protagonist. Thus, information in the foreground of the model along with the protagonist was more available than other pieces of information. Responses were slower when the room the objects were located in was either the one the protagonist had started from or an unmentioned room along the protagonist's path of travel. Response time was mediated by the distance between the protagonist and the room the objects were in. (See O'Brien & Albrecht 1992, and Wilson et al. 1993 on the importance of having a focus on the protagonist.) These results suggest that information gradually falls away from the foreground of the model as the situation focus shifts, and that situation models can capture complex aspects of situations, such as room divisions.

Finally, we would like to mention one further study by Morrow and colleagues that demonstrated that this pattern of results is not exclusively tied to a story protagonist's spatial location. In one experiment, observations were based on the room the protagonist was thinking about, rather than the room the protagonist was in. For example, in one passage, while the protagonist was said to be located in the reception room, the probe objects were presented immediately after the sentence "He thought the library should be rearranged to make room for a display of current research." Subjects responded to objects in the room that was being thought about 180 ms faster than to objects in other rooms. Therefore, it appears that the foreground of a situation model is capable of shifting to portions of the model other than the protagonist's spatial location.

Summary
The results of these studies show that the retrieval of situation-specific information from a situation model during on-line processing is guided by the structure of the model and by the current focus within that situation model. The structure of the situation model is analogous to the structure of a situation in the world that it represents. In other words, the availability of information about different parts of a situation is mediated by functional relations of a situation, such as spatial characteristics, and by whether entities and relations are foregrounded in the model.

MEMORY RETRIEVAL FROM FIXED SITUATION MODEL STRUCTURES

In addition to influencing information retrieval from working memory, the organization of information into situation models can also affect the retrieval of information from long-term memory. This is an important issue to consider because we often need to draw on information about situations other than the one that currently has our attention. Studies of this aspect of situation models have explored the extent to which the representation captures either gist or verbatim information, as well as how the storage of information in either one or several situation models affects the ease with which that information can be retrieved.

Gist representation
A central characteristic of situation models is that they represent the situation described by a text rather than the text itself or the propositions composing that text (Johnson-Laird 1983, Kintsch 1994, Glenberg et al. 1987). As such, information retrieval from situation models stored in long-term memory should reflect this gist-like nature. One prediction is that recognition test confusion errors (false alarms) should occur for statements that potentially describe the same situation, but are propositionally distinct.

In a classic demonstration of this effect, Bransford et al. (1972) had people listen to one member of a list of pairs of sentences. For example, they heard either the sentence "Three turtles rested *on* a log and a fish swam beneath them" or "Three turtles rested *beside* a log and a fish swam beneath them". On a subsequent recognition test, people were given the original sentence and a distractor sentence. For the distractor sentence, the last word was changed from "them" to "it". People who had originally heard the first sentence were less accurate than people who had heard the second. This suggests that a representation that conveys the gist of a described situation is relied on to make these decisions: a situation model (see also Garnham 1982, and Radvansky et al. 1990).

This notion has been expanded by Taylor & Tversky (1992) from single-sentence stimuli, open to a large number of interpretations because of a lack of context, to lengthy descriptions of a spatial layout. According to our view, the structure of a spatial situation model should correspond to the structure of an actual spatial framework such that all of the relevant spatial characteristics of the situation are represented in the model. Provided that the person is not trying to take the perspective of an observer within the situation, this situation model should be perspective-free. As a result, retrieval time should be unaffected by the original perspective embedded in the narrative. That is, attempts to retrieve information from the model will be dependent on the spatial relations among the entities in that situation, and not on the position of some hypothetical or ideal observer.

In a series of experiments, Taylor & Tversky (1992) asked subjects to read descriptions of environments, such as a resort or a zoo. An example of the zoo layout can be seen in Figure 7.6. Subjects were instructed to memorize these layouts from a description given in a text and without the benefit of a map (i.e. they never saw the layout in Figure 7.6). Half of the subjects were given *route descriptions* that gave the reader a perspective of the environment of a person walking through the area. To emphasize this perspective, the spatial descriptions used viewer-relative spatial terms such as "to the right" or "in front of". The other half of the subjects were given *survey descriptions* that gave an overview perspective of the environment, as though one were viewing a map of the area. To encourage subjects to adopt this perspective during encoding, the survey descriptions used spatial terms such as "to the south", or "in the centre".

Immediately after reading the descriptions, subjects were given a recognition test for phrases used in the description. The results are presented in Figure 7.7. As can be seen, verbatim statements were verified faster when they conformed to the original perspective. This was explained as the use of a propositional representation (discussed in more detail below) that more accurately preserved the original wording than the situation model. The important result is the performance on the inference statements. In particular, subjects were as fast and as

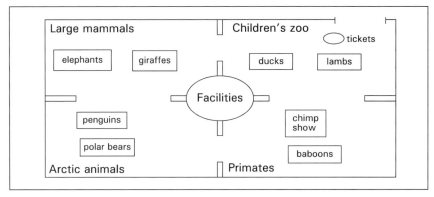

FIG. 7.6.   Sample layout of a zoo. Originally presented in Taylor & Tversky (1992). Copyright © 1992 by Academic Press, Inc. Reprinted with permission.

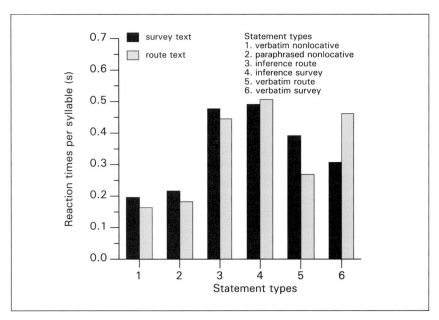

FIG. 7.7.   Reaction times per syllable to memory probes, for description types and test statement types. Originally presented in Taylor & Tversky (1992). Copyright © 1992 by Academic Press, Inc. Reprinted with permission.

accurate for inference statements conforming to either perspective regardless of the form of the original text. Taylor & Tversky (1992) concluded that spatial situation models were being used that captured the major spatial characteristics of the described environments but were perspective free.

Information integration

A single situation model is capable of representing several pieces of information that pertain to a single situation. However, in order for information to be integrated into a situation model, relevant task goals must be present, and it must be clear that all of the pieces refer to the same situation. Integration does not occur when it is unclear that several facts refer to the same situation. Under such circumstances, subjects rely on separate representations. This characteristic of the creation of situation models should have an effect on the retrieval of information from long-term memory. In particular, memory performance should be better when the information can be easily integrated into one situation model than when it cannot, resulting in the information being stored across a number of representations.

A demonstration of this effect was provided by Mani & Johnson-Laird (1982). Subjects were presented with descriptions of four or five objects with the task of remembering these descriptions. These descriptions referred to the placement of objects with respect to one another in a two-dimensional plane. The objects formed arrangements such as the following:

A   B   C
D

A description that indicated a coherent and unique arrangement of the objects allowed for the creation of a single situation model. For example, the following three sentences uniquely describe the arrangement above: (a) A is behind D, (b) A is to the left of B, and (c) C is to the right of B. In other words, this description refers to one and only one possible situation in the world, namely the one depicted in the diagram.

However, descriptions that do not refer to a unique set of circumstances, but are consistent with a number of situations do not result in the creation of a single situation model. The following three sentences are an example of such a description for the arrangement above: (a) A is behind D, (b) A is to the left of B, and (c) C is to the right of A. Like the previous example, this description can refer to the arrangement of objects in the diagram. However, unlike the first example, this description can also refer to other possible arrangements. As such, it is unlikely that people will notice that all these statements refer to the same situation.

Descriptions that conformed to a single situation showed more evidence of gist memory on a subsequent recognition test than descriptions that could refer to multiple situations. That is, for descriptions like the first example above, subjects were more likely to accept inference statements as having been presented than was the case for descriptions such as the second example. This suggests that the integration of situation-specific information occurs only when a set of facts clearly refers to a single situation, not when it refers to several different situations. Furthermore, the success or failure in integrating a set of information into a single situation model has an effect on the nature of the representation used during long-term memory retrieval. Knowledge that can be integrated is more amenable for the recognition of any consistent description, whereas knowledge that cannot be integrated is more "frozen" in the sense that accurate recognition occurs only for more verbatim items.

Retrieval set size

When we speak of retrieval set size, we are referring to the number of situation models involved in the retrieval set. Memory retrieval is affected by the number of situation models composing a search set. In particular, retrieval is influenced by whether a set of facts, that are related by virtue of overlapping concepts, refers to a single situation, and thus a single model, or to multiple situations, and thus several models. In a series of experiments, we (Radvansky & Zacks 1991, Radvansky 1992, Radvansky et al. 1993, 1996 in press) have used a fan-effect paradigm to assess such an impact of situation models on memory retrieval. A *fan effect* is an increase in retrieval time with an increase in the number of associations with a concept in a memory probe (Anderson 1974).

The general idea is that a fan effect emerges in cases where a set of related facts refers to several situations, and therefore these facts are stored across several situation models in long-term memory. During memory retrieval, all of those models containing the concepts expressed in the memory probe are activated. Provided the subject is engaging in more than just a familiarity test, one model must be selected to be brought into working memory to have its contents verified. The activation of multiple situation models produces competition and retrieval interference, leading to a fan effect. The greater the number of irrelevant situation models that contain concepts present in the memory probe, the longer the response time. In contrast, a fan effect does not emerge when a set of related facts refers to a single situation, and is therefore stored in a single situation model. During memory retrieval, there are no additional competing representations to produce interference. As a consequence, response time is unchanged and no fan effect is observed. (This argument assumes that the models themselves are relatively simple; otherwise the complexity of the structure of the model will also have an impact on response time.)

In the most basic experiment, subjects memorized a list of 18 sentences about objects in locations, such as "The potted palm is in the hotel". These sentences were studied one at a time and in a random order, so that any organization was imposed by the subject. Across the entire list, each object and location had 1 to 3 associations. An illustration of the object and location concepts, along with the associations used to generate the study sentences is presented in Figure 7.8. These sentences can be classified into three types. Those sentences in which an object is in several locations, but each location has only a single object are in the *multiple-location* condition. Those sentences in which an object is in only one location and the location contains many objects represent the *single-location* condition. The rest of the sentences with several associations for both the object and location concepts provide the appropriate number of associations in the single- and multiple-location conditions and otherwise serve as *fillers*.

Let us consider the multiple-location and single-location conditions in more detail. In the multiple-location condition, a single object is described as being in several locations. For example, a "potted palm" may be in a "hotel", a "cocktail lounge", and a "high school". In the real world, it is unlikely that such an object will travel from place to place as part of a single situation. As a result, a separate situation model is created for each of those situations corresponding to the different locations of the object. During retrieval, when the subject is required to verify a multiple-location fact, not only is the appropriate situation model activated, but so are the other situation models that also contain

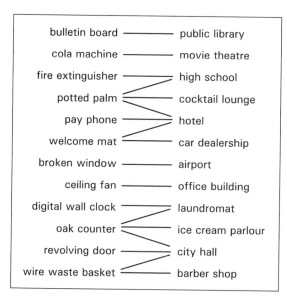

FIG. 7.8. Structure of the study list associations for objects and locations in situation model fan-effect experiments.

the concepts in the memory probe. For example, in verifying the fact "The potted palm is in the hotel", not only is the hotel model activated, but so are the cocktail lounge and high school models, although to a lesser degree. These associated but irrelevant situation models interfere with a subject's ability to retrieve the desired representation. As a result, there is an increase in retrieval time accompanying an increase in the number of these distracting models, hence a fan effect.

Now consider the single-location condition in which several objects are in a single location. For example, in the "city hall" there may be an "oak counter", a "revolving door", and a "waste basket". Unlike the multiple-location condition, these facts are all consistent with a single situation in the real world, and only a single situation model needs to be created. During retrieval, only one model is activated; there are no related distractor models. As a result, response time is relatively constant with an increase in the number of objects associated with the location. The pattern of data for multiple- and single-location conditions is illustrated in Figure 7.9.

This pattern of retrieval times holds across a variety of circumstances. It does not change when the nature of the articles used is manipulated, making them either definite (i.e. "the") or indefinite (i.e. "a" or "an") (Radvansky et al. 1993), or with the order of the concepts in the sentences (Radvansky & Zacks 1991, Radvansky et al. 1993, 1996). It is also unaffected by instructions to overtly try to organize a set of

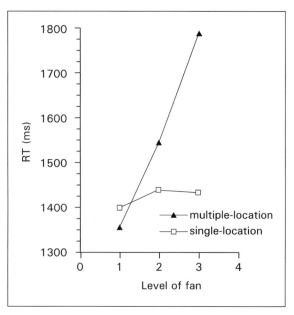

FIG. 7.9.   Typical pattern of response times for single- and multiple-location conditions. Data taken from a study originally reported in Radvansky et al. (1993).

facts based on one method or another (Radvansky & Zacks 1991), by the transportability of the described objects (Radvansky et al. 1993), and by whether the subjects are college students or elderly people (Radvansky et al. 1996).

It is important to note that in this series of experiments, subjects are not presented with a structure at encoding, such as a narrative. Instead, organization into situation models is imposed by the subjects themselves. In other words, even in the absence of cues to organization and structure, subjects actively evaluate what situations are described by the facts they are memorizing, and they organize the information around those situations.

One question about these studies relates to the fact that other research has found that the structure of the situation model, while it is in working memory, affects the availability of information from that representation (e.g. Morrow et al. 1987, 1989). Intuitively, one would expect that as the situation model itself becomes more complex (i.e. as more objects are included in a single location), it should be more difficult to access any one part of the model and this should influence retrieval times. Yet, in the Radvansky et al. experiments, there was no effect of the number of objects (fan level) in the single-location condition. We believe this apparent difference from the studies described earlier relates to differences in the complexity of materials used. Typically, in the working memory retrieval studies a described situation is very complex. In contrast, in our long-term memory retrieval studies, the situation models are much simpler. Some evidence that we have gathered (Radvansky & Shoben 1994) also suggests that with more complex information, for single-location conditions, response time may increase with model complexity (i.e. a fan effect emerges). However, this increase in retrieval time does not approach the size of the effect observed when information is stored across several situation models.

Nonspatial situation models

In many of the studies that have been described in this paper, the situation models have been either explicitly or tacitly based on some sort of spatial representation. Consequently, some readers may infer that situation models are almost exclusively location-based or that perhaps they are little more than souped-up mental images. If this were true, then the study of how situation models affect memory retrieval would be better framed as a consideration of how spatial memory representations affect memory retrieval discarding, all of the baggage about situations. However, there are two other types of situation models that have been evaluated using our procedure, both of which focuses on person-based situations, not location-based situations.

Small locations

In one study (Radvansky et al. 1993), subjects memorized lists of facts about people in locations, such as "The banker is in the phone booth". The person concepts were referred to by their occupational title, such as banker, lawyer, or farmer. Unlike the large locations used in the experiment described above, the locations were small ones that typically contain only a single person at one time, such as a phone booth, a witness stand, or the bathroom on a Greyhound bus. Because it is unlikely that more than one person will occupy one of these locations at one time, a location-based organization is implausible. However, it is possible for a person to travel from place to place. As a result, subjects create situation models that are person-based[2]. Therefore, facts about a person going from place to place are integrated into a single model, whereas facts about several people occupying a small location are stored across separate models. On a recognition test, a fan effect is observed for multiple-person–single-location conditions, but not for single-person–multiple-location conditions. This pattern exemplifies the distinction between situation models of states-of-affairs and courses-of-events (Barwise & Perry 1983). Sets of facts, such as "The oak counter is in the city hall", "The revolving door is in the city hall", and "The waste basket is in the city hall" are more consistent with state-of-affairs situations, whereas sets of facts such as "The banker is in the phone booth", "The banker is on the witness stand", and "The banker is in the Greyhound bus's bathroom" are more consistent with course-of-events situations.

Ownership

A course-of-events is not the only type of situation that would lead to a person-based organization. In another study (Radvansky et al. in press), a person-based organization was observed when the situations were states-of-affairs rather than courses-of-events. The situations in this case used the abstract relation of ownership, rather than the spatial relation of containment. Subjects memorized facts about people buying objects. The objects were all ones that can be purchased in a drugstore, such as "toothpaste", a "magazine", or "candy". A person-based organization was then observed on the subsequent recognition test with a fan effect for conditions with a single object being bought by several people, but not for conditions with a single person buying several objects.

However, the ownership relation is not adequate in and of itself for the creation of person-based organizations. The information is only integrated when it potentially refers to a single situation, such as buying a collection of items at a drugstore. No such organization is observed when the objects are typically purchased at different times and in different locations, such as a "house", a "computer", or a "car". In that case, the person cannot become the basis for organization because people tend not to buy these sorts of objects in the same situation.

Summary

Situation models impact on the way information is retrieved from long-term memory. In general, memory for information stored in a situation model reflects the fact that the model captures the gist of the situation, not the specific information used to originally construct it. Furthermore, when a set of related facts is understood as being part of a single situation, the facts are integrated into a single situation model. Because the information has been integrated, it will be easier to retrieve it at a later point in time. In contrast, when a set of facts have a common concept, but refer to several situations in the world, or it is unclear how they describe a single situation, these facts will be stored across several situation models. As a result, during memory retrieval, it will be more difficult to retrieve any one of those facts.

WHEN SITUATION MODELS ARE NOT USED

We have outlined some of the ways situation models can affect memory retrieval. However, it is not always the case that an influence will be observed. Most obviously, it will not be observed when the information is not situation-specific. However, it is also possible that situation models will not affect retrieval even though they have been created. Two circumstances where this may occur are considered. First, certain memory tasks may not access the model, but may use another type of representational code, such as a propositional or mental image code. Second, the task may not focus attention on the situation represented by the model. Finally, we consider some arguments which maintain that situation models are not stored in long-term memory and so would not affect long-term memory retrieval.

Type of memory test

Situation models do not dominate all aspects of memory retrieval. Memory retrieval tasks that do not require a subject to focus on the situations as a whole may result in the use of other representational codes. For example, in a study by Radvansky (1992), subjects memorized a list of facts about people in small places, such as "The banker is in the phone booth", similar to the study described above in the section on small locations. After memorizing the sentences, subjects were given both recognition and free recall tests. The striking result was that two different types of organization were observed for the same subjects. The recognition test data reflected a person-based organization, consistent with a course-of-events situation, as found in the earlier studies. Specifically, a fan effect was observed for the single-location–multiple-person condition, but not for the multiple-location–single-person condition. In contrast, a location-based organization was observed on the free recall test. Subjects strongly tended to recall together sentences that referred to a common location.

The explanation for this finding is based on the notion that situation models were affecting retrieval under only one of these conditions. In particular, the situation model affected recognition, but not free recall. During recognition, the subject does not need to engage in an extensive search of all of the situation models that were created earlier. Instead, only those models that contain concepts in the memory probe are activated (e.g. all of the models containing the *banker* and *phone booth* concepts). So, any difference in response time can be attributed to the organization of the information into situation models.

In contrast, during free recall, subjects need to access all of the information in such a way that would allow them to recover all of the facts. Situation models would be a poor choice for accessing this information because each representation is stored separately from the others. The notion that the situation models were not used is supported by the fact that a person-based organization was not observed. According to our view, there are two other representational codes that could be used to retrieve the needed information: propositional and mental image codes.

One alternative is that, during free recall, subjects may rely more on information stored in a propositional network. In such a case, the facts would all be interconnected in the representation, making it easier to access the entire set. However, a problem with this explanation is that it does not directly account for why the observed organization was location-based, rather than person-based, or some other organization. Another possible explanation is that subjects may have been using mental images to guide their fact retrieval. This could explain why the free recall data was location-based. Visual mental images would appear to be largely location-based because location provides a framework in which an image can be created. By changing the person, the image needs to be changed less than by keeping the person constant and changing the surrounding location. The problem with this second explanation is that it does not account for how all of the needed images were recalled. In order to do this, some sort of location-based retrieval plan needs to be hypothesized. However, this is not too large a step since the creation of such retrieval plans during free recall is well known.

The situation model is not the most relevant

Another reason that situation models may not impact on memory retrieval is that subjects may not need to rely on them in certain circumstances. Although the retrieval task does not preclude their usage, there may be cases in which the target information is more easily accessed from another source (O'Brien & Albrecht 1992, Wilson et al. 1993). In these cases, a propositional or mental image code may be used. For example, in a study similar to those done by Morrow et al. (1987, 1989), Wilson et al. had subjects memorize the layout of a building. Afterwards, subjects read a narrative about a person walking through that building. Occasionally during the course of reading the narrative, subjects were given memory probes in which they were asked to say whether two objects were located in the same room or not. For half the subjects, the narrative protagonist was included in the probe set, whereas for the other half, it was left out. The results are summarized in Figure 7.10. Response time was affected by situation model foregrounding only for the group that had probes that contained the protagonist.

It appears to us that subjects are relying on a situation model when the protagonist is included in the probe set. This is because it is only the situation model that contains a token for the protagonist, whereas a general spatial map of the location does not. As a result, the foregrounding of information in the situation model affects retrieval. In contrast, for the other group, because the protagonist was not included in the

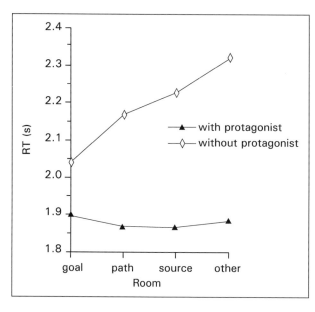

FIG. 7.10.   RT for verifying that target object pairs are in the same room, relative to the room a protagonist is currently in when protagonist is either included or excluded from probe set. Derived from Wilson et al. (1993).

memory probe set, subjects did not need to access the situation model for the verification task. Instead, the subjects needed only to use a general spatial map of the building that they had built up earlier (a building schema), or perhaps even a propositional representation that encoded the object locations in a more abstract fashion. As a result, foregrounding in the situation model would have no effect on retrieval times. The notion that a more abstract representation is being used by the protagonist-absent group is supported by the fact that their response times are faster relative to the protagonist-present group.

Another example of this type of finding comes from the study by Taylor & Tversky (1992) described earlier. As can be seen in Figure 7.7, subjects verified verbatim statements faster than inference statements. Taylor & Tversky argued that the verification of verbatim statements relied more on a propositional representation that had this verbal information directly encoded into it than on a situation model. In contrast, for the inference statements, verification required a more complex understanding of the spatial arrangement. As a result, subjects were forced to use a more complex spatial situation model, which consequently took a longer period of time.

In sum, the use of a situation model to access information during memory retrieval is affected by whether the task either requires a person to consider the entire situation, or whether the task is readily accommodated by the structure of a situation model. When situation models do not most readily yield the required information, subjects may opt to use some other representational form, such as a propositional or mental image code.

Arguments against the long-term storage of situation models

While the research we have reviewed here seems to suggest that situation models are stored in long-term memory and that they directly influence memory performance, there are other opinions. Recently, some theorists have argued that situation models are used in working memory, but are not stored in long-term memory. Instead, what is stored in long-term memory is a propositional representation that is derived from the situation model(s) created earlier (Glenberg & Langston 1992), perhaps along with the set of procedures that were used to create the situation model (Payne 1993). These procedures would allow for the easy reconstruction of the situation model at a later time. However, situation model structure could have no direct effect on memory retrieval itself. (This view is similar to Kosslyn's (1983) theory of imagery in which it is thought that images themselves are not stored in long-term memory, but exist only in working memory, and can be created from previously stored propositions.)

Glenberg & Langston (1992: 147–8) argue for their view on the basis of parsimony, stating that "...we need not propose a new type of long-term representation format (or even a separate long-term representation of the situation model), and we can take advantage of the tremendous literature supporting propositional representational formats." While all good scientists should strive for parsimony whenever possible, the parsimony argument may not be applicable in the present context. Although propositional codes are well known in cognitive psychology, they are certainly not the only long-term representation that has received serious consideration. Also, in order to accept Glenberg & Langston's position, one needs to consider the storage, somehow, of the processes that translate the information from a situation model into a propositional representation (and vice versa). If not, all of the information that is gained by constructing a situation model would be lost. In such a case, it may be better to retain the situation model construct.

Payne (1993) has also argued against the long-term memory storage of situation models, based on a replication and extension of the study by Mani & Johnson-Laird (1982). In Mani & Johnson-Laird's original study, it was found that gist memory was better for descriptions that were consistent with a single situation, whereas verbatim memory was better for descriptions that were not consistent with a single situation. Payne not only failed to replicate Mani & Johnson-Laird's results, but also showed that recognition memory was mediated by the number of overlapping propositions and the order in which propositions were encountered. This led him to theorize that what was stored in long-term memory was not a situation model, but a propositional code along with the processes that were used in the original creation of the situation model, such as the order in which the idea units were encountered, and the manner in which they overlapped. While Payne's data raises doubts about whether situation models are stored in long-term memory, it may be that he failed to find any evidence of situation models because the task he used did not successfully tap into stored models (Radvansky 1992). Only future research will be able to answer this question. Until such a time, we find the arguments for the influence of situation models on memory retrieval to be more compelling than those against their consideration.

SITUATION MODELS, PROPOSITIONS, AND MENTAL IMAGES

As stated earlier, we assume that in addition to creating situation models, people also may use other representational codes to capture different aspects of situation-specific information. In this section we consider how two other representational codes, propositional networks and mental images, represent situation-specific knowledge, how information is structured in these codes, and what mechanisms are used during memory retrieval.

Propositional networks

Characteristics of propositional networks

Propositional representations have received a great deal of attention over the last few decades. Propositions themselves are simple idea units that have some sort of argument structure to convey the important concepts and the associative relations among them. For example, the sentence "The yuppie is in the BMW dealership" is comprised of a single proposition containing the concepts "yuppie" and "BMW dealership" that are associated by a containment relation. Furthermore, the sentence "The yuppie is in the BMW dealership in Cleveland" is composed of two propositions, "the yuppie is in the BMW dealership" and "the BMW dealership is in Cleveland".

For the present discussion, we will limit ourselves to propositional network models of the adaptive character of thought (ACT*) variety (Anderson, 1983). A propositional network is a complex of nodes and links. The nodes correspond to the concepts and the links represent the associations among the concepts. A combination of two nodes and an associative link forms a single proposition. Each concept can be linked to a wide variety of other concepts, leading to a network structure. This form of propositional representation is attractive to researchers because information can be organized rather directly in the network. Specifically, concepts that are related to one another have this relation explicitly encoded in the network. As such, the network is a purely abstract representation of the situation with few or no analogue qualities.

Propositional networks attempt to capture situation-specific information through the distinction between type and token nodes. Type nodes refer to concepts in general, whereas token nodes refer to specific instances of those concepts. For example, a person could have a type node that refers to hotels in general (i.e. general knowledge), and a token node that refers to a specific hotel.

Propositional networks are appealing because it is relatively straightforward to see how knowledge can be built up from a collection of simple propositional units. When a new piece of information is learned, it is simply added to the structure of propositions that are already connected in memory. In an ideal representation, no pieces of information would be left out. Information is structured in a propositional network in terms of the concepts and relations that have been expressed.

Information is retrieved from a propositional network through a process of spreading activation. During retrieval, the nodes for the currently relevant concepts are activated. This activation then spreads along the links until an intersection occurs. At that point, a person can verify a fact is known. In the case of an unknown fact, if an initial plausibility check is passed (Reder & Ross 1983), the activation spreads throughout the network for a certain waiting period (King & Anderson 1976). At the end of that period, a person can verify that the fact is not known. This prevents activation from spreading indefinitely through the network, avoiding the possibility of spurious intersections.

Limitations of propositional networks

A propositional network view would have difficulty predicting or accounting for some of the research done on situation models. For example, in the research by Franklin & Tversky (1990), Glenberg et al. (1987), and Morrow et al. (1987, 1989) this type of theory would have trouble accounting for data suggesting that the availability of information is mediated by the structure of the situation. It is also unclear how and why a propositional network would differentiate among changes in the orientation of an observer, the foregrounding of information, and the increased availability of portions of a situation that a story protagonist has recently passed through, but were left unmentioned in the text.

Despite this it may be possible to modify a propositional network model to account for viewer orientation effects. This is largely attributable to the fact that such models can represent just about anything, psychologically plausible or not. For example, there may be elaborations that alter various node and link strengths whenever the viewer changed orientation or location. However, such additions would result in an increasingly cumbersome model, and are tantamount to using a situation model explanation with the extra assumption that the situation model itself is composed of a complex of propositions. We think that a situation model view provides a better perspective from which to draw predictions and answer questions about how viewer orientation may affect memory retrieval.

Another argument against using propositional networks as the sole representational code to explain a person's understanding of situations is based on what these networks exactly represent. A propositional network conveys how concepts are related to one another. However, the representation does not directly convey how these relations correspond to the relations among entities in the world. For example, if a person encoded the ideas that "George is to the left of Scott" and "Scott is to the left of Roger", the idea that "George is to the left of Roger" would not be encoded in the network. However, this information should be stored directly in a situation model. Network representations, like ACT[*], are viewed by some theorists as being little more than verbal/linguistic translations of information (Johnson-Laird, Herrmann & Chaffin, 1984).

This limitation of propositional networks can be seen in the experimental work by Radvansky & Zacks (1991, Radvansky et al. 1993). In particular, it is not easy to determine how the structure of a propositional network would be constrained by whether a set of information pertained to a single situation or multiple situations. Presumably, a propositional network would represent both situations similarly. According to a propositional network view, the availability of information should be mediated by the number of associations with each concept, the relative strength of the different concepts and associations based on frequency of usage, and/or whether that part of the network is currently in an active state (in working memory). The number of situations involved is not considered to be a factor[3].

However, before rejecting the capability of network codes just yet, it should be noted that some provision has been made for propositional networks to handle thematically related concepts (McCloskey & Bigler 1980, Reder & Anderson 1980). Specifically, it has been argued that sets of thematically related ideas are clustered in the network by means of associative links joining the related concepts to a common concept or *theme node*. This theme node is strategically placed in the network so that it serves to reduce the number of associative links that need to be searched during memory retrieval. However, this mechanism still does not specify which thematic relations correspond to situations in the world. In the case of the Radvansky & Zacks (1991) study, there does not appear to be any *a priori* reason to select object or locations concepts as theme nodes. Why should the hotel concept be more likely to serve as a theme node for a set of facts about a hotel than the cola machine for a set of facts about a cola machine? The factor that apparently identifies which facts are organized together is whether the sentences refer to a common situation in the world. A propositional network would be required to take on all of the procedures used to structure a situation model in order to account for such a pattern of results.

Mental images

Characteristics of mental images

Mental images are internally generated perceptual events that roughly correspond to real perceptual events of some real or imagined situation (although some theorists argue that mental images can be accounted

for by propositions, e.g. Pylyshyn 1984). Despite the close correspondence between real perceptual experiences and visual images, there are
important differences. For example, mental images are typically less
detailed than visual events.

Like situation models, mental images represent single situations. It
is easy for people to conjure up an image of a single event in the world.
People do not form images that simultaneously correspond to two different situations, such as forming an image of a state fair and a jury
trial. Furthermore, situation models and mental images are similar in
that information is represented in an analogue form. In mental images,
this refers to the notion that the structure of the image corresponds to
the structure of a perceptual event. The analogue form of images is evident from research that suggests that people may scan mental images
in a manner similar to scanning perceptual scenes (Kosslyn et al. 1978),
that people manipulate mental images in a fashion similar to perceptually available displays (Shepard & Metzler 1971), and that mental imagery tasks can interfere with similar analogue perceptual processing
(Brooks 1968).

Information is thought to be retrieved through a process of scanning
the mental image. Characteristics of this scanning process should be
evident in memory retrieval tasks. It has been found that it takes
longer to scan a large distance in a mental image than a short distance
(Kosslyn et al. 1978). Furthermore, the access of information from a
mental image can be affected by the other components of the images,
such as the size of other entities in the imagined situation. For example, it is easier to identify the parts of a rabbit when the rabbit is embedded in an image along with a fly, than if the rabbit is embedded in an
image along with an elephant (Kosslyn 1983).

While the notion of a mental image is useful, it does not provide a
complete account of how people mentally represent situations. A mental
image may be able to represent visual aspects of a situation, such as
space and possibly time, but it has difficulty representing aspects of a
situation that are not perceptual. For example, a mental image cannot
easily or directly incorporate abstract relations and concepts such as
ownership and kinship relations. In contrast, a situation model does
represent such relations (Radvansky et al. in press).

Franklin & Tversky's (1990) spatial framework findings are also
inconsistent with a mental imagery account. Mental imagery theory
would predict that information directly in front of the viewer should be
most available. Information would become less available the more an
observer needs to rotate in the scene. This is not the case. As a reminder,
it was found that information along the above–below axis was the most
salient. This is accounted for by the strong salience of gravity. Further-

more, if one assumes that mental rotation to directions other than ahead of the viewer is involved, then the identity of objects to the left or right should be more available than the identity of objects behind the viewer. Again, this prediction was not upheld. Instead, the retrieval of object information appears to be mediated more by the functional relations among objects along primary axes oriented around an observer.

Finally, the results of the studies by Radvansky et al. (1993, in press), particularly those from the small location and ownership studies, are difficult to explain using only an imagery-based account. If subjects use mental images, rather than situation models, a location-based organization should always be observed. This is because a location provides an appropriate frame from which to construct a mental image and organize information, whereas a person travelling from place to place provides a poor image frame. Also, there is no provision for incorporating abstract relations such as ownership into a mental image. Instead, what is observed is that situation models are formed based on concepts other than location, such as person concepts, and that these situation models represent relations that would not be represented in a mental image, namely ownership.

Multiple representational codes

While propositional and mental image codes have competed with situation models as the means by which situation-specific knowledge is stored and structured, the view advocated by most situation model theorists is that these other codes coexist with situation models (e.g. Johnson-Laird 1983, Kintsch 1994). That is, the situation model view argues for "...the existence of at least three types of mental representation: propositional representations which are strings of symbols that correspond to natural language, [situation] models which are structural analogues of the world, and images which are perceptual correlates of models from a particular point of view" (Johnson-Laird 1983: 165) (see also Schmalhofer & Glavanov 1986). Each of these representational codes is assumed to play a different role in mental processing.

While all three different representational codes may be used, one or more codes may be absent, depending on the nature of the information. For example, while some situation-specific information may have a large imagistic component, such as "The weathered red life-boat is tied to the long dock out on the frozen lake", others may have a minimal or nonexistent imagery component, such as "Someone owns the television", "I am the President's half-brother", or "All artists are beekeepers".

We would also like to emphasize that the creation and use of situation models is not an automatic process, but only proceeds when the person is motivated to consider the situations described. Additionally, attention can be directed to other representational codes depending on the current task demands (Graesser et al. 1994, Singer et al. 1994). Such effects were observed in the Taylor & Tversky's (1992) experiments where subjects verified previously seen statements from a description of a spatial environment. Specifically, verbatim probes were verified faster than inference statements. Taylor & Tversky argued that verbatim statements could be identified more directly using a propositional code, whereas the verification of inference probes required a more elaborate model of the situation. Moreover, a series of experiments by Wilson et al. (1993) found that situation model structure influenced memory retrieval only under certain conditions. These experiments were based on the paradigm developed by Morrow et al. (1987, 1989) in which a narrative was read about a person travelling through a previously memorized space. Subjects were intermittently interrupted with probes of two objects from the space and had to indicate whether the objects were in the same room in the building. Wilson et al. found that distance effects were not observed if the story protagonist was not included in the set of memory probe items. Under such circumstances, people may be less willing to use a situation model to verify the location of entities when they can use a general mental map they constructed during the initial learning period.

LIMITATIONS OF OUR SITUATION MODEL VIEW

In this chapter we have proposed a version of a theory of situation models and how they affect memory retrieval. Evidence was provided to support this view, and reasons were given for why a situation model view is superior to propositional network or mental imagery explanations alone. At this point we would like to address some of the gaps in our theory and in some future directions of research.

Structure of situation models

Earlier in this chapter, we considered some characteristics that are important aspects of situation model structure. Despite those efforts, as well as the efforts of other situation model theorists, the precise nature and underlying structure of situation models is still unclear. For example, in Kintsch's (1994) construction–integration theory, situation models can be made up of propositions, mental images, procedural codes, or abstract codes. A situation model captures spatial frameworks (Franklin & Tversky 1990), but it is more than just a spatial or any other framework. It captures both perceptual (e.g. spatial extent, Morrow et al. 1989), and abstract relations (e.g. ownership, Radvansky, et al. in press), but it is not clear by what mechanism this is accomplished, only that the representation should serve this function. As such, situation model theory bases its ideas of organizational structure and how this structure impacts on memory retrieval more on the function the representations serve rather than on an account of the specific structure of the memory representations themselves.

Creation of situation models

A requirement for describing how situation models are created is the need to adequately describe what is and what is not part of a situation. However, this is a difficult task. For example, would a situation of a person placing luggage into her car include the entire driveway? The yard? The neighbour's yard? Because the structure of situations cannot be easily identified, it may sometimes be difficult to determine how information is used to construct a situation model. Recently, this issue has received some attention. Graesser et al. (1994) were able to place limits on the types of inferences that people make when constructing a situation model, thereby constraining the scope of the model. Specifically, a situation model contains only those elements, properties, and relations that can be simply derived, such as backwards causal inferences (a person is putting luggage into her car because she is going on a trip), but not more open-ended aspects of a situation, such as forward causal inferences (the person is going to the airport), or detailed information that, while probably true, is not central to understanding the situation (the person has an operating digestive system).

Presently, we are limited to investigating memory for information that can be clearly classified into certain types of situations. However, some exploration is being made in cases where the situation boundaries are not so clear cut. For example, in studies on ownership relations, we have found that situation model organizations are observed for facts referring to people buying objects commonly found in a drugstore (magazines, toothpaste, and candy), but not when the relation between the people and objects is described as "owns" rather than "is buying", nor when the items are typically purchased in different locations (e.g. compact disc, toothpaste, and diamond ring) (Radvansky et al. in press). This suggests that situation models are more easily constructed when the information refers to a particular region in space (e.g. a drugstore), and a particular region in time ("is buying" is more likely to refer to a discrete event than "owns").

Memory retrieval from situation models

The focus of this chapter has been on the retrieval of information from situation models. We have provided an outline for some of the major factors that we think can influence retrieval. However, there is still further clarification and specification to be done. For example, it is unclear by what mechanisms memory retrieval is accomplished. What procedure is used when the internal structure of a situation model is searched while the model is in an active state (i.e. in working memory)? How is it that a portion of a situation model can be "foregrounded" with respect to the rest of the model? Is long-term memory retrieval accomplished entirely through an activation process, or is it some combination of activation and inhibitory mechanisms (Anderson & Bjork 1994, Hasher & Zacks 1988)?

As far as the last question goes, we have begun a series of studies using an ignored-distractor priming (negative priming) paradigm (e.g. Tipper 1985) in a standard recognition test. In these studies, those situation models that contain concepts overlapping those contained in the target representation are treated as distractors. For example, consider a situation in which a person knows that a potted palm is in the hotel and in the barber shop. Presumably, two situation models would be created, one for the hotel and the other for the barber shop (Radvansky & Zacks 1991). In the course of verifying the fact that the potted palm is in the hotel, interference from the barber shop model is observed. The question is what should happen concerning retrieval of the fact that the potted palm is in the barber shop? One possibility is that retrieval of the barber shop model will be facilitated as a result of lingering activation from the previous trial. This would be positive priming. The other possibility is that retrieval of the barber shop model will be delayed as a result of this information having been suppressed on the previous trial as part of the effect to isolate the correct representation from related competitors. This would be negative priming. Although we cannot come to a clear conclusion at this point, some pilot data that we have collected suggests that negative priming will be observed.

SUMMARY AND CONCLUSIONS

Over the course of this chapter we have looked at how situation models affect memory retrieval. It has been argued that situation models capture important aspects of described situations and can affect memory retrieval depending on whether the relevant information is stored in a single situation model or across several situation models. Effects of situation models are observed, it has been argued, during both on-line processing and when the knowledge representation is already fixed in memory. Furthermore, the situation model view allows predictions to be made that are not easily derivable from either propositional network or mental image views alone. Propositional networks do not provide insight into how situations are structured and separated. Mental imagery does not account for how abstract situation-specific information will be organized. Although some aspects of the situation model view are in need of further elaboration, we believe there is strong evidence of a central role for situation models in memory retrieval.

NOTES

1. We are concerned here with research where the term *mental model* has been used to refer to situation-specific representations, but not to research where the term is used to describe a person's understanding of a physical device (e.g. Gentner & Stevens 1983), such as an electrical circuit or the thermostat in their house. Although there have been attempts to link these two uses of the term (Johnson-Laird 1989), we consider them to be separate applications.
2. If large locations are used, the data reflect no specific organization, presumably because both location-based and person-based organizations are plausible.
3. One argument that we have encountered on more than one occasion is that, while it is generally true that a fan effect occurs as the number of associations with a concept increases, there are some exceptions. Specifically, Anderson (1976) described a characteristic of his network model called the *min* effect. The *min* effect refers to the notion that a fan effect may be attenuated or absent when one of the concepts has only a single association. Because the object concepts in the single-location condition each have only a single association, the lack of a fan effect could be seen as an instance of the *min* effect. The flaw in this logic is that the location concepts in the multiple-location condition, like the object concepts in the single-location condition, have only a single association. So, a *min* effect should also be observed in this condition, but it is not. In short, the *min* effect cannot be used to explain away our results.

REFERENCES

Anderson, A., S. C. Garrod, A. J. Sanford 1983. The accessibility of pronomial antecedents as a function of episode shifts in narrative text. *Quarterly Journal of Experimental Psychology* **35A**, 427–40.

Anderson, J. R. 1974. Retrieval of propositional information from long-term memory. *Cognitive Psychology* **6**, 451–74.

Anderson, J. R. 1976. *Language, memory, and thought*. Hillsdale, New Jersey: Erlbaum.

Anderson, J. R. 1983. *The architecture of cognition*. Cambridge, Mass.: Harvard University Press.

Anderson, M. C. & R. A. Bjork 1994. Mechanisms of inhibition in long-term memory: a new taxonomy. In *Inhibitory Processes in Attention, Memory, and Language*, D. Dagenbach & T. H. Carr (eds), 265–325. New York: Academic Press.

Barwise, J. 1989. *The situation in logic*. Stanford, Calif.: Center for the Study of Language and Information.

Barwise, J. & J. Perry 1983. *Situations and attitudes*. Cambridge, Mass.: MIT Press.

Bransford, J. D., J. R. Barclay, J. J. Franks 1972. Sentence memory: a constructive versus interpretive approach. *Cognitive Psychology* **3**, 193–209.

Brooks, L. 1968. Spatial and verbal components of the act of recall. *Canadian Journal of Psychology*, **22**, 349–68.

Bryant, D. J., B. Tversky, N. Franklin 1992. Internal and external spatial frameworks for representing described scenes. *Journal of Memory and Language* **31**, 74–98.

Bryant, D. J., B. Tversky, M. Lanca, B. Narasimhan 1993. Mental spatial models guide search of observed spatial arrays. Paper presented at the 34th Annual Meeting of the Psychonomic Society, Washington DC.

Carlson-Radvansky, L. A. & G. A. Radvansky (1996). Functional relations and spatial terms. *Psychological Science*, **7**, 56–60.

Franklin, N. & B. Tversky 1990. Searching imagined environments. *Journal of Experimental Psychology: General* **119**, 63–76.

Garnham, A. 1982. Mental models as representations of text. *Memory and Cognition* **9**, 560–5.

Garrod, S. & A. Sanford 1983. Topic dependent effects in language processing. In *The process of language understanding*, G. B. Flores d'Arcais & R. J. Jarvella (eds). New York: John Wiley.

Gentner, D. & A. L. Stevens 1983. *Mental models*. Hillsdale, New Jersey: Erlbaum.

Gernsbacher, M. A., H. H. Goldsmith, R. W. Robertson 1992. Do readers mentally represent characters' emotional states? *Cognition and Emotion* **6**, 89–111.

Glenberg, A. M. & W. E. Langston 1992. Comprehension of illustrated text: pictures help to build mental models. *Journal of Memory and Language* **31**, 129–51.

Glenberg, A. M., M. Meyer, K. Lindem 1987. Mental models contribute to foregrounding during text comprehension. *Journal of Memory and Language* **26**, 69–83.

Graesser, A. C., M. Singer, T. Trabasso 1994. Constructing inferences during narrative text comprehension. *Psychological Review* **101**, 371–95.

Hasher, L. & M. Griffin 1978. Reconstructive and reproductive processes in memory. *Journal of Experimental Psychology: Human Learning and Memory* **4**, 318–30.

Hasher, L & R. T. Zacks 1988. Working memory, comprehension, and aging: a review and a new view. In *The Psychology of Learning and Motivation* vol. 22, G. H. Bower (ed.), 193–225. New York: Lawrence Erlbaum Associates.

Hintzman, D. L. 1986. "Schema abstraction" in a multiple-trace memory model. *Psychological Review* **93**, 411–28.

Johnson-Laird, P. N. 1983. *Mental models: towards a cognitive science of language, inference and consciousness*. Cambridge, Mass.: Harvard University Press.

Johnson-Laird, P. N. 1989. Mental models. In *Foundations of cognitive science*, M. I. Posner (ed.), 469–500. Cambridge, Mass.: MIT Press.

Johnson-Laird, P. N. 1992. Propositional reasoning by model. *Psychological Review* **99**, 418–39.

Johnson-Laird, P. N., D. J. Herrmann, R. Chaffin 1984. Only connections: a critique of semantic networks. *Psychological Bulletin* **96**, 292–315.

King & Anderson, J. R. 1976. Long-term memory search: an intersecting activation process. *Journal of Verbal Learning and Verbal Behavior* **15**, 587–605.

Kintsch, W. 1994. The psychology of discourse processing. In *Handbook of Psycholinguistics*, M. A. Gernsbacher (ed.), 721–39. San Diego: Academic Press.

Kosslyn, S. M. 1983. *Ghost in the mind's machine: creating and using images in the brain*. New York: W. W. Norton.

Kosslyn, S. M., T. M. Ball, B. J. Reiser 1978. Visual images preserve metric spatial information: evidence from studies of image scanning. *Journal of Experimental Psychology: Human Perception and Performance* **4**, 47–60.

Logan, G. D. 1995. Linguistic and conceptual control of visual spatial attention. *Cognitive Psychology* **28**, 103–74.

Mani, K. & P. N. Johnson-Laird 1982. The mental representation of spatial descriptions. *Memory and Cognition* **10**, 181–87.

McCloskey, M. & K. Bigler 1980. Focused memory search in fact retrieval. *Memory and Cognition* **8**, 253–64.

McKoon, G. & R. Ratcliff 1992. Inference during reading. *Psychological Review* **99**, 440–66.

McNamara, T. P., J. K. Hardy, S. C. Hirtle 1989. Subjective hierarchies in spatial memory. *Journal of Experimental Psychology: Learning, Memory, and Cognition* **15**, 211–27.

Minsky, M. L. 1986. *The society of mind*. New York: Simon and Schuster.

Morrow, D. G., G. H. Bower, S. L. Greenspan 1989. Updating situation models during narrative comprehension. *Journal of Memory and Language* **28**, 292–312.

Morrow, D. G., S. L. Greenspan, G. H. Bower 1987. Accessibility and situation models in narrative comprehension. *Journal of Memory and Language* **26**, 165–87.

O'Brien, E. J. & J. E. Albrecht 1992. Comprehension strategies in the development of a mental model. *Journal of Experimental Psychology: Learning, Memory and Cognition* **18**, 777–84.

Payne, S. J. 1993. Memory for mental models of spatial descriptions: an episodic-construction-trace hypothesis. *Memory and Cognition* **21**, 591–603.

Pylyshyn, Z. W. 1984. *Computation and cognition*. Cambridge, Mass.: MIT Press.

Radvansky, G. A. 1992. Recognition, recall, and mental models. Unpublished dissertation, Department of Psychology, Michigan State University.

Radvansky, G. A. & E. J. Shoben 1994. Mental model complexity. Unpublished data.

Radvansky, G. A., L. D. Gerard, R. T. Zacks, L. Hasher 1990. Younger and older adults use of mental models as representations for text materials. *Psychology and Aging* **5**, 209–14.

Radvansky, G. A. & R. T. Zacks 1991. Mental models and the fan effect. *Journal of Experimental Psychology: Learning, Memory, and Cognition* **17**, 940–53.

Radvansky, G. A., D. H. Spieler, R. T. Zacks 1993. Mental model organization. *Journal of Experimental Psychology: Learning, Memory, and Cognition* **19**, 95–114.

Radvansky, G. A., R. S. Wyer, J. M. Curiel, M. F. Lutz in press. Mental models and abstract relations. *Journal of Experimental Psychology: Learning, Memory, and Cognition*.

Radvansky, G. A., R. T. Zacks, L. Hasher 1996. Fact retrieval in younger and older adults: the role of mental models. *Psychology and Aging* **11**, 258–71.

Ratcliff, R. & G. McKoon 1989. Similarity information versus relational information: differences in the time course of retrieval. *Cognitive Psychology* **21**, 139–55.

Reder, L. M. & J. R. Anderson 1980. A partial resolution of the paradox of interference: the role of integrating knowledge. *Cognitive Psychology* **12**, 447–72.

Reder, L. M. & B. H. Ross 1983. Integrated knowledge in different tasks: the role of retrieval strategies on fan effects. *Journal of Experimental Psychology: Learning, Memory, and Cognition* **9**, 55–72.

Schank, R. C. & R. P. Abelson 1977. *Scripts, plans goals and understanding*. Hillsdale, N. J.: Erlbaum.

Schmalhofer, F. & D. Glavanov 1986. Three components of understanding a programmer's manual: verbatim, propositional, and situational representations. *Journal of Memory and Language* **25**, 279–94.

Shepard, R. N. & S. Chipman 1970. Second-order isomorphism of internal representation: shapes of states. *Cognitive Psychology* **1**, 1–17.

Shepard, R. N. & J. Metzler 1971. Mental rotation of three-dimensional objects. *Science* **171**, 701–3.

Singer, M., A. C. Graesser, T. Trabasso 1994. Minimal or global inference during reading. *Journal of Memory and Language* **33**, 421–41.

Taylor, H. A. & B. Tversky 1992. Spatial mental models derived from survey and route descriptions. *Journal of Memory and Language* **31**, 261–92.

Tipper, S. P. 1985. The negative priming effect: inhibitory effects of ignored primes. *Quarterly Journal of Experimental Psychology* **37A**, 571–90.

Tulving, E. 1985. How many memory systems are there? *American Psychologist* **40**, 385–98.

Wilson, S. G., M. Rinck, T. P. McNamara, G. H. Bower, D. G. Morrow 1993. Mental models and narrative comprehension: some qualifications. *Journal of Memory and Language* **32**, 141–54.

Zwaan, R. A. 1994. Effect of genre expectations on text comprehension. *Journal of Experimental Psychology: Learning, Memory, and Cognition* **20**, 920–33.

PART FOUR
Autobiographical memory

CHAPTER EIGHT

Representations of autobiographical memories

Stephen J. Anderson & Martin A. Conway

In this chapter we describe and evaluate various approaches to the representation of knowledge in long-term memory. Our focus is on how adequately different approaches treat the representation of specific experiences, i.e. autobiographical memories (AMs). Three broad "schools" of knowledge representation are discussed: semantic networks, scripts, and connectionist models. The ability of the three approaches to account for a critical list of "facts", which in our view must be accommodated by any serious theory of AM, is appraised, (see Conway 1990, 1995a,b, and Conway & Rubin 1993, for reviews of AM research). We should say at the outset that this is something of an unfair exercise as none of the models we consider below (with the possible exception of scripts) were explicitly designed to model AMs. Moreover, the data from which our list of AM facts have been drawn were reported only recently, and after the models were first proposed. Nevertheless, all the models we consider make at least some attempt to specify the representation of experiences in long-term memory and, therefore, should be able to account for at least some of our AM facts. A final section briefly considers the form that a full model of AM would have to take and raises issues relating to the roles of the self and central control processes in mediating remembering.

AUTOBIOGRAPHICAL MEMORY: SOME FACTS

We are concerned with a specifically psychological model of AM and, at a very minimum, we want this model to explain various aspects of AM that we know about from empirical studies. (Ultimately, of course, we want a model that will guide empirical research and exhibit interesting properties that give new insights into AM.) Consider the following two descriptions, the first of which was provided by a colleague and the second by a subject taking part in an AM retrieval experiment in our laboratory.

> I was reminded of my own flashbulb memory for the declaration of the second world war which occurred in September 1939 when I was aged 6 years and 6 months. I have a clear image of my father standing on the rockery of the front garden of our house waving a bamboo garden stake like a pendulum in time with the clock chimes heard on the radio which heralded the announcement. More hazily, I have an impression that neighbours were also out in the adjoining gardens listening to the radio and, although my father was fooling around, the feeling of the memory is one of deep foreboding and anxiety. I have never discussed this memory with anyone and very rarely thought about it. (G. Cohen, personal communication 1994).

> ...Ah, now this was when I uh worked in an engineering factory and we ... well we used to fool around a lot...and there'd be a lot of singing...people used to sing loudly in these sort of pressure vessels they were working on ...or whistle ...and it would echo and be amplified and there was one guy people used to pick on a little. He was walking through this huge vessel like a giant tube open at both ends but about 20 feet in diameter and maybe 40 feet long and we sort of set it up so when he got to about the middle ... we were all standing down the side ... we started banging the sides with hammers. The noise just built and built and he was shaking when he got out I can see him standing there shaking and his face was white ... I was glad when I left there. (Protocol collected from a subject recalling a memory to the cue word hammer. Note that the subject was required to report anything that went through his mind while generating this memory.)

These accounts illustrate a number of important features of autobiographical memories. For instance, each memory contains both general and specific information, i.e. *when I was 6 years old, when I worked in an engineering factory*, and also *the bamboo stake* and the *white face of the deafened workmate*. This mix of general and specific knowledge is a hallmark of autobiographical remembering and has been noted by many researchers (Brown et al. 1986, Linton 1975, Conway & Berkerian 1987, Barsalou 1988, Conway 1992, 1995a,b,c,d, Schooler & Herrman 1992, Treadway et al. 1992, Conway & Rubin 1993, Anderson & Conway 1994). One possibility is that general information contained in a report of an autobiographical memory frames highly event-specific details in the context of a rememberer's own autobiography.

It is also of interest that general information typically precedes the report of specific information. There may of course be many reasons for this, some of which are to do with narrative conventions governing the public presentation of memories (e.g. Neisser 1982). However, a number of lines of research suggest that such conventions are secondary to the retrieval of a memory, i.e. a memory is first retrieved and only then put into a suitable form for presentation (Anderson & Conway 1994). Instead, prior presentation of general information in a description of a memory may expose part of the memory retrieval process in which the access of specific autobiographical knowledge is contingent upon first accessing general knowledge. In addition to this, both descriptions suggest that autobiographical memory retrieval is effortful, and this too is a common feature of memory retrieval. Unlike the access of factual semantic knowledge, which in laboratory experiments typically takes about 1 to 2 seconds, retrieval of AMs ranges over periods of anything up to 15 seconds, averaging about 4 seconds in laboratory tasks (Conway 1992, 1995c). Moreover, retrieval is often characterized by false starts, redundant information, and retrieval blockages (Williams & Hollan 1981, Burgess & Shallice 1995). Taken together these characteristics indicate that AM retrieval is a complex process in which memories are effortfully constructed rather than retrieved as whole, fully formed, units.

One difference between the two example memories is that the first memory is far older than the second. Indeed, the first memory was put forward by the rememberer as an example of a *flashbulb memory*. Flashbulb memories are vivid, highly detailed memories that endure, apparently unchanged, for many years (Brown & Kulik 1977). This type of AM is usually associated with experiences that were high in personal importance and that involved strong emotions (see Conway 1995d, for a review of the flashbulb memory literature). Thus, AMs may vary in their vividness and durability, and a model of AM must also be able to accommodate this. More generally, descriptions of AMs very frequently feature self-evaluative comments and/or comments relating to emotion and mood. This would seem to implicate the role of the self in autobiographical remembering and, again, research has established that factors relating to the self strongly influence both the encoding and construction of AMs (Conway 1995a, Strauman 1990).

Finally we must mention what is arguably one of the most striking findings of AM research. When subjects are asked to recall memories across their lifespan and the subjects are older than about 35 years, then the number of memories recalled varies as a function of the subject's age at the time the memory was formed (Rubin 1982, Rubin et al. 1986). Figure 8.1. shows an idealized curve illustrating the probability of memories recalled in each of 10 five-year blocks for a typical 50-year-old subject. It can be seen from Figure 8.1 that there are three components to the lifespan retrieval curve. The period from zero to about 5 years of age is known as the period of *childhood amnesia* and most people simply cannot recall many memories from this period (see Pillemer & White, 1989, for a review). In fact, the distribution of memories recalled from the period of childhood amnesia can be fitted by an exponential function (Wetzler & Sweeney 1986) in which the number of memories recalled rapidly decreases with diminishing age of the rememberer at the time of encoding. The second component of the lifespan retrieval curve is often referred to as the *reminiscence bump* because there is an increase in the number of memories recalled from the period of about 15 to 25 years of age. Conway & Rubin (1993) proposed that this period may be differentially sampled because it is a critical period in the formation of self and identity. Finally, the third

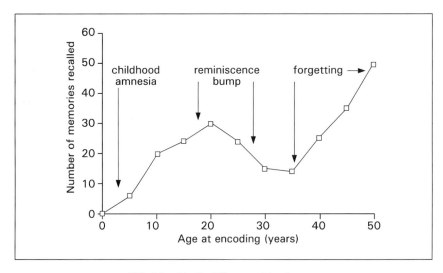

FIG. 8.1.   Idealized lifespan retrieval curve.

component essentially shows monotonically increasing forgetting, from good recall of recent memories to poor recall of more remote memories.

Thus, models of autobiographical memory should at least be able to offer mechanisms that account for at least some, if not all, of the following characteristics:

(a) the mix of general and specific knowledge in all memories;
(b) effortful retrieval and memory construction;
(c) differences in the vividness of different memories;
(d) the three components of the lifespan memory retrieval curve.

There are, of course, many other characteristics of AM that we have not discussed here. For example, memories can be wrong (Neisser 1982, Loftus 1993, Loftus & Ketcham 1994, Conway et al. 1995), they can become impaired in intriguing ways following brain damage and in psychogenic disorders (Conway 1993, 1995c), and they may vary in their phenomenological sequelae (Nigro & Neisser 1983, Conway et al. 1995). However, the short list of four characteristics is sufficient as one set of criteria that must be met by a general model of autobiographical memory.

NETWORK MODELS

Tulving (1972) drew a distinction between episodic/autobiographical memory and semantic memory. Autobiographical memory, as we have seen preserves contextual knowledge of an experienced event. In contrast, semantic memory does not preserve knowledge of encoding contexts but rather represents decontextualized conceptual knowledge about, for example, the meanings of words, numbers, and world knowledge. A metaphor that has often been used to illustrate this distinction is that AM is like a diary whereas semantic memory is like an encyclopaedia. Theories of the representation and processing of encyclopaedic or conceptual knowledge have been expressed in semantic network models (see Rumelhart & Norman 1983, for an excellent review), one of the first of which was due to Quillian (1968, Collins & Quillian 1969). Although Quillian's model was primarily concerned with semantic knowledge it also included the representation of AMs. Figure 8.2 depicts an example of a Quillian-style network for conceptual knowledge of *animals*.

This type of semantic network embodies a number of important aspects of network models. Concepts are represented as nodes in a network, and each node has attached to it a number of semantic

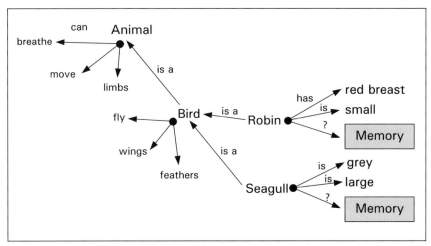

FIG. 8.2.   A semantic network for *birds* (after Quillian 1968).

features or properties. Nodes in the network are interconnected by links or labelled relations to other nodes. In Quillian's model, the concept nodes are hierarchically organized and in Figure 8.2 the concept *robin* is subordinate to *bird*, which in turn is subordinate to *animal*. In other words the nodes are subsets of each other. More generally this introduces the idea of type–token relationships. Thus, in Figure 8.2, *robin* is a token or instance of the type *bird*, and *bird* is a token or instance of the type *animal*. In the Quillian model the hierarchical relations between types and tokens support the *inheritance of properties*. Tokens inherit the properties of concepts that are their types. So, the concept *robin* inherits the property *has wings* from its type concept *bird*. Property inheritance is an efficient or cognitively economic form of representation as properties do not have to be redundantly represented several times over. Property inheritance also supports inference. For example in order to verify a novel statement such as *Napoleon had toes* it is only necessary to know that Napoleon was a man and access the node for man and retrieve the property *has toes* (Kintsch 1980).

One further mechanism, introduced later by Collins & Loftus (1975), is that of spreading activation. Consider how a statement such as *a seagull is a bird* might be processed in a network similar to the one depicted in Figure 8.2. According to the spreading activation account, as the concepts *seagull* and *bird* are mapped onto their corresponding nodes in the network, the two nodes become activated above their resting level. Activation spreads out along paths leading from each node and as it spreads it dissipates becoming progressively weaker. A consequence of this is that closely associated nodes receive greater activation than more distantly associated nodes. As activation spreads from two or more nodes the different sources of activation eventually intersect. It is this intersection that supports the processing of the currently active set of concepts. Activation spreading from the nodes for *Bird* and *Seagull* will rapidly intersect because these two nodes are closely linked (in Collins & Quillian's (1969) terminology they are only two levels apart). When this occurs, the statement *a seagull is a bird* can be then judged true.

How does this model handle AMs? It can be seen from Figure 8.2 that memories are allocated to nodes at the lowest level in conceptual hierarchies. They are treated as holistic units of knowledge with, presumably, little structure and are accessed by traversing the links of the semantic network. From our earlier characterization of AM this is, of course, wholly implausible. Nevertheless, let us assume for a moment that the semantic network shown in Figure 8.2 is an accurate model of AM representation. Now consider the following memory, reported by a 40-year-old male subject in response to the cue word "seagull".

One holiday at Z we sat out on a sort of large balcony attached to a hotel on the seafront. This balcony was about 40 feet above a rocky shoreline and looked out over the sea. It was sunny and the children and I sat drinking lemonade while these huge seagulls strutted along the high stone parapet a few feet away or wheeled around screeching in the air. The kids threw them crisps and the gulls became frantic and started to fight.

Why should this memory be encoded in terms of the concept *seagull*? It could have been encoded in relation to any of the other concepts in the event, for example, *hotel, lemonade, holiday at Z, crisps, the children, the sea*, and so forth. Certainly all these concepts, and many more, would have been active during the actual period when the event was encoded into long-term memory. Perhaps the memory has labelled relations in the network to all the nodes that became active during the experience and any one of these can be used to access the memory. For instance, if the cue had been *lemonade* or *holiday at Z* then maybe the same memory would have been retrieved. One possibility is that all memories are summary records of the knowledge activated during their encoding and have labelled links to the nodes most centrally involved in processing the original experience. If this were the case then semantic knowledge might be conceived as "resting" on a very large pool of AMs that form the lowest level in the network. Links between memories and nodes representing concepts will vary in their degree of association and, therefore, some links between memories and concept nodes will be close whereas others will be distant. For whatever reason, the example memory appears to have a close association with the concept *seagull* and activation spreading from the *seagull* node would have raised the resting activation level of this particular memory and made it available for retrieval.

There is some attraction to the idea that semantic knowledge rests, as it were, upon a large pool of AMS, as undoubtedly semantic and auto-biographical knowledge must be strongly interrelated (Tulving 1983). One implication is that when nodes in a semantic network become acti-vated then at least some activation must spread to representations of AMS. If semantic knowledge structures terminate in distinctive features and AMS then those nodes lowest in the network, at the base of hierar-chical knowledge structures, should activate AMS strongly and directly. For example, in Figure 8.2 activation of the node *seagull* should acti-vate memories more strongly than does activation of the node *bird* which, in turn, activates memories more strongly than does activation of the superordinate *animal*. Conway & Bekerian (1987) tested this as-sumption in a series of primed AM retrieval experiments. In these stud-ies subjects retrieved memories to cue words such as "seagull". On some occasions, just prior to the subject's seeing the memory cue, a related word or prime, was presented which the subject simply read. Primes were always types and memory cue words always tokens, e.g. furni-ture–chair, vehicle–bus, bird–robin, and so on. On other occasions no related prime was presented and instead the word "ready" was used, e.g. ready–chair, ready–bus, ready–robin, and so on. It was reasoned that if AMS are represented in a way similar to that depicted in Figure 8.2, then when a related prime is presented this will activate an associ-ate and at least some activation will spread from the associate to any related AMS. When the primed memory cue word is then presented it will increase activation of its own node and raise the activation level of associated memories even further. Under these conditions an AM should be quickly retrieved. In contrast, when the prime is unrelated then the associated node of the memory cue word does not receive prior activa-tion nor are any more distantly associated memories primed, conse-quently memory retrieval should be slowed compared to the primed case. However, no semantic priming effects were detected in any of Conway & Bekerian's (1987) experiments and memory retrieval times to primed and unprimed cues did not differ. Thus, a central prediction of the semantic network model of AM representation was not supported.

The evidence then does not support the semantic network account of AM representation, nor does this account have anything to say concern-ing the mix of general and specific knowledge in AMS and differences in memory clarity. This is because memories are conceived of as undifferentiated whole units attached to the base of hierarchical knowledge structures. Moreover, this assumption of "holistic" storage finesses the problem of memory construction. It is also difficult to envisage how this approach might be used to account for the reminiscence bump and pattern of retention of recent memories that are characteristic of the lifespan AM retrieval curve (Figure 8.1). Despite these shortcomings, the hierarchical network approach might, nonetheless, be used in a more general way to provide some insight into the phenomenon of childhood amnesia. Assume again that AMs have paths to the concepts used in their original processing, i.e. when actually experienced during encoding. Recent research has established that children below the age of 5 years and even below the ages of 2 and 3 years have AMs and a fairly rich set of autobiographical knowledge (see for example the papers collected in Fivush 1994, or Pillemer & White 1989). We know that the majority of these memories will not be available when the child becomes adult. One possibility is that AMs are in fact somehow linked to semantic knowledge, but not as the base of hierarchical knowledge structures. Perhaps there are other paths between concepts and memories that we have overlooked (cf. Conway 1990). The semantic network of a pre-5-year-old is undoubtedly very different from the same network in the adult. Assuming then that memories are in some sense a record of semantic processing and are encoded and retrieved in terms of the links and nodes of a network then, as the semantic network itself changes so will access to memories encoded in terms of a previous version of the net. Thus, memories that were formed below the age of 5 years may become progressively inaccessible as conceptual knowledge develops and the nodes and their links in the semantic network are added to, deleted, or transformed in other ways by new knowledge and new learning.

Overall, the Quillian-style hierarchical semantic network does not appear appropriate to modelling AM, although it can give rise to intriguing suggestions, i.e. that memories are records of semantic processing and therefore must be connected to semantic knowledge. Other semantic network models have made different assumptions and these too give rise to equally intriguing insights. The LNR research group (Norman & Rumelhart 1975) expanded the hierarchical type–token relationship so that verbs as well as nouns could be modelled in network form. In order to do this they defined verbs as tokens and particular actions as types or instances of verbs. Figure 8.3 illustrates this scheme for the two propositions *James fed the seagulls* and *Stephen fed the cat*. Figure 8.3(**a**) shows how these propositions would have been represented in earlier networks and it can be seen that this type of representation does not discriminate between who fed what. Figure 8.3(**b**) shows how the LNR approach allows discrimination between actors, actions, and objects, by allowing nodes for verbs to stand as tokens of which specific actions are instances. In the example of the "seagulls" memory the fact that James and Stephen gave crisps to different seagulls can be represented by the scheme shown in Figure 8.3(**c**). These N-ary relations, so called because a node can have an indefinite number (N) of relations, provide a more flexible way in which to represent AMs. Other approaches such as Schank's (1975) *conceptual dependency* go even further and attempt to analyze meanings into conceptual primitives. Dependencies between the primitives can then be used to model the meaning of events and propositions.

Unfortunately none of these later models readily specify how we might model the four characteristics of AM singled out earlier as critical to a model of AM. The N-ary relational format certainly provides a way in which to model actions but still leads to a view of AMs as holistic units. Moreover it is difficult to envisage how such an approach accommodates more general personal knowledge of the type *Our holiday in Z,*

FIG. 8.3.   Three representational schemes using types and tokens (after Rumelhart & Norman 1983: Figure 2.5). (**a**) and (**b**) represent the sentence "James fed the seagull and Stephen fed the cat". Only (**b**) represents these correctly. (**c**) correctly represents the sentence "James and Stephen fed the seagulls". See text for comment.

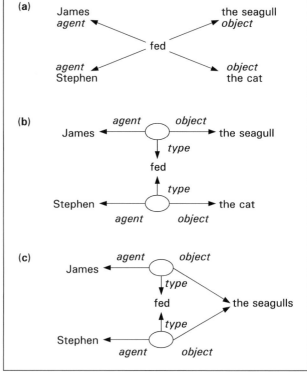

When I was 6 years old, When I worked in a factory. Perhaps one way in which this could be achieved would be by defining these periods as nodes or tokens that take individual memories as types. Thus when a memory containing specific information is activated so are corresponding nodes containing general information; we will return to this point later. General autobiographical knowledge is also a problem for the analysis of experience and meaning into primitives, for it is simply not clear what the primitives would be for representations of the form *when the children were little*, which is a common lifetime period listed by older subjects (Conway & Bekerian 1987).

Finally, Anderson's ACT (1976, 1983) model introduces a new notion that is highly relevant to the idea that memories are constructed rather than retrieved. In ACT knowledge is represented in a semantic network and the network is accessed or "read" by a *production system*. We do not describe the production system approach here (see Newell & Simon 1972), but rather note that in ACT the production system is used as a type of short-term or working memory. In Anderson's model, then, activated knowledge can be maintained in an "active list" (in short-term memory) otherwise activation declines very rapidly. The advantage of this, for models of AM, is that general and specific knowledge can be entered into an active list as a memory is generated. Thus, memories do not have to be pre-stored as whole units in the network and, instead, they can be constructed on-line. As this appears to correspond to how people actually create memories, then ACT clearly is an advance on the previous models in that it provides a way in which we can think about how to model at least one of our four critical AM criteria: memory reconstruction. How this model could be used without many further assumptions and additions to account for general and specific knowledge, memory clarity, and the lifespan retrieval curve, is not, however, immediately apparent.

Semantic networks were developed to model word meanings, simple propositions, and short narratives. That they can be applied at all to AM is something of an achievement. The emphasis on the organization of knowledge, a common processing assumption (spreading activation), and the notion of an active short-term memory, allow the modeller some initial way in which to approach the complex issue of AM. But, arguably, the most pressing problem with the semantic network approach is that it is too atomistic. Knowledge is arbitrarily divided into small units, such as verbs and nouns, or into equally arbitrary primitives, and then combined by simple type–token relations. Within this context it is difficult to construct convincing accounts of AMs with wide explanatory power and, consequently, AMs when modelled by semantic networks appear arbitrary and *ad hoc*.

SCRIPTS AND MEMORY ORGANIZATION PACKETS (MOPS)

In the mid-1970s there was a general move by a number of the most influential network theorists towards representations with larger structures (see Rumelhart & Norman 1983). Of particular relevance to AM was the introduction by Schank & Abelson (1977) of the notion of scripts. A script is a representation of a stereotypical sequence of actions that are temporally ordered. The much cited example of Schank & Abelson (1977) is that of a script for *eating at a restaurant*. The restaurant script consists of a setting (a restaurant), various props (menus, tables, etc.), and various actors (waiter, customers, etc.). Importantly, scripts have goals and the restaurant script goal might be to *eat a meal*. (Of course, all scripts will have multiple goals.) In this general restaurant frame there are certain action sequences that characterize a typical meal in a restaurant. For instance, there are actions typical of *entering the restaurant and finding a table*, *ordering the meal*, *eating the meal*, and *paying the bill*. Each of these action sequences or scenes, which together define the restaurant script, help guide behaviour and determine expectations at each point in the action sequence. Thus, scripts are an ordered (usually temporally ordered) sequence of scenes. In Schank & Abelson's original proposal, scripts were primarily passive data structures that contained expectations. One problem, however, with a passive notion of scripts is that when expectations are not fulfilled then the script can no longer guide behaviour. In an attempt to obviate this problem Schank & Abelson (1977) proposed that there may be "tracks" of alternative event sequences that stem from a main script. If a diner orders a meal but that item is no longer available then a "re-order meal" track can be activated and followed for that scene. But this solution is unsatisfactory as it results in large and unwieldy scripts in which all script deviations and expectation alternatives must be represented.

In order to solve the problems posed by script expectation failures Schank (1982) formulated a new version of script theory in which event memory was recast as a dynamic form of memory supported by a complex range of knowledge types and knowledge structures. For instance, Schank (1982) considers that the first time a person visits, say, a dentist the experience will be stored in memory as a discrete, whole unit, (rather in the way the earlier network theorists supposed). However, as further experiences of dental health care accrue, the resulting experiential or autobiographical information (AMs) is reorganized and transformed into generalized schema, which Schank (1982) called *scenes*. Scenes are instantiated by scripts or, put another way, scripts are specific versions of scenes. So, for example, a scene for *eating at a restaurant* is instantiated by a number of more specific scripts such as *eating at a French restaurant*, *eating at a Mexican restaurant*, and even, *a romantic dinner for two*, or *family meal at a restaurant*. Scripts are abstracted from specific experiences whereas scenes are abstracted from specific scripts. Idiosyncratic experiences, perhaps in the form of script violations or expectation failures, are stored in terms of their differences to the corresponding script and/or scene prototype. Schank comments that a scene is "a memory structure that groups together actions with a shared goal, that occurred at the same time. It provides a sequence of general actions. Specific memories are stored in scenes, indexed with respect to how they differ from the general action in the scene" (Schank 1982: 95). Note that as with the original versions of scripts, the versions of scenes and scripts also have goals and plans for actions appropriate to the events that they represent.

It is also important to note that Schank (1982) distinguished between different types of scenes. In particular, he proposed that there were three different types of scenes: physical scenes, societal scenes, and personal scenes. Physical scenes are like "snapshots" in that they define how things happened and what they looked like. By contrast, societal scenes are defined as social situations existing between two people for a particular purpose. Finally, personal scenes consist of an individual's private goals and plans. These different types and levels of representation, scenes, scripts, and memories, are further organized by *memory organization packets* or MOPS.

Schank's definition of a MOP is that it "consists of a set of scenes directed towards the achievement of a goal. A MOP always has one major scene whose goal is the essence or purpose of the events organized by the MOP" (Schank 1982: 97). Consider a MOP for *visiting a friend in London*, a subgoal of which is *to travel to London arriving early evening*. Unless this is a frequently experienced event there will be no existing MOP and therefore one must be created from the available scenes, scripts, and memories, e.g. *scenes for purchasing rail tickets*, *travelling by train*, *arriving in London*, *taking the Tube*, and so forth. Each scene will be associated with various scripts. For the *purchasing rail tickets* scene there might be a script for, say, *buying rail tickets at Bristol Parkway Station*. In fact, if one lived in Bristol (England) where there are two mainline stations, there would also be attached to the *purchasing rail tickets* scene a script for *Buying rail tickets at Bristol Temple Meads Station*. In short there will be many choices made in creating a MOP for *visiting a friend in London*, but once made the MOP itself provides the organizational structure that sequences in the appropriate scenes and scripts at the correct time.

In Schank's (1982) view the process of MOP construction and the way in which a MOP guides behaviour is highly interactive and dynamic. Scenes and scripts may be accessed directly, or through associated MOPs. MOPs in turn may access other MOPs and many MOPs may be active at any one time. After all, visiting a friend in London will entail many other, probably disjunct action sequences, and feature multiple goals. Indeed, Schank proposed that there are three distinct types of MOPs, physical, societal, and personal, corresponding to the three different types of scenes. Moreover, different types of MOPs may share common scenes. For example, the scene for *buying an item of clothing* can belong to both a physical MOP, i.e. the physical act of buying something, as well as to the societal MOP of buying a birthday present for someone.

Finally, Schank proposes that there are meta-MOPs. These are envisaged to be templates by which MOPs are constructed. Once again meta-MOPs are abstract knowledge structures. They, like specific MOPs, do not contain memories, but rather consist of generalized scenes. Thus, a hierarchical but dynamic structure is described by Schank (1982) that consists of meta-MOPs that organize MOPs and MOPs that organize scenes. Scenes have scripts attached to them and it is scenes that finally organize memories. The MOP structure supports the generation of plans for goal attainment and the representation in memory of experiences that relate to those goals. However Schank (1982) also wanted a system that could account for the ability to draw analogies and derive similar meanings from unrelated experiences. In order to do this, one further type of higher order organizing structure was proposed: the thematic organization packet or TOP. TOPs are domain-independent knowledge structures (unlike MOPs which are domain-specific) that represent abstract knowledge drawn from one or more episodes. Schank proposes that TOPs support abstract analogies between different experiences by grouping otherwise disjunct memories in terms of a common, but abstract, goal.

In summary, Schank (1982) proposed a dynamic memory system that incorporated five basic types of knowledge structures: memories, scripts, scenes, MOPs and TOPs. Once appropriate scripts, scenes, MOPs and TOPs are established, AMs are not stored holistically. Rather, they are derived from information contained within scenes and scripts. Scripts are specific instantiations of scenes and contain knowledge about goals as well as the general actions described by the scene. MOPs are goal-based, contain information about which scenes are commonly found together, and are used to index relevant scenes and scripts. Finally, there are TOPs. These are the very highest level of knowledge structures and consist of clusters of memories organized around a high level theme. In this dynamic model of memory, AMs are reconstructed from scenes and scripts.

Schank's (1982) view of dynamic memory brings together a number of general principles that underpin current thinking about AM. Most influential have been the ideas that memories are reconstructed from various sorts of knowledge (general and specific); that memories are represented in terms of goals, and that thematic knowledge may play an important role in the representation of AMs. However, dynamic memory was not a specifically psychological model of memory in the sense that it sought to account for a large body of empirically derived data. Indeed, Schank's aim had always been to develop a memory system that could support inference and generalization and, so, comprehend language. A specific realization of dynamic memory that attempted to be psychologically plausible was developed by Kolodner (1983a,b, 1984). Kolodner implemented many of the principles outlined by Schank in a computer model that contained knowledge, in separate databases, of the diplomatic activities of two American politicians: Cyrus Vance, a former secretary of state, and Edmund Muskie (the programme was called CYRUS). CYRUS's output simulated AMs of either of the two politicians with respect to important diplomatic meetings, negotiations and conferences. Kolodner identified two central issues that had to be addressed in CYRUS: (a) how is new information integrated into a memory system, and (b) how are pre-existing items of information retrieved? In designing CYRUS Kolodner assumed, following Schank (1982), that memory must have some internal organization. In CYRUS, memory is organized in terms of categories of shared meaning, or so called conceptual categories. These categories represent both prototypical information or "norms" about the types of events contained within the category as well as other structures that organize the category-specific events by their differences. These normative event categories correspond to Schank's concept of scenes. Norms are connected to one another by indices based on the salient features of the categories. Indexing supports several tasks. For example, indexing allows categories to be subdivided into smaller, more easily manageable, subcategories, as well as allowing category members to be easily accessible through cross-indexing (the referencing of an item in many different ways) and sub-indexing (an item is given a unique set of pointers that makes it more easily discriminable).

The basic unit, or knowledge structure, used by Kolodner to represent classes of events is the event-memory organization packet or E-MOP (see Figure 8.4). E-MOPs correspond to Schank's (1982) notion of scripts. One important point to note here is that successful searches of E-MOPs for target events can only be achieved if the search process is directed in some way. In CYRUS this is achieved through a locking system. Each E-MOP is "locked" by the indices that accessed it and can only be unlocked by locating knowledge that corresponds to the indices. Thus, as

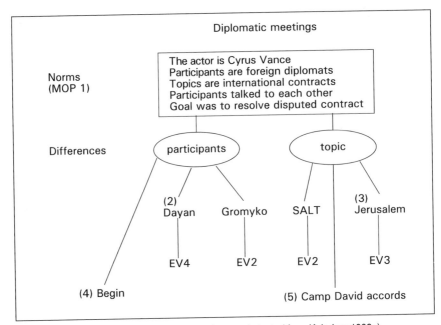

FIG. 8.4.   Knowledge structures in CYRUS (adapted from Kolodner 1983a).

each index contains labels that specify the differences between the E-MOPS, an index can only be successfully traversed if it has its labels met by the search requirements of the retrieval process. For example, in Figure 8.4, if the index "Jerusalem" cannot be accessed by the retrieval process then CYRUS cannot "remember" that "he" attended a meeting in Jerusalem. Note that, "Jerusalem" is an index or label that specifies the difference, or uniqueness, of that meeting and so distinguishes it from other meetings.

Moreover, an event type or "context for search" (Koldoner 1983b: 303) must be specified by the retrieval process for memory retrieval to occur. Thus, if CYRUS was asked to remember an event and was only given the cue "Dayan" then CYRUS would fail, as the cue does not specify an event type or E-MOP. In practice, however, CYRUS actually makes use of several different strategies when faced with this type of situation, to infer an E-MOP from pre-existing information. For example, in the case of "Dayan" an E-MOP can be inferred from pre-stored "participant" knowledge. The actual strategy used by CYRUS is to access stored knowledge, i.e. associated E-MOPS, and then evaluate which, if any, are associated with the current search context. This use of a search context against which stored knowledge can be evaluated is critical to the memory reconstruction both in CYRUS and in human AM (Conway 1995a).

Overall, then, CYRUS reconstructs memory by accessing information at different levels in the E-MOP structure and compiling it in some type of short-term store. Moreover, memories consist of both normative, or prototypical, information as well as the specific event details that distinguish one memory from another. However, for CYRUS to generate memories at all contextual information is needed, and if contextual information is not present then CYRUS infers context from stored knowledge. Essentially, CYRUS's search process operates by narrowing the initial search context until a level of information that constitutes a specific memory is accessed. If the given search context does not lead to a specific memory CYRUS then reformulates the initial context and begins the search process again.

Undoubtedly the main advantage of CYRUS over the earlier network models is that it exhibits properties found in human memory. Through its indexing system, only certain event types, or combinations of event types can be accessed at any one time. This makes CYRUS an efficient system. Second, indexing also accounts for why people sometimes forget, get confused and make false starts in memory as well as often only being able to reconstruct an event poorly. For example, you may be able to remember a party but be unable to remember whose birthday it was, who was there and what you were wearing. However, the memory for that same party may be distinctive because of some unusual feature. Thus, indexing via differences between events also seems to make intuitive sense as events are often memorable to us because of their distinctive qualities, i.e.what sets this particular party apart from all the others you have been to. Finally, indexing also accounts for our abilities to infer and generalize from one given event type to any number of seemingly unrelated memories. For example from a memory of a party, to a flood, to a white Christmas, to a bicycle trip, and so on. This is because memories can be accessed by numerous combinations of paths between different E-MOPs provided that their indices can be unlocked by accessing relevant knowledge.

The Schank–Kolodner model of dynamic memory provides ways in which to model at least three of the four critical AM characteristics outlined earlier. The mix of general and specific knowledge naturally falls out of the dynamic memory approach, as according to this view specific knowledge is organized and indexed by more abstract knowledge. AM retrieval is effortful and memories are constructed by successively sampling the knowledge base. Differences in memory vividness may depend upon the distinctiveness of an experience and how this gives rise to the encoding of that experience in terms of its difference from normative event knowledge pre-stored in long-term memory. The dynamic memory view does not, however, provide any easy purchase on the problem of accounting for the lifespan AM retrieval curve. In particular, it is especially difficult to envisage how this approach could explain the reminiscence bump, that is the increased recall of memories from when a rememberer was 15 and 25 years of age (see Figure 8.1). There are also other questions we might raise concerning key components of the approach. For example, what exactly is the relation between scripts and scenes? Is there evidence in human AM that autobiographical knowledge is structured in these terms? In Kolodner's model, activities and action play a central role in organizing knowledge; is this also the case in human AM? In the next section we briefly consider how these questions have fared in empirical investigations.

CONTEXTS AND ACTIONS

Not all of Schank's and Kolodner's claims for dynamic memory can be directly tested. But certain aspects, especially those to do with retrieval processes, can be and have been investigated—with mixed results. In a series of experiments Reiser et al. (1985) examined the type of knowledge structures used in the retrieval of autobiographical memories. Following Kolodner (1983a,b, 1984), Reiser et al. proposed that memory is organized in terms of contexts that vary in their specificity. They reasoned that retrieving a specific memory to a cue such as *finding a seat*, should be more difficult than retrieving a specific memory to the cue *going to the cinema* + *finding a seat*. This is because the latter cue specifies a context in which a general action occurs, whereas the former cue only specifies a general action. Here Reiser et al. are equating their notion of general actions with Schank's (1982) notion of generalized scenes. As generalized scenes, *finding a seat*, *waiting*, and *paying*, for example are equally applicable to many different contexts, they should be poor cues to memory retrieval. But when placed within a specific context (a script), such as *going to the cinema*, then memory retrieval should be facilitated.

In order to explore these proposals Reiser et al. conducted a series of experiments in which autobiographical memories were retrieved to various types of cues. In one experiment subjects retrieved specific memories to compound cues that named either a context followed by a general action, e.g. *going to the cinema* + *finding a seat*, or a general action followed by a context, e.g. *finding a seat* + *going to the cinema*. The clear prediction of this manipulation was that when a context is presented first followed shortly after by a general action, then memory retrieval should be speeded because the context has already initiated a search of knowledge structures in which memories are encoded. In contrast, when the general action is presented first, the memory search commences by accessing general normative knowledge structures that do not directly index AMs, and consequently memory retrieval is slowed. Reiser et al. found that memory retrieval was indeed faster when subjects were given context cues first rather than given general action cues first. Thus, the findings of Reiser et al. suggest that memories are indeed organized in terms of the contexts (scenes, norms) and general actions (scripts, E-MOPs), much as Schank and Kolodner originally suggested.

Subsequent studies have not, however, supported the context plus action view of AM. For instance, Conway & Bekerian (1987) in a series of primed autobiographical memory retrieval experiments, using a procedure that differed slightly from that employed by Reiser et al., were unable to replicate the earlier findings. In the Reiser et al. studies the first cue was shown for a period of 5 seconds prior to the presentation of the memory cue. However, in the Conway & Bekerian experiment the first cues were only presented for 1.5 seconds prior to presentation of the second cue and memory retrieval. This minor difference was sufficient to abolish the advantages in retrieval time of context plus general action over general action plus context cues. Nevertheless, with these presentation times Conway & Bekerian found robust priming effects when cues were drawn from individual personal histories. Thus, when a prime named a period from a person's life, e.g. *when I lived in city "Y"*, and the memory cues named a general event from that period, e.g. *holiday in "Z"*, then memory retrieval was extremely fast compared to a general event preceded by a neutral prime, e.g. *ready* (prime), followed by *holiday in "Z"* (memory cue). Thus, memory retrieval can be influenced by different types of cues but only when these correspond to the content of an individual's autobiographical knowledge.

Conway & Bekerian concluded that contexts and activities do not form the central organizing indices of autobiographical memory. Instead, they proposed that autobiographical memories are organized through an abstract personal history. Furthermore, they suggested that one level within personal histories consists of knowledge structures that represent *lifetime periods* and they refer to these as autobiographical memory organization packets or A-MOPs. It is suggested that A-MOPs map onto and index the general events or E-MOPs (Kolodner 1983a). However, Conway & Bekerian argue that there are several differences between their conceptualization of A-MOPs that index E-MOPs that in turn index specific memories, and the Reiser et al. context plus action model. First, Conway & Bekerian found that neither lifetime periods nor general events simply named activities. Instead lifetime periods and general events contain information about actors, locations, places, and temporal information, as well as information about activities. The differential use of these components in memory retrieval was not apparent and they appeared to feature equally often. Thus, activities do not play the central role in organizing autobiographical memory assigned them by Reiser and his colleagues. Furthermore, if E-MOPS are accessed through A-MOPS, as Conway & Bekerian propose, then all cues, including context/scene/script cues such as *eating at a restaurant*, have to be elaborated through the initial access of A-MOP knowledge in the process of memory construction. These types of cues cannot gain direct access to A-MOP structures because there is is no lifetime period to which they correspond. Cues naming contexts and activities require elaboration prior to any search of memory. When presented with the cue *eating at a restaurant* an initial search would be made for a lifetime period containing associated information, and only once this has been located can the indices of autobiographical knowledge be searched for appropriate specific knowledge, i.e. a single instance of eating at a restaurant.

The view that contexts and activities are not a predominant form of AM organization has also been evaluated by Barsalou (1988). Barsalou proposed that underlying the models of Kolodner and Reiser et al. is what he called the "activity dominance hypothesis". According to the activity dominance hypothesis autobiographical remembering should be dominated by activity-based memories and memory retrieval should be faster when the retrieval process features retrieval cues that name activities. In addition to this, the activity dominance hypothesis also proposes that AMS will consist largely of generic knowledge and this is because memories are derived from generalized knowledge structures such as Kolodner's E-MOPS. In the free recall of events from the summer vacation period, Barsalou found that the dominant type of recall was not memories of specific events. Instead the dominant category of recall was that of general or "summarized" events, e.g. *summer hikes to meadows, a trip to Paris*, and so on. In later experiments the advantage of general over specific events was maintained, and this aspect of Barsalou's findings supports the dynamic memory emphasis on the role of general or normative knowledge in the construction of memories.

Other aspects of Barsalou's findings do not, however, fit well the dynamic memory view and the activity dominance hypothesis. For instance, Barsalou had subjects retrieve memories to composite cues similar to those employed by Reiser et al. These cues named either activities, persons, locations and times and these were arranged so that all possible pair combinations were represented, i.e. activity/person, activity/location, activity/time, person/location, person/time, location/time. Cue pairs were presented in both forward and reverse orders, thus simulating the main manipulation in the Reiser et al. experiment.

However, Barsalou found no differences in retrieval time for the different orderings of cue pairs or between the different types of cue pairs. Clearly these findings lend no support to the Reiser et al. claim that the underlying structure of autobiographical knowledge is in terms of contexts and activities. In fact Barsalou found that fastest production of memories occurred to participant cues followed by location, time, and activity cues (see also Wagenaar 1986). It would seem from this that memories are, if anything, organized more in terms of "others" than in terms of activities.

One further problem relating specifically to the Reiser et al. study is that there is an alternative explanation for the findings. Anderson (1993) and Anderson & Conway (1994) found that temporal order plays a significant role in the organization of autobiographical knowledge, and in particular in the organization of specific memories. Indeed knowledge in specific memories appears, at least in part, to be represented in forward chronological order, preserving the order in which the various aspects of a memory were actually experienced. One possibility is that the effects observed by Reiser et al. may be due to temporal order effects rather than due to the effects of context. Consider again the cue type *going to the cinema + finding a seat*. This cue presents actions that are in forward temporal order whereas the cue *finding a seat + going to the cinema* presents actions in backward temporal order (an order found by Anderson & Conway 1994, to be least conducive to memory retrieval). The differences in retrieval times between context plus action and action plus context cues may then have arisen because of differences in temporal order in the cues rather than because of differences in contexts and actions. In this way, the findings of Reiser et al. may actually reflect the dominance of temporal order as an underlying organizer of autobiographical knowledge rather than any influence of contextualizing activities.

To explore this possibility Anderson (1993) repeated the experiment of Reiser et al. (1985) and added a new manipulation. A new class of cues was created in which a general action naturally preceded its associated context and so retained forward temporal order in the composite cue. The composite cues *bought a ticket* (general action) + *caught a train* (context) and *parked the car + went to the cinema* are representative of this new type of cue. If temporal order is the dominant organizer in structuring specific autobiographical memories, rather than contextualizing actions, then retrieval of AMS to composite cues that name a *general action + context* should be as fast as retrieval to composite cues that name a context first such as: *going to the cinema + finding a seat*, as long as the cues preserve temporal order. When the composite cues are then reversed, and placed out of temporal order, then retrieval times should be much slower in both conditions. By contrast, if context is the dominant organizer in structuring specific autobiographical memories rather than temporal order, then retrieval of specific memories to composite cues that name a *general action* + *context* should be slower than retrieval to cues that name *context* + *general action*, regardless of temporal order. The results of this study showed a reliable effect of temporal order with the mean memory retrieval time for cues presented in temporal order being 2064 ms, whereas for cues presented out of temporal order it was 2604 ms. This finding shows that when cues are presented in forward temporal order then memory retrieval is quicker than when the cues are out of temporal order, regardless of cue type. Thus, these results provide support for the idea of temporal order as an organizer of memory, a finding compatible with Conway & Bekerian's (1987) and Barsalou's (1988) models of memory, but incompatible with dynamic memory models that focus only on contexts and actions.

Dynamic models of AM arising from Schank's (1982) work do seem to be a clear advance over the types of AM models derivable from the semantic network approach. However, the advantage in dynamic models of AM rests largely in the broader principles underlying Schank's work rather than in specific implementations. Notions of memory construction, knowledge structures that encompass both general and specific knowledge, and a focus on the types of knowledge that might serve as organizers of AMs, are all useful general propositions that can guide research and the construction of AM models.

CONNECTIONIST MODELS

Connectionist models of long-term memory have been concerned with an issue that is central to the study of autobiographical memory: namely how to represent both specific and general knowledge. McClelland & Rumelhart (1985, 1986) deal directly with this problem and it is their distributed memory model that we briefly discuss in this section. Within the general approach of connectionist distributed memory systems, knowledge is represented as a pattern of activation across a set of units. As McClelland & Rumelhart point out, it may be convenient in certain types of model to let the units represent certain sorts of conceptual primitives. For example, in modelling AM, primitives such as those proposed by Schank (1975) or primitives common in later AM models, i.e. objects, actions, actors, locations, feelings, and time, might be employed. But why certain primitives should be chosen over others, and how in the case of AM primitives, these might be implemented in a distributed memory system remains obscure. Instead, the features to be modelled might better be conceived as patterns of activation over a set of units. In McClelland & Rumelhart's model, sets of units are organized into modules and within a module the units are richly interconnected. Modules receive inputs from and send outputs to other modules. Modules contain many units, in the order of thousands or more, and some modules mainly take input from information streams arising from sensory processing whereas others have the majority of their inputs from more abstract processing modules. According to McClelland and Rumelhart each module can be thought of as a "synthesis" of states of all other modules from which it receives inputs.

Taking this approach, memories can be viewed as a pattern of activation across a set of modules. Some of the modules will represent quasi-sensory features associated with the memory and other modules more abstract features. The patterns of activation for any given feature are represented in the model by changes in the weights of the connections between the units in modules and presumably in connections between modules (the model described by McClelland & Rumelhart 1986 uses only one module). Thus, it is possible to represent the features of many different memories as different weight-change patterns across the same set of units and modules. Within this general framework, memory retrieval consists of the partial reinstatement of pre-stored patterns of activation in response to a cue. A cue is itself represented as a set of weight changes distributed over the connections within units and between modules. A memory is "retrieved" when the representation of a cue reinstates patterns of activation representing stored experiences. A "cue" in this case will always be an internally derived representation, possibly arising directly from externally presented information, but more usually arising from a sequence of internally constructed patterns of activation.

In the demonstration model designed by McClelland & Rumelhart the concept of a "dog" is represented in a single module 24-unit distributed memory. It is assumed that the network will have a number of experiences with a range of different dogs and each experience will give rise to a representation of each animal. A set of input units, with each unit taking a positive or negative value, codes, say, perceptual features of the first dog encountered. Other dogs, which must be perceptually similar to the first dog, are coded by random changes to a subset of the original input pattern, e.g. some of the original units are flipped from positive to negative or vice versa. The weights between all the individual units in the network are then adjusted until a stable pattern of activation is established that represents the input. In retrieval, only part of an original input pattern is presented and this causes corresponding weight changes in the connections between units. These changes are incremented according to the delta rule (see McClelland & Rumelhart 1986: 178) until a stable pattern of activation is again achieved. In the case of this particular model, the module represents a prototype for dogs, abstracted across all input patterns, and it represents recent input patterns particularly well. Furthermore, it is able to reinstate original input patterns in response to partial input patterns and does this more accurately for recently learned inputs and for input patterns that are more distant from the prototype.

Quite evidently these are the sorts of core properties that a model of AM must exhibit: the ability to abstract a prototype from repeated similar experiences and at the same time the ability to retain knowledge of specific experiences, particularly recent ones. However, general knowledge in autobiographical memory does not only take the form of schematic representations of repeated experiences. General knowledge such as *when I lived with "Y", our trip to city "Z"*, and so forth, does not arise through similarity of repeated experiences. Instead, this type of general knowledge arises through shared meanings and the temporal contiguity of experiences. Possibly, these types of general knowledge could be represented in other modules that are more concerned with abstract knowledge and have inputs to and take inputs from, modules that represent more specific features of events. Moreover, and as McClelland & Rumelhart point out, there must be some procedure for feeding back patterns of activation to sets of modules as a search unfolds over time. In other words there must be some sort of retrieval plan that shapes the whole pattern of weight changes across and within modules.

We have not provided a detailed account of the McClelland & Rumelhart distributed memory model here, as the aim was to simply illustrate some of the potential of this approach (McClelland & Rumelhart 1986, provide a particularly lucid account). Nor have we explored any of the more technical problems with this particular model (especially the linear predictability constraint). Connectionist models of AM have yet to be developed and until this occurs evaluation is premature. Nevertheless, the distributed memory approach with sets of units in interconnected modules provides something like a base architecture for thinking about the representation of specific autobiographical knowledge. Exactly what form this should take, and how stable patterns of activation across many different modules can be established, are questions to be dealt with in more fully developed connectionist models of AM (but see McClelland (1995) for a recent very interesting connectionist approach to AM).

CONSTRUCTING AUTOBIOGRAPHICAL MEMORIES: A FRAMEWORK

Conway (1992, 1995a), Conway & Rubin (1993), and Anderson & Conway (1993) have developed an account of how AM construction might take place. The impetus for this account comes from findings in the laboratory and from findings arising from the neuropsychological impairment of AM (Conway 1993, 1995d). These findings cannot be considered in detail here (see Conway 1995a, and Conway & Rubin 1993, for reviews) and instead we confine ourselves to simply outlining the main features of the approach. In their review of the literature, Conway & Rubin (1993) identify several general characteristics of AMs that have been persistently observed in a number of studies. For instance, AMs contain different types of knowledge. Some of this knowledge is sensory-perceptual in nature and can constitute a highly accurate record of at least some of the features of an event. In contrast, other knowledge is more abstract and decontextualized, relating more to an individual's personal history than to the features of any specific experience. Thus, AMs can be accurate, but accuracy in this case means accurate both in terms of the self and in terms of the basic knowledge of a remembered event. AM knowledge can be thought of as residing in an autobiographical knowledge base. The AM knowledge base is structured and contains at least three layers of knowledge. The first layer, *lifetime periods*, refers to lengthy periods of time, typically measured in years, and represents the goals, plans, and themes of the self during particular periods. Goals, plans, and themes are reflected in knowledge of significant others, records of goal attainment, and general knowledge of actors, actions, and locations characteristic of the period. The second layer, *general events*, is more specific and consists of records of extended and repeated events that occurred over periods of weeks and months. General events contain knowledge that can be used to access *event-specific knowledge* (ESK) of sensory-perceptual details. In addition, general events may themselves be further organized into small sets of thematically related events (Robinson 1992). Specific memories are represented by chronologically ordered lists of memory details, and memory details may themselves consist solely of ESK knowledge. Indeed, Anderson (1993) found that subjects, when asked to list highly specific details of memories responded by describing images, sensations, smells, thoughts, and other sensory-perceptual features associated with a given memory detail. Finally, across the three layers of knowledge, hierarchical knowledge structures may be formed such that cues available in a lifetime period index a particular, usually large, set of general events that in turn index other general events and ESK.

The AM knowledge base is accessed by a complex retrieval process modulated by central control processes. The retrieval process is cyclic and is driven by a mental model of current task demands. The task model is generated and constantly updated by the central executive of working memory. The task model imposes constraints on cyclic retrieval by specifying the type of sought-for-knowledge. In cyclic retrieval a cue is first elaborated (perhaps according to constraints set by the task model) and then knowledge structures in the AM knowledge base are accessed. Activation is channelled through the knowledge base by the indices available at different layers in accessed knowledge structures. For example, once a search accesses a lifetime period such as *when I lived with "X"* and activation is then channelled by cues available at this level to some set of associated general events, e.g. *our trip to "Z", the day we went shopping at "Y",* then the search phase itself cannot break out from this local organization unless central control processes intervene. Thus, the third phase of cyclic retrieval is an evaluation phase in which accessed knowledge is assessed for the probability that satisfies the constraints of the task model. If the probability is low then a new cycle of retrieval may be initiated with a different cue. When accessed knowledge is judged to be likely to lead to information that satisfies the centrally imposed task constraints, then a new cycle of retrieval is initiated using the evaluated knowledge (cf. Norman & Bobrow 1979, Norman & Shallice 1980, Williams & Hollan 1981, Burgess & Shallice 1995). By this process of access and evaluation, the search process is fine-tuned until knowledge that satisfies the task constraints is finally accessed. Once this occurs a stable pattern of activation is established across the appropriate set of knowledge structures in the AM knowledge base and a memory is "retrieved".

Here then, AMs are transitory patterns of activation dynamically generated by the staged retrieval process and consist of both a stable, but temporary, pattern of activation of AM knowledge as well as a task model that guides retrieval. Thus, the process of memory construction is dynamic and unfolds over time and results in complex mental representation. It might be concluded that memory construction is somewhat unwieldy in that it is effortful and may make extensive demands on processing resources. Undoubtedly this is the case on at least some occasions, and everyone has experienced the effort required to recall general events and ESK. However, the autobiographical knowledge base may be exquisitely sensitive to cues and, possibly, patterns of activation may be continually stabilizing and dissipating within the knowledge base. Central control processes may turn to other tasks, having initiated a memory search, and switch rapidly back and forth between co-ordinating memory construction and modulating other processing sequences. Moreover, it is not assumed that the retrieval process requires conscious mediation, although this may often be the case. Rather, memories may be constructed, as it were, in the background, and only emerge into conscious awareness at some appropriate moment or when other tasks have been completed. In this way memories may spontaneously "pop" into mind (Salaman 1970) or a person may be unexpectedly reminded of a previously experienced event (Schank 1982).

The main advantage of this model of memory construction over the earlier approaches is that it can be used to conceptualize the diverse pattern of findings from many different studies (Conway & Rubin 1993). As central control processes modulate the operation of the retrieval cycle this also allows the current themes and discrepancies of the self to influence memory construction (Conway 1995a). This is possible as the model assumes that current preoccupations of the self are part of central control processes. As many features of the model are drawn from aspects of network and schema theories, it has been possible to use the strengths of these without encompassing their weaknesses. Thus, the model employs the notion of knowledge structures, indexing, and spreading activation, without making strong commitments to type–token relations, actions and contexts, or representation by primitives. The main disadvantage, compared to earlier approaches, is that this account of memory construction has not been implemented in any computational form, and so its status as a model rests solely on its ability to provide useful insights into empirical findings. For instance, it provides a good account of the four features of autobiographical memory outlined at the start of this chapter (see Conway 1995a, for a more detailed account).

CONCLUSIONS

In this chapter we have given an outline sketch of how various approaches to the representation of knowledge might be used to model the representation of autobiographical memory. None of the approaches yield satisfactory solutions but all provide interesting insights into the problems of modelling this type of knowledge. Overall, it may be the case that autobiographical remembering is simply too complex a form of cognition for current models of knowledge representation. Nonetheless, in making the attempt new and informative issues are discovered.

REFERENCES

Anderson, J. R. 1976. *Language, memory, and thought*. Hillsdale, N. J.: Lawrence Erlbaum Associates.

Anderson, J. R. 1983. *The architecture of cognition*. Hillsdale, N. J.: Erlbaum.

Anderson, S. J. 1993.*Autobiographical memory organization*. PhD dissertation, Department of Psychology, University of Lancaster, Lancaster, England.

Anderson, S. J. & M. A. Conway 1993. Investigating the structure of autobiographical memories. *Journal of Experimental Psychology: Learning, Memory, and Cognition* **19**, 1178–96.

Anderson, S. J. & M. A. Conway 1994 Are autobiographical memories stable? Under review.

Barsalou, L. W. 1988. The content and organization of autobiographical memories. In *Remembering reconsidered: ecological and traditional approaches to the study of memory*. U. Neisser & E. Winograd (eds), 193–243. Cambridge: Cambridge University Press.

Brown, N. R., S. K. Shevell, L. J. Rips 1986. Public memories and their personal context. In*Autobiographical Memory*, D. C. Rubin (ed.), 137–58. Cambridge: Cambridge University Press.

Brown, R. & J. Kulik 1977. Flashbulb memories. *Cognition* **5**, 73–99.

Burgess, P. W. & T. Shallice 1995. Confabulation and the control of recollection. *Memory* **4**, 359–412.

Collins, A. M. & E. F. Loftus 1975. A spreading activation theory of semantic processing. *Psychological Review* **82**, 407–28.

Collins, A. M. & M. R. Quillian 1969. Retrieval time from semantic memory. *Journal of Verbal Learning and Verbal Behaviour* **8**, 240–47.

Conway, M. A. 1990. *Autobiographical memory: an introduction*. Buckingham: Open University Press.

Conway, M. A. 1992. A structural model of autobiographical memory. In *Theoretical perspectives on autobiographical memory*, M. A.Conway, D. C. Rubin, H.Spinnler, W. A. Wagenaar, (eds), 167–94. Dordrecht, The Netherlands: Kluwer Academic Publishers.

Conway, M.A., 1993. Impairments of autobiographical memory. In*Handbook of neuropsychology*, F.Boller & J.Grafman (eds) vol. 8, 175–91. Amsterdam: Elsevier.

Conway, M.A. 1995a.Autobiographical memories and autobiographical knowledge. In *The construction of autobiographical memory*, D. C.Rubin (ed.). Cambridge: Cambridge University Press, in press.

Conway, M. A. 1995b. Autobiographical memories. In *Handbook of perception and cognition, Vol.10: Memory*, E. Bjork & R. Bjork (eds). Orlando Fla.:Academic Press, in press.

Conway, M. A. 1995c. Failures of autobiographical remembering. In *Basic and applied memory: theory in context*, D. Herrmann, M. Johnson, C. McEvoy, C. Hertzog & P. Hertel (eds), Hillsdale, NJ: Erlbaum, in press.

Conway, M.A. 1995d. *Flashbulb memories*. Hove, UK: Lawrence Erlbaum Associates Ltd.

Conway, M.A. & D. C. Rubin 1993. The structure of autobiographical memory. In, *Theories of memory*, A. E. Collins, S. E. Gathercole, M.A. Conway & P. E. M. Morris (eds) 103–37. Hove, UK: Lawrence Erlbaum Associates Ltd.

Conway, M. A. & D. A. Bekerian 1987. Organization in autobiographical memory. *Memory & Cognition* **15**(2), 119–32.

Conway, M. A., S. J. Anderson, S. F. Larsen, C. M. Donnelly, M. A. McDaniel, A. G. R. McClelland, R. E. Rawles, R. H. Logie 1994. The formation of flashbulb memories. *Memory & Cognition* **22**, 326–43.

Conway, M. A., A. F. Collins, S. E. Gathercole, S. J. Anderson 1995. Recollections of true and false autobiographical memories. *Journal of Experimental Psychology: General* **125**, 69–95.

Fivush, R. (ed) 1994. Long-term retention of infant memories. *Memory* **2**, 337–457.

Kintsch, W. 1980. Semantic memory: a tutorial. In *Attention and performance*, vol. VIII, R. S. Nickerson (ed.), 595–617. Hillsdale, N. J.: Lawrence Erlbaum.

Kolodner, J. L. 1983a. Maintaining organization in dynamic long-term memory. *Cognitive Science* **7**, 243–80.

Kolodner, J. L. 1983b. Reconstructive memory: a computer model. *Cognitive Science* **7**, 281–328.

Kolodner, J. L. 1984. *Retrieval and organizational strategies in conceptual memory*. Hillsdale, N. J.: Lawrence Erlbaum Associates.

Linton, M. 1975. Memory for real-world events. In *Explorations in Cognition*, D. A. Norman & D. E. Rumelhart (eds), 376–404. San Francisco: W. H. Freeman.

Loftus, E. F. 1993. The reality of repressed memories. *American Psychologist* **48**, 518–37.

Loftus, E. F. & K. Ketcham 1994. *The myth of repressed memory*. New York: St. Martin's Press.

McClelland, J. L. 1995. Constructive memory and memory distortions: a parallel distributed processing approach. In *Memory Distortion: How Minds, Brains, and Societies Reconstruct the Past*, D. L. Schacter (ed.), 69–90. Cambridge, Mass.: Harvard University Press.

McClelland, J. L. & D. E. Rumelhart 1985. Distributed memory and the respresentation of general and specific information. *Journal of Experimental Psychology: General* **114**, 159–188.

McClelland, J. L. & D. E. Rumelhart 1986. A distributed model of human learning and memory. In *Parallel distributed processing. Explorations in the microstructure of cognition. Volume 2: psychological and biological models*. J. L. McClelland, D. E. Rumelhart, and the PDP Research Group (eds), 170–215. Cambridge, Mass.: MIT Press.

Neisser, U. 1982. Snapshots or benchmarks? In *Memory observed: remembering in natural contexts*, U. Neisser (ed.), 43–48. San Francisco: W. H. Freeman.

Newell, A. & H. Simon 1972. *Human problem solving*. Englewood Cliffs, N. J.: Prentice Hall.

Nigro, G. & U. Neisser 1983. Point of view in personal memories. *Cognitive Psychology* **15**, 467–82.

Norman, D. A. & D. G. Bobrow 1979. Descriptions and intermediate stage in memory retrieval. *Cognitive Psychology* **11**, 107–23.

Norman, D. A. & D. E. Rumelhart 1975. *Explorations in cognition*. San Francisco: Freeman.

Norman, D. A. & T. Shallice 1980. Attention to action: willed and automatic control of behaviour. University of California, San Diego: Technical Report No. 99.

Pillemer, D. B. & S. H. White 1989. Childhood events recalled by children and adults. *Advances in Child Development and Behaviour* **21**, 297–340.

Quillian, M. R. 1968. Semantic memory. In *Semantic information processing*, M. Minsky (ed.). Cambridge, Mass.: MIT Press.

Reiser, B. J., J. B Black, R. P. Abelson 1985. Knowledge structures in the organization and retrieval of autobiographical memories. *Cognitive Psychology* **17**, 89–137.

Robinson, J.A. 1992. First experience memories: contexts and functions in personal histories. In *Theoretical perspectives on autobiographical memory*, M. A. Conway, D. C. Rubin, H. Spinnler, W. A. Wagenaar (eds), 223–39. Dordrecht, The Netherlands: Kluwer Academic.

Rubin, D. C. 1982. On the retention function for autobiographical memory. *Journal of Verbal Learning and Verbal Behavior* **21**, 21–38.

Rubin, D. C., S. E. Wetzler, R. D. Nebes 1986. Autobiographical across the lifespan. In *Autobiographical Memory*, D. C. Rubin, 202–21. Cambridge: Cambridge University Press.

Rumelhart, D. E. & D.A. Norman 1983. Representation in memory. *CHIP Technical Report (no. 116)*. San Diego: Centre for Human Information Processing, University of California.

Salaman, E. 1970. *A collection of moments: a study of involuntary memories*. London: Longman.

Schooler, J. W. & D. J. Herrmann 1992. There is more to episodic memory than just episodes. In *Theoretical perspectives on autobiographical memory*, M.A. Conway, D. C. Rubin, H.Spinnler & W. A. Wagenaar (eds), 241–62. Amsterdam: Kluwer Academic.

Schank, R. C. 1982. *Dynamic memory*. New York: Cambridge University Press.

Schank, R. C. (ed.) 1975. *Conceptual information processing*. New York: Elsevier.

Schank, R. C. & Abelson, R. P. 1977. *Scripts, plans, goals, and understanding*. Hillsdale, N. J.: Erlbaum.

Strauman, T. J. 1990. Self-guides and emotionally significant childhood memories: a study of retrieval efficiency and incidental negative emotional content. *Journal of Personality and Social Psychology* **59**, 869–80.

Treadway, M., M. McCloskey, B. Gordon, N. J. Cohen 1992. Landmark life events and the organization of memory: evidence from functional retrograde amnesia. In *The handook of emotion and memory: research and theory*, S. Christianson (ed.), 389–410. Hillsdale, N. J.: Lawrence Erlbaum Associates.

Tulving, E. 1972. Episodic and semantic memory. In *Organization of memory*, E. Tulving & W. Donaldson (eds). New York: Academic Press.

Tulving, E. 1983. *Elements of episodic memory*. New York: Oxford University Press.

Wagenaar, W. A. 1986. My memory: a study of autobiographical memory over six years. *Cognitive Psychology* **18**, 225–52.

Wetzler, S. E. & J. A. Sweeney 1986. Childhood amnesia: an empirical demonstration. In *Autobiographical Memory*, D. C. Rubin, 191–201. Cambridge: Cambridge University Press.

Williams, D. M. & J. D. Hollan 1981. The process of retrieval from very long-term memory. *Cognitive Science* **5**, 87–119.

CHAPTER NINE

The relationship between prospective and retrospective memory: neuropsychological evidence

Paul W. Burgess & Tim Shallice

INTRODUCTION

Recently, there has been an enormous increase in interest in the field of "prospective memory" (PM), especially amongst neuropsychologists. The term refers to a hypothetical cognitive ability (or set of abilities) that enables people to carry out their intentions at a future time. So, for instance, prospective memory functions would be strongly involved in enabling someone to remember to post a letter at some future time, or in remembering to go to the shops on your way home (if this is not usually the time you shop).

One of the key theoretical questions in this area concerns the relationship between such prospective memory functions, and those that are involved in remembering things that have occurred in the past (called retrospective memory, or RM). Are the same mental processes involved in remembering to do things in the future as are used in remembering things we have done in the past, or are quite different cognitive abilities used in the two situations (see e.g. Rabbitt 1996)? Currently, there are some very different views on this matter. Some maintain that prospective remembering shares little in terms of processing resources with RM (e.g. Ellis 1996, Kvavilashvili 1987), while other theorists have argued, in the words of Dalla Barba (1993:245) that "much of the evidence does not support a clear cut distinction between prospective memory and other kinds of memory" (see also Baddeley &

Wilkins 1984, Hitch and Ferguson 1991). There are also more complex views. For instance, Roediger (1996: 150–1) maintains that "it is clear (and no surprise to anyone) that the processes involved in prospective memory tests are quite different from those underlying implicit memory tasks" whilst also suggesting that "there seem to be no cases of principles emerging that would cause us to change our thinking of how memory works or to believe that prospective tasks differ fundamentally from retrospective tasks".

A NOTE ON TERMINOLOGY

Some of the disagreement about whether PM is a memory form distinct from RM may have arisen because of terminological difficulties. Use of the term prospective memory perhaps seems to suggest that memory for intended behaviour is a different form of memory altogether from RM. It does not, however, necessarily require that the user hold this position: currently "prospective memory" refers as much to a particular type of experimental paradigm as it does to a hypothetical mental ability. Although the details of the experimental procedures vary widely, they all require that a subject to carry out a behaviour at some time following intention creation. Thus the term "prospective memory" need not carry any particular theoretical orientation, just as terms such as "free recall" or "forced-choice recognition" need not; they are shorthand for types of experimental procedures rather than theoretical positions. Of course if "prospective memory" refers to an area of intellectual enquiry relating to certain types of tasks, we then need a term to refer to the particular behaviours and experiences involved in them from the subject's own standpoint. This we will call "prospective remembering" or PR.

If one accepts this usage i.e. that "prospective memory" describes a type of experimental paradigm rather than a type of memory, then the position that "the loss of the term prospective memory would leave us better off" (Crowder 1996: 144) perhaps seems a little strong; after all, few memory theorists would strongly advocate loss of the term "free recall".

In this chapter we therefore take the view that PR refers to behaviour produced under certain circumstances, and examine how evidence from neuropsychology might inform an understanding of how retrospective memory abilities are used under these circumstances. In doing so we will adopt a similar position to that advocated by Bisiacchi (1996: 297), who maintains that "the problem is not to demonstrate the prospective memory is different from short-term memory … or long-term memory

...but to define which processes are involved in PM, or which task requirements are present in a certain PM test".

PROSPECTIVE REMEMBERING REQUIRES RETROSPECTIVE MEMORY

A few years ago, one of the present authors was working with a patient (GAS; Alderman & Burgess 1993) who had suffered herpes simplex encephalitis, which had left him with a dense and relatively pure amnesia. This patient's anterograde memory problem was so severe that he would have no recollection for events that had happened to him more than 30 minutes previously; often he would not be able to remember even more recent events. On formal neuropsychological testing, GAS failed all memory tests, whatever form, including the PR components of the Rivermead Behavioural Memory Test (RBMT; Wilson et al. 1991), and simple investigations of his PR abilities (such as asking him to clap his hands in 10 minutes' time, or when a timer sounded a bell) consistently failed to find any ability to carry out an intention beyond the span of his RM abilities. Under these circumstances, it did not appear to be the case that he was aware, given the cue, that there was something he needed to be doing, but that he could not remember what. Instead, in the example above, he just looked at the timer and commented that it was ringing, and he was surprised that the investigator was not stopping it.

One interpretation of GAS's difficulties might be that the processes underlying the ability to realize a delayed intention and those supporting RM are potentially dissociable (in other words, that one can be impaired when the other is intact), but that this patient has coincidental damage to both systems. But clinical evidence (see, e.g. Davies & Binks 1983, Wilson 1987, Kapur 1988) suggests that GAS's everyday behaviour is typical of dense amnesics; without training in the use of appropriate aids, such patients cannot remember to carry out an intention at a future time. At the time at which the intention should be resurrected, they have forgotten ever having had such an intention, the circumstances in which that intention was formed, why it was formed, or the future situation in which it was to be activated.

In this chapter we therefore take the position that at the extremes, RM and PR abilities are not doubly dissociable (where a double dissociation would mean that the two abilities do not share common resources; see Shallice 1988, Bisiacchi 1996, Einstein & McDaniel 1996). However we take the view that a single dissociation (PR impaired with intact RM) may occur. This pattern occurs because PR ability presupposes a degree of RM functioning; indeed, we will argue that PR often involves a special application of the processes used in RM, especially in recollection.

RETROSPECTIVE AND PROSPECTIVE MEMORY:
ARE THESE CONSTRUCTS INDEPENDENT?

The general conclusion from studies investigating PR–RM relationships using normal subjects is that the RM "component" in PR is relatively small (e.g. Wilkins & Baddeley 1978, Einstein & McDaniel 1990, Meacham & Leiman 1982, Kvavilashvili 1987, Maylor 1990). In other words, while remembering to perform things in the future may require the ability to remember things that have happened in the past, this retrospective component is only a small part of what is required. However, although this may (empirically) be the case for controls, it does not necessarily mean that a stronger relationship would not appear if individuals with impaired RM were examined. If we assume that the ability to realize a delayed intention requires a number of processes other than those involved in retrospective memory, and that the RM resource needs only to be above a comparatively low threshold for adequate performance, variability in PR task performance in normal subjects will measure mainly those processes not shared between PR and RM[1]. However people with RM impairments (e.g. amnesic patients or perhaps even some of the very elderly) may fail the PR task due to either degradation of the RM or of other PR processes. If this scenario is correct, one might predict that only a single dissociation between RM and PR should ever be found: people with very significant RM problems would always be poor at PR tasks, but not all people with PR problems would necessarily have RM difficulties. Is there any evidence that this is the case?

An interesting study by Bisiacchi (1996) found that in a factor analysis of normal subjects who were under 70 years old, scores on prospective memory tasks were loaded on a factor orthogonal to factors upon which other cognitive measures (e.g. planning test scores and IQ) were loaded. However, in a group of more elderly subjects this was not the case. For these subjects, PR task performance was loaded on the same factor as scores on the planning test and, critically for the present argument, performance on a task of free recall. One interpretation of this result might be that only when a group of individuals who show a marked range of impairment in RM tasks are tested will the role of RM in PR performance be demonstrated, since only in these cases might PR performance be noticeably constrained by RM ability (see Burgess & Shallice 1994) for further argument on this point).

IMPAIRED PR WITH INTACT RM:
THE STRATEGY APPLICATION DISORDER

So far, this chapter has argued that patients with neuropsychological deficits might reveal relationships between RM and PR that do not make themselves apparent in controls. Furthermore, we have considered the possibility that only two patterns of performance may be found in patients with profound RM or PM deficits: both ability to remember past events and to realize delayed intentions being severely impaired, or intact RM with impaired PR. The former pattern can tell us little about the relationship between PR and RM, since the impairment in both areas may be an epiphenomenon. The latter pattern is however informative, and we will now consider the neuropsychological evidence for such a pattern, before examining the evidence for the pattern we have so far rejected, that is severely impaired RM with intact PR.

Shallice & Burgess (1991a) reported three head injury patients in whom there was CT (computerized tomography) evidence of focal frontal lobe damage. All had IQs between 120 and 130 on the Wechsler Adult Intelligence Scale. On 13 neuropsychological tests held to be sensitive to frontal lobe dysfunction, two of the patients were well within the normal range on all 13 tests, but one patient (C) was below the normal range on three. One patient (A) performed well on a wide range of traditional neuropsychological memory tests. Patient B however was impaired on some visual memory tests (e.g. Rey's (1964) figure reproduction that requires free recall of a complex design), but was well within the normal range on a variety of verbal memory tests. Patient C also performed well on a variety of memory tests (e.g. Coughlan & Hollows' (1985) list learning), but was impaired on certain others (e.g. Wechsler's (1945) Memory Scale hard paired associates). In summary, all three patients had preserved general intellectual abilities, were not markedly dysexecutive (Baddeley & Wilson 1986) on traditional tests and showed little or no impairment of retrospective memory. However all three patients showed little spontaneous organization in everyday life, and two at least had made a number of gross errors of judgment with major practical consequences. In this sense they were similar in everyday life to other frontal lobe patients reported in the literature (e.g. Eslinger & Damasio 1985, Goldstein et al. 1993, Duncan et al. 1995).

As part of the investigation into these patients' problems, two tests were developed that measured their ability to schedule a number of relatively straightforward activities in a restricted period of time. Thus in one test they had to carry out six open-ended but not difficult tasks in 15 minutes (the Six Element Test or SET); two involved dictating routes, two involved writing down the names of pictures of objects, and two involved the carrying out of a series of fairly simple arithmetic problems. However, completing all six tasks would take much longer than the limited time available. The patients had to judge how much time to devote to each task so as to optimize their performance, given some simple rules. They were not allowed to do two subtasks of the same type one after another, and the points system guaranteed diminishing returns on a task as it continued to be carried out; for example the initial sums scored more than later ones.

Normal subjects of comparable age and IQ switched between the tasks, tackling on average 5.7 (SD 0.5) of them and spent an average of 5 minutes 35 seconds (SD 53 seconds) on the task to which they devoted most time. The three patients were outside the normal range on both measures except for one score (A, 3, 7 minutes 30 seconds; B, 5, 10 minutes 11 seconds; C, 3, 7 minutes 18 seconds). In addition they performed in a qualitatively inappropriate fashion. Thus A started the test by making notes for 4 minutes, which he never subsequently used, and B spent 10 minutes on one task and did not even tackle a second that was very similar. These findings have been recently replicated in further studies of neurological patients (Burgess & Taylor, in preparation, Burgess et al 1996a), where it was not uncommon for patients to say that they had intended at the beginning of the test to switch tasks every 2 minutes or so, but then "completely forgot" to do so at the appropriate time.

Shallice & Burgess's (1991a) three patients performed equally poorly on the second test (Multiple Errands Test or MET), which involved scheduling a set of simple shopping activities in real time in a shopping area close to the hospital. Certain aspects of this test had a strong PR component. For instance, the subjects had to remember to come over to the experimenters every time they left a shop and one test item required them to be in a specific place at a certain time.

It was not possible to explain the poor performance of these patients on these two tests in terms of memory, motivational or other basic cognitive problems. Thus they worked at a normal rate on the problems that they tackled on the SET, and completed very satisfactorily complex and demanding tasks such as Raven's Matrices unsupervised. Moreover, they were generally able to recall adequately, after the test, rules and task constraints which they had just broken. Their deficit lay within a different level of supervisory processing.

It appeared instead that these patients' difficulties were most marked in situations which required that their behaviour be guided by explicit intentions generated previously, or where there was a need to conform with broad rules or decisions outlined at an earlier time; that is, where PR was required. We developed a hypothesis relating to such intention- or rule-retrieving situations that would explain the inappropriate behaviour of the patients both within the experimental tasks and in everyday life. We proposed that "temporal markers" are activated when intentions are created or rules temporarily set up, which will be triggered if a relevant situation occurs, and that these patients have lost the facility to activate or trigger such markers. More standard tests of executive function are carried out in the same way as typical psychometric tests, in that an experimenter is present and closely involved, and the task material directs the attention of the subject to the task. We therefore presumed that such marker activation and triggering would be required less in the more standard tasks, so explaining the preserved performance of two of our patients on them.

A schematic representation of the relationships between these

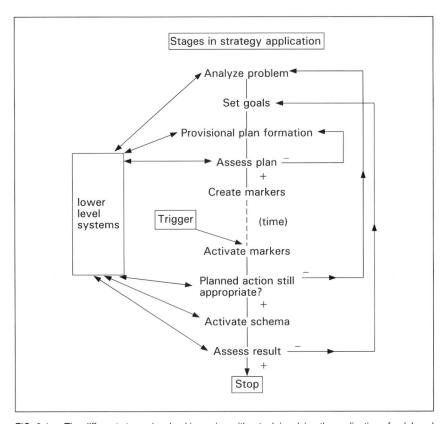

FIG. 9.1.   The different stages involved in coping with a task involving the realization of a delayed intention. Performance at each stage is supported by supervisory or "executive" cognitive processes, which interact with nonexecutive cognitive processing systems (represented as lower level systems).

stages in PR performance is given in Figure 9.1. It takes as its framework the Norman–Shallice model of action and thought control (Norman & Shallice 1986, Shallice 1988), and is derived from standard approaches to problem-solving (e.g. Ben-Yishay & Diller 1983, De Groot 1965; more detailed expositions of these ideas can be found in Shallice & Burgess, 1991b, 1993).

Although the three patients described above all showed impairments on tasks that relied heavily upon the formation of appropriate intentions and their realization, it was difficult in any one case to localize their failures to any one, or particular set of, the stages outlined in Figure 9.1. Clinically, A's deficit appeared to be most severe at marker creation and triggering stages, and C's problem seemed to lie more at the stages of goal setting, plan formulation and evaluation. However no clear predictions were made as to the characteristic behaviours to be observed with the different types of deficit.

These patients do however provide critical evidence that patients with apparent PR problems (at least in complex situations) do not necessarily suffer from RM deficits. But what of patients who do have RM problems? Do they necessarily have PR deficits?

WHEN RM IS IMPAIRED, WHAT HAPPENS TO PR?

The complementary issue is the PR performance of patients with RM impairments. A recent study in our laboratory (Burgess & Taylor, in preparation) examined the influence of differing levels of impairment in RM abilities on performance on the Six Element Task (SET). A total of 30 patients who had suffered brain damage (from a variety of pathologies, predominantly head injury) were tested on a modified version of the task, which included a rather more complex method of administration. Before the patients started the test, we measured the ease with which they were able to learn the task rules (called "Learning" score). The patients were then asked if they had any plan in mind that they intended to follow in carrying out the test itself. The sophistication of their plan was assessed using a "Planning" score. The patients then set about the test itself, and by watching what they actually did compared with what they said they were going to do, we derived a measure of how closely they followed their original plan ("Sticking-to-plan" score). Directly after the patients had performed the test itself, they were asked to describe exactly what they had just done. The accuracy of this description we termed the "Monitoring" score. Finally the patients were asked to recall the task rules, which was used as a measure of their RM abilities ("Retrospective memory" score).

The broad range of patient pathologies meant that this group included some patients whose primary neuropsychological impairment was in the domain of executive function[2] (and therefore they were likely to show PR failures), while other patients showed impairments that were relatively greater in the RM domain. Thus the study allowed one to examine how degrees of RM impairment might affect performance on the task overall and, critically, from the point of view of the present argument, how RM dysfunction might affect the PR component of the task. The Sticking-to-plan score represented a measure of this component, as it is assumed (at the simplest level) that PR abilities must mediate at some level the ability to follow a planned course of action.

The results were most interesting. Should RM functions be only minimally involved in a person's ability to carry through a planned course of action, then one would expect that at least a few patients whose RM abilities (as measured by Memory scores) were very poor, would be able to follow their original plan in an intact fashion. Dissociations would be expected between measures of PR and RM. In fact no such pattern occurred in any of the 30 patients, taking the criterion for a dissociation between scores as being where "intact" required the subject to be at least at the mean of a group of age- and reading-IQ-matched (National Adult Reading Test; Nelson 1982) controls on one measure, and "impaired" required them to be at least 2 SDS below the controls' mean on the other[3].

Of course this lack of finding could be attributed to a lack of sensitivity of the measures, but in fact, other dissociations occurred (no less than 6 separate single dissociations between the measures, plus 3 double dissociations), including ones that involved Sticking-to-plan and Memory. Moreover, the overall correlation across patients between Memory score and Sticking-to-plan was –.58 (significantly different from zero at $p < .005$). It could be argued that this association was a consequence of generalized impairment across the patients (i.e. associated deficits), but four of the correlations between scores did not reach significance in this group. Critically, the corresponding correlation between Memory and Sticking-to-plan scores in the controls did not approach significance ($r = -.18$). The difference between these correlations is significant at the .05 level.

In summary, in a patient group that included memory-impaired individuals, plan-following (i.e. PR) behaviour was significantly correlated with RM abilities. In a group of unimpaired controls however, there was little or no relationship between RM abilities and plan-following behaviour. This would seem to support the methodological point made earlier: the relationship between PR and RM might be seen most clearly when one considers patients with primary RM deficits (i.e. a classic amnesic syndrome).

At this point in the argument, we therefore have two findings to consider. The first is that patients with poor PR but intact RM can be found (e.g. the strategy application disorder cases above). The second is that patients with RM deficits tend also to show poor PR (given that one accepts that plan-following behaviour is a measure of PR). One possible, and plausible, explanation for these two findings would be that RM abilities are a prerequisite for PR behaviour, but not vice-versa.

What then might be the role of RM in PR? The most obvious one would be in maintaining the representation of the intention over the retention interval, or perhaps in recalling which action was to be performed. However the possibility exists that RM is involved in PR performance in a less obvious way.

THE ROLE OF RM IN CONTEXT-SETTING

Ellis (1996) divides the stages in the realization of a delayed intention into five general phases (corresponding to the first five stages in Figure 9.1): (a) formation and encoding of intention and action; (b) the retention interval (the delay between encoding and start of the performance interval, represented as a dotted vertical line in Figure 9.1); (c) the performance interval, i.e. the period during which the intended action should be retrieved (this most closely corresponds to the time over which the "trigger" is active in Figure 9.1); (d) the initiation and execution of intended action (marker activation to schema activation stages in Figure 9.1); and (e) the evaluation of outcome (result assessment in Figure 9.1). Ellis (1996) argues that the RM component of performance of an intended future action lies with stage (a), the formation and encoding of the intention and action. By contrast Einstein & McDaniel (1990) suggest that the RM component of a task refers to the ability to retain the basic information about action and context. Our observations of patients with amnesia clearly support Einstein & McDaniel's view that, for instance, remembering to give a message to a friend requires remembering the message and the friend to whom it is to be given. But let us consider Ellis's more complex view that RM is primarily involved in the formation and encoding of intention and action.

This processing is held to be composed of a minimum of three pieces of information, concerning the action (what you want to do), an intent (that you have to do something), and a retrieval context that describes criteria for marker activation (when you should perform the action). But what are the processing operations involved in putting these three pieces of information together? We will consider here only situations that are (a) naturalistic, in the sense that the task constraints are not directly signalled by an experimenter, and (b) are fairly non-routine (see Kvavilashvili & Ellis 1996, Dalla Barba 1993, for discussion of PR in more routine situations).

In neuropsychological terms, the decision about what action needs to be performed, and creation of the intent to carry it out fall within the traditional domain of executive function. There would appear, *prima facie*, to be little involvement of RM at these stages if one considers only episodic memory, since the operations do not involve recall of past events, but decisions regarding what to do in the future. Amnesic cases have been reported who show normal or near-normal learning on problem-solving tasks (e.g. Kinsbourne & Wood 1975, Cohen 1984), so there is no easy relationship between problem-solving (e.g. deciding upon an appropriate way of dealing with a novel situation) and episodic memory. Even if one were to broaden the definition of RM to include semantic memory, there would still be little obvious shared processing resources between the stages of action formulation/intent creation and RM. Certainly the problem-solving and goal-setting operations that need to be carried out at these stages require semantic knowledge (in the sense that one might draw on past experience to guide a decision about an appropriate course of action), but neurological patients with primary deficits in novel problem-solving do not generally have semantic memory impairments; their difficulty lies instead with the adaptation of existing knowledge to new situations (e.g. Shallice & Evans, 1978). However it is less certain what part RM might play in the development of the third piece of information, i.e. the retrieval context. This will now be discussed.

RETRIEVAL CONTEXT AND AUTOBIOGRAPHICAL RECOLLECTION

The retrieval context serves to describe the characteristics of a future situation which should prompt the activation of the delayed intention (Ellis 1996). It is thought that there are a number of distinct types of context, such as events, activities, times, people, locations and so forth (see, e.g. Harris & Wilkins, 1982), and whilst retrieval contexts that consist of only one of these forms do exist, often the context is a much more complicated combination of various forms. Thus a complex retrieval context consists not only of a set of representations but, critically, must also describe the relationship between them. For instance, consider the example of intending to mail a letter on your way home tomorrow evening, at a mailbox that you have used before. This retrieval context includes time (tomorrow evening), location (on the route home) and objects (the mailbox you know). Any of these could be used as a retrieval context in their own right (e.g. I will mail a letter sometime tomorrow evening), but this specific retrieval context is defined by the combination of all the characteristics.

Furthermore, the individual context representations themselves are drawn from memory. In the example given, all the representations can be drawn directly from RM. However some intended actions are to be performed in contexts that have not been encountered before, or even where key objects in the scenario are novel. For instance, consider the following example. You are travelling by train to Croyde village and on leaving the station you need to purchase some surfboard wax. If you know Croyde village, and have encountered surfboard wax before, you can easily imagine both. You may not have actually experienced buying surfboard wax in Croyde, but you can imagine the scenario quite well. This scenario has been "constructed" from familiar images. In the situation where both the village and the item are unfamiliar, the complex set of representations that would form the retrieval context will have to be constructed from a combination of available and imagined circumstances. Indeed, in this situation it might be better to try and remember your intention by "anchoring" it to a situation that is most like one you can imagine clearly, such as getting off the train (this argument is one plausible explanation of why people turn "steps" into "pulses"; cf. Ellis 1988, Ellis et al., in preparation). We will examine the similarities between this "construction" process in naturalistic situations and those involved in autobiographical recollection, and argue that both cognitive events are supported by similar sets of processes, albeit applied to different circumstances or modes of operation.

RECOLLECTION AS ACTIVE RECONSTRUCTION

As part of a study that aimed to explain the neuropsychological phenomenon of confabulation, Burgess & Shallice (1996a) investigated the manner in which people control or constrain their recollection when answering questions about events that had happened to them some time previously. Eight normal subjects were asked a series of 14 questions such as "Describe the last time you had dealings with the police", or "when was the last time you cleaned your car?". The subjects were instructed to describe their thought processes and the memories/images that came to mind as they answered. If possible each new idea was to be given a single-word label only. This "voicing aloud" was tape-recorded. Subjects were asked to continue for up to one-and-a-half minutes for each question, although no effort was made to enforce this guideline. After the subjects had finished an answer, the tape-recording was replayed so that they could elaborate their brief labels and comment on what they had said, especially as regards its accuracy. The original answers and the commentary were then transcribed word-for-word for each subject. This procedure was employed so as to reduce as far as possible the interference that producing a protocol necessarily entails in the primary task, and to allow subjects to check the accuracy of their initial recall process.

The transcripts were used to investigate the hypotheses put forward by a number of memory theorists (e.g. Norman & Bobrow 1979, Williams & Hollan 1981, Morton et al. 1985, Shallice 1988, Conway 1992) who maintain that recollection involves stages of forming a description for retrieval, followed by post-retrieval verification procedures. Pilot studies had shown that various sections of the verbal recollection protocols contained elements that corresponded to these processes of description and verification, as well as those that are aimed at resolving impasses or memory failures. The study aimed to characterize some forms of confabulation in neurological patients as being due to impairment in these memory control processes.

The verbal protocols were split into small sections, each of which was then independently rated by two judges as belonging to one of 25 different categories of element type. There was satisfactory agreement between the judges. The 25 element types could be grouped into four different[4] broad categories of types of process.

The first type were memories themselves; the second were verification processes (where the subject is assessing a retrieved memory for accuracy, suitability or giving notice of recall failures or confusions); the third related to the formation of general descriptions or hypotheses about what is to be recalled; the last category consisted of pure strategic, problem-solving elements, termed "mediator elements".

By examining the frequency with which a given element was followed by another across all the subjects' protocols, it was possible to calculate those combinations that occurred more frequently than chance. This data was then used to form a model of the most common forms of recall structure. The results indicated that, for instance, elements linked to the verification procedures often directly preceded or followed the retrieval of a memory, and these memory elements in turn tended to appear with greatest frequency towards the end of recollection. "Description" elements, however, were less closely linked to memories (that is, that there was more often at least one other element between a description one and a memory) and appeared with especially high frequency in the early stages of the subjects' answers to the questions. The mediator elements were particularly interesting. These elements are evidence that recollection sometimes involves inferential reasoning as well as frank problem-solving. For instance it was not uncommon for subjects to answer the question "what was the weather like yesterday morning" by trying to remember first what they were wearing, thus giving a hypothesis that they could "try out" on their memory store. On other occasions, subjects made direct calculations about, say, the timing of a particular episode in a more straightforward fashion. Other mediator elements (which tended to be even further away from memories in the recall structure, occurring primarily at the start of autobiographical recollection of an episode) included meta-cognitive judgments of the difficulty of the retrieval task before recall had started ("the last time I cleaned my car... *Oh, this is going to be difficult* ...let me think") or notice that a particular memory is not available, but is likely to be in the future. In summary, autobiographical recollection did not appear to consist of instant, easy access to a memory, which was then recalled in its entirety and without error. Instead there was a general tendency towards the use of strategic and problem-solving procedures at the beginning of recall (when the memory was not yet available), followed by the formation of precise specifications (descriptions) for recall, which then enabled the recall of candidate memories. Output was then subject to a range of checking and error-correction procedures at each stage.

That these control processes (descriptions, verifications and mediations) are necessary in recollection appears to be a direct consequence of the way event memories are represented. Recollection appears not to proceed by the activation of an invariant "record" or an event; the process is more one of deliberate reconstruction as many authors have underlined (Bartlett 1932, Norman & Bobrow 1979, Williams & Hollan 1981, Reiser et al. 1986, Barslou 1988, Conway 1990, 1992). The complexity of the processes involved in recollection was emphasized by some interesting phenomena shown by subjects in this study. Subjects quite often made errors in recall, with relatively common mistakes being the incorrect insertion of personal semantic information in a memory (eg. see the example given in Box 9.1), and the conflation of memory experiences (where two, often similar, events are mixed up). Moreover at times subjects were aware of not being able to remember certain details of an event that were retrieved later, or thought that they had recalled all the elements of an event when in fact they had not.

The results from this study were explained according to the model presented in Figure 9.2. In this model, autobiographical recollection occurs through the action of two processes. A generic representation derived from perceptual and cognitive input, (termed here an *input template*) activates key nodes within the long-term store, where a node

---

BOX 9.1   Example of an analyzed protocol from subject JS. Letters refer to the subsequent classification of the element.

Question: When was the last time you went to the coast?

JS: "The last time I went to the coast [O]/ – the last time I went to the coast would be the last time I went on holiday, I would think [D]/ Which was last summer. [A]/ I went to the coast down to Plymouth to catch a fer... [A; NB, incorrect]/ No! I didn't go to Plymouth at all, did I? [B]/ Bloody hell no [B]/ I went to Dover [B]/ to Dunkirk [A; NB, incorrect]/ with you two bods [A]/ to Italy [A]/ so that would have been the last time [O]/ – I mean technically it would have been on the way back of course. [B]/ I can't remember going to the coast since then [D]/ Um, on any trips of any variety [D]/ no rock climbing, [D]/er, I haven't visited any relations on the coast. [D]/ Haven't been to Blackpool. [D]/ No, I haven't been anywhere on the sea at all, [O]/ I don't think ... [B]/ Oh [B]/ well technically I suppose crossing the Forth Bridge up to Scotland at New Year ... [B]/ I mean, that was a river estuary so that could technically be the coast. [B]/ But, er, other than that it was definitely last summer when I was on holiday in Italy. [O]"

Note: In the commentary on this answer, JS admitted that not only was his first memory of Plymouth incorrect [corrected in protocol] but his subsequent recall of Dover was also incorrect. In fact, he had travelled from Ramsgate on this occasion, but Dover was his more usual route.

Element types: A, memories; B, verifications; C, descriptions; D, mediator processes; O, other processes not related to memory.[4]

---

is a context-independent representation. These nodes are linked by connections of differing associative strength carrying pre-existing semantic association. Recall of semantic information proceeds through activation of these nodes. For autobiographical recollection, however, a second input is equally important. This proceeds through activation of these nodes by means of a descriptor process. The descriptor defines a set of nodes in the net that correspond to aspects of types of events. Recollection itself involves an iterative process of the production of descriptors in such a way as to "explore" the net. The input templates are continually refreshed by the ongoing outputs of the net and verification procedures are necessary to detect incompatibilities either within the recall structure or between the original description and the output representation. Resolution of these incompatibilities, impasses or failures in activation can also require problem-solving routines initiated by the mediator, to which the other cognitive systems are enslaved. The products of these supervisory processes are used to form new descriptions (see Burgess & Shallice 1996 for further description).

The importance of control processes, involving descriptors and particularly verification, in the retrieval of episodic memories is indirectly supported by recent positron emission tomography (PET) studies. In Shallice et al. (1994) the scanning period in the experimental

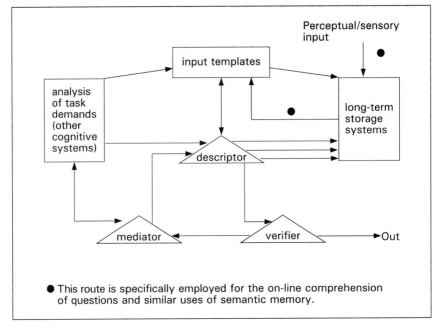

FIG. 9.2.   Relationship between memory control processes (in triangles) and other memory and cognitive systems.

condition involved only the retrieval of item responses cued by their category labels with which they had been paired in a previous learning trial. This condition was compared with one in which the category labels were presented and any exemplar could be produced without any preceding trial. Two areas were significantly more activated in the first (episodic memory) compared with the second (semantic memory) condition: the right frontal lobe and an area high on the medial surface of the parietal lobe, the precuneus. In a later study (Fletcher et al. submitted) it was shown that the latter area but not the former was particularly activated when highly imageable pairs were recalled (compared to low imageability pairs), suggesting that it was specifically involved in the retrieval of images in episodic recall. A similar pair of locations were found in a task involving the recognition of sentences (Tulving et al. 1994). One obvious possibility for the right frontal activation would be that this area of the brain supports the verification processes involved in both recognition and recall, as in both tasks descriptor processes require minimal resources. When however a more complex retrieval task was scanned by Fletcher et al. (in preparation), the task being retrieval of random paired associates compared with semantically related paired associates, then both frontal lobes were significantly activated[5]. This might suggest a left frontal involvement for producing descriptions (as well possibly as right frontal) to complement the right frontal locus of the verification process[6].

CONTEXT-SETTING IN PR AS AN APPLICATION OF CONTROL-DRIVEN RECOLLECTION

Context-setting in PR appears to require, *prima facie*, similar processing to that which is involved in autobiographical recollection. Consider again the example of mailing a letter on the way home tomorrow at a mailbox you have used before. If one introspects about what comes to mind when one "sets up" this intention (in the same way as the Burgess & Shallice subjects were asked to do) it becomes apparent that one is engaged in some sense in recollection. This is not an actual recall of a specific event, but construction of an imagined scenario based upon episodic and semantic memories. One can imagine the journey home, the street and surroundings of the mailbox, possibly the box itself, and so forth. These memories are drawn from RM, even though they may never have been experienced in the particular combination one is currently imagining. The parallel can be emphasized if one contrasts the mental experience of answering the RM question, as in the Burgess & Shallice paradigm, "describe what happened the last time you mailed a letter on your way home" with that which one has for answering the question "describe what goes through your mind as you plan how you would mail a letter on your way home". Very possibly, this act of cognition shares similarities with other mental events such as "imagining" scenarios, fantasizing, or creative "daydreaming", although the purpose is more obviously goal-directed.

Of course it is possible to create a retrieval context without such visualization of the future scenario. However Koriat et al. (1990: 568) have argued that the "imaginal-enactive properties of ... envisaged acts" explains the superiority in memory for to-be-performed compared with to-be-recalled tasks since the encoding of sensorimotor properties in the former perhaps facilitates the activation of memory by an appropriate external scenario (e.g. the view of the mailbox). In other words it would appear that the most effective retrieval context is one where as many of the aspects as possible of the anticipated future scenario have been considered and imagined.

As regards the development of these retrieval contexts, it is axiomatic that not all situations will be equal in this respect, and we considered here fairly naturalistic ones, i.e. where the subject has considerable freedom, with many differing possibilities for action, and which therefore load highly upon self-initiation (see e.g. Rabbitt 1996). Given that complex retrieval contexts are formed by using many of the same cognitive mechanisms as are involved in autobiographical recollection, "temporal marking" i.e. the formation of a message to treat some aspect of an imagined future scenario as requiring non-routine action, will proceed through a process of construction of a mental representation of the contingencies of this situation. Thus, typically, many markers will be set up at any one time, the number and strength of which will be determined by the degree of planning (in the sense of foresight) involved at the initial stages of intention encoding.

The account given here of the mechanisms involved in autobiographical recollection was developed initially as an explanation of the neuropsychological phenomenon of confabulation. This memory disorder was held to be due to a failure in the control mechanisms underlying recollection. Curiously, Dalla Barba (1994) has reported that a confabulating patient of his, MB, produced confabulatory intentions which he tried to carry out. On one occasion, MB said that he was looking forward to the end of his experimental session because he had to go to the general store to buy some new clothes. At the end of the session MB actually attempted to leave his hospital room, claiming that there was a taxi waiting for him downstairs. The remarkable behaviour of this case opens up a whole new range of possibilities for neuropsychological investigation of intention realization.

From a neuropsychological perspective, the view outlined above is that executive control systems facilitate not only the early stages of intention creation, but also mediate in the development of complex retrieval contexts. However it is likely that these control systems also facilitate the activation of temporal markers (i.e. intention activation) (Shallice & Burgess 1991a, 1991b). Goschke & Kuhl (1993) have suggested that such a view might be one possible explanation for their intriguing finding of intention-superiority effects. In their study, subjects were quicker at recognizing words from a to-be-performed script compared with those from a to-be-memorized one, even when the effects of encoding strategies were accounted for. Goschke & Kuhl (1993) argue that representations of intentions exist at a heightened level of subthreshold activation in long-term memory, and that one possible explanation of this effect might be that the storage of temporal markers might be a separable memory operation that is mediated by the frontal cortex. On the account here, the representation of a temporal marker is equivalent to the specific combination of nodes that have been activated (by executive cognitive control processes) in the long-term store. Thus an intention is stored with episodic material, but its status (activation-wise) is different.

EXECUTIVE PROCESSES AND INTENTION ACTIVATION

This leaves the matter of how intention activation occurs. Mantyla (1996) argues that retrieval sensitivity effects in PR reflect the influence of three factors (and interactions between them): the activation level of the underlying event representations; the characteristics of the cue event for triggering the planned behaviour, and the availability of attentional resources for task monitoring and self-initiated retrieval operations. Considering the first factor, Mantyla argues that the level of activation of the intention representation might be a function of the degree of planning involved. That patients with executive dysfunction can show deficits in planning ability has been known for some time (e.g. Luria 1973, Shallice 1982, 1988), and that these problems can affect performance in certain memory situations has also been demonstrated (e.g. Milner et al. 1985). More direct empirical evidence exists for the link between planning and realization of delayed intentions. Cockburn (1995a) has argued that the failures in prospective remembering in her patient (who had bilateral frontal lobe infarcts) were the result of executive problems, including planning ones. Additionally, in the study by Burgess & Taylor (in preparation) reported above, there was (in controls) a significant correlation between the sophistication of the plan subjects formed, and the closeness with which their subsequent actions matched that plan. Thus there is both theoretical and empirical evidence to support Mantyla's first assertion, and the neuropsychological evidence suggests that frontal lobe structures might play a significant part in supporting the processes involved.

Neuropsychological support exists also for Mantyla's third[7] possible influence upon retrieval sensitivity, that of the availability of an individual's attentional resources for self-monitoring and task initiation. Whilst in Burgess & Taylor's study, the controls showed a high degree of correlation between the sophistication of their plans and subsequent plan-following behaviour, this was not necessarily the case for the neurological patients, and the overall correlation in this group between planning and sticking-to-plan scores was not significant. In other words, unlike the controls, patients who planned well were not necessarily more likely to follow their plan later. This lack of association is perhaps a result of damage to those processes supporting intention activation as Mantyla suggests. In fact, Mantyla's characterization of these processes as those involved in "task monitoring" is strongly supported by a further piece of evidence from this study: in the patient group, the "monitoring" score (i.e. a measure of how well the patients were able to describe what they had just done in the SET) was significantly correlated with how closely they had followed their original plan. Whether it is the case that self-monitoring skills facilitates intention activation, or vice-versa, remains to be investigated.

FURTHER COMPLEXITIES: MULTIPLE MEMORY SYSTEMS

The account about the role of RM in PR which we have developed so far, is that the successful realization of a delayed intention requires some basic functioning of RM abilities. Specifically, the primary function of retrospective memory is twofold: it is required to be able to recognize the retrieval context, and to remember what the intention was. However there is a third, less straightforward way in which RM processes are used. This is that the same processes that facilitate retrospective recollection are used but in a different cognitive mode the in "planning for the future" mode, in setting up the retrieval context. In other words, we are suggesting that imagining a future scenario uses the same processes as remembering a past one. This is not to say that the two cognitive operations are equivalent in every way—clearly they are not—only that many of the mechanisms are shared.

According to this account, a patient who is very amnesic (i.e. has poor RM abilities) should always be poor at PR tasks, but those that are poor at PR tasks may not necessarily be amnesic (e.g. Shallice and Burgess 1991, Goldstein et al. 1993, Cockburn 1995a, Duncan et al. 1995). This is a rather bold position: it could be refuted quite easily by the finding of a classic amnesic who performs a wide range of PR tasks at a normal level. But this assumes, of course, that there is a perfect overlap between the retrospective memory functions that are used in realizing a delayed intention, and those that are damaged in amnesic patients.

An interesting case reported by Cockburn (1995b) suggests that the situation is likely to be more complex. Cockburn's patient (MG) was a 38-year-old man who had suffered a rupture of an anterior communicating artery aneurysm. Early in this patient's recovery, his prospective and retrospective memory functions were both similarly, and severely, impaired. However the patient recovered the ability to do a number of PR tasks, despite much less improvement in his scores on memory tests. The PR tasks involved realizing a range of actions over a filled delay of between 2 and 10 minutes, where the retrieval cue was either the end of the filler task, or a timer sounding. (There were also examples of everyday PR behaviour, but these are more difficult to interpret.) Of course, these PR tasks were carried out over rather shorter retention intervals than is common for many situations in everyday life, and the tasks presented a clear retrieval cue, either in the form of the end of a task, or a timer bell. Nevertheless, the results are potentially most instructive.

It is notable that the only memory test items that MG was able to perform at a grossly normal level were the easy pairs of the verbal paired associates test. One possible explanation for MG's pattern of PR–RM functions might therefore be that relatively easy cue–behaviour associations (as used with MG) might be represented in the same way as are easy paired associates. An alternative explanation is that RM tasks and PR tasks share no cognitive processing resources, and that MG's pattern of performance is a mere epiphenomenon. However, given the natural task similarity of forming cue–behaviour associations and forming paired-associate associations, this second explanation seems, *prima facie*, less likely. It is apparent that neuropsychological data of this sort is likely to be particularly instructive in revealing the cognitive processing similarities between different PR and RM tasks.

CONCLUSION

In this chapter, we have taken the view that the term "prospective memory" is best considered as referring to a set of behaviours in certain situations, rather than being the outward sign of the activity of an informationally encapsulated "module" or hypothetical construct whose operation is orthogonal to the cognitive systems that enable a person to remember past experiences (see Dobbs & Reeves 1996, for a similar view). In this way, "prospective memory" perhaps just refers to an area of psychological enquiry, with "prospective remembering" referring to the personal experience and outward behaviours involved in realizing a delayed intention.

In pursuit of empirical support for this position, we have considered neuropsychological evidence that suggests that while some patients may show impaired prospective remembering with unimpaired episodic RM, the converse pattern is not observed[8]. It is suggested that these findings are compatible with the view that RM processes play a critical part in PR, but that PR involves additional, non-mnestic processes. We would agree with Ellis (1996) who argues that the term "prospective memory" is too narrow, preferring instead to discuss "realizing delayed intentions". As pointed out by Roediger (1996), this broader view emphasizes the involvement of these non-mnestic cognitive processes (such as intention-and-goal creation, and planning, problem-solving as well as motivational factors). Perhaps one of the most obvious applications of neuropsychological data to the understanding of PR is in consideration of the interface between these non-mnestic and mnestic processes (see, e.g. Cockburn 1995a, Cohen and O'Reilly 1996, Glisky 1996). It seems likely that Robinson's (1986: 23) observation that "autobiographical memory is not only a record, it is a resource" is particularly apt in this respect.

NOTES

1. This argument makes two assumptions. First there is a generally positive correlation between cognitive abilities in the intact brain; or at least strong double dissociations do not occur (see Burgess, in press). Secondly, the distributions of ability across the various component processes are roughly equivalent.

2. The term "executive functions" is used in neuropsychology to refer to the cognitive processes that are involved in controlled, conscious and usually goal-related behaviour. Often they are characterized in terms of the way that attentional resources are allocated (e.g. Shallice 1988). Currently, many theorists hold that these processes are most heavily taxed in novel situations, and that executive processes are probably not, in a strict sense, informationally encapsulated (see Burgess, in press). From a neuroanatomical viewpoint, executive processes are, to a large degree, held to be supported by frontal lobe structures in humans.

3. A similar finding occurs if the criteria for "intact" requires the score to be better than 1 SD below the mean of the controls, with "impaired" being at least 3 SD below the mean.

4. There was actually a fifth category that consisted of elements that were a function of the social interaction involved in the experimental procedure itself, but these will be ignored as being basically irrelevant to the recollection process.

5. The random paired associates had been presented more frequently in the learning phase, to equalize the retrieval rate in the two conditions.

6. This latter localization also fits with neuropsychological evidence on paramnesic syndromes (see Burgess et al. 1996b) and on excessive repetitions in verbal free recall (see Stuss et al. 1994).

7. We will ignore for the moment the influence of the characteristics of the cue event (Mantyla's second influence) for action triggering, as in experimental situations this is likely to be equivalent for all subjects, and in the naturalistic situations considered here it is likely to be extremely complex.

8. Here the archetypal episodic RM impairment would be a pure classical amnesia. This claim is likely to be less true for other types of memory impairment, such as material-specific ones (see McCarthy & Warrington 1990).

REFERENCES

Alderman, N. & P. W. Burgess 1993. A comparison of treatment methods for behaviour disorder following herpes simplex encephalitis. *Neuropsychological Rehabilitation* **4**, 31–48.

Baddeley, A. D. & A. Wilkins 1984. Taking memory out of the laboratory. In *Everyday memory, actions and absentmindedness*, J. E. Harris & P. E. Morris (eds), 1–17. London: Academic Press.

Baddeley, A. D. & B. A. Wilson 1986. Frontal amnesia and the dysexecutive system. *Brain and Cognition* **7**, 212–30.

Barsalou, L. W. 1988. The content and organization of autobiographical memories. In *Remembering reconsidered: ecological and traditional approaches to memory*, U. Neisser & E. Winograd (eds), 193–243. Cambridge: Cambridge University Press.

Bartlett, F. C. 1932. *Remembering: a study in experimental and social psychology*. Cambridge: Cambridge University Press.

Ben-Yishay, Y. & L. Diller 1983. Cognitive remediation. In *Rehabilitation of the head injured adult*, M. Rosenthal, E. R. Griffith, M. R. Bond, J. D. Miller (eds), 376–80. Philadelphia: F. A. Davies.

Bisiacchi, P. S. 1996. A neuropsychological approach in the study of prospective memory. See Brandimonte et al. (1996), 297–318.

Brandimonte, M. A., G. O. Einstein, M. A. McDaniel (eds) 1996. *Prospective memory: theory and applications*. Hillsdale, N. J.: Erlbaum.

Burgess, P. W. Theory and methodology in executive function research. In *Methodology of frontal and executive function*, P. Rabbitt (ed.). Hove, UK: Lawrence Erlbaum Associates Ltd, in press.

Burgess, P. W. & T. Shallice 1994. Fractionnement du syndrome frontal. *Revue de Neuropsychologie* **4**, 345–70.

Burgess, P. W. & T. Shallice 1996. Confabulation and the control of recollection. *Memory* **4**, 359–411.

Burgess, P. W., N. Alderman, H. Emslie, J. Evans, B. A. Wilson, T. Shallice 1996a. The modified six element test. In *The behavioural assessment of the dysexecutive syndrome*, B. A. Wilson, N. Alderman, P. W. Burgess, H. Emslie, J. Evans. Bury St Edmunds: Thames Valley Test Company.

Burgess, P. W., D. M. Baxter, M. Rose, N. Alderman 1996b. Delusional paramnesic misidentification. In *Case studies in cognitive neuropsychiatry*, P. Halligan, J. Marshall (eds), 51–87. Hove, UK: Lawrence Erlbaum Associates Ltd.

Cockburn, J. 1995a. Task interruption in prospective memory: a frontal lobe function? *Cortex* **31**, 87–97.

Cockburn, J. 1995b. Dissociation between prospective and retrospective memory in amnesia. Paper presented at British Psychological Society Annual Conference, Warwick, England.

Cohen, J. D. & R. C. O'Reilly 1996. A preliminary theory of the interactions between prefrontal cortex and hippocampus that contribute to planning and prospective memory. In *Prospective memory: theory and applications*, M. A. Brandimonte, G. O. Einstein & M. A. McDaniel (eds), 267–96. Hillsdale N. J.: Erlbaum.

Cohen, N. J. 1984. Preserved learning capacity in amnesia: evidence for multiple memory systems. In *The neuropsychology of memory*, L. R. Squire & N. Butters (eds), 419–32. New York: Guilford.

Conway, M. A. 1990. *Autobiographical memory: an introduction*. Buckingham, England: Open University Press.

Conway, M. A. 1992. A structural model of autobiographical memory. In *Theoretical perspectives on autobiographical memory*, M. A. Conway, D. C. Rubin, H. Spinnler & W. A. Wagenaar (eds), 167–93. Dordrecht, The Netherlands: Kluer.

Coughlan, A. K. & S. E. Hollows 1985. *The adult memory and information processing battery (AMIPB)*. Leeds: St James' University Hospital.

Crowder, R. G. 1996. The trouble with prospective memory: a provocation. See Brandimonte et al. (1996), 143–8.

Dalla Barba, G. 1993. Prospective memory: a new memory system? In *Handbook of Neuropsychology*, F. Boller and J. Grafman (eds), vol. 8. New York: Elsevier.

Dalla Barba, G. 1994. Confabulation: remembering "another" past. In *Broken memories*, R. Campbell and M. Conway (eds). Oxford: Blackwell.

Davies, A. D. M. & M. G. Binks 1983. Supporting the residual memory of a Korsakoff patient. *Behavioural Psychotherapy* **11**, 62–74.

De Groot, A. D. 1965. *Thought and order in chess*. The Hague: Mouton.

Dobbs, A. R. & M. B. Reeves 1996. Prospective memory: more than memory. See Brandimonte et al. (1996), 199–226.

Duncan, J., P. W. Burgess, H. Emslie 1995. Fluid intelligence after frontal lobe lesions. *Neuropsychologia* **33**, 261–8.

Einstein, G. O. & M. A. McDaniel 1990. Normal ageing and prospective memory. *Journal of Experimental Psychology, Learning Memory and Cognition* **16**, 717–26.

Einstein, G. O. & M. A. McDaniel 1996. Retrieval processes in prospective memory: theoretical approaches and some new empirical findings. See Brandimonte et al. (1996), 115–42.

Ellis, J. A. 1988. Memory for future intentions: investigating pulses and steps. In *Practical aspects of memory, volume 1: Current research and issues*, M. M. Gruneberg, P. E. Morris & R. N. Sykes (eds), 371–6. Chichester: Wiley.

Ellis, J. A. 1996. Prospective memory or the realisation of delayed intentions: a conceptual framework for research. See Brandimonte et al. (1996), 1–22.

Ellis, J. A. & T. Shallice. Memory for, and the organisation of future intentions. Manuscript submitted for publication.

Eslinger, P. J. & A. R. Damasio 1985. Severe disturbance of higher cognitive function after bilateral frontal lobe ablation: Patient E. V. R. *Neurology, Cleveland* **35**, 1731–41.

Glisky, E. L. 1996. Prospective memory and the frontal lobes. See Brandimonte et al. (1996), 249–66.

Goldstein, L. H., S. Bernard, P. B. C. Fenwick, P. W. Burgess & J. McNeil 1993. Unilateral frontal lobectomy can produce strategy application disorder. *Journal of Neurology, Neurosurgery, and Psychiatry* **56**, 274–6.

Goschke, T. & J. Kuhl 1993. Representations of intentions: persisting activation in memory. *Journal of Experimental Psychology: Learning, Memory and Cognition* **19**, 1211–26.

Harris, J. & A. J. Wilkins 1982. Remembering to do things: a theoretical framework and illustrative experiment. *Human Learning* **1**, 1–14.

Hinton, G. E. & T. Shallice 1991. Lesioning on attractor network: investigation of acquired dyslexia. *Psychological Review* **98**, 74–95.

Hitch G. J. & J. Ferguson 1991. Prospective memory for future intentions: some comparisons with memory for past events. *European Journal of Cognitive Psychology* **3**, 285–95.

Kapur, N. 1988. *Memory disorders in clinical practice*. London: Butterworths.

Kinsbourne, M. & F. Wood 1975. Short-term memory processes and the amnesic syndrome. In *Short-term memory*, D. Deutsch & J. A. Deutsch (eds). New York: Academic Press.

Koriat, A., H. Ben-Zur, A. Nussbaum 1990. Encoding information for future action: Memory for to-be-performed tasks versus memory for to-be-recalled tasks. *Memory and Cognition* **18**, 568–78.

Kvavilashvili, L. 1987. Remembering intention as a distinct form of memory. *British Journal of Psychology* **78**, 507–18.

Kvavilashvili, L. & J. Ellis 1996. Varieties of intention: some distinctions and classifications. See Brandimonte et al. (1996), 23–52.

Luria, A. R. 1973. *The working brain*. New York: Basic Books.

McCarthy, R. & E. K. Warrington 1990. *Cognitive neuropsychology: a clinical introduction*. London: Academic Press.

Mantyla, T. 1996. Activating actions and interrupting intentions: mechanisms of retrieval sensitization in prospective memory. See Brandimonte (1996), 93–114.

Maylor, E. A. 1990. Age and prospective memory. *Quarterly Journal of Experimental Psychology* **42A**, 471–93.

Meacham, J. A. & B. Leiman 1982. Remembering to perform future actions. In *Memory observed: remembering in natural contexts*, U. Neisser (ed.) 327–36. San Francisco: Freeman.

Milner, B., M. Petrides, M. L. Smith 1985. Frontal lobes and the temporal organization of memory. *Human Neurobiology* **4**, 137–42.

Morton, J., R. H. Hammersley, D. A. Bekerian 1985. Headed records: a model for memory and its failure. *Cognition* **20**, 1–23.

Nelson, H. E. 1982. *The national adult reading test*. NFER–Nelson.

Norman, D. A. & D. G. Bobrow 1979. Descriptions: an intermediate stage in memory retrieval. *Cognitive Psychology* **11**, 107–23.

Norman, D. A. & T. Shallice 1980. Attention to action: willed and automatic control of behaviour. Center for Human Information Processing (Technical Report No. 99). Reprinted in revised form in R. J. Davidson, G. E. Schwartz, D. Shapiro (eds), 1986, *Consciousness and self-regulation*, vol. 4, 1–18. New York: Plenum Press.

Rabbitt, P. 1996. Why are studies of "prospective memory" planless? See Brandimonte et al. (1996), 239–48

Reiser, B. J., J. B. Black, Kalamarides 1986. Strategic memory search processes. In *Autobiographical memory*, D. C. Rubin (ed.), 100–21. London: Cambridge University Press.

Rey, A. 1964. *L'examen clinique en psychologie*. Paris: Universitaires de France.

Robinson, J. A. 1986. Autobiographical memory: a historical prologue. In *Autobiographical memory*, D. C. Rubin (ed.). Cambridge, UK: Cambridge University Press.

Roediger, H. L. 1996. Prospective memory and episodic memory. See Brandimonte et al. (1996), 149–56.

Shallice, T. 1982. Specific impairments of planning. *Philosophical Transactions of the Royal Society of London B*, **298**, 199–209.

Shallice, T. 1988. *From neuropsychology to mental structure*. Cambridge, UK: Cambridge University Press.

Shallice, T. & P. W. Burgess 1991a. Higher order cognitive impairments and frontal lobe lesions in man. In *Frontal lobe function and injury*, H. S. Levin, H. M. Eisenberg, A. L. Benton (eds), 125–38. Oxford: Oxford University Press.

Shallice, T. and P. W. Burgess 1991b. Deficits in strategy application following frontal lobe damage in man. *Brain* **114**, 727–41.

Shallice, T. & P. W. Burgess 1993. Supervisory control of action and thought selection. In *Attention: selection, awareness and control*, A. D. Baddeley & L. Weiskrantz (eds). Oxford: Oxford University Press, 171–87.

Shallice, T. & M. E. Evans 1978. The involvement of the frontal lobes in cognitive estimation. *Cortex* **14**, 294–303.

Shallice, T., P. Fletcher, C. D. Frith, P. Grasby, R. S. J. Frackowiak, R. J. Dolan

1994. Brain regions associated with acquisition and retrieval of verbal episodic memory. *Nature* **368**, 633–5.

Stuss, D. T., M. P. Alexander, C. L. Palumbo, L. Buckle, L. Sayer, J. Pogue 1994. Organizational strategies of patients with unilateral or bilateral frontal lobe injury in word list learning tasks. *Neuropsychology* **8**, 355–73.

Tulving, E., S. Kapur, H. J. Markowitsch, F. I. M. Craik, R. Habib, S. Houle 1994. Neuroanatomical correlates of retrieval in episodic memory: auditory sentence recognition. *Proceedings of the National Academy of Sciences*, USA **91**, 2016–20.

Wechsler, D. 1945. A standardized memory scale for clinical use. *Journal of Psychology* **19**, 87–95.

Wilkins, A. J. & A. D. Baddeley 1978. Remembering to recall in everyday life: an approach to absent-mindedness. In *Practical aspects of memory*, M. M. Gruneberg, P. E. Morris, R. N. Sykes (eds), 27–34. New York: Academic Press.

Williams, M. D. and J. D. Hollan 1981. The process of retrieval from very long-term memory. *Cognitive Science* **5**, 87–119.

Wilson, B. A. 1987. *Rehabilitation of memory*. New York: Guilford.

Wilson, B. A., J. Cockburn, A. D. Baddeley 1991. *The Rivermead Behavioural Memory Test*, 2nd edn. Bury St Edmunds, UK: Thames Valley Test Company.

ACKNOWLEDGEMENT

Paul W. Burgess is supported by grant number 38964\Z\93\1.5 from the Wellcome Trust.

PART FIVE
Neurobiology

CHAPTER TEN

Implementing a mathematical model of hippocampal memory function

Jonathan Foster, John Ainsworth, Peyman Faratin
& Jonathan Shapiro

The purpose of this chapter is to present a review of one aspect of the contemporary neuroscientific investigation of human memory. In our investigations, we have adopted a computational perspective in order to address the question of how causal interactions at the neuronal and brain systems levels provide the basis for adaptive interactions between the organism and the external world. In a general sense, computational neuroscience seeks to explain how neuronal information (subserved by the chemical and electrical signals that permit communication between neurons) is harnessed to accomplish a particular psychological task. More specifically, in the work conducted in our laboratory, we have sought to investigate how discrete environmental episodes (mediated via distinct patterns of sensory activity within the nervous system) are represented within the brain in a form that makes them available for subsequent utilization by the organism. In other words, we are interested in how complex macroscale phenomena, such as memory, emerge from the relatively simple microscale elements that constitute our brains.

Computational modelling of the brain is founded on the principle that high level psychological properties can be understood in terms of the functional characteristics of low level constituents, combined with the assumption that the brain functions as a complex processor of information (i.e. cognitive tasks are computationally tractable and can be formally analyzed and simulated). The fundamental rationale guiding such an approach is that by modelling neurons and their interconnections, the broad dynamic principles operating in the brain may be elucidated. The findings of these simulations can then be interrelated with more detailed neuroscientific data, which may constrain the ways in which such operating principles can be implemented in the brain. From a complementary perspective, the information derived from simulations may also be used to guide further empirical investigation. For example, it may illuminate research into the candidate biological mechanisms and brain regions involved in representing environmental events within the central nervous system.

Historically, the central focus of computationally based thought (as applied to neuroscience) has been in the domain of memory. The starting point of a computational perspective is the principle of association, which states that memory constitutes a process of establishing adaptive mappings among different psychological states. These states in turn correspond to specific patterns of neuronal activation, which may undergo a strengthening of their interconnections, leading to the formation of functionally important "cell assemblies" (Hebb 1949). Over

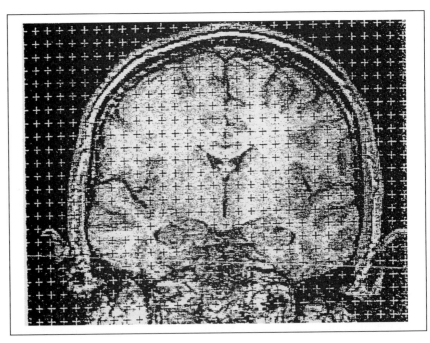

FIG. 10.1.   Magnetic resonance image of the brain. The right hippocampus is denoted by the region just above the right temporal lobe in which the overlaid grid of "+" marks has been deleted. (Although clearly visible beneath the grid, the left hippocampus has not been so identified.)

the past few decades, a wealth of data has emerged concerning the neuroanatomical loci of such assemblies.

One such candidate region is the medial temporal region and the regions that it overlies, specifically the limbic system and, in particular, the hippocampus (see Figure 10.1 for an illustration of the location of the hippocampus in the brain). A number of independent lines of evidence have now implicated the hippocampus, lying deep to the medial temporal region, in the mediation of long-term declarative memory functioning (see Squire 1992, for a review of both human and nonhuman hippocampal research). Several models have been proposed to account for the precise role of the hippocampus in mnemonic function. One of the most influential of recent mathematical formulations is that proposed by Treves & Rolls 1992.

This chapter will report a number of simulations that have been conducted to evaluate the operational viability of the Treves & Rolls model. The heuristic utility of the Treves–Rolls mathematical-computational approach to the elucidation of hippocampal mnemonic functioning will also be considered. The chapter will further discuss the significance of our findings with respect to the general question of the computational role of the hippocampus in memory.

BACKGROUND

The structure of the human nervous system is radically different from that of typical man-made digital computers, in that the nervous system has a massively parallel architecture constructed out of many simple processors (i.e. neurons), whereas a digital computer centres upon one very complex processor, which performs numerous serial operations. Furthermore, whereas digital computers are general purpose and capable of being programmed to run any algorithm, the brain appears to consist of many dedicated systems, each one of which is designed to be very efficient at a particular task (see Fodor (1983) for a development of this modular account of brain organization).

During the past decade, there has been renewed interest in the proposition that the brain may be modelled heuristically using networks of such simple computational units, or artificial neural networks. Inspired by the organizational principles of the brain, these networks typically comprise a large number of interconnected simple processing units (or "neurons") across which information is distributed. These units work collectively on a given computational problem and are connected by synapse-like links. An event is represented in such a parallel network by the collective activity of an ensemble of these neuron-like elements and stored as the weights (or strength of connections) between the individual units.

This parallel, distributed approach to information representation therefore contrasts markedly with alternative symbolic conceptualizations, in which complex information is represented more discretely, through the activity level of particular units or, in extreme cases (the "grandmother cell"), in which information can be embodied by an individual unit. By comparison, the computational properties of parallel distributed networks are largely determined by the ways in which the processing units are interconnected. According to this principle, neural networks have been designed that are able to perform computationally nontrivial tasks such as pattern recognition and the representation of content-addressable memories, for which conventional serial computers have generally proven unsuitable.

Building upon this parallel processing framework, mathematical modelling techniques have been applied over the past decade to important questions in psychology and related areas of neuroscience. Specifically, in response to the wealth of data generated in the neurosciences, researchers have attempted to develop explicit formulations of the principles of associative cell assembly first espoused by Hebb. The models derived from these formulations are additionally often designed to capture the essential features of a particular component of the relevant neuroanatomical circuitry (Marr 1969, 1970, 1971; Willshaw et al. 1969, Kohonen 1972). However, although such models are ultimately important in directing conceptualization and informing empirical research, there has been little attempt to test such models in order to evaluate their functionality. In particular, the values of key parameters, which may critically determine the operational efficiency of a model, are often not specified. If values are cited, the parameters themselves are often couched in such general terms that their utility is not always apparent.

This chapter will focus on a mathematical formulation of hippocampal function, proposed by Edmund Rolls and Alessandro Treves and their colleagues. This model is most clearly articulated mathematically by Treves & Rolls (1992). An account will be presented of our attempts to implement this model empirically. By simulating and testing the Treves & Rolls theoretical framework, we have attempted to address some of the issues raised above. In particular, we have attempted to identify key parameter values of the model and to investigate whether any further predictions can be made about the necessary features of the real system from the operating characteristics of the simulations.

Whereas other chapters presented in this volume deal predominantly with modelling at the cognitive or functional level of explanation, the material presented in this chapter will deal with explanation at the neuroanatomical and neurophysiological level. Some biological background (or at least affinity) on the part of the reader will therefore be required. In Marr's (1982) terminology, we will be referring to explanation at the *implementation* level of analysis (i.e. at the level of physical realization of the algorithm), whereas other types of model may deal with higher level explanations at the level of *computational* theory (i.e. identifying the overall goals of the computation) or at the level of the *representation and algorithm* (i.e. functional implementation of the computational theory). Marr believed that each level is independent of the one below. Thus, in computer science, there are many different algorithms which may be used to implement a particular computational theory. However, the reader may wish to reflect upon the degree to which different levels of explanation may be mutually constraining in the real system; for example, the degree to which the spatial configuration of the available neuronal hardware may restrict the number of possible algorithms available to achieve a particular computational goal (for a discussion of this question, see Churchland & Sejnowski 1992).

NEUROPSYCHOLOGICAL DATA

Neuropsychological evidence obtained from the study of both human and nonhuman animals has implicated the hippocampus in the mediation of memory, and provide the ultimate motivation for the simulations reported herein (see Squire 1992, Squire & Butters 1992). It is now over four decades since the discovery that a profoundly amnesic disorder typically occurs following brain damage restricted to the medial temporal lobes, including the hippocampus and associated structures lying deep to this region (Scoville & Milner 1957). Data obtained subsequently from the study of other brain-damaged humans, together with lesion data from nonhuman primate and rat studies, have provided evidence to support the notion that the hippocampus is critically involved in the mediation of memory. Indeed, ensuing debates in the neuropsychological memory literature have focused not so much on whether the hippocampus is actually involved in memory, but on the precise kinds of mnemonic function that the hippocampus is thought to subserve.

These debates have continued to the present day (see Squire 1992, Squire & Butters 1992). However, a consensus of opinion is now amassing that the human hippocampus is particularly implicated in subserving long-term declarative memory. This relatively broad type of memory comprises semantic and episodic facts (see Cohen & Squire 1980). Declarative memory can be contrasted with procedural memory, which is concerned with the acquisition of skills, habits and conditioning, and which does not appear to be reliant upon the integrity of the hippocampus.

The empirical evidence suggests that the hippocampus does not represent the ultimate storage location for this declarative information, but rather that it constitutes a temporary store. Thus, amnesic individuals with selective hippocampal damage are able to access information to which they were exposed some time before the occurrence of the brain damage, but not that deriving from more recent experience (MacKinnon & Squire 1989). These observations imply that the hippocampus is necessary for establishing declarative memories, but does not constitute their final destination. Memories may be stored in the hippocampus at the time of the initial experience, and for a temporary period thereafter, but they are subsequently transferred to other brain regions, with the neocortex representing the primary candidate location for this more permanent storage. Supportive evidence for the hypothesis of time-limited hippocampal memory function is also available from other sources; for example, from a consideration of the gradient of retrograde amnesia typically observed following selective hippocampal lesions in the monkey (Zola-Morgan & Squire 1990).

HIPPOCAMPUS AND RELATED STRUCTURES

Architecturally, this region of the brain can be divided into four functional components: the cortical afferent system, the parahippocampal gyrus, the hippocampal formation proper and the cortical efferent system (see Figure 10.2 for a schematic representation of the relevant corticohippocampal circuitry).

Afferent and efferent connectivity

There are *prima facie* reasons for the hippocampus to be implicated in memory functioning because of the particular features of its input and output connectivity with the rest of the brain. Located deep within the temporal lobes, it is in a unique position to receive afferents from almost all association areas of neocortex. The inferior temporal cortex, posterior parietal cortex and prefrontal cortex (regions involved in the high level processing of multimodal information) all feed into the hippocampus via the main input station, the entorhinal cortex (EC). These cortical regions are themselves activated as part of a cascade of infor-

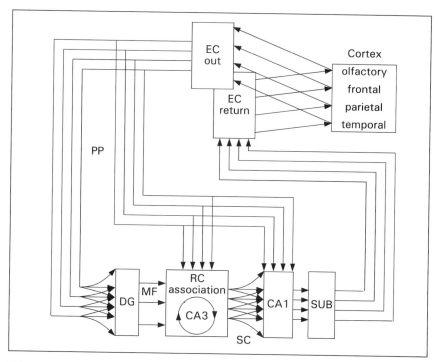

FIG. 10.2.   Schematic representation of the relevant corticohippocampal architecture and connectivity. The illustration shows the converging and diverging flow of information into and then out of the hippocampus, via the entorhinal cortex (EC). This information is thought to originate in the distributed regions of the neocortex which are responsible for representing different perceptual elements of the to-be-remembered episode (e.g. visual, spatial, auditory, olfactory). The information is processed and held in the hippocampal system for a finite period (during which memory for the relevant episode is susceptible to hippocampal damage). Information representing a particular event is thought ultimately to be returned to neocortical regions for long-term storage (after which time memory for the original episode may be accessed independently of the hippocampal system). (See text for further explanation of the abbreviations used in this representation. SUB = Subiculum.)

mation initiated by a particular environmental event. The original episode comprises characteristic visual, auditory, olfactory, gustatory and kinaesthetic elements, as represented by the activation of relevant primary sensory cortices. During its course through the brain, this information is transformed and subsequently represented by the higher association cortices downstream, and is then communicated to EC. Once funnelled through EC, the information is processed by the hippocampus. Following hippocampal processing, information may be relayed back to the entorhinal cortex, and then through a highly divergent pathway on to the neocortical regions that originally represented the episode.

In addition to its inputs from EC, there are also intrinsic connections to the hippocampus from a small population of (mainly inhibitory) interneurons, in addition to extrinsic connections with other subcortical structures, such as the amygdala. However, within the Treves–Rolls framework, these inputs are believed to play only a generic modulatory role in regulating the activity of hippocampal cells, rather than in providing specific memory-related information.

Communication within the hippocampus

The hippocampus is, in turn, composed of three main cytoarchitectonic fields, known as the dentate gyrus (DG), CA1 and CA3 (Fig. 10.2). Information is conveyed to the hippocampus via the excitatory perforant path from the entorhinal cortex, and is processed in a nonreciprocal, unidirectional manner from EC to DG, from DG to CA3, and from CA3 to CA1. In addition, there is a direct perforant path projection from EC to CA3, and a projection from EC to CA1.

For the purposes of the current exposition, we shall concentrate upon the excitatory connections between EC, DG and CA3 ("the trisynaptic pathway"), on which the Treves–Rolls framework is based. Of the projections from EC, some axons synapse at DG (synapse 1), while others proceed to make direct synapses on the apical dendrites of the pyramidal cells of CA3 (synapse 2; the direct perforant path PP route). The DG cells independently send axons, known as mossy fibres, to CA3 (synapse 3). In addition, CA3 cells send recurrent collateral (RC) projections to other CA3 cells. The mossy fibres seem to carry ostensibly the same information as the direct perforant path projection to CA3, although of course relayed via the dentate gyrus (see Figure 10.3 for an illustration of the internal hippocampal circuitry).

The pattern of connectivity and the properties of the synapses within the hippocampus determine the way in which information is processed. Notably, the number of cells first increases from EC to DG, and then decreases from DG to CA3. Specifically, in the human hippocampus, it is estimated that there are approximately 1.6×10^6 EC cells, 8.8×10^6 granule cells and 2.3×10^6 CA3 pyramidal cells. The mossy fibre (MF) projections from DG to CA3 are thought to be very limited in number, although precise data are not currently available for humans. However, relevant data are available for the rat hippocampus, in which Amaral et al. (1990) have estimated that each dentate granule cell contacts approximately 14 CA3 pyramidal cells only. In other words, each CA3 pyramidal cell receives inputs from roughly 46 granule cells. By contrast, it has been estimated (again in the rat) that each CA3 pyramidal cell may receive up to 3750 direct perforant path inputs from EC. Furthermore, it is estimated that each CA3 cell receives approximately 12000 intrinsic inputs

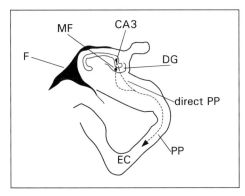

FIG. 10.3. The internal circuitry of the right hippocampus. F, fimbria; MF, mossy fibre input from DG to CA3; DG, dentate gyrus; PP, perforant path; direct PP, direct perforant path projection from EC to CA3. This figure can be related to Figure 10.1, which shows the right hippocampus at a more anterior location in the brain.

▼ represents pyramidal cell.

Incoming information flows from EC to DG and CA3.

from recurrent collaterals. In other words, the number of recurrent collateral synapses to each CA3 pyramidal cell is approximately four times the number of connections provided by the direct perforant path input, which is, in turn, approximately three times the number of inputs provided by DG along the MF route. As stated by Treves & Rolls (1992): "the CA3 system therefore is, uniquely within the hippocampus, a system in which intrinsic, recurrent excitatory connections are, at least numerically, dominant with respect to excitatory afferents".

The degree of synaptic plasticity within the hippocampus is also an important consideration. The MF synapses are presumed to be strong and display a form of long-term activity-dependent potentiation (LTP) that is nonassociative (Zalutsky & Nicoll 1990). The change in the efficacy (weight) of a network connection contingent upon previous activation approximates to LTP in the real biological system (the synaptic mechanisms underlying LTP in the brain are still controversial but shall not directly concern us here). At a nonassociative network connection, such has been postulated here for the MF synapses, this change in efficacy depends on the activity in either the "presynaptic" terminal and/or on the conditions prevailing at the "postsynaptic" site, but not on their multiplicative interaction. By contrast, in the biological system the RC and direct PP synapses are thought to be individually weak, and of the NDMA type. This variety of synapse has been implicated elsewhere in an associative type of plasticity (Brown et al. 1990). Associative plasticity (a "Hebbian" mechanism) signifies that the change in efficacy of the synapse depends on both presynaptic and postsynaptic levels of activity in a multiplicative manner.

Artificial neural networks that employ a Hebbian learning rule typically exhibit powerful forms of learning and self-organization (Hopfield 1982, Hopfield & Tank 1985, Kohonen 1988, Sejnowski & Tesauro 1989). These features appear to be intrinsic to the Treves & Rolls formulation. In the biological system, the LTP mechanism may be induced rapidly (see Baudry & Davis 1991), but it does not appear to produce permanent synaptic enhancement. It has been observed to persist for up to weeks or months (Morris et al. 1988), but seems to decay naturally over this time period (see Baudry & Davis 1991). Thus, it does not seem feasible as a mechanism for indefinite storage of information, but it is a prime candidate as a mechanism underlying fast-learning and time-limited storage of information.

To summarize, interdisciplinary data from the fields of neuropsychology, neuroanatomy and neurophysiology would all seem to support the notion that the hippocampus acts as a temporary store for declarative memories. Lesion data, the highly connected, matrix-like architecture of the CA3 cell field and the prevalence of LTP within the hippocampus all suggest that this structure may play a critical role in subserving memory. Furthermore, studies of retrograde amnesia, the nature of the backprojections for the hippocampus to the neocortex, and the nonpermanent nature of the synaptic changes induced by LTP all add weight to the hypothesis that the hippocampus represents a temporary site for the storage of memories. Finally, the preservation of procedural memory and the loss of declarative memory in amnesics with hippocampal damage, the funnelling of polymodal information into the hippocampus from all areas of association neocortex, and the nonsegregation of these inputs within the hippocampus all add credence to the view that the hippocampus represents a critical node in the chain of structures processing afferent information into long-term declarative memories.

THEORETICAL VIEWPOINTS

We have seen how evidence from neuropsychological, neuroanatomical and neurophysiological investigations have all provided supportive evidence for the notion that the hippocampus functions as a time-limited store for declarative memories. Some computational approaches to hippocampal functioning will now be discussed.

Successful models are based upon combining coherent theoretical formulations with the relevant empirical data. In other words, within the present context, they must explain how the anatomy and the physiology of the hippocampus can perform the mnemonic functions that are suggested by the psychological literature. A variety of such models have been proposed to integrate the available empirical data on hippocampal memory functioning into a theoretical understanding, and, more specifically, to relate the functional properties of the hippocampus to its anatomical and physiological characteristics.

The majority of models of hippocampal processing have adopted the principles of associative memories as their foundation (although there are some alternative approaches; for example, Sclabassi et al. 1988, Schmajuk 1988). Several of these models have taken the results from artificial neural networks and modified them, incorporating findings from neuroanatomical studies, in order to produce a biologically plausible model that manifests the processing features of the real system. Important current models include McNaughton's model of spatial memory (1989), Marr's temporary memory (1971) and the Treves & Rolls (1992) formulation. This chapter will concentrate upon the Marr & Treves-Rolls models only. Both of these models: (a) use an autoassociative architecture, and (b) seek to incorporate established anatomical and physiological data.

In the early 1970s, Marr proposed a model of the hippocampus, based upon earlier neuroscientific data, in which the hippocampus was seen as a source for temporary content-addressable memory. According to this framework, memories of events are represented as patterns of activity across the "cells" of the model, and are stored as modifiable "synapses" of the network. A representation of the event could then be recalled by prompting the network with a small fraction of the original pattern. Marr arrived at such a network by imposing numerical and computational constraints upon its design. The numerical constraints were derived either intuitively, or from neurobiological data (such as the estimated number of cells in a particular field of the hippocampus), whereas the computational constraints were derived from existing neural network models of memory.

Through these considerations, Marr arrived at a model of memory with three layers of units, and some topographical organization of the connections between them (in particular, recurrent connections within the third layer). Marr then related this model to the structure of the hippocampus, identifying the three layers of units with the neocortex, entorhinal cortex and the CA3 cell field.

Although Marr's model has been very influential, the relationship between Marr's theory and the actual structural features of the hippocampus is somewhat tenuous. Marr's framework lacks any representation of the EC–DG–CA3 trisynaptic circuit, and the physiological properties of the units and their interconnections bear little resemblance to those of real synapses and neurons. For instance, the units and their connections are binary, i.e. they can be in one of only two states: "on" or "off". This does not take into account the continuous activity of neurons in the brain, embodied through their temporal coding properties.

By contrast, Edmund Rolls and his colleagues have developed a more anatomically detailed framework, in which they relate hippocampal mnemonic function to the physiological properties of the anatomical neural networks comprising the hippocampus (Rolls 1989a, 1990). This model represents the hippocampus as the fulcrum of a complex information storage and retrieval system. In particular, the theory assigns a critical role to the CA3 cell field in representing memories of discrete episodes. Rolls and his associates propose that any to-be-remembered event ultimately evokes a specific representation as the firing pattern of CA3 pyramidal cells, upon which memory for the original event is founded. When the organism experiences a particular to-be-remembered episode, a constellation of stimuli is deemed to be processed along various sensory pathways. This subsequently produces a collection of neural representations of different elements of the episode. These highly elaborated patterns are considered to be rich in information content, and to be channelled towards the hippocampus through overlying regions of neocortex.

According to the Treves–Rolls framework, during encoding, the entorhinal input into the hippocampus is thought ultimately to elicit a specific firing pattern in the CA3 pyramidal cells, constituting a unitary representation of the original episode. From this viewpoint, neural representations of numerous different episodes may be stored on the modifiable synapses of the CA3 recurrent collateral projections. The change in the efficacy of these and other connections (such as those between the EC and CA3 cells) is considered by Treves & Rolls to depend upon the level of activity of the pre- and postsynaptic cells during learning. These synaptic modifications are thought to represent a relatively long-term memory trace, and to persist (superimposed with subsequent modifications) as the system is exposed to new episodes. The CA3 region is deemed to function as an autoassociative network, i.e. by virtue of the extensive recurrent connections within CA3, it is proposed that, in retrieval, the original episode may be retrieved via the subsequent presentation of a fragment of the initial pattern. This fragment, or partial cue, can be conceptualized in psychological terms as corresponding to a memory for a subset of elements of the original episode. For example, a specific dinner taking place in a particular restaurant may comprise gustatory, olfactory, visual, spatial, auditory and tactile elements. When one tries to remember the evening in question, partial information pertaining to the episode may be present in one, several or all of these forms; for example, the pleasantly distinctive odour of the dessert, the idosyncratic feel of the cutlery or the appealing face of the waitress. From each of these individual elements, a psychologically unitary memory of the original event may be summoned.

In the Treves–Rolls scheme, such a cue is represented at the hippocampal level by an afferent signal that has some degree of correlation with the signal that reached the hippocampus during the original episode. The cue is thought to be able to elicit a firing pattern that is strongly correlated with that which represented the original event in CA3. Moreover, in subsequent versions of the model it is postulated that this cued memory retrieval may itself subserve the consolidation of longer term forms of memory storage in regions extrinsic to the hippocampus.

Rolls and his associates have therefore presented a coherent framework describing the ways in which information may be represented, processed and stored within biological networks. According to this framework, memory representation is deemed to be sparse, i.e. each episode is represented by the firing of a relatively small number of CA3 neurons, so that the patterns can be relatively orthogonal to each other. In other words, the architecture is fully distributed, in so far as any neuronal unit may, in principle, be active in any pattern (although, in practice, few CA3 neurons are actually involved in representing any particular episode). This arrangement minimizes cross-talk and increases the number of patterns that can be stored or associated in the hippocampal network. Moreover, in contrast to Marr's earlier model, this framework permits units to adopt more realistically neuronal (i.e. graded rather than binary) firing behaviour (Treves 1990).

Further to the proposal of the original model, it has been extended and elaborated by Edmund Rolls and Alessandro Treves (Treves & Rolls 1992). In this later formulation, Treves & Rolls seek to integrate the specific afferent inputs of the hippocampus into a more detailed mathematical version of the CA3 autoassociative framework. Specifically, in addition to the numerous collateral CA3 connections, they attempt to ascribe a computational role to the two major input systems to CA3; namely, the direct perforant path projection from entorhinal cortex and the mossy fibre projection from DG. However, the central property of the proposed model remains the ability of the CA3 system to perform as an autoassociative memory in selectively retrieving a specific firing pattern among several stored on the same set of synaptic efficacies. This is regarded as a highly nontrivial capacity, if the system is able to operate in the presence of both intrinsic noise and the interference effects of the storage of many patterns. Furthermore, Treves & Rolls contend that a mathematical requirement arises for two extrinsic input systems to CA3. (These should possess the qualitative information-processing features that empirically characterize the direct perforant path and mossy fibre inputs.) Whereas the direct PP input comprises associatively modifiable synapses with characteristics (in particular, average synaptic strength) similar to the RC synapses, the MF input is a potentially much stronger synapse, lacking the type of plasticity suitable for associative learning. Treves & Rolls contend that an auto-associative memory system requires both this weak but associative form of input, and the strong but nonassociative form, each with a distinct role, in order to mediate successful learning and retrieval.

Although the Treves & Rolls framework seems feasible, in the context of the known anatomy and physiology of the hippocampus, it is important that any theoretical model is implemented to test its computational validity, by determining if it will function adequately across a wide range of its parameter space. If it does, then it can be classified as a generic model. If it does not, however, then its general utility must be called into question. We also hoped that our computer simulations would add more concrete detail to the model; specifically, by identifying the value of key numerical parameters of the Treves & Rolls formulation, and their relative interdependence, and by studying the effects of varying the value of the parameters from their optimal value on the overall functional efficiency of the model. Finally, it was also hoped that the results of the simulations might generate testable predictions about the empirical features of the real neuronal system.

THE SIMULATIONS

Initially, we attempted to test the Treves–Rolls formulation by implementing networks of limited complexity. The rationale of this approach was that simulating the full EC–DG–CA3 system might have been unsuccessful due to an inappropriate choice of one of the many parameter values. This could have initiated malfunctioning of one component of the system, the consequences of which would then propagate throughout the entire network. In addition to the benefit of lucidity, we considered that it would be more tractable to demonstrate the principles underlying the Treves & Rolls model if it were first separated into component subsystems.

The CA3 autoassociative memory system was the obvious starting point for the simulations, as it lies at the heart of the Treves & Rolls formulation. If a set of parameters could be determined that permitted the CA3 network to function as prescribed by the Treves & Rolls framework, then the MF and direct PP inputs could subsequently be grafted on. In addition, the direct PP projection could be modelled in isolation in order to test its ability to form a mapping between different input patterns and their CA3 representation, and hence provide a cue for the CA3 autoassociative memory system. If these separate simulations indicated that the individual components of the model were functioning as prescribed by Treves & Rolls, it would then be possible to combine them into one dynamic simulation of the hippocampus.

A further consideration concerned the selection of those parameter values that needed to be assigned in the implementation. As a number of the parameter values were not specified explicitly in the Treves & Rolls formulation, we selected plausible values by making realistic estimations based upon the relevant empirical literature. Hence, the simulations did not explore the operation of the model under all available conditions, but only under those that were neurobiologically feasible.

The patterns of activation that were presented to the network in these studies were either binary or continuous. Patterns of activation comprise a number of units, which are either active or quiescent. For binary patterns, the magnitude of the activations was either zero or one, while for continuous patterns, the magnitude of the individual elements could take any value within a continuous range from zero to one (Treves & Rolls 1991). All patterns presented to the network were randomly generated by computer, according to either a binary pattern probability distribution or a continuous pattern probability distribution (Fig. 10.4). A total of 10–20 binary patterns and 10–20 continuous patterns were presented to separately implemented networks and permitted to propagate through the network. The level of sparseness (i.e. the percentage of nonzero activation units in each pattern) was constant across patterns: there were 50/500 (i.e 10%) active units per input pattern.

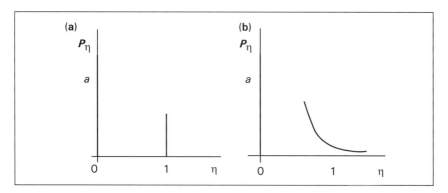

FIG. 10.4.   (a) Binary and (b) continuous firing rate probability distributions. η is the level of unit activation in pattern η; $P(\eta)$ is the probability of a unit in pattern η with the given level of activation, and a is the overall level of sparseness of pattern η. In the binary partterns, each unit was either switched on (activation = 1) or off (activation = 0). In the continuous patterns, the activity value of each of the units varied between 0 and a value considerably greater than 1. However the mean level of unit activation was the same in both pattern distributions.

Partial cues, which were used to initiate retrieval, were based upon Marr's criterion, which states that, in order to mimic the real system, there should be a correlation of approximately 30% (i.e. 15 active units) between the cue and the original pattern. These fragments were created by randomly selecting an active element from the originally presented pattern and re-setting its value to zero. This procedure was repeated until the requisite number of active elements had been removed. Having been created from the original pattern, the partial cue was continuously presented to the network in order to initiate retrieval.

The dynamics of the network were then allowed to commence. In order to test the similarity between the original pattern and what was

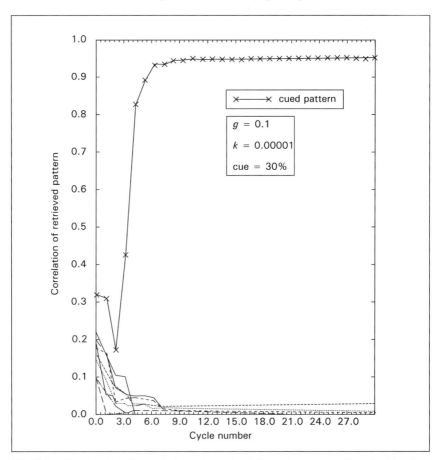

FIG. 10.5.   Correct retrieval to a partial cue of a previously learned pattern over 30 cycles. Note that, even though the cue is ultimately correctly classified, there is an initial reduction in the level of correlation to the cue, due to global system inhibition. *g* is the gain variable, and *k* is the modulatory variable.

retrieved, and hence gauge the accuracy of retrieval, a correlation was computed after each full cycle of the network in order to compare the state of the network after presentation and propagation of the original pattern, and the state of the network after presentation and propagation of the cue. The output of the network was plotted after each full cycle in order to produce a temporal trace of the network's dynamic evolution. This was continued until the network reached a definable attractor state, i.e. where the activation of all the units had stabilized, and the network had finished retrieving. Correct retrieval of a pattern to a partial cue is shown in Figure 10.5.

There were many free parameters arising from the Treves & Rolls formulation. The value of these had to be chosen before any of the implementations could be executed. Some typical values are shown in Tables 10.1–10.3. These values were chosen in order to satisfy the following conditions: wherever possible, they should be (a) neurobiologically plausible, and/or (b) computationally sensible and/or (c) generous, with respect to the appraisal of the Treves–Rolls model. For example, the number of patterns was severely limited (i.e. between 10 and 20), so that the network should have been operating well below its critical loading, but was storing a meaningful amount of information. The value of the sparseness of the patterns selected also indicated that the degree of cross-talk between different patterns should have been minimal in a network of this size. Hence, the network should have been

TABLE 10.1
Typical parameter values assigned for network implementation (1).

Variable	Description	Value
DG Θ	DG threshold	0.25
CA3 Θ	CA3 threshold	0.0
g	Gain variable	0.1
k	Modulatory variable	10^{-5}
a^{EC}	Sparseness of EC input	0.1
p	Number of patterns stored	10
C^{EC}	Connectivity of EC→DG	2%
C^{MF}	Connectivity of MF	0.6%
C^{RC}	Connectivity of RC	100%
C^{PP}	Connectivity of PP	25%
J^{RC}_{ini}	Initial RC weight	1.0
J^{PP}_{ini}	Initial PP weight	1.0
J^{MF}_{ini}	Initial MF weight	10
Learn rule	Learning rule used	Covariance
η^{CUE}	Cue pattern size	30%/50%

TABLE 10.2
Typical parameter values assigned (2).

Variable	Description	Value
DG Θ	DG threshold	0→X
CA3 Θ	CA3 threshold	0.0
a^{EC}	Sparseness of EC input	0.1/0.8
C^{EC}	Connectivity of EC→DG	2%
C^{MF}	Connectivity of MF	0.6%

Table 10.3
Typical parameter values assigned (3).

Parameter	Description	Values used
N^{EC}	Number of EC units	500
N^{CA3}	Number of CA3 units	500
L^{PP}	Fraction of connectivity of PP	0.25
L^{CA3}	Fraction of connectivity of CA3	1
p	Number of patterns stored	20
a^{EC}	Sparseness of EC pattern	0.1
a^{CA3}	Sparseness of CA3 pattern	0.05
g	Gain of CA3 units	0.1
Θ	Threshold of CA3 units	0.0
$b(X)$	Modulation term	$-k\left(\sum_i V_i - N^{CA3}a\right)^3$
k	Modulation constant	0.0001
J^I	Initial values of weights	0.2
d	Decay term	1
	Pattern type	binary

Note: V_i is the activation value of unit i and a is the sparseness value

working under nearly optimal conditions. Values of terms that could not be selected using the aforementioned principles were investigated experimentally, such as the network inhibition term, k.

The simulations were of two different types. First, as already mentioned, simplified local network analyses were conducted, in which the EC–DG–CA3 trisynaptic system was unpacked and then reassembled, and the primary focus was upon the performance of the CA3 system alone. The local systems analyses comprised: (a) the CA3 model; (b) the afferent mossy fibre inputs to CA3 for learning; (c) the direct PP model; (d) the combined CA3 and direct PP system, and (e) combined CA3 and direct PP system with afferent mossy fibre input. These simulations focused upon the question of adequate conditions for retrieval, given appropriate storage of patterns in the CA3 network.

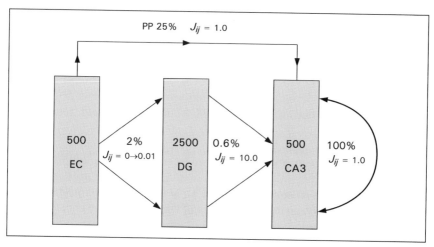

FIG. 10.6.   Typical network architecture and parameters for the simulations reported. As shown, 500 EC units projected with a connectivity of 2% to 2500 DG units. These in turn projected with a connectivity of 0.6% to 500 fully intraconnected CA3 units. Note the relative divergence of unit activity from EC to DG and re-convergence from DG to CA3. Along the direct PP input route, the 500 EC units projected with a connectivity of 25% to the 500 CA3 units. (J_{ij} is the weight or synaptic efficacy between units i and j.)

Secondly, simulations of the entire EC–DG–CA3 system were conducted in order to identify the parameter values that permitted a set of mutually orthogonal patterns to be produced and stored on the CA3 cells, and correct retrieval to be subsequently initiated by the direct PP route and maintained by the RCs.

The network architectures varied slightly between simulations (for example, number of components, initial weights, network connectivity). However, the default parameters (from which there was minimal divergence) were as shown in Figure 10.6, with 500 EC units, 2500 DG units and 500 CA3 units. In other words, the real human hippocampal system was scaled down by factors of 200, 400 and 200, respectively. This was found to be the optimum scale for emulating the limited MF connectivity and at the same time constraining the processing time within reasonable limits.

All simulations were run extensively in order to determine performance efficiency to an adequate level of accuracy. During retrieval, each network was run 400 times, so that individual patterns were cued on between 20 and 40 separate occasions (depending upon the number of patterns in the original learning set).

LOCAL SIMULATIONS

Network parameters that are representative of those used in all the local simulations reported in this section are shown in Table 10.1. However, in some of the simulations several of these parameters are not relevant, as the corresponding component of the network was not implemented (for example, EC in the CA3 model reported below.)

The CA3 model

The first set of these analyses concentrated upon implementing the CA3 system in isolation. The general principles applied in this simulation apply to all the others reported. Thus, many free parameters arose out of this implementation, the values of which had to be chosen before any simulations could be performed. For example, the threshold of each unit was set to zero, in order to simplify the network's operation, and the gain was set to 0.1. Other parameter values were selected to ensure that the network was operating well below its critical loading, but was storing a meaningful quantity of information. The connectivity of the CA3 network was 100% (i.e. a standard Hopfield network); in other words, every unit connected with every other unit. The value of the modulation term followed from the work of Treves (1990), and allowed for generalized inhibition when the overall network activity was too high, and global excitation when the network activity was too low. During learning, the weights of the network were modified according to a Hebbian covariance learning rule. During retrieval, the initial starting point of the network was determined by imposing the activation pattern of the cue onto the units in the CA3 network.

The dynamics of the network were then allowed to commence. On each occasion that the activity values of the CA3 units had been updated, the current activation state of the network was correlated against all of the originally stored patterns. The correlations after each full cycle were then plotted in order to produce a trace of the network's dynamic evolution. This was continued until the network reached a stable state (basin of attraction). The measure that was used to establish the degree of correlation between a stored and a retrieved pattern was based upon a cosine measure of the difference between pattern representations (the normalized dot product). A value of 1 signifies that the vectors that describe the two patterns are identical whereas a value of 0 indicates that they are mutually orthogonal. The criterion for correct retrieval of a particular pattern was that the vector correlation between the original CA3 representation and that which was reinstated at CA3 by the retrieval cue was equal to or greater than a normalized dot product value of 0.9 (corresponding to an inter-pattern percentage similarity of approximately 80%). A total of 20 different patterns were used in all the local simulations that were conducted.

The results of this first set of local simulations showed that the CA3 model was able to store and retrieve binary patterns (unit activity = 0 or 1) efficiently, scoring at an average of 86% correct retrieval over all the binary patterns stored (see Figure 10.7). However, the CA3 implementation was relatively poor at retrieving more neurobiologically feasible continuous patterns (in which unit activity was free to vary between 0 and 1). Average performance with these patterns was in the order of 46% (see Figure 10.8), with the network tending to end up in one of its "favoured" states, probably due to some patterns having a larger basin of attraction than others. It remains possible from our findings that the CA3 model may work well for some combinations of parameters when

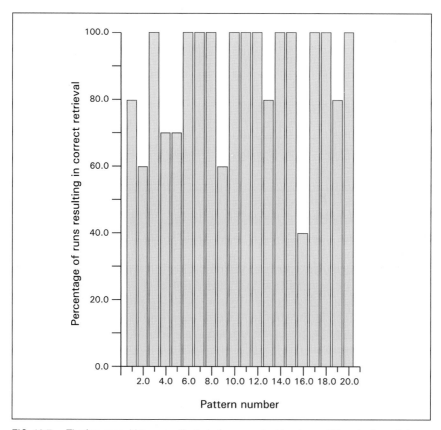

FIG. 10.7. The frequency histograms illustrate the percent retrieval over 400 cycles to partial cues for each of the 20 different patterns learned by the system. In this set of simulations all cues represented binary patterns of activation. The overall level of correct pattern retrieval was 86%.

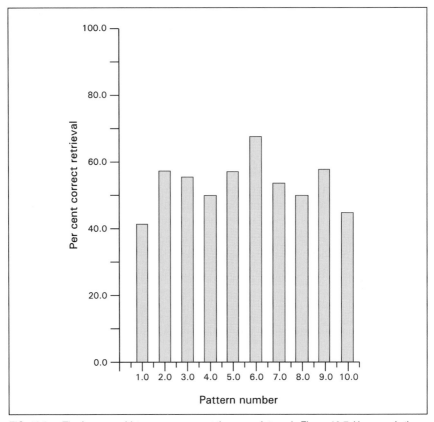

FIG. 10.8.   The frequency histograms represent the same data as in Figure 10.7. However, in these simulations all cues represented continuous patterns of activation. The overall level of correct pattern retrieval was 46%.

storing and retrieving continuous patterns, but we concluded that the system must be so sensitive to a particular combination of parameter values as to render it functionally somewhat implausible.

Because of the failure of the system to work reliably with continuous patterns, binary patterns were used for all local system simulations conducted hereafter.

Afferent input to CA3 for learning

The aim of the second set of simulations was to test whether a strong input of the MF type was indeed necessary for new information storage to occur. The Treves & Rolls formulation requires a learning input that is able to force the CA3 network out of an existing attractor state and into a new state determined by the afferent input, thus permitting the network to learn this new pattern. During the encoding of a new pattern, the dynamics of the ongoing iterative CA3 processing are deemed to introduce interfering randomizing effects to the storage of novel information. For this reason, in the Treves & Rolls framework, a weak input (similar to the direct perforant path input) is not considered capable of storage, whereas the strong input attributed to the mossy fibres is considered to be capable of performing this function.

In these simulations, the network was therefore provided with a cue, in order to retrieve one of the previously stored binary patterns, and was then allowed to cycle. A new input (i.e. pattern 21) was then applied to the network. This pattern had been previously unseen, and therefore not stored in the network. The strength and duration of this new input was parametrically varied by altering the relevant system variables. After presenting an input to the network, the network was allowed to continue its dynamic evolution and correlations between the current pattern of CA3 activation and those representing the 20 previously stored patterns and the new afferent input pattern were tracked across iteration of the network.

The findings of simulations demonstrated that a strong binary MF-type input to CA3 can force it out of an existing attractor basin and into a novel state for learning. However, this seemed to depend further on the size of the afferent exceeding a critical threshold (Fig. 10.9). Secondly, it was found that the feedback of the CA3 RCs could not be overcome unless a new input was applied continuously. Under these conditions, the findings obtained from the local simulation of the afferent binary input to CA3 were consistent with the notion advanced by Treves & Rolls that the MF-type input is able preferentially to direct information storage.

Direct perforant path simulations

The hypothesized role of the PP input to CA3 was tested in the third set of simulations. The Treves and Rolls formulation requires that, during learning, the direct perforant path input to CA3 learns a mapping between the EC input pattern and the corresponding pattern that is stored on CA3, so that a cue presented at EC can subsequently be used to initiate the retrieval process. Parameter values were initially chosen for consistency with the previous simulations, but were then varied in order to assess their effect on the functioning of the direct perforant path network. Each EC unit was connected to the CA3 units at random. The binary CA3 pattern used had lower arithmetic sparseness values (i.e. it was "more sparse" in colloquial parlance) than the corresponding binary EC patterns, as the mossy fibre encoding input is thought to supply patterns that contain less information (in terms of the number

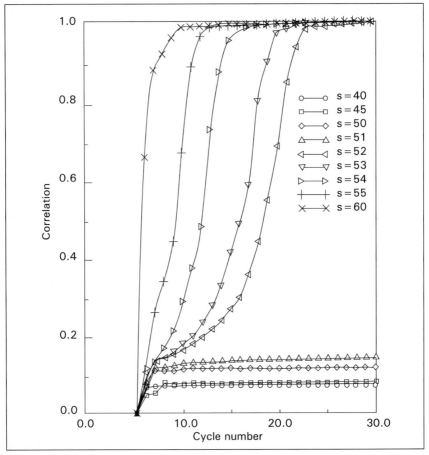

FIG. 10.9.   Various strengths (s) of the mossy fibre-type input to CA3 and their relative effects, when persistently applied. Note that the input strength required to force the CA3 network out of its current state of retrieval and into a new basin of activity must be ≥52.

of participating units) than the corresponding EC pattern, due to the orthogonalizing effect of the EC–DG–CA3 input pathway. The direct PP weights between the EC and CA3 units were then modified according to the designated Hebbian covariance learning rule, so that a mapping was created between the corresponding EC and CA3 patterns of activity. By the tenets of the Treves & Rolls framework, supplying a partial cue to the EC units should then have enabled a particular CA3 pattern to be partially recreated by the direct PP input, due to the information represented in the learned EC–CA3 weights. From this partially retrieved pattern, it is postulated that the CA3 network will then be able to retrieve the original pattern of activation in its entirety.

In order to initiate retrieval, a cue was applied to the network and allowed to propagate through the direct PP pathway. Note that the CA3 units were not permitted to cycle in this set of simulations. Rather, the degree to which the CA3 activations were affected by the direct PP input alone were investigated. The activation state vector of the CA3 units was correlated with the stored vector derived from the original CA3 pattern. From this, it could be determined to what extent the direct PP projection was able to recreate a particular CA3 pattern from a partial EC cue. Furthermore, in order to investigate how this ability degraded with the number of mappings stored in the network, further pairs of patterns were presented to the EC and CA3 units, and learning took place, as before. In order to evaluate the effects of sequential additions of new patterns, after each new pattern had been learned, a cue to the pattern learned first was presented to the EC units, the network was updated accordingly and the appropriate correlations were calculated. From these data, graphs were plotted showing the correlation between the current activation state of CA3 and the original activation state, against the number of pairs of patterns stored in the direct PP network. These simulations were repeated for many different values of the free parameters, so that the performance of the network under a whole range of conditions could be gauged.

In this third set of simulations, retrieval of binary patterns was again broadly as prescribed by the Treves & Rolls framework: the network performed efficiently to a cue presented at EC for propagation along the direct PP route to CA3. However, it was found that the quality of the cue provided to CA3 by the direct PP input was dependent upon the number of patterns stored in the EC–CA3 synapses, with the quality of a given value cue decreasing when more patterns had been learned. This was no doubt due to the degree of interference between the stored patterns. The quality of the cue also seemed to be related to the fraction of direct PP–CA3 connectivity. Specifically, lower connectivity resulted in a proportionately smaller cue for CA3. Finally, even if the connections were allowed to decay (in a manner thought to be broadly analogous to the decline in LTP over time), then the ability of the direct PP input to supply a useful cue to CA3 was nevertheless sustainable.

CA3 and direct perforant path simulations combined
Having examined the ability of the CA3 and direct PP systems to perform in relative isolation, the next logical phase was to combine these components in order to determine whether they were able to function in tandem, with CA3 being permitted to iterate, as in the real system. These simulations were implemented according to the mathematical descriptions of the CA3 and direct PP models, as previously

implemented. The values of the parameters that were selected were chosen for consistency with previous simulations, and because they were known to permit the individual systems of the model to perform well with binary patterns.

Pairs of binary patterns were imposed on the EC and CA3 units. As in the earlier direct PP simulations, the CA3 patterns were allocated a lower sparseness value (i.e. they were, as one would say, "more sparse") than the EC patterns. However, in these simulations both the weights between EC and CA3 and the weights between the CA3 units (corresponding to the RC connections) were modified according to the covariance rule, for each of the 20 pairs of EC and CA3 paired patterns in turn. Thus, mappings between the EC and CA3 patterns were created in the direct PP network and, in addition, the patterns were effectively stored within the CA3 autoassociative network.

At retrieval, the network was then presented with a cue at EC to one of the 20 stored patterns. This cue was allowed to propagate along the direct PP path to CA3. The total input to each of the CA3 units was then calculated sequentially, as in the earlier direct PP simulations. However, by contrast with the previous set of simulations, the activation vector of the CA3 units provided by the direct PP input was then utilized as a cue by the CA3 network, which was permitted to cycle according to its intrinsic dynamics. The EC cue was persistently applied, since the direct PP input is regarded as a temporally continuous influence on the CA3 network. The usual trace of the network's evolution towards a particular basin of attraction was then made in order to determine whether the network had functioned effectively to retrieve the pattern for which it had been cued. This fourth set of simulations again demonstrated that the direct PP–CA3 network could retrieve binary patterns efficiently from cues presented at EC, indicating that the CA3 network is capable of retrieving iteratively from a partial cue propagated along the direct PP route.

CA3 and direct perforant path networks combined with mossy fibre input

In the fifth and final set of these local simulations, the implementation was as in the previous section, but now an afferent input, simulating the original MF input to CA3, was added. It was anticipated that these simulations would demonstrate whether or not a new pattern could be imposed on the CA3 network to force it out of an existing attractor network, as previously described, then learned and retrieved via the direct perforant path input to CA3. There was a critical difference between these simulations and those described previously in the second set of local simulations. This distinction concerned the learning of the 21st pattern by the network and subsequent retrieval of this pattern to

a partial binary cue presented at EC (rather than simply the requirement of the 21st pattern to force CA3 out of an existing basin of attraction). These simulations therefore tested the principles of new learning
and retrieval that lie at the heart of the Treves & Rolls dual input
hippocampal formulation. Thus, 20 binary patterns were stored in the
weights of both the direct PP and CA3 networks, as in the fourth set of
simulations. The network was then presented with a cue at EC to one of
these learned patterns, which was propagated along the direct PP
retrieval route, and the CA3 network was allowed to cycle and retrieve
a pattern to this cue.

After 10 time cycles, a 21st binary pattern, which the network had
not yet learned, was presented at EC, and the corresponding more
sparse version of this pattern was applied at CA3 (via the mossy fibre
input). This 21st pattern was of an appropriate input strength, as determined in the first set of simulations. As before, both the EC version and
MF-type input version of the new pattern were continuously applied for
10 cycles. Then, from the total input to CA3 (including the direct PP contribution from EC), the activation values of the CA3 units were computed according to the relevant transfer function. This process was permitted to continue for a further 10 cycles, following which the weights of
the direct PP and RC networks were modified by applying the
covariance rule to the activations of the EC and CA3 units at that time.
The activation vector of the EC units was simply the new pattern that
had been presented, and it was expected that the activation pattern of
the CA3 units would reflect the characteristics of the transformed version of the new pattern imposed via the MF-type input. The inputs to
the CA3 network were then re-zeroed, the MF-type input was removed
and the CA3 network was allowed to stabilize. Finally, on the 31st cycle,
a partial cue (corresponding to the recently learned new pattern) was
presented to the EC units, and the direct PP projection was allowed to
propagate the cue to CA3, which then cycled towards an attractor state.

In this phase of testing, each simulation therefore consisted of 10
cycles in which one of the original 20 patterns was retrieved, followed
by 10 cycles in which the new pattern was encoded, followed by 10
cycles of CA3 cycling and RC and EC–PP weight-setting, followed on
the 31st cycle by partial cueing of the new pattern along the EC–PP
route and the cycling of CA3 towards an attractor state.

The results of this final set of simulations illustrated that, similar to
what had been observed previously, the CA3 network was able to learn
reliably a new directly imposed binary pattern and effect a mapping
between this pattern and the corresponding EC binary pattern. Then,
using a partial cue at EC, supplied to CA3 along the direct PP route, the
network was able to retrieve this new pattern successfully. This final

set of local simulations therefore again demonstrated that, in principle, the dual input theory of Treves & Rolls is valid for the learning and retrieval of binary patterns.

WHOLE SYSTEM

Having conducted these local analyses, the next set of implementations looked at the whole network, from encoding of new patterns along the EC–DG–CA3 route, to storage in CA3, to retrieval along the EC–CA3 direct PP projection.

Encoding: orthogonality versus sparseness

These simulations focused on the encoding of new patterns. In particular, they examined the assumed role of DG in producing a sparse and mutually orthogonal set of patterns on the CA3 cells through the implementation of the bisynaptic EC–DG–CA3 input pathway. The connectivity, weights and other parameter settings were again dictated by neurobiological plausibility and/or reasonable supposition, and the values were closely related to those used in the local simulations presented above (see Table 10.2).

In these full system simulations, only ten binary activity patterns were initially presented to the network and, after EC–DG–CA3 processing had taken place, the CA3 representation of each pattern was measured in terms of the value of the vector cosine measure relative to the other patterns. The CA3 patterns of activity were also related to the DG threshold, which was varied across different simulations. Furthermore, the ability of DG processing to orthogonalize the separate EC patterns was further evaluated by presenting two different sets of inputs to the network, one having little cross-correlation between the individual members of the EC pattern set ("highly sparse") and another that showed high pattern intercorrelations ("less sparse").

The finding of these simulations demonstrated that DG processing did indeed produce orthogonal representations on the CA3 cells, irrespective of the initial level of intercorrelations of the EC input patterns. However, our findings indicated that the restricted connectivity between DG and CA3 cells alone was not sufficient for distinctive CA3 representations to be produced. An additional condition appeared to be the requirement that the DG cells were carefully thresholded. Specifically, by setting the threshold of the DG cells to a value of approximately 0.25, the subsequent representations of the original EC patterns at CA3 became sparse and mutually orthogonal (Fig. 10.10).

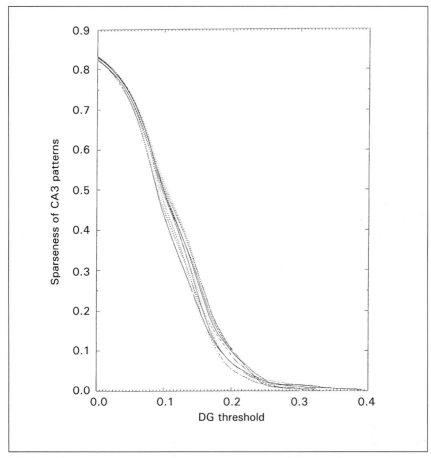

FIG. 10.10. Sparseness of CA3 patterns produced by the propagation of 10 EC patterns of average intercorrelation 0.8. Note that as the DG threshold approaches a value of 0.25, the patterns reach an acceptable level of sparseness. Beyond this level of activity threshold, sparseness tends towards zero as fewer and fewer units are active in each pattern at DG.

Storage and retrieval of continuous patterns

Having adequately encoded orthogonal continuous patterns (with appropriate DG thresholding) at CA3, the ability of the network to retrieve these continuous patterns to a partial cue was then examined.

In this next set of simulations, the network parameters were once more dictated by a combination of the Treves & Rolls stated values, biological plausibility and reasonable assumptions, together with the findings of the EC–DG–CA3 encoding simulations just reported (see Table 10.3). Thus, the DG threshold was set to its previously determined optimal value of 0.25, thereby producing sparse and orthogonal representations of each input pattern on the CA3 cells. Having set the network parameters, ten input patterns were again sequentially presented to the EC cells. For each EC pattern, the resulting CA3 representation, after EC–DG–CA3 processing, was stored on the RC weights of the CA3 cells and on the direct PP projection from EC.

The retrieval of a pattern consisted of presenting to the network a fragment of a previously presented EC input pattern and then allowing CA3 to iterate until it converged to a stable state. Cues were again generated utilizing a function that randomly changed an active EC unit from the original EC pattern into an inactive one. This process continued until the required 30% of the original pattern remained, in accordance with Marr's criterion of realistic cue size. Once generated, the cue was presented to the network via the direct PP projection. The CA3 network was then permitted to cycle until it settled into a basin of attraction. The contribution of the direct PP fragment completion to the retrieval cue was included during iteration. Correct retrieval was again determined by computing the final correlation of the retrieved CA3 pattern with that which had been originally encoded and stored at CA3. In these full system correlations, the criterion of correct retrieval for the cosine vector measure was set, slightly more liberally than in the separate systems analyses, to a value of 0.8 (corresponding to a pattern similarity of approximately 64%).

As found in the local simulations, the findings obtained with the whole system demonstrated that few of the stored continuous CA3 patterns could be consistently retrieved from the network. Indeed, despite fine-tuning of the network parameters, the maximum overall level of retrieval was of the order of 45%. Furthermore, increasing the size of the cue from 30% to 50% of the original pattern did not improve the overall performance of the network, even though some of the individual patterns did seem to be retrieved slightly better. Nor did modifying other network parameters significantly improve performance. For example, the performance of the network declined appreciably from 45% when the value of the inhibition term, k, was altered from its optimal value. Even a small step in either numerical direction through the parameter space had a deleterious effect upon performance.

DISCUSSION

Implementation of the Treves & Rolls formulation of hippocampal memory functioning produced a somewhat heterogeneous collection of findings. Support was obtained for certain components of the model, but a number of weaknesses were also discovered. These flaws in the model were apparent despite the fact that the learning and retrieval algorithms that were implemented were chosen to be favourable towards the Treves & Rolls formulation. Several salient points were raised by these simulations. Most notably, when implemented, the network was consistently unable to retrieve biologically feasible continuous patterns, thus casting doubt upon the neurobiological validity of the Treves & Rolls formulation. This was a somewhat surprising finding, given the model's stated goal of embodying considerable anatomical and physiological realism. Moreover, it was apparent that there was somewhat imprecise specification of key parameters in the Treves & Rolls framework, rendering explicit testing problematic. The network was also extremely sensitive to the values of principal variables, such that divergence from optimal levels caused a precipitous decline in its functional efficiency.

In the encoding phase, fine-tuning the threshold on the DG units enabled the system to perform as prescribed, i.e. orthogonalization of different patterns was achieved through the establishment of sparse representations. Furthermore, it was apparent that a MF-type input was indeed necessary in order to force the CA3 units out of an existing attractor state and learn a new pattern of activity. In addition, during retrieval, if CA3 had been entrained into a binary pattern of activity, a partial binary cue at EC reliably retrieved the appropriate pattern along the direct PP route in a viable manner. In other words, the complete system appeared able to form the requisite mapping between EC and binary patterns of activity represented in CA3 in order to mediate subsequent retrieval.

On a less positive note, only 40–50% retrieval efficiency was achieved by the complete system if neurobiologically plausible continuous patterns of activity were stored in CA3, even if the patterns were proximally cued at CA3 (as in the first of the local simulations). Bearing in mind that the system was taught only 10–20 patterns (a figure well below the capacity predicted by the formal mathematical analyses of such networks; see Treves & Rolls 1991), and that this level of performance was achieved only when the system parameters were highly tuned, a 40–50% success rate would seem to be a disappointing outcome for the Treves–Rolls model. By contrast, Marr's (1969) criteria indicate that, at a conservative estimate, a comparably sized network should be able to store approximately $10^5/400$ separate events successfully, or 250 patterns. This number is over an order of magnitude greater than the largest number of patterns used in the current simulations. Furthermore, the EC–DG–CA3 trisynaptic pathway lies, according to Treves & Rolls, at the very core of the episodic memory system. The performance efficiency of this network would therefore seem to represent a potentially limiting factor on the efficiency of the episodic memory retrieval system as a whole.

The observation that the performance of the system was considerably better using binary rather than comparable continuous patterns is informative, with respect to the issue of where in the system any deficiencies are located. Our findings indicate that the failings of the model are related specifically to the nature of the representations, rather than indicating a fundamental flaw in, for example, the architecture of the Treves & Rolls framework.

Divergence from the optimal, empirically determined values of key parameters (such as the gain and inhibition terms) caused a further decline in the efficiency of the model from the level already stated for continuous patterns. Indeed, with nonoptimal parameter values, the network often would not converge to any stable state during retrieval. The model therefore seemed to be rather "brittle", embodying relatively few degrees of freedom, and requiring very precise tuning in order for it to search the parameter space in an appropriate manner. The network's apparent sensitivity and instability is emphasized when one considers that the findings were similar when a relatively liberal criterion was employed to denote "correct" retrieval (i.e. a critical dot product threshold of 0.8) and when a more stringent (0.9) criterion was applied. Moreover, given the myriad afferent inputs to the hippocampus (only some of which are specified in the Treves–Rolls formulation), it is questionable whether the hippocampus would function in such a finely tuned manner *in vivo*, given its physiologically labile surroundings. An additional point regarding the model's overall level of performance is that the retrieval of a rather limited number of overlearned patterns was tested over multiple independent simulations, with no appreciable differences in the outcome of separate sets of simulations.

From a practical perspective, the somewhat imprecise specification of key parameters of the Treves–Rolls model rendered testing problematic and time-consuming. For example, appropriate values for the DG threshold, gain, inhibitory term and degree of sparseness of the initially encoded pattern were not specified. We were therefore forced to adopt a combined approach of adopting a neurobiologically appropriate range of variables, and exploring the parameter space at great length in order to determine an optimal combination of parameter values.

CONCLUSIONS

We conclude from the results of these simulations that the principal concept underlying the Treves & Rolls formulation appears to be viable, i.e the CA3 region of the hippocampal formation is, under certain circumstances, able to function as an autoassociative memory mechanism, utilizing two distinct input routes. One of these routes is appropriately designated for encoding of new patterns (mossy fibres), while the other is appropriately designated for retrieval (direct perforant path).

However, although the system conditions would seem to have been favourably disposed towards the Treves–Rolls formulation, none of the simulations using neurobiologically plausible continuous patterns produced a high level of performance. Therefore, paradoxically, although the Treves–Rolls formulation is ostensibly a neurobiologically motivated model, its efficiency deteriorated markedly when the biological plausibility of the patterns was increased.

The apparent failure of the system to retrieve biologically valid continuous patterns over multiple independent simulations represents a potentially serious flaw in the Treves & Rolls formulation. Moreover, given the degree of fine-tuning that was required in order for the model to converge to a stable retrieval state for continuous patterns, it seems debatable whether the model can be regarded as a generic memory model. In addition, the heuristic value of the Treves & Rolls framework is weakened by the lack of specific detail concerning the values of key parameters.

The comments made so far are in essence computationally, rather than empirically, motivated. Thus, the findings of these investigations do not represent a critique of the Treves & Rolls model from a directly neuropsychological, neuroanatomical or neurophysiological perspective. Rather, our aim was to test a formal computational model of hippocampal memory function through its implementation. However, the neuroscientific aspects of the Treves & Rolls model must, of course, also be considered in evaluating its overall heuristic utility. For example, the evidence derived from studying the consequences of experimental lesions of the hippocampal formation suggests that the CA1 region may play a more critical role in subserving memory than CA3. Indeed, the work of Len Jarrard and his associates using selective neurotoxic lesions in the rat has indicated that CA3 damage may not, in fact, induce a profound and enduring amnesia (see Jarrard 1986). In addition, the substantial amnesic effects of the intraventricular administration of LTP blocking agents (Lyford et al. 1993) also appears to be consistent with the view that the CA3 region may not be as centrally important as is proposed in the Treves–Rolls framework, given that this technique should render LTP intact in CA3.

A further point to consider when evaluating the Treves & Rolls formulation concerns its implications for the long-term consolidation of memories into neocortex. It appears to follow both from the core version of the Treves & Rolls framework (implemented here), and more complex versions (in which the CA1 region of the hippocampus is cited as a relay for information flow back to neocortical regions) that a particular CA3 representation will not be transformed into a long-term memory of an event unless a critical condition is satisfied; namely, that the representation is re-accessed ("remembered") within the critical time period during which patterns are held in the hippocampus. Re-accessing of the information is deemed necessary in order to activate the neocortical modules that originally represented the episode, thus setting in motion the sequence of events that culminate in true long-term storage. If this condition is not satisfied, the representation of the episode in CA3 will ultimately be overwritten by new input patterns, and thus lost irretrievably from storage. This hypothesis is potentially testable, but would seem, *prima facie*, to be questionable on psychological grounds.

Finally, the apparent realism of the Treves & Rolls formulation seems, as with other such models, to embody both its essential strengths and weaknesses. As stated by Sejnowski et al. (1988): "as the model is made increasingly realistic by adding more variables and more parameters, the danger is that the simulation ends up as poorly understood as the nervous system itself". In accordance with this assertion, the reasons underlying the failure of the network consistently to retrieve continuous patterns are somewhat nebulous because of the size of the multidimensional parameter space in which the simulations were executed.

FUTURE DIRECTIONS

In the future, further searches of the parameter space may permit elucidation of the critical obstacles to efficient performance with continuous patterns in the implementation of the Treves & Rolls formulation. It may also prove of benefit in future to incorporate supplementary components and/or mechanisms into the network; for example, the CA3 output to CA1 has been espoused by some theorists (O'Reilly & McClelland 1994). Furthermore, as noted, data from the empirical lesion literature would seem to implicate the CA1 region more than the CA3 subfield in the mediation of episodic memory.

Additional questions that need to be addressed more explicitly in future mathematical models of hippocampal functioning concern the issues of timing, sequencing and switching. For example, which mechanism/s is/are responsible for the synchronization of inputs from DG and along the direct PP route, in order that an appropriate mapping is effected between EC and CA3? Perhaps the most significant question concerns the mechanism that is responsible for switching off the MF input during retrieval, thus preventing the cue being encoded as a novel pattern in its own right. Once the fundamental computational memory mechanisms have been established, further simulations should aim to increase the size of the networks in order to model with greater biological realism the anatomy and physiology of the hippocampus.

REFERENCES

Amaral, D. G., N. Ishizuka, B. Claiborne 1990. Neurons, numbers and the hippocampal network. *Progress in Brain Research* **83**, 1–11.

Baudry, M. & J. L. Davis 1991. *Long-term potentiation: a debate of the current issues*. Cambridge, Mass.: MIT Press.

Brown, T. H., E. W. Kairiss, C. L. Keenan 1990. Hebbian synapses: biophysical mechanisms and algorithms. *Annual Review of Neuroscience* **13**, 475–511.

Churchland, P. S. & T. J. Sejnowski 1992. *The computational brain*. Cambridge, Mass.: MIT Press.

Cohen, N. J. & L. R. Squire 1980. Preserved learning and retention of pattern analysing skills in amnesia: dissociation of knowing how and knowing that. *Science* **210**, 207–9.

Fodor, J. 1983. *The modularity of mind*. Cambridge, Mass: MIT Press.

Hebb, D. O. 1949. *The organization of behavior*. New York: John Wiley.

Hopfield, J. 1982. Neural networks and physical systems with emergent collective computational abilities. *Proceedings of the National Academy of Sciences USA* **81**, 3088–92.

Hopfield, J. & D. Tank 1985. "Neural" computation of decisions in optimization problems. *Biological Cybernetics* **52**, 141–52.

Jarrard, L. 1986. Selective hippocampal lesions and behaviour: implications for current research and theorizing. In *The hippocampus*, K. Pribram & R. Isaacson (eds) vol. 4, 93–122. New York: Plenum Press.

Kohonen, T. 1972. Correlation matrix memories. *IEEE Trans. Comp.*, **C–21**, 353–9.

Kohonen, T. 1988. *Self organization and associative memory*. Berlin: Springer-Verlag.

Lyford, G. L., S. A. Gutnikov, A. M. Clark, J. N. P. Rawlins 1993. Determinants of non-spatial working memory deficits in rats given intraventricular infusions of the NMDA antagonist AP5. *Neuropsychologia* **31**, 1079–98.

MacKinnon, D. & L. R. Squire 1989. Autobiographical memory in amnesia. *Psychobiology* **17**, 247–56.

McNaughton, B. L. 1989. Neuronal mechanism for spatial computation and information storage. In *Neural connections, mental computations*, L. Nadel, A. Cooper, P. Culicover, R. Harnish (eds). Cambridge, Mass: MIT Press.

Marr, D. 1969. A theory for cerebral cortex. *Journal of Physiology London*, **202**, 437–70.

Marr, D. 1970. A theory for cerebral neocortex. *Proceedings of the Royal Society of London, B* **176**, 161–234.

Marr, D. 1971. Simple memory: a theory for archicortex. *Philosophical Transactions of the Royal Society of London, B* **262**, 24–81.

Marr, D. 1982. *Vision*. New York: W. H. Freeman.

Morris, R. G. M., E. R. Kandel, L. R. Squire 1988. The neuroscience of learning and memory: cells, neural circuits and behaviour. *Trends in Neuroscience* **11**, 125–7.

O'Reilly, R. C. & J. L. McClelland 1994. Hippocampal conjunctive encoding, storage and recall: avoiding a tradeoff. Parallel distributed processing and cognitive neuroscience technical report PDP.CNS.94.4. Pittsburgh: Carnegie Mellon University.

Rolls, E. T. 1989a. Functions of neural networks in the hippocampus and neo-cortex in memory. In *Neural models of plasticity*, J. H. Byrne & W. O. Berry (eds), 240–65. San Diego, California: Academic Press.

Rolls, E. T. 1989b. The representation and storage of information in neural networks in the primate cerebral cortex and hippocampus. In *The computing neuron*, R. Durbin, C. Miall, G. Mitchison (eds), 125–59. Wokingham: Addison-Wesley.

Rolls, E. T. 1990. Functions of the primate hippocampus in spatial processing and memory. In *Neurobiology of comparative cognition*, D. S. Olton & R. P. Kesner (eds), 339–62. Hillsdale, N. J.: Erlbaum.

Schmajuk, E. L. & J. W. Moore 1988. The hippocampus and the classically conditioned nictitating membrane response: a real time attentional-associative model. *Physiobiology* **16**, 20–35.

Sclabassi, R. J., J. L. Eriksson, R. L. Port, G. B. Robinson, T. W. Berger 1988. Non-linear systems analysis of the hippocampal perforant path-dentate projection. I. Theoretical and interpretational considerations. *Journal of Neurophysiology* **60**, 1066–76.

Scoville, W. B. & B. Milner 1957. Loss of recent memory after bilateral hippocampus lesions. *Journal of Neurology, Neurosurgery and Psychiatry* **20**, 11–21.

Sejnowski, T. J., C. Koch, P. S. Churchland 1988. Computational neuroscience. *Science* **241**, 1299–306.

Sejnowski, T. J. & G. Tesauro 1989. The Hebb rule for synaptic plasticity: algorithms and implementations. In *Neural models of plasticity: experimental and theoretical approaches*, J. H. Byrne & W. O. Berry (eds), 94–103. San Diego, Calif.: Academic Press.

Squire, L. R. 1992. Memory and the hippocampus: a synthesis from findings with rats, monkeys and humans. *Psychological Review* **99**, 195–231.

Squire, L. R. & N. Butters 1992. *Neuropsychology of memory*. 2nd edn. New York: Guilford Press.

Treves, A. 1990. Graded-response neurons and information encoding in autoassociative memories. *Physiological Review, A* **42**, 2418–30.

Treves, A. & E. T. Rolls 1991. What determines the capacity of the auto-associative memories in the brain? *Network* **2**, 371–97.

Treves, A. & E. T. Rolls 1992. Computational constraints suggest the need for two distinct input systems to the hippocampal CA3 network. *Hippocampus* **2**, 189–99.

Willshaw, D. J., O. P. Buneman, H. C. Longuet-Higgins 1969. Non-holographic associative memory. *Nature* **222**, 960–962.

Zalutsky, R. A. & R. A. Nicoll 1990. Comparison of two forms of long-term potentiation in single hippocampal neurons. *Science* **248**, 1619–24.

Zola-Morgan, S. & L. R. Squire 1990. The primate hippocampal formation: evidence for a time-limited role in memory storage. *Science* **250**, 288–9.

ACKNOWLEDGEMENTS

This work was conducted as part of the research requirement of the MSc in Cognitive Science in the University of Manchester (John Ainsworth and Peyman Faratin). Preliminary findings were presented at the London meeting of the Experimental Psychology Society in January 1994. We are grateful to Nick Rawlins for his comments on the empirical evidence regarding the roles of the CA1/CA3 cell fields in memory.

PART SIX
Models of age-related changes in memory

CHAPTER ELEVEN

Memory aging as frontal lobe dysfunction

Tim Perfect

INTRODUCTION

> There is a striking similarity between the functional deficits seen in frontal lobe syndrome and those seen in normal aging. (Veroff 1980: 260).

> Because there is also evidence that the prefrontal cortex may be particularly vulnerable to the effects of aging, the implication is that "normal" aging is associated with cognitive impairments that are essentially the same as, though milder than, those seen in patients with frontal lobe lesions. (Craik et al. 1990: 149).

There is considerable current interest in the idea that the cognitive changes that can be observed in old age are the same as those observed in frontal lobe patients. The aim of this chapter is straightforward; it is to examine the parallels between the deficits in memory performance that accompany old age with the deficits that are due to frontal lobe damage. The model under consideration is that of memory aging as dysexecutive syndrome (Baddeley & Wilson 1988) or working-with-memory deficit (Moscovitch & Winocur 1992). For the remainder of this chapter I will refer to the model as the MAAFLD (memory aging as frontal lobe dysfunction) model.

There are distinctions that can be made as to exactly how much correspondence to expect between aging and frontal lobe impairment. The strongest possible version of the MAAFLD model is that the two are one and the same, i.e. that memory aging can be fully understood as a deterioration in frontal lobe functioning, and the deficits seen in older adults are precisely those found in frontal patients, with no other deficits apparent. However there are weaker versions of the model that offer theoretical mileage to the MAAFLD model: older adults may show greater deficits on frontal than nonfrontal cognitive tests or they may show deficits on particular subsets of frontal tests that are greater than their deficits on nonfrontal tests. It is the relative deficits of frontal and nonfrontal tests that are crucial if the MAAFLD model is to be of value; showing that older adults are poorer than younger adults at frontal tests is not enough, since this may be only a part of a general cognitive decline. There is an ongoing debate in the cognitive gerontological literature concerned with the issue of global and local theories of aging and the means for distinguishing between them (e.g. see articles by Cerella 1994, Fisk & Fisher 1994, Myerson et al. 1994, Perfect et al. 1994 in a recent special issue of the *Journal of Gerontology*). Local models are those that propose specific cognitive deficits that arise during the process of aging (e.g. a retrieval deficit), whilst global models propose that all cognitive processes are equally affected by age (e.g. all processes become slower). If the MAAFLD model is to be advanced as the latest global model of cognitive aging, it will need to be able to deal with the criticisms aimed at previous global models such as speed or processing resources. This chapter is dedicated to evaluating the current status of the MAAFLD model with particular attention to this issue.

The remainder of the chapter will focus on the range of memory functions that have been associated with the frontal lobes. The first section will examine the performance of older adults on clinical tests of frontal functioning, and the section that follows will examine aspects of memory performance in cognitive tests that have been associated with frontal functioning. The aim through these two sections will be to see whether a clear "frontal" pattern of performance by older adults emerges. The final section of the chapter will discuss the status of the MAAFLD model as a global model of cognitive aging. In order to help the reader through the wide range of evidence, an overview of the tests that will be reviewed is given in Table 11.1. The taxonomy of the tests is not definitive, mainly because many of the tests used can be conceptualized in many ways: for instance, successful word fluency performance involves planning or strategy use in order to generate candidate items, suppression of inappropriate responses, avoidance of perseveration (repetition of items already produced) and so forth. However, it does

TABLE 11.1
A taxonomy of frontal lobe tasks, loosely based upon Daigneault et al. (1992).

Task	Requirements of task
Planning sequencing	
Self-ordered pointing/ sequential programming of motor functions	The planning, coordination and execution of sequences of motor responses
Finger tapping	Speed of finger tapping; designed to test co-ordination of motor control
Self-regulation of behaviour / suppression of interference	
Wisconsin Card Sort	Alternation between sorting strategies for sets of cards
Porteus Mazes	Discovery of a route through a maze, without repetition of errors
The Stroop test	Naming of ink colours whilst suppressing colour word names
Brown–Peterson	Recall of trigrams, following interference. This involves suppression of responses to previous trials
Fluency	
Verbal fluency	Time-constrained generation of verbal responses to specified word association cues
Design fluency	Time-constrained generation of pictorial responses to specified cues
Alternative uses	Time-constrained generation of alternative uses for common objects
Spatiotemporal segmentation and organization of events	
Recency judgments	Judgment of which of two memory items was encountered most recently
Contextual judgments	Judgments of the context (e.g. which list, which room) in which an item was encountered
Source monitoring	Judgments of the source of an event (e.g. which of two people, which modality)
Visuospatial integration	Segmentation of visuospatial performance

give a flavour of how researchers have sought to operationalize frontal test performance.

THE PERFORMANCE OF OLDER ADULTS ON CLINICAL TESTS OF FRONTAL FUNCTIONING

Before discussing the literature on cognitive aging and frontal lobe functioning, it is perhaps worth briefly mentioning why there is reason to expect that frontal lobe functioning in particular declines with age.

Ivy et al. 1992 recently reviewed the neurophysiological changes that occur in old age and reported that the most marked atrophy of tissue loss observed in the human brain is in the frontal cortex, and that the greatest decreases in neuron density are in the frontal and temporal lobes, with up to 50% decrease across the adult lifespan. Therefore there is good reason to expect that the greatest age-related deficits should be in those behaviours subsumed by the frontal lobes in particular.

Perhaps the most obvious prediction of the MAAFLD model is that neuropsychological tests that have been shown to be sensitive to frontal damage should be age-sensitive also. However, as mentioned above, in order to support the MAAFLD model, one needs to demonstrate that frontal measures are more age-sensitive than nonfrontal measures of performance. While there have been several studies that have assessed the performance of older adults on frontal measures, surprisingly few have contrasted frontal and nonfrontal measures. One paper that does explicitly include both types of measures is that by Whelihan & Lesher (1985). They tested young-old adults (60–70 years) and separate groups of normal and cognitively impaired old-old adults (76–92 yrs) on a battery of frontal (Wisconsin Card Sort, the Stroop test, verbal fluency, visuospatial integration, Wechsler Adult Intelligence Scale (WAIS) similarities, sequential programming of motor function and finger tapping) and nonfrontal measures of cognitive performance. For the normal elderly, all frontal and some nonfrontal tests showed decline with age. A comparison amongst the two old-old groups showed that with cognitive impairment, there were declines on both frontal and nonfrontal tests. Unfortunately, however, this paper did not report any estimates of effect size, relying instead on the pattern of significant and nonsignificant differences across the two test domains in order to draw conclusions. It may be the case that the nonfrontal tests failed to give effects because of floor or ceiling effects. Also left open is the extent to which the tests presented in the paper do indeed neatly fall into frontal and nonfrontal tests as the authors argue, since no factor analysis techniques were used to justify the split between the two categories of test.

Daigneault et al. (1992) tested young (20–35 years) and older (45–65 years) adults on a battery of frontal tests (Wisconsin Card Sort, self-ordered pointing, Porteus Mazes, a word association test, verbal and design fluency, and Stroop interference). They examined perseverative and nonperseverative performance separately. For perseverative errors, they found age-related declines in all tests bar word associations and Stroop. For nonperseverative errors, they found age-related declines on all tests bar word associations and design fluency. They conclude that their data support the notion of an age-related decrease in the ability to "regulate behavior on the basis of plans, abstract concepts, environmental feedback or one's own responses" (Daigneault et al. 1992: 99). However, since they include no nonfrontal tests in their battery, it is hard to know what to conclude regarding the MAAFLD model.

Using a different frontal battery (Wisconsin Card Sort, Stroop, Brown–Peterson and the FAS test) Brauer Boone et al. (1990) found only moderate age-related declines in a sample of healthy adults (50–80 years). For the Wisconsin Card Sort test, there was no significant age decline overall, although there were declines on number of categories achieved and total errors that were due to the oldest age group. Interestingly the significant differences on the Stroop test were on the speeded reading, and colour-naming sections, but not in the interference condition. There were no age effects at all on the Brown-Peterson task or the FAS fluency task. Thus these data do not confirm the pattern reported above. However, Daigneault et al. (1992) have argued, that for the Wisconsin Card Sort test at least, on the basis of their data, the youngest group in the Brauer Boone et al. study might have declined already. Whilst this is a possibility, it does not explain why decline does not continue after 50, and it does not offer the MAAFLD model much support given the neurophysiological decline that is supposed to occur after 50 years of age. It also does not account for the data from an earlier study by Haaland et al. (1987). The latter studied Wisconsin Card Sort performance in a group of young controls (17–25 years) as well as in four groups of healthy elderly (64–69, 70–74, 75–79, 80–87 years). Only two measures of performance showed age-related declines: the number of categories achieved, and the total number of errors. *Post hoc* tests indicated that the declines were only significant for the oldest sample (80+). Thus the pattern of findings in this study is almost exactly the same as in Brauer Boone et al. (1990).

Parkin & Walter (1991) examined the performance of young (mean age 33.9 years) and old (mean age 80.0 years) subjects on the Brown–Peterson task, and related this to their performance on frontal tests of Wisconsin Card Sort test performance and verbal fluency (FAS test). They found that the older group were poorer at the Brown–Peterson memory task and both "frontal" tests. They also found that for the old group, once IQ had been partialled out, both FAS fluency, and Wisconsin total errors, and nonperseverative errors (but interestingly not perseverative errors) correlated with Brown–Peterson performance. On the basis of their data the authors conclude: "A significant aspect of age-related memory loss arises through atrophy of the frontal lobes" (Parkin & Walter 1991: 178). However, once again, no nonfrontal tests were included as a test of global decline.

Therefore the evidence regarding the performance of older adults on frontal test batteries is suggestive, though not compelling. There is evidence that older adults have problems with tests of frontal lobe functioning, but it is by no means a clear picture. Only one study directly compares frontal and nonfrontal tests in older adults, and whilst this is consistent with the MAAFLD model, the split between frontal and nonfrontal tests is not justified by any analytic process. The remainder of the studies looking at performance on a battery of tests have only examined frontal test performance, and these have revealed a complex pattern, with different studies showing different declines, on different tests, starting at different ages. It remains to be convincingly demonstrated that these problems are in excess of a global decline.

THE PERFORMANCE OF OLDER ADULTS ON COGNITIVE TESTS ASSOCIATED WITH THE FRONTAL LOBES

Recall versus recognition

There is a good deal of evidence that frontal lobe patients are impaired at free recall tasks, in contrast to relatively preserved recognition memory performance[1]. It is thought that this reflects a lack of recall strategies, or lack of spontaneous use of retrieval cues by frontal lobe patients (see Stuss et al. 1994, for a review). For example Jetter et al. (1986) studied the performance of frontal and nonfrontal patients on free and cued recall and recognition for categorized word lists. They found that the two groups were matched on cued recall and recognition, but the frontal group were poorer at free recall after one day. The authors argued that the cued recall and recognition data suggests that the frontal patients encode the information normally, and so they have a particular retrieval deficit associated with the generation of suitable retrieval cues. This idea was supported by the finding that the frontal patients recalled words from fewer semantic categories. One further possibility is that the frontal lobe patients are simply more "impaired" than the nonfrontal group, and so their deficit emerges on the "difficult" memory test of free recall. Two recent case studies have directly examined this issue, by using the Calev (1984) procedure that matches the difficulty of recall and recognition. Hanley, Davies et al. (1994) report a case study of a patient who presented with a frontal syndrome following an anterior communicating artery aneurysm. This patient showed severe recall deficits but normal recognition performance on recall and recognition tests that control subjects find equally difficult. Parkin et al. (1994) report a similar case; however, whilst their patient showed the same pattern as the patient of Hanley et al. (impaired free recall coupled with normal recognition memory performance with forced choice recognition tests), he also showed marked recognition memory impairment when sequential item-by-item Yes/No recognition was used. Parkin et al. (1994) suggest that the patient relies more on familiarity-based judgments of prior occurrence, rather than on recollection of the original experience, and further that this only allows judgments of relative familiarity. Thus the implication that follows from consideration of frontal lobe patients, with some exceptions, is that frontal lobe damage impairs free recall, and the recollective aspects of recognition memory, but leaves familiarity based recognition unimpaired. The Parkin et al. (1994) data suggest that this familiarity process only allows for relative judgments across items.

The relative impairment of recall performance in contrast to recognition performance in old age is regarded as one of the "classic" patterns of memory aging. Almost all studies comparing the two tests have shown this difference; for a review of this area, see Craik (1977) or Craik & Jennings (1992). There is good evidence that this recall–recognition distinction is more than a mere scaling artifact. For example, Craik & McDowd (1987) compared cued recall and recognition performance in a divided attention paradigm. Subjects were presented with a list of 12 phrase–word pairs (e.g. *A body of water–pond*) and then tested either by recall of the target from the phrase cue or recognition of the cue–target pair presented on headphones, whilst at the same time performing a visual reaction time secondary task. Two aspects of this data are noteworthy. First, they found that older adults were worse than the young at cued recall, but were as good as the young at recognition, even though for both age groups cued recall performance was higher than recognition performance, in contrast to the normal pattern. Thus this represents an age deficit in retrieval that cannot be explained in terms of task difficulty and strongly supports the notion of a particular retrieval deficit in old age. Secondly they showed that cued recall causes disproportionately more slowing on a secondary task than recognition for old compared to young subjects. The effect of the memory task on secondary task performance was examined by looking at the proportional increase over baseline visual response time. There was a significant interaction between test type and age, indicating that recall was proportionately a more effortful task for older subjects than it was for younger subjects. Thus, for cued recall but not for recognition, the old were impaired in comparison to the young both in terms of how many items were remembered, and how resource-demanding the memory task was. Converging evidence that the frontal lobes are associated with a particular retrieval deficit in the elderly comes from Parkin & Lawrence (1994) who have shown that the discrepancy between recall and recognition performance in a sample of older adults is predicted by Wisconsin Card Sort errors, although not by measures of fluency.

However, there is good evidence that recognition memory performance is also affected negatively by increased age. Parkin & Walter (1992) have suggested that while recognition memory in older people may not be quantitatively very different from that in younger adults, qualitatively, however, older adults perform very differently. Parkin & Walter utilized the procedure pioneered by Tulving (1985) in which subjects are asked about the nature of recollective experience for those items they claim to recognize. Subjects are asked to say whether they actually recollect an item's prior occurrence (an R response) or whether they merely find it familiar, or know it was presented earlier, without recollecting specific details (a K response). Parkin & Walter found that if older adults are asked about how they recognize an item as old, compared to young subjects, they report many fewer occasions of recollective experience and many more occasions on which they find an item familiar only. This pattern has been replicated in more recent work by Perfect et al. (1995). More intriguingly for present purposes, Parkin & Walter (1992) show that the likelihood of an older individual reporting recollective experience is correlated with measures of their frontal functioning, as measured by performance on the Wisconsin Card Sort task, although not verbal fluency. Interestingly both Parkin & Walter (1992) and Perfect et al. (1995) tested their elderly subjects using parallel presentation of the test items. If we remember that Parkin et al. (1994) reported that a patient with frontal impairments showed normal recognition with parallel presentation and impaired recognition with sequential (Yes/No) presentation, then an intriguing possibility arises: perhaps the pattern reported by Parkin & Walter (1992) and Perfect et al. (1995) for older adults only holds for a particular form of recognition test.

Thus we see that in terms of relative impairment on recall and recognition, older adults appear similar to frontal patients. Further, this relative impairment for older adults is more than a scaling effect, since it emerges when recall exceeds recognition, and the difference between recall and recognition is predicted by tests sensitive to frontal functioning. Finally for recognition, while there is evidence that older adults perform reasonably well, there is a suggestion that the quality of their recollective experience is impaired, and the degree of impairment is associated with frontal functioning.

Memory for source

There have been several demonstrations that frontal lobe patients are impaired at making judgments of source. For example, Janowsky et al. (1989a) presented frontal patients and control subjects with general knowledge questions (e.g. "What is the body of water that lies between Russia and Iran?"). If subjects failed to answer, they were told the answer by the experimenter. This continued until each subject had been presented with the answers to 20 questions they had originally not been able to answer. After a delay of 6–8 days, subjects were retested, and asked to make source judgments about the items (i.e. subjects were asked where they had most recently learned the information). Frontal patients made many more source errors than either young or old control subjects, despite matched memory performance for the target facts. In a second experiment, the subjects were presented with the facts incidentally, as part of a categorization task, and tested after a 10-minute delay. Once again, frontal lobe patients showed higher levels of source-monitoring errors, although this time they did not differ from the elderly group, who were (marginally) significantly worse than the young group. Similarly, patient ROB of Hanley et al. (1994) showed source-monitoring performance to be essentially at chance when asked to distinguish which of two sources (one man, one woman) spoke a target sentence. ROB also showed lower levels of target recall than a group of control subjects, but when contextual judgments were conditionalized on correct recall, ROB remained at chance, whilst control subjects achieved 71%.

Older adults have been reported as being impaired at memory for source: Schacter et al. (1991) reported a study in which young and older subjects were presented with novel trivial pieces of information (e.g. "Bob Hope's father was a policeman") by one of two people. Even when performance for cued fact recall was matched across age, older subjects were poorer at identifying the source of the memory when the information was blocked. This replicated the pattern of findings by McIntyre & Craik (1987) in a nonmatched situation (i.e. older adults showed deficits in fact recall and source memory). There was a complication, however, in that the elderly did not show a disproportionate deficit when the source of the information was random. Older adults have also been shown to be poorer than young subjects at deciding the sex of a speaker (for verbal presentation) or whether a word was in capitals or small letters (Kausler & Puckett 1980, 1981). They are also more susceptible to the false-fame effect, in which they misattribute experimental familiarity with a name to celebrity status, indicating faulty source monitoring (Dwyan & Jacoby, 1990). Craik et al. (1990) found that the degree of source amnesia in an elderly sample was correlated significantly with the number of perseverative (but not nonperseverative) errors on the Wisconsin Card Sort test, and with verbal fluency, both of which are tests of frontal functioning.

Spencer & Raz (1994) studied the performance of young and older adults on fact memory, source monitoring (proportion of correctly recalled facts that were correctly attributed to source), source familiarity (proportion of correct source attributions irrespective of target status), and context (number of correct descriptions of which room, which set of cards or the colour of the stimuli) over a period of 8 weeks. The results indicate that the rate of loss of source memory and contextual details was accelerated in the older group. Spencer & Raz (1994: 155) concluded "Unlike time-dependent decay of factual memory, which is observed in young and old people, the tendency to forget the source even when the fact is retained may be a specific feature of cognitive aging." However, Spencer & Raz did not find evidence that this loss of source and context was associated with frontal lobe functioning in the older group. They argue that perhaps the measures of frontal function used, whist being suitable for neuropsychological assessment, are not optimal for healthy older adults.

Not all studies have reported an age decrement in source monitoring however: Denney & Larsen (1994) argue that older adults do not have a particular problem in encoding context. Instead they favour the explanation that older adults have a general encoding deficit that undermines performance for target and contextual information. They compared two conditions in which older and younger subjects were presented with words superimposed on a background of cityscapes. In one condition subjects were told only to study the words, and in the other they were instructed to remember the word–picture pairs. All subjects were tested for the word–city pairs using recognition, with distractors made up of novel pairs, a novel item with an old item, and two old items that were previously not paired. Denney & Larsen (1994) found that older adults were poorer at recognizing old items, more likely to make false-positives, and there was an interaction of age and distractor type, indicating that older adults were more prepared to accept novel pairings if the items had appeared before individually. However, crucially, there was no age interaction with encoding conditions. If anything, the age difference on memory for the cityscapes was greater under deliberate study conditions, contrary to the view that older adults suffer from a contextual memory deficit. On this basis Denney & Larsen concluded that older adults have a problem in remembering connections between items, whether or not those items are target or context, and this represents a general episodic memory deficit rather than a specific contextual encoding deficit. That is they argue that there is a general memory problem in old age, not just a problem in associating a particular target with the context in which it was encountered.

It is hard to know what to make of the above paper. There is a confound between deliberate and incidental study conditions, and whether the cityscape was target or context. One could argue that the data show that older adults do not benefit as much from deliberate study as younger adults, rather than focus on the issue of target versus context.

This would not be an entirely novel point: White (cited in Craik 1977) showed, using the classic levels of processing paradigm, that whereas younger subjects performed best under deliberate study conditions, older subjects performed best under incidental semantic processing conditions, with deliberate study only producing performance at the same level as with incidental rhyme encoding. Further in the Denney & Larsen (1994) study it seems unlikely that subjects in the incidental condition would not have questioned why the words they have been instructed to learn are being superimposed on a cityscape. Nonetheless, the paper does draw attention to an important question: does failure to remember context represent a particular deficit, or is it just part of a global episodic memory deficit? Proponents of the context deficit view would argue that the fact that older adults show impaired performance on context when matched on target information implies a particular deficit. However, there are two arguments against this interpretation. First, it could be that the contextual judgment is simply a more sensitive measure since it is a harder task, and hence it shows a greater age decrement. This is akin to the argument outlined above concerning recall and recognition. What is needed is a demonstration of impaired contextual memory, when absolute level of performance on the two tests (memory for target and context) is matched. However, this is problematic, since to remember the context for an item, one has to remember the item itself. A second possibility is that both target and context memory are impaired with age, but that they are independent memory processes. If this were the case, then demonstrations showing that memory for context is impaired when memory for target is matched are simply showing that it is possible to manipulate performance for target and context independently. It might be possible to show that other factors improve memory for context, but not target; it would then follow that matching for contextual memory would show an impairment for target memory with age. As far as I am aware this idea has never been tested.

Reality monitoring

A particular version of memory for source concerns the distinction between remembering an external event, and remembering an internal event: i.e. distinguishing "real" or perceived events from those that were merely imagined. Johnson et al. (1993) have argued that the confabulations of patients with frontal lobe damage can be understood as impairments of source monitoring. However, as far as I can determine, there has been no laboratory testing of frontal patients on formal tests of reality monitoring. However, there have been a number of studies that have demonstrated older adults are poorer at distinguishing between events that were originally experienced either externally or internally. Cohen & Faulkner (1989) compared young subjects with young-old (60–68 years) and old-old (72–83 years) subjects on their ability to remember whether a particular action (e.g. "Place the book on the table") had been performed by themselves, performed by the experimenter, or had been imagined. While there was no age effect on recognition of the actions, both elderly groups were more prone to making source errors, compared to the young, including reality monitoring errors (confusing what was performed or seen with what was imagined and vice versa), but the errors were greatest for the oldest group. Rabinowitz (1989) compared young and old on their ability to judge whether a word they recognized had previously been read, or generated from a word-stem cue. As with Cohen & Faulkner (1989) older adults were more likely to confuse what they had produced with what they had seen. Hashtroudi et al. (1989) reported a different pattern however. They compared younger and older adults on their ability to discriminate between two classes of internally generated events (items that they spoke themselves, and items they imagined being spoken), and two externally generated events (words being spoken by two experimenters). They found that whilst overall there was an age difference in source monitoring, this was due to the intraclass conditions, in which subjects had to discriminate between two internal, or two external events. Interclass discriminations (which can be classed as reality monitoring errors) did not produce age declines, in contrast to the work described above. However, in none of these studies was there an attempt to correlate the likelihood of this kind of error with any measures of frontal functioning.

Memory for temporal information

Memory for temporal information can be tested in a number of ways. Subjects can be asked to make judgments of recency (of which of two events happened more recently), to reproduce the temporal order of events, or to estimate the frequency of occurrence of particular events. It is claimed that frontal lesions lead to impairments on all these tasks.

Kesner et al. (1994) presented frontal lobe patients and control subjects with lists of six items, which came from a set of 16 possible items. There were four versions of this test: words, spatial locations, abstract shapes, and hand positions. After each presentation, subjects were presented with two items and asked either to decide which had been shown (recognition discrimination between a target and a distractor), or which was shown earliest (temporal judgment between two targets). A total of 24 trials were conducted per test. With the exception of hand positions, there were no deficits for the frontal patients on tests of item recognition, but in contrast, the frontal patients were impaired on all measures of temporal order of presentation. Consistent with this finding, Eslinger & Grattan (1994) reported a study which demonstrated that frontal patients, unlike nonfrontal patients matched on recall, showed no serial position effects in a series of repeated recall tests, again suggesting impairment of temporal (and sequential) information about the items. However, this time, this is manifest not in impaired temporal knowledge for recalled items, but in failure to show the benefit of temporal order for primacy and recency items that can aid recall.

Smith & Milner (1988) studied the ability of frontal patients to make judgments of the frequency of occurrence of events. Subjects were presented with a series of abstract designs that differed in terms of the frequency of presentation. At the end of the list, subjects were asked to judge the frequency of occurrence for each design in a new list, consisting of targets and new distractors. Recognition was assessed by examining the number of false-positives (giving a frequency count to a distractor) and the number of misses (saying "new" to previously presented items) separately. Patients with frontal lobe lesions did not differ from controls on either measure. However, in judgments of frequency of occurrence, the frontal lobe patients were as accurate as normal controls up to frequency 3, but thereafter (frequencies 5, 7 and 9) they were significantly impaired, grossly underestimating frequency each time.

A number of studies have examined the ability of older adults to make judgments of frequency. Contrary to Hasher & Zacks' (1979) assertion that item frequency is encoded automatically, and hence is maintained with increased age, the majority have found age-related impairments. For example, Kausler et al. (1981) presented subjects with lists of words that varied in frequency, under conditions that either involved a secondary task or not and deliberate or incidental encoding of frequency. At the end of the list, subjects had to decide, between pairs of items, which had been presented most often. Whilst there was no main effect of deliberate versus incidental study, supporting the notion of automaticity, there was a main effect of age on frequency judgment, with older subjects (55–86 years) performing more poorly than their younger counterparts (17–27 years), contrary to Hasher & Zacks' (1979) position. Salthouse (1991) reviewed the literature concerning the performance of older adults on tests requiring frequency judgments of items. Of the 14 studies he identified, three found no age differences, whilst 11 found that older adults were impaired at frequency estimation. His review also concluded that there is a similar age related impairment on memory for temporal order, with four studies showing age-related decline, and a further two showing nonsignificant differences in favour of younger adults.

Memory for spatial location

Schacter (1987) argued that frontal impairment leads to impairments of memory for spatial location. However, there is as yet insufficient evidence to support this claim (see Stuss et al. 1994, for a review). Shoquierat & Mayes (1991) found that spatial impairment, although present in a group of mixed aetiology amnesic patients, was unrelated to their level of frontal functioning. However, there is clearer evidence regarding the performance of older adults. For example Puglisi et al. (1985) compared younger (17–30 years) and older (59–80 years) adults on location tasks for objects and words. They reported consistent age deficits on correctly locating items, and on identifying which locations had been used, despite matched recognition for the items (though recall was impaired with age). Salthouse's (1991) review of older adults also examined performance in studies requiring location of items presented in memory tests. As with temporal information he found that most studies found age-related impairment in memory for spatial location, contrary to Hasher & Zacks' (1979) assertion that spatial location is another aspect of automatic encoding that is age-invariant. A recent meta-analysis by Foisy (1994) suggested that the effect of age on intentional memory for spatial location is large, with older adults on average performing 0.81 standard deviations below the mean for younger subjects.

Metamemory

The impairments of metamemory functioning in frontal lobe patients are less clear cut, perhaps reflecting the broadness of the concept. There is evidence that frontal lobe patients are impaired at "feeling-of-knowing" judgments. Janowsky et al. (1989b) found that Korsakoff's amnesics were impaired at predicting their later recognition in a standard recall–judgment–recognition task for episodic information, but they were not impaired at judgments for general knowledge (see Shimamura 1994, for a review). Shallice & Evans (1978) reported that patients with frontal lobe damage are particularly poor at making cognitive estimates based on memory, such as estimating the length of a man's back, or the height of a bus, a test that could be seen as a form of memory monitoring.

There is little evidence that older adults have poorer metamemory functioning than younger adults (see Light 1991, for a review). There is evidence that young and old share beliefs about appropriate strategies (e.g. Loewen et al. 1991), even though they may not always appear to use the same strategies (Light 1991). Older adults are just as accurate as younger ones in making confidence judgments about their memory (Perfect 1989), and in making feeling-of-knowing judgments (e.g. Lachman et al. 1979). Harris-Peterson & Boyd (1991) failed to show a deficit in older adults' cognitive estimates, using an American version of the Shallice & Evans (1978) test, although it must be said that their "older" adults ranged only up to 74 years old. It may be the case that cognitive estimation as a skill only declines in the very elderly. There is also a suggestion that any deficits in metamemory that are observed may be secondary to overall memory performance. Perfect & Stollery (1993) used a paired associate paradigm to test the accuracy of predictive and postdictive judgments of performance over five learning trials. Older adults showed poorer recall across all trials, and were less accurate in their predictions of performance, although just as accurate at postdictions. However, when level of recall was controlled for, the predictions of older adults were just as accurate as the younger group, suggesting that the apparent deficit in predictive accuracy comes from the recall deficit, and is not a separate problem.

This last point is reflected in a recent critique of studies that have attempted to localize metamemory functioning to the frontal lobes. O'Shea et al. (1994: 643) question the sophistication of attempts to separate out executive knowledge of function from the memory functioning itself, suggesting that "this is not unlike the problems attendant upon the diagnosis of apraxia in the presence of a paralyzed limb". They also argue that there is no evidence to support the notion of localization of metamemory functioning to the frontal lobes since the term metamemory has been inappropriately expanded from its initial definition as a theory of one's own memory functioning. As O'Shea et al. (1994: 640–1) point out "the notion of an acquired neurogenic deficit in a theory of the operation of one's own memory function appears to be unreasonable". This seems a convincing argument, given the diversity of functions that have been given the appellation "metamemory": feeling of knowing, judgments of learning, memory search time, recall readiness, responses to cognitive failure questionnaires, and so forth. It is hard to believe that all such functions will be subsumed by the same cognitive module. O'Shea et al. (1994) propose that some of these putative "metamemory" functions are better thought of as executive processes, which may or may not be localized to the frontal lobes. However, at present, perhaps the safest conclusion is that we need to develop a taxonomy of metamemory tasks prior to attempting to localize any of them to particular brain regions.

DISCUSSION

As the above review shows, there is a reasonable degree of overlap between the deficits observed in frontal lobe patients, and the cognitive problems associated with old age. However, it is clear that the strongest version of the MAAFLD model cannot be accepted, although perhaps there is enough evidence to warrant further consideration of a weaker version of the model. At present there are too many inconsistencies between studies for one to put too much faith in any particular experimental result. Perhaps one of the most evident differences between the studies discussed above is the putative "starting age" for decline in frontal functioning. For example Daigneault et al. (1992) reported declines on a range of frontal measures in a group of elderly who ranged between 45 and 65 years old, yet Brauer Boone et al. (1990: 215) tested subjects aged between 50 and 80 years on a similar battery of frontal tests and found "minimal evidence of age difference in frontal lobe abilities". Cohen & Faulkner (1989) found significant declines in reality monitoring only for an old-old group (72–83 years old) but not in a young-old group (60–68 years old) even though this age range represents the upper age range (and beyond) of the Daigneault et al. study. Parkin & Walter (1992) found that the pattern of decreased recollective and increased familiar responses was found for both "middle old" (mean age 67.7 years) and "old–old" (mean age 81.6 years) subjects, although in this study there were age declines on two "frontal" tests (the Wisconsin, and embedded figures), but not on a third (FAS fluency). This in turn contrasts with Harris-Peterson & Boyd (1991) who found no decline in the frontal measure of cognitive estimation ability in a group that ranged up to 74 years. An additional complication for the Parkin & Walter (1992) study was that they found that frontal test performance correlated with likelihood of recollective experience only for the old-old group; the middle-old group showed marked change from the young on recollective experience without corresponding "frontal" correlations.

Proponents of the MAAFLD model might wish to argue that there is no reason to expect that recollective experience should correlate with cognitive estimates, for example. However, to argue this is to accept that the idea of a monolithic age decline in frontal ability, that underlies these separate aspects of age decline in memory performance, cannot be correct. In fact, when faced with the full range of tasks it would be foolish to claim so; however the piecemeal accumulation of studies such as those discussed above has led a number of researchers to claim that their findings of age differences are "frontal". Hence the strong version of the MAAFLD model has begun to take hold, as evidenced by the quotes that started this chapter. Sadly, only when one contrasts the studies directly does one realize that the different authors cannot be talking about the same thing since they disagree with each other. Though the strong version of the MAAFLD model cannot be right, this does not rule out the possibility that the weaker version has value. Most fruitful is likely to be a multicomponential approach to memory and the frontal lobes, in which one can ask questions not about whether all aging is frontal, but ask what aspects of age-related decline can be attributed to what aspects of frontal lobe deterioration. From this point one might expect differential rates of aging across tasks, and differential sensitivity to different "frontal" tests across memory tests. Parkin & Lawrence (1994) have recently made a similar proposal.

> Human memory and frontal lobe functions are both complex entities and it seems unlikely, on intuitive grounds at least, that the relation between them should be unidimensional. More likely both memory and frontal function are multi-componential so that any given memory function might be associated with a particular subset of frontal functions. This idea has not yet received any investigation because there has been little development of frameworks within which an idea of this kind might be expressed. (Parkin & Lawrence 1994: 1524)

Before this can be accepted however, there are two particular issues that deserve consideration: individual differences and global versus local models of aging.

Individual differences

It is well established that variance in performance in most domains increases with increased age (Morse 1993). The majority of the studies cited above have discussed average performance of older adults (and indeed frontal lobe patients). This leaves open the question regarding the extent to which frontal lobe deficits are typical of the entire population; the MAAFLD may be true only for a subset of the population. Conceptually this is similar to the "terminal drop" issue. Riegel & Riegel (1972) retrospectively analyzed data from subjects who did or did not die within 5 years of an original test session. Those who had died in the intervening 5 years had performed significantly poorer than the rest of their cohort in the original test, suggesting that at the original test they were in a period of cognitive decline that ultimately would lead to their death within 5 years. One implication of such a rapid pre-death decline in cognitive performance is that the average performance for a cohort is reduced by the number of its members in the terminal drop phase, and this proportion is likely to increase with increased age of the cohort. More importantly, whilst average performance reduces with age, this does not necessarily imply that healthy (non-terminal-drop) adults are showing the same pattern of performance as the average, and may show less, or no age-related decline. Exactly the same point can be made regarding frontal test performance. A decline in average performance for a population on frontal lobe tests may either reflect the fact that all members of the population are showing frontal decline, or that a sub-population is showing pathological decline, whilst the majority remain at the same levels as their younger age. The fact that variance increases with increased age strongly supports this notion that individuals may "age" at different rates at specific tasks. An acknowledgement of this fact is implicit in studies that correlate neuropsychological assessment of frontal performance with putative frontal lobe functions in cognitive tests. Whilst the data from such studies indicate that variance in performance on source monitoring, for example, can be explained in terms of Wisconsin Card Sort performance, or verbal fluency performance, it does little to answer the critical questions the MAAFLD model needs to answer: do all adults show frontal decline; are all age declines due to frontal lobe decline; do all older adults behave like frontal patients?

Global versus local deficits

Much of the research reported here has been of a confirmatory nature, i.e. researchers have sought to confirm that putative frontal functions decline with age, or in some cases, that certain memory deficits are associated with frontal lobe integrity. However, science does not advance by seeking to confirm a hypothesis, but by seeking to falsify it, and several of the studies cited above have not adequately sought to do this. For example, take the study by Parkin & Walter (1992). They tested recollective experience in a group of older and younger subjects, and sought to test the prediction that recollective experience would be associated with performance on tests of frontal functioning, in particular fluency, embedded figures, and card sort performance. However, what they did not do was check that recollective experience did not correlate with nonfrontal tests of performance, i.e. they did not seek to determine whether the amount of recollective experience in older adults was predicted by tests such as perceptual speed, simple reaction time, or mental rotation. One might argue that they could have disconfirmed their hypothesis regarding frontal lobe function by failing to find a correlation between recollective experience and the frontal tests. However, there are two arguments against this. First, they did fail to find a correlation for fluency, but this was not taken as counter-evidence to the MAAFLD model since other frontal tests did correlate (see below for further discussion of this point). More important, however, is the fact that the most obvious alternative hypothesis to the MAAFLD model is that there are global intellectual declines with age. This would predict that recollective experience would correlate with all age-sensitive cognitive measures, and hence would correlate with all frontal measures. Thus what Parkin & Walter failed to do was to distinguish between the MAAFLD hypothesis, and its most obvious competitor. Before I leave this point, let me stress that this argument by no means applies only to Parkin & Walter (1992). Similar criticisms can be levelled against other studies cited above that correlate neuropsychological tests with cognitive tests of frontal function in older adults (e.g. Schacter et al. 1991).

An insight into the scope of the global memory deficit in aging can be gained from a recent meta-analysis by Verhaeghen et al. (1993). They reviewed evidence for age-related declines on five tasks: speed of STM search, memory span, word-list recall, paired associate recall and prose recall, from a total of 180 studies. Their aim was to determine whether moderator variables such as characteristics of the material, the instructions, or test conditions would alter the age-related change in performance. They found that, despite ubiquitous and large main effects of age that:

> virtually none of the moderator variables associated with the presumed application of memory strategies yielded significant differences in effect size (categorizability in list recall and review possibility in list recall are the sole exceptions). If the decrease in memory proficiency in old age were a question of not spontaneously using strategies, one would expect larger age differences for those conditions under which the use of that particular strategy is less expected. (Verhagen et al. 1993: 167)

There are two points one can make from this. First, one would have to ask whether a "frontal" model of aging would predict the pattern found, given the putative role of the frontal lobes in planning, metacognition and strategy usage (see the earlier section on recall versus recognition). A second point is that any piecemeal consideration of the evidence—simply looking at scanning speed for example—could be used to support a particular local hypothesis. However, when one looks at the broader scope then it is clear that local hypotheses cannot suffice. It is this latter point that the MAAFLD model needs to address; evidence is accumulating that points to parallels between aging and frontal lobe function, but no overview has been achieved to determine whether these patterns are independent examples of a coherent whole, or are merely further examples of global decline.

If one abandons the obsession with frontal lobe tests then it is very easy to find global models that have sought both convergent and divergent evidence. Perhaps the most eminent is Salthouse's neural speed hypothesis. He has argued (e.g. Salthouse 1993, 1994) that the general cognitive deficits of older adults can be understood as being due to basic CNS slowing. To this end he has sought to determine whether age differences on various complex tasks can be removed by partialling out estimates of CNS speed taken from simple independent tests. (For examples see Lindenberger et al. 1993, Salthouse 1993, 1994, Salthouse & Coon 1993, 1994). This is a different enterprise from simply showing a deficit on test X when performance on test Y is matched. This suggests a more rigorous test of the MAAFLD model: neuropsychological tests of frontal function should be used to partial out "frontal" variance in age-related deficits in putative frontal functions. If age differences are removed, then this is stronger support for the MAAFLD model, but if they are not, then there must be more to the decline than simple frontal integrity.

There is one further point that is worthwhile making on the subject of global and local deficits, and that relates to the nature of theory building. To the cognitive gerontologist, burdened with methodological and artifactual explanations for every age-related change, neuropsychological theorizing seems very appealing. Our findings are always open to the criticism that age effects are simply manifestations of social expectations of age-related decline, or some other such factor; it is much more comforting to be able to draw upon biological data to buttress our claims. However, we must be careful not to throw the baby out with the bathwater. A read through the literature on frontal lobe damage and memory performance, gives the impression of an interesting yet relatively disjointed set of knowledge. It is certainly not the case that the memory performance of frontal lobe patients is as well mapped, or as well understood, as that of older adults. It therefore seems slightly odd to explain the performance of the latter in terms of the former. Whilst this buys cognitive gerontologists some biological credentials, it does so at the cost of some precision. Given the range of memory deficits that frontal patients show, it is sometimes hard to know what the MAAFLD model would predict.

The same argument can also be made at the level of tasks; in terms of task decomposition, it is usual to attempt to understand complex tasks in terms of simpler building blocks. Consideration of the range of frontal lobe tests (fluency, planning, attention shifting) would not lead one to describe frontal tests as simple, or even entirely theoretically coherent, and thus it seems slightly strange to attempt to use performance on such tests as tools with which to understand age-related change on other cognitive tasks. Thus, it appears that the endeavour of explaining memory aging as changes in frontal lobe performance, is an attempt to explain a well mapped domain of knowledge with a less well mapped one. No doubt there are benefits, but these seem related to localization rather than theoretical coherence. If one wishes to develop a theory of memory aging related to frontal lobe performance, then one needs a psychologically well founded theory of frontal lobe function.

CONCLUSION

It is not the intention here to outline a theory of frontal lobe functioning: for that the reader is directed to the recent review by Stuss et al. (1994). What I have attempted to do is to give an overview of the growing area of research linking cognitive aging and neuropsychology, applying some of the rigour of the former to the latter. However, the final paragraph of a chapter does seem an appropriate place to consider nailing one's colours to the mast. Is memory aging all frontal? It seems hard to accept this, on current evidence, although it does appear a fruitful avenue of research to pursue. There are certainly some intriguing parallels between frontal lobe patients and older adults that could be more rigorously analyzed. There are also some glaring inconsistencies, and large gaps in knowledge. What is needed is a clearer taxonomy of frontal tasks, and the testing of strong predictions regarding age differences. Too much research to date has lacked the power to rule out frontal explanations of age differences, partly because only correlations with frontal tests have been sought, and partly because the term "frontal" is too loose and offers many hypotheses to test. Perhaps the safest conclusion to make is that which is available to jurors in the Scottish legal system: neither guilty nor not guilty, but case not proven.

NOTE

1. There have been exceptions to this pattern, however. Delbecq-Derousné et al. (1990) report a case of a patient with frontal lobe damage that led to impaired recognition performance with (relatively) intact recall. As well as this pattern, the patient showed many confabulations, very high confidence in his answers (correct and incorrect alike), and a lack of insight into his memory problems. The authors argue that this patient suffers from an impairment in the subjective experience of remembering.

REFERENCES

Baddeley, A. & B. Wilson 1988. Frontal amnesia and the dysexectuive syndrome. *Brain and Cognition* 7, 212–30.
Brauer Boone, K., B. L. Miller, I. M. Lesser, E. Hill, L. D'Elia 1990. Performance

on frontal lobe tests in healthy, older individuals. *Developmental Neuropsychology* **6**, 215–23.

Calev, A. 1984. Recall and recognition in chronic nondemented schizophrenics: use of matched tests. *Journal of Abnormal Psychology* **93**, 172–7.

Cerella, J. 1994. Generalized slowing in Brinley plots. *Journal of Gerontology: Psychological Sciences* **49**, 65–71.

Cohen, G. & D. Faulkner 1989. Age differences in source forgetting: effects of reality monitoring and on eyewitness testimony. *Psychology and Aging* **4**, 10–17.

Craik, F. I. M. 1977. Age differences in human memory. In *Handbook of the psychology of aging*, J. E. Birren & K. W. Schaie (eds) 348–420. New York: Van Nostrand Reinhold.

Craik, F. I. M. & M. Byrd 1982. Age and cognitive deficits: the role of attentional resources. In *Aging and cognitive processes*, F. I. M. Craik & S. E. Trehub (eds), Hillsdale, N. J.: Plenum Press.

Craik, F. I. M. & J. M. Jennings 1992. Human memory. In F. I. M. Craik & T. A. Salthouse (eds). *The Handbook of Aging and Cognition*. Hillsdale, New Jersey: Lawrence Erlbaum Associates.

Craik, F. I. M. & J. M. McDowd 1987. Age differences in recall and recognition. *Journal of Experimental Psychology: Learning, Memory and Cognition* **13**, 474–9.

Craik, F. I. M., L. W. Morris, R. G. Morris, E. R. Loewen 1990. Aging, source amnesia, and frontal lobe functioning. *Psychology and Aging* **5**, 148–51.

Daigneault, S., C. M. J. Braun, H. A. Whitaker 1992. Early effects of normal aging on perseverative and non-perseverative prefrontal measures. *Developmental Neuropsychology* **8**, 99–114.

Delbecq-Derousné, J., M. F. Beauvois, T. Shallice 1990. Preserved recall versus impaired recognition: a case study. *Brain* **113**, 1045–74.

Denney, N. W. & J. E. Larsen 1994. Aging and episodic memory: are elderly adults less likely to make connections between target and contextual information? *Journal of Gerontology: Psychological Sciences* **49**, 270–5.

Dwyan, J. & L. L. Jacoby 1990. Effects of aging on source memory: differences in susceptibility to false fame. *Psychology and Aging* **5**, 379–87.

Eslinger, P. J. & L. M. Grattan 1994. Altered serial position learning after frontal lobe lesion. *Neuropsychologia* **32**, 729–39.

Fisk, A. D. & D. L. Fisher 1994. Brinley plots and theories of aging: the explicit, muddled and implicit debates. *Journal of Gerontology: Psychological Sciences* **49**, 81–9.

Foisy, P. 1994. Age-related deficits in intentional memory for spatial location in small scale space: a meta-analysis and methodological critique. *Canadian Journal on Aging* **13**, 353–67.

Guttentag, R. E. & R. R. Hunt 1988. Adults' age differences in memory for imagined and performed actions. *Journals of Gerontology: Psychological Sciences* **43**, 107–8.

Haaland, K. Y., L. F. Vranes, J. S. Goodwin, P. J. Garry 1987. Wisconsin card sort test performance in a healthy elderly population. *Journal of Gerontology: Psychological Sciences* **42**, 345–46.

Hanley, J. R., A. D. M. D. Davies, J. J. Downes, A. R. Mayes 1994. Impaired recall of verbal material following rupture and repair of an anterior communicating artery aneurysm. *Cognitive Neuropsychology* **11**, 543–78.

Harris-Peterson, M. R. & T. M. Boyd 1991. Cognitive estimation in young adult and elderly subjects. Paper presented at the annual conference of the International Neuropsychological Society, San Antonio, Texas.

Hasher, L. & R. T. Zacks 1979. Automatic and effortful processes in memory. *Journal of Experimental Psychology: General* **108**, 356–88.

Hashtroudi, S., M. K. Johnson, L. D. Chrosniak 1989. Aging and source monitoring. *Psychology and Aging* **4**, 106–12.

Ivy, G. O., T. L. Petit, E. J. Markus 1992. A physiological framework for perceptual and cognitive changes in aging. In *The handbook of aging and cognition*, F. I. M. Craik & T. A. Salthouse (eds). Hillsdale, N. J.: Lawrence Erlbaum Associates.

Janowksy, J. S., A. P. Shimamura, L. R. Squire 1989a. Source memory impairment in patients with frontal lobe lesions. *Neuropsychologia* **27**, 1043–56.

Janowksy, J. S., L. R. Shimamura & L. R. Squire 1989b. Memory and metamemory: comparisons between patients with frontal lobe lesions and amnesic patients. *Psychobiology* **17**, 3–11.

Jetter, W., U. Poser, R. B. Freeman, H. Markowitsch 1986. A verbal long-term memory deficit in frontal lobe damaged patients. *Cortex* **22**, 229–42.

Johnson, M. K., S. Hashtroudi, D. S. Lindsay 1993. Source monitoring. *Psychological Bulletin* **114**, 3–28.

Kausler, D. H. & J. M. Puckett 1980. Adult age differences in recognition memory for a non-semantic attribute. *Experimental Aging Research* **6**, 195–99.

Kausler, D. H. & J. M. Puckett 1981. Adult age differences in memory for modality attributes. *Experimental Aging Research* **7**, 117–25.

Kausler, D. H., R. E. Wright, M. K. Hakami 1981. *Bulletin of the Psychonomic Society* **18**, 195–97.

Kesner, R. P., R. O. Hopkins, B. Fineman 1994. Item and order dissociation in humans with prefrontal cortex damage. *Neuropsychologia* **32**, 881–91.

Lachman, J. L., R. Lachman, C. Thronesbery 1979. Metamemory through the adult life span. *Developmental Psychology* **15**, 543–51.

Light, L. L. 1991. Memory and aging—four hypotheses in search of data. *Annual review of Psychology* **42**, 333–76.

Lindenberger, U., U. Mayr, R. Kliegl 1993. Speed and intelligence in old age. *Psychology and Aging* **8**, 207–20.

Loewen, E. R., R. J. Shaw, F. I. M. Craik 1990. *Experimental Aging Research* **16**, 43–8.

McIntyre, J. S. & F. I. M. Craik 1987. Age differences in memory for item and source information. *Canadian Journal of Psychology* **41**, 175–92.

Milner, B., M. Petrides, M. L. Smith 1985. Frontal lobes and the temporal organization of memory. *Human Neurobiology* **4**, 137–42.

Morse, C. K. 1993. Does variability increase with age? An archival study of cognitive measures. *Psychology and Aging* **8**, 156–64.

Moscovitch, M. & G. Winocur 1992. The neuropsychology of memory and aging. In *The handbook of aging and cognition*, F. I. M. Craik & T. A. Salthouse (eds). Hillsdale, N. J.: Lawrence Erlbaum Associates.

Myerson, J., D. Wagstaff, S. Hale 1994. Brinley plots, explained variance, and the analysis of age differences in response latencies. *Journal of Gerontology: Psychological Sciences* **49**, 72–80.

O'Shea, M. F., M. M. Saling, P. F. Bladin 1994. Can metamemory be localized? *Journal of Clinical and Experimental Neuropsychology* **16**, 640–6.

Parkin, A. J. & A. Lawrence 1994. A dissociation in the relation between memory tasks and frontal-lobe tests in the normal elderly. *Neuropsychologia* **32**, 1523–32.

Parkin ,A. J. & B. M. Walter 1991. Aging, short-term memory, and frontal dysfunction. *Psychobiology* **19**, 175–9.

Parkin A. J. & B. M. Walter 1992. Recollective experience, normal aging, and frontal dysfunction. *Psychology and Aging* **7**, 290–8.

Parkin, A. J., J. Yeomans, C. Bindschaedler 1994. Further characterization of the executive memory impairment following frontal lobe lesions. *Brain and Cognition* **26**, 23–42.

Perfect, T. J. 1989. *Age, expertise and long term memory.* PhD thesis, University of Manchester.

Perfect, T. J. 1994. What can Brinley plots tell us about cognitive aging? *Journal of Gerontology: Psychological Sciences* **49**, 60–4.

Perfect, T. J. & B. T. Stollery 1993. Memory and metamemory performance in older adults: one deficit or two? *Quarterly Journal of Experimental Psychology* **46A**, 119–35.

Perfect, T. J., R. B. Williams, C. Anderton-Brown 1995. Age differences in recollective experience are due to encoding differences, not response bias. *Memory* **8**, 169–86.

Puglisi, J. T., D. Park, A. D. Smith, G. W. Hill 1985. Memory for two types of spatial location: effects of instructions, age, and format. *American Journal of Psychology* **98**, 101–18.

Rabinowitz, J. C. 1989. Judgements of origin and generation effects: comparisons between young and elderly adults. *Psychology and Aging* **4**, 259–68.

Riegel, K. F. & R. M. Riegel 1972. Development, drop and death. *Developmental Psychology* **6**, 306–19.

Salthouse, T. A. 1991. *Theoretical perspectives on cognitive aging.* Hillsdale, N. J.: Lawrence Erlbaum Associates.

Salthouse, T. A. 1993. Speed mediation of adult age differences in cognition. *Developmental Psychology* **29**, 722–38.

Salthouse, T. A. 1994. The nature of the influence of speed on adult age differences in cognition. *Developmental Psychology* **30**, 240–59.

Salthouse, T. A. & V. E. Coon 1993. Influence of task-specific processing speed on age differences in memory. *Journal of Gerontology: Psychological Sciences* **48**, 245–55.

Salthouse, T. A. & V. E. Coon 1994. Interpretation of differential deficits: the case of aging and metal arithmetic. *Journal of Experimental Psychology: Learning, Memory, and Cognition* **20**, 1172–82.

Schacter, D. L. 1987. Memory, amnesia, and frontal lobe dysfunction. *Psychobiology* **15**, 21–36.

Schacter, D. L., A. W. Kasniak, J. F. Kihlstrom, M. Valdiserri 1991. The relationship between source memory and aging. *Psychology and Aging* **6**, 559–68.

Shallice, T. & M. E. Evans 1978. The involvement of the frontal lobes in cognitive estimation. *Cortex* **14**, 294–303.

Shimamura, A. P. 1994. The neuropsychology of metacognition. In *Metacognition: knowing about knowing*, J. Metcalfe & A. P. Shimamura (eds). Cambridge, Mass.: MIT Press.

Shimamura, A. P., J. S. Janowsky, L. R. Squire 1990. Memory for the temporal order of events in patients with frontal lobe lesions and amnesic patients. *Neuropsychologia* **28**, 803–13.

Shoquireat, M. A. & A. Mayes 1991. Disproportionate incidental spatial memory and recall deficits in amnesia. *Neuropsychologia* **22**, 749–69.

Smith, M. L. & B. Milner 1988. Estimation of frequency of occurrence of abstract designs after frontal or temporal lobectomy. *Neuropsychologia* **26**, 297–306.

Spencer, W. D. & N. Raz 1994. Memory for facts, source, and context: can frontal lobe dysfunction explain age-related differences? *Psychology and Aging* **9**, 149–59.

Stuss, D. T. & D. F. Benson 1987. The frontal lobes and control of cognition and memory. In *The frontal lobes revisited*, E. Perecman (ed.), 185–210. New York: IRBN Press.

Stuss, D. T., G. A. Eskes, J. K. Foster 1994. Experimental neuropsychological studies of frontal lobe functions. In *Handbook of neuropsychology*, vol. 9, F. Boller & J. Grafman (eds). Amsterdam: Elsevier Press.

Tulving, E. 1985. Memory and consciousness. *Canadian Psychology* **26**, 1–12.

Verhaeghen, P., A. Marcoen, L. Goossens. 1993. Facts and fiction about memory aging—a quantitative integration of research findings. *Journal of Gerontology* **48**, 157–71.

Veroff, A. 1980. The neuropsychology of aging: qualitative analysis of visual reproductions. *Psychological Research* **41**, 259–68.

Whelihan, W. M. & E. L. Lesher 1985. Neuropsychological changes in frontal functions with aging. *Developmental neuropsychology* **1**, 371–80.

CHAPTER TWELVE

Constraint satisfaction models, and their relevance to memory, aging and emotion

Philip T. Smith

OVERVIEW

This chapter has a diverse set of aims. The core will be the examination of a particular connectionist constraint satisfaction model, and it will be argued that by understanding some of this model's properties, we gain some insight into a variety of phenomena, including memory retrieval, the functions of emotions, and some aspects of aging. For example, we will suggest that "tip-of-the-tongue" phenomena, the association between quality of autobiographical memory and emotional state, and the existence of false memories can all be understood within this same framework.

The general argument runs as follows. A process such as memory retrieval is a particular example of *constraint satisfaction*. Recalling an autobiographical memory (whom did I see in London last week, what did I have for breakfast, where did I go on holiday last year, when did I last see my father) involves coming up with a solution to a who-what-where-when type of question, subject to various constraints, such as specific times or places. If I succeed in remembering an event I get the reassuring feeling of a coherent experience that fits consistently into the rest of my life. It is as if I have put a number of whos, whats, whens and wheres into a number of simultaneous equations and come up with a solution, this solution being my memory for an event.

Multiple constraint satisfaction is a way of life: in the physical world, when we sit down, raise a glass to our lips, ride a bicycle, strike a ball with a tennis racket, success depends on simultaneously meeting various restrictions imposed on us by the laws of physics and physiology (gravity, conservation of energy and momentum, etc.); in the intellectual world, solving a crossword puzzle and writing a sonnet involve finding solutions within the limitations imposed by the puzzle setter or poetical conventions; in the social world, running a political party and keeping a family of small children happy involve trying to limit irreconcilable disagreements among conflicting standpoints. Not all these processes involve similar mechanisms, but it is the thesis of this chapter that multiple constraint satisfaction at the level of basic perceptuo-motor and mnemonic processes, the very building blocks of cognition, works in a particular way, via simple optimization techniques that we are about to describe.

Solving problems involving several simultaneous constraints can be tackled in a number of ways. Analytic solutions, if they are available, are the best: linear equations, for example, can be solved directly, via well-known methods developed in matrix algebra. Another method that is sometimes successful is the method of serial constraint satisfaction: given a problem with constraints $a, b, c, ...$, which is too difficult to solve as a whole, then it is sometimes possible to reach the solution by first seeking to find the solution that best satisfies constraint a only, then to take this partial solution and adapt it so that it best satisfies constraint b, then taking this as a starting point, adapt the solution so that it best satisfies solution c and so on. The entire cycle of constraints might have to be repeated many times to obtain the most satisfactory solution, that simultaneously satisfies all the constraints as nearly as possible. The process is like successively sawing off the ends of a four-legged table to make it stable, and with complex problems, where the constraints are interdependent, there is no guarantee that a complete solution will be found: the method can be successful, however, in certain areas of statistics (e.g. Ten Berge et al. 1993).

A more general method, which will sometimes succeed when more analytic methods are not available, is *hill climbing*. This involves trying to find a maximally satisfactory solution to a problem by successive improvements on an interim solution, usually by seeking which solutions similar to the interim solution offer improvement. It is like searching for the top of a hill when one is blindfolded, by trying to go uphill wherever possible. We give this method a more careful examination in the next section.

When computer scientists use a hill-climbing algorithm to solve numerical problems, a number of crucial decisions need to be made to ensure the algorithm works efficiently. For example, a decision needs to be taken about *step size*, that is, the amount by which the interim solution is changed to try to find an improvement. If the step size is too small the algorithm will take too long to find a solution; if it is too large the optimal solution might be missed. Another decision involves the *stopping rule*: when can we be confident that any further searching will not lead to a significant improvement (stop too soon and a better solution is missed; carry on searching for too long and effort is wasted)? Now the act of hill climbing is *local*, that is to say if we are blindfolded we can make decisions only on the basis of local conditions, however general considerations about step size, persistence and other strategic aspects are *global*, that is, they represent conditions that exist throughout the task. It is not enough to invoke a hill-climbing algorithm and sit back and let it do its work: additional strategic global decisions need to be made. It is argued that similar considerations apply to human cognition, where, for example, there is more to problem solving or memory retrieval than application of an algorithm: issues about speed, persistence, etc. also come into play. The suggestion in this chapter is that the global features in hill-climbing algorithms correspond, in terms of their functions, to emotions in living organisms.

One particular class of hill-climbing model is examined in the third section of this chapter. It is a *connectionist* model. The term "connectionist" implies a network of interconnected units. Each unit might correspond to a particular entity (*Martin*, *Bristol*, *July*, etc.), in which case the representation is *local*, or groups of units might represent particular entities, with every relevant piece of information being represented by at least two different units: such a representation is *distributed*. In such a system, a "memory" is retrieved, if an input to certain units (a "prompt") leads to the activation of other units (so, the activation of units corresponding to *Bristol* and *July* might lead to the activation of *Martin*). The memories in such a system are encoded via the connections between units. So because I met Martin in Bristol in July, the connections between the groups of units corresponding to these entities are positive; in contrast, because I did not meet Martin in Manchester in August, the connections between the corresponding groups of units are absent or negative. Problems arise when I need to keep several memories distinct: I also met Martin in Reading in October, and I also met Tim in Bristol in July and in Reading in November, so how can I avoid "false" memories, such as Martin-in-Reading-in-July? With a realistic number of such memories, serial checking of such possibilities would be arduous: the attraction of a network model is that all possibilities are checked in parallel, and usually only those combinations that satisfy all the constraints lead to maximal activation in the system.

One of the advantages of distributed representations is that they exhibit *graceful degradation*: removal of a small number of units or connections does not lead to catastrophic failure, since most of the relevant information represented by a unit or a connection is also coded by units and connections that have not been removed. This leads to another strand in this chapter, where we examine the effects of degrading networks that represent knowledge, in the hope that this will give us some clues to the degradation we all suffer, sometimes more gracefully than others, as our brains grow older.

In summary, we are going to examine the notion that memory retrieval can be characterized as a solution to a multiple constraint satisfaction problem and which can be implemented by a connectionist model. Solutions are found in this network by a hill-climbing algorithm associated with global parameters that are functionally equivalent to emotions. This entire framework might permit us to characterize the aging process in various ways and to understand why memory retrieval appears to decline with age.

PROBLEM SPACES AND HILL-CLIMBING

We begin with an apparent digression about one way to characterize problem solving. Cognitive scientists make use of the concept of a *problem space*. This is a collection of states representing all possible intermediate steps involved in solving a problem. Figure 12.1 gives the familiar example of noughts and crosses. The game starts with an empty 3 × 3 matrix and ends when one of the players has a line of noughts or crosses, or when no further moves are possible. Each intermediate step in the game is a *point* in problem space, and the sequence of steps in a game is a *path* in problem space. In a standard game (one in which both players are trying to win) end states where there are three crosses in a line are *goal states* for player 1 (and three noughts in line are goal states for player 2). The aim for player 1 of winning the game can be re-described as finding paths through problem space that lead to a goal state.

There are three problems with goals: creating them, organizing efficient searches for them and recognizing them when we find them. The creation of goals in noughts and crosses is rather limited: most of the time we want to win, but there might be occasions (playing against a five-year-old?) when our goal is to lose. Searching for winning lines is a simple matter in noughts and crosses but by no means trivial even for well defined problems such as chess. In principle, one could win at chess by listing all possible games (paths) with, say, less than 100 moves, and

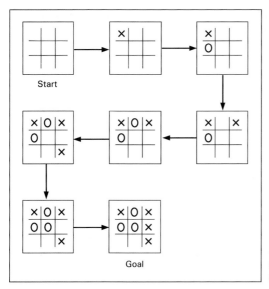

FIG. 12.1.   A path through problem space for the game of noughts and crosses.

then choose only those paths that led to wins (goal states). But the absurdity of this strategy is obvious: not only life but the universe is too short to carry out such a programme. With chess, however, at least we know when we have won or lost. In a less well defined task, such as painting a picture or recalling a memory, how do I know when I have finished?

A solution to these difficulties is to attach an *evaluation measure* to each point in problem space. The evaluation measure tells us how satisfactory the current situation is, and the process of finding a goal state can be re-described as that of finding a point in problem space where the evaluation measure is a maximum. Powerful analytic methods exist for finding maxima when the function relating evaluation measure (y) to location in problem space (x) is well-defined. For example, if $y = 1 - x^2$, we can use differential calculus to prove that y is a maximum when $x = 0$. In noughts and crosses, the evaluation measure "largest number of crosses forming an uninterrupted line" will tell us we have won when this measure equals 3. When analytic processes to find solutions are not possible, because an explicit function relating evaluation measure to location is not known, it is often possible to obtain a solution by a series of successive approximations. Consider a real life example: I wish to create a good painting, and start applying paint to canvas. From time to time I stop and see how I am progressing: at one stage I evaluate the painting as "quite good" but consider the tree on the left needs balancing with some object on the right; further work might make my evaluation "good", but a brighter colour is needed for the central figure; still further work might make it "excellent" and I would stop. On another occasion I might rate the painting "poor"; further work might lead to the rating "still poor" and I might abandon my attempt and scrap the painting. This oversimplified account of how to paint a picture nonetheless contains two realistic elements: (a) at every stage we know roughly how well we are doing, and (b) we sometimes can make good guesses about how to improve the situation. These two elements are at the basis of the *hill-climbing* algorithm for achieving a maximum of the evaluation measure. This algorithm moves from point to point in problem space by attempting to select successive points that are improvements on their predecessor (i.e. they have higher evaluation measures). In some circumstances such a procedure leads to "the top of the hill", that is, to a maximum of the evaluation measure, which in its turn may be a goal state.

Problem solving, then, can be seen as the process of moving across a surface (a "terrain") with the aim of finding a maximum ("scaling the highest peak"). The theory of emotions presented in this paper is simple. Emotions are devices for the creation of problem spaces and for successful navigation in problem spaces. They come in at least five forms:

(1) *motivations* which attach evaluation contours to an otherwise flat environment (winning the Nobel Prize is a peak, being boiled in oil is a trough);
(2) *energizing emotions* that give us the energy to move around the space (the power to drive the "mountain bike" on which we intend to climb the hill);
(3) *state emotions*, that tell us how well we are doing (altimeters to tell us how high we are);
(4) *persistence emotions* that set criteria for how thoroughly we search for the goal state;
(5) *strategic emotions* that choose the type of algorithm for attacking the problem (the characteristics of the path we choose, the options to take if our path is blocked).

Figure 12.2 illustrates the functions of these emotions. We make no apology for such a heterogeneous set of entities all being labelled "emotions", since we believe this reflects the heterogeneity of functions in human emotions. Debate about the functions of emotions from a cognitive science perspective goes back to Simon 1967, and there have been several proposals about the role of emotions in guiding and disrupting planning, for example Oatley & Johnson-Laird (1987). The distinctiveness of the proposals in this chapter is that they are firmly linked to the

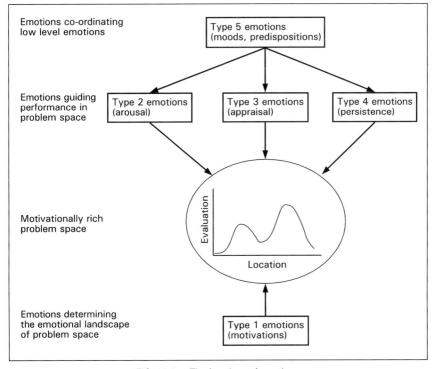

FIG. 12.2. The functions of emotions.

operations of a hill-climbing algorithm, but they are part of this functionalist tradition.

The next step in the paper is to present neural network models that operate in ways similar to those described in the preceding paragraphs. We shall identify parameters that are crucial to the efficient operation of these systems, and explore what happens when these parameters are inappropriately chosen. The parameters are identified with the five types of "emotion" described in the previous paragraph. We shall then attempt to link the behaviour of these systems and their parameters to the behaviour, both normal and abnormal, of human beings.

SIMULATED ANNEALING

Simulated annealing is a procedure that has been developed to find a goal state in problem space. In the particular application we discuss, that of "harmony theory" (Smolensky 1986), a probabilistic search is conducted in problem space. At any point, the decision to move to another point is governed by a probability that is proportional to exp($-H/T$), where H, the *harmony* at a particular point in problem space, is a measure of how good the current provisional solution is. H achieves a maximum (a small positive value) only at a goal state. T, the *temperature* of the system, is a positive number; in the standard applications T begins as a large number and is gradually reduced ("cooling" takes place). For high values of T, the probability of moving to a different point in problem space is high; for low values of T and positive harmony, the probability of change is small. If we adopt a schedule of gradual reduction of T, this will have the effect of the search through problem space starting very vigorously and almost at random, but as T reduces the system will often "relax" into an optimal (goal) state, with the probability of further changes being small. Such a cooling schedule is called *simulated annealing*, by analogy with a process in physics whereby some substances can be best crystallized by first melting them and then cooling them slowly.

This rather abstract characterization can be illustrated as follows. Consider, in Figure 12.3 four frogs jumping around a hilly terrain in search of the hill top. All the frogs jump at random, but with a bias to go to higher ground rather than lower ground. Frog A initially takes large jumps, but gradually reduces the size of the jump. Frog B always takes large jumps. Frogs C and D take only small jumps. Frog A does better than all the others: frog B keeps overshooting the summit; frog C gets to the summit, but slowly; frog D never gets to the summit, being marooned at the top of a lesser hill or *local maximum*. Frog A is following a simulated annealing schedule by gradually reducing jump size. The other frogs illustrate what would happen if this additional flexibility is not included.

In this framework, H is a type 3 emotion (see Figure 12.2), the altimeter telling us how well we are doing, and T is a type 2 emotion, determining how vigorously problem space is searched. (In our frog analogy, H is the height of the frog on the hill and T is the size of the frog's jump.) There is one other conceptual link between simulated annealing and emotions, and that is the *annealing schedule*. There are many different ways to arrange for T to change over time. The usual procedure is to set T to a large number and let it decrease over time to near zero. For example, in the application of Smolensky's model that is the starting point for our investigations, T starts at 1 and decreases linearly to 0.05 in 200 cycles. This is a procedure that almost always finds a goal state, but it is not necessarily always the best schedule and many others are possible (for example, reducing T more rapidly to zero or even allowing T to vary nonmonotonically). Each annealing schedule is, in our terminology, a type 5 emotion, that is, a strategy for exploring problem space.

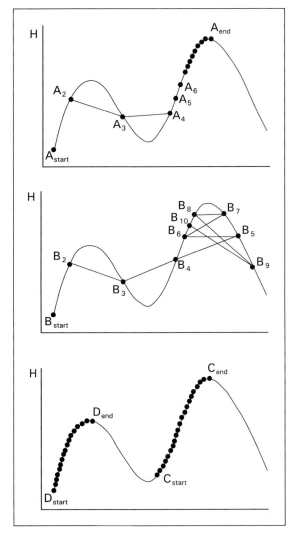

Figure 12.3. Various hill-climbing schedules. All the frogs begin at the point marked *start* and continue until *end* is reached. Intermediate positions are indicated by subscripts. Thus frog A starts at A_{start} and continues through A_2, A_3, A_4, etc. until A_{end} is reached. There is no end marked for frog B, because it will rarely reach the summit. Intermediate points for frogs C and D are not indicated because they are too close together. These diagrams should be regarded as schematic: with the actual simulations, the terrain is more complex and the number of steps larger.

(Frogs A, B and C each show different annealing schedules, with only Frog A showing the gradual reduction in jump size which is character-istic of classical simulated annealing.) We have placed the type 5 emo-tions (analogous to annealing schedule) above the other emotions in Figure 2 because they are more strategic, determining the patterns of variation of lower level emotions (such as T). In human terms, a chroni-cally anxious person (predisposition, type 5) has a lowered threshold for detecting fear-provoking stimuli (fear is a mixture of an arousal emo-tion, type 2, and an appraisal emotion, type 3) or a bad-tempered person (type 5) is more likely to take offence at an insult (anger, types 2 and 3).

We start with the example that Smolensky (1986) gives in his chapter, and which is implemented in the McClelland & Rumelhart (1988) computer package. The task is to solve problems related to a simple electrical circuit (Figure 12.4). The program is fed the information that one or more of the variables in the circuit have changed (in the example discussed by Smolensky, 1986, which we call Problem 1 in this chapter, R_2 is increased: see Fig. 12.4). The program's job is to discover what happens to the other variables in the system, i.e. the resistance R_1, the total resistance R_{total}, the total voltage V_{total}, the voltage drop V_1 across the resistance R_1, the voltage drop V_2 across the resistance R_2, and the current I. The laws governing electrical circuits put the following constraints on these variables:

(C1) $V_1 + V_2 = V_{total}$
(C2) $R_1 + R_2 = R_{total}$
(C3) $I \times R_1 = V_1$
(C4) $I \times R_2 = V_2$
(C5) $I \times R_{total} = V_{total}$

A point in problem space can be conveniently represented by a 3×5 matrix. Each row of the matrix corresponds to a different constraint (C1 to C5), and the elements of each row tell us what happens to the three variables specified in the constraint. Each element can take the value u (the variable goes up), d (the variable goes down), s (the variable stays the same) or 0 (don't know).

The solution to problem 1 (what happens in Figure 12.4 when R_2 is increased?) is given by the following point in problem space:

$$\begin{bmatrix} dus \\ suu \\ dsd \\ duu \\ dus \end{bmatrix}$$

This should be read as follows. Row 1 (referring to constraint C1): V_1 goes down, V_2 goes up, V_{total} stays the same; Row 2 (referring to constraint C2): R_1 stays the same, R_2 goes up, R_{total} goes up; and so on, for the remaining 3 rows. Most of us would solve this problem analytically, first deducing from C2 that if R_2 goes up then R_{total} will go up, then deducing from C5 that if R_{total} goes up then I will go down, and so on through the constraints until the behaviour of all the variables is identified. The program approaches the problem differently: given that it

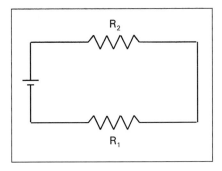

FIG. 12.4.   The electrical circuit examined by Smolensky (1986). Reproduced by permission from Rumelhart, McLelland et al. Parallel Distributed Processing: Explorations in the Microstructure of Cognition. Volume 1: Foundations. Cambridge, MA: MIT Press.

finds itself at a particular point in problem space, it computes the value for H at this point and uses this to determine the probability that it should move to another point. The relationship between H, T and the probability of moving (proportional to $\exp(-H/T)$) often leads to the system coming to rest at or near a goal state, as T becomes small. That is, as the system cools, it relaxes into an appropriate state.

Whether this is a good analogy for how humans solve this sort of physics problem is questionable, but it seems a very promising analogy for a number of processes in perception and memory where a large number of constraints are to be satisfied simultaneously. For example, with binocular fusion the brain needs to compute the alignment of the eyes that maximizes the correspondences between them; with retrieval of a proper name from long-term memory we might make several inaccurate or incomplete attempts until we hit on the solution, which immediately "feels" right.

So our concern in examining this Smolensky problem in this section is not due to an obsessional interest in electrical circuits, but rather because it is an example of a general type of problem, *multiple constraint satisfaction*, which is a central part of much psychological processing.

Local maxima, multiple solutions and annealing schedules
The electrical problem we have just described is not always solved by the program, at least not within an acceptably short space of time. For example, in Problem 1, using an annealing schedule where T starts at 1 and declines linearly to 0.05 in 200 cycles, in a series of 50 simulations we carried out the solution was found within 400 cycles on 92% of occasions. The median number of cycles to find the solution was 201. On the remaining 8% of occasions the program became stuck in a *local maximum*, that is, a region where H is quite large but has not achieved its overall maximum, and where small changes in location in problem space do not lead to any improvements in H: at low temperatures the

Table 12.1
The solution, and some local maxima, for Problem 1.

Matrix of changes			Solution $H = 1.25$	$H = 1.00$	Local maxima $H = 0.75$	$H = 0.75$	$H=0.75$
V_1	V_2	V_{total}	dus	sss	dus	000	uds
R_1	R_2	R_{total}	suu	suu	000	000	suu
I	R_1	V_1	dsd	000	000	sss	usu
I	R_2	V_2	duu	dus	suu	suu	000
I	R_{total}	V_{total}	dus	dus	sss	sss	000

program finds it very difficult to leave such regions. Some local maxima for Problem 1 are shown in Table 12.1.

Two questions arise: can we improve on the 92% success rate, and can we reduce the median number of cycles needed to reach the solution, by changing the annealing schedule? We have investigated this by examining five annealing schedules.

Schedule A: T starts at 1 and declines linearly to 0.05 in 200 cycles.
Schedule B: T remains at 0.05 throughout testing.
Schedule C: T starts at 1 and declines to 0.05 in 100 cycles.
Schedule D: T starts at 1 and declines to 0.01 in 200 cycles.
Schedule E: T starts at 0.05 and stays there, except for cycles 51, 101, 151, 201, 251 and 301 when $T = 1$.

The rationale behind this choice of schedules is as follows: Schedule B is designed to see what happens when annealing is omitted; Schedule C is designed to see if annealing can usefully be speeded up; Schedule D is designed to see if anything can be gained by cooling to a lower final temperature, and Schedule E, the "frustration" schedule, requires the system to stay cool most of the time, but, if progress is not being made, a brief high temperature outburst is permitted.

Table 12.2 shows the performance of the system under these various schedules. The poor hit rate for Schedule B (becoming stuck at local maxima on 46% of occasions) shows that some variation of T is beneficial. The modest performance of Schedules C and D shows that annealing can be too rapid and the final state should not be too rigid. But the star performer is Schedule E, which is superior to all the other schedules examined, both in ability to avoid becoming stuck at local maxima and in speed to reach goal. This shows that strict annealing (monotonic decrease of T with time) is not necessarily the best schedule; for this problem, occasional switches to high temperature is a more efficient

TABLE 12.2
Performance of the "harmony" model, using various annealing schedules in Problem 1.

Schedule label	Change in T	Number of simulations	Per cent occasions solution found within 400 cycles	Median cycles to goal
A	1 to 0.05 in 200 cycles	50	92	201
B	0.05 constant	50	54	195
C	1 to 0.05 in 100 cycles	10	70	114.5
D	1 to 0.01 in 200 cycles	10	60	195.5
E	0.05, except $T = 1$ every 50 cycles	50	98	100.5

solution. Returning to our frog analogy, Figure 12.5 shows frog E, personifying Schedule E; the frog's occasional large jumps ensure it will not stay long in a non-optimal area, but the small jumps that follow on from each large jump ensure that if it lands near the summit it will be able to locate the summit rapidly and accurately.

Thus far we have demonstrated that annealing schedule can influence the efficiency with which a unique solution is found. It is also possible to show that where there are multiple solutions, the annealing schedule influences which solution is found. Staying with the circuit in Fig. 4, consider *Problem 2*, where we wish to know what happens when, simultaneously, R_1 is raised, R_2 is lowered, and V_{total} is raised. The problem has 11 solutions, shown in Table 12.3; that is, it is possible to find particular values of R_1, R_2 and V_{total} satisfying the constraints of the problem that lead each of the 11 distinct patterns of changes shown in Table 12.3. If we chose values of R_1, R_2 and V_{total} at random then the solutions would usually be those numbered 1 to 5. Solutions 6 to 10 are

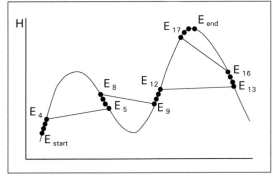

Figure 12.5. The hill-climbing schedule for frog E. The frog begins at E_{start} and continues until E_{end}. Intermediate positions are indicated by subscripts (there is not room to show them all). Step size is small except that at every fourth trial a large leap is made. The diagram should be regarded as schematic; with the actual simulations, the terrain is more complex and the large leap is made every 50th trial.

more subtle, since they require one pair of changes to balance each other: for example solution 8 has the increase in R_1 exactly matched by the decrease in R_2, so R_{total} remains unchanged. Solution 11 is unique in that *two* pairs of changes balance each other: the increase in R_1 matches the decrease in R_2, so that R_{total} stays the same, and the increase in I matches the decrease in R_2, so that V_2 stays the same. We call solutions 1 to 5 *0-match solutions*, solutions 6 to 10 *1-match solutions* and Solution 11 the *2-match solution*.

We have shown that the solution obtained and the annealing schedule chosen interact. This was achieved by running 55 simulations each with Schedules A (T falls from 1 to 0.05 in 200 trials) and B (T remains constant at 0.05). Schedule A is less good at finding 1-match solutions and hopeless at finding the 2-match solution, but within each solution type it spreads itself fairly evenly. In contrast Schedule B is better than Schedule A at reaching the 1- and 2-match solutions, but within each type of solution shows strong biases. (Simple chi-square tests establish all these statements as statistically significant.) How do these differences come about? Well, Schedule A is more energetic, and in its random wanderings round problem space is less likely to show biases, but its energy hampers it with respect to the more subtle solutions that occupy less area in problem space, since it is less likely to cool down in an area close to a subtle solution. Schedule B, on the other hand, searches much less of problem space, and thus shows biases; its slower exploration strategy means it is less likely to overlook a subtle solution.

Degradation of the network

Much of the material we have so far examined could form the basis for a discussion of individual differences. If the Smolensky's harmony model is viewed as an analogy for how humans solve multiple constraint satisfaction problems, then we might expect individual differences in the willingness or ability of a particular subject to select a particular annealing schedule to lead to observable differences in performance. The depressive might be confined to low temperature schedules, the anxious person might be unable to cool sufficiently, etc. With normal aging, one speculation is that an "energetic" schedule, with repeated raising and lowering of T, such as Schedule E discussed above, might become too demanding as we grow older.

There is, however, another dimension that relates rather directly to aging, and that is the condition of the network. Smolensky's problem is tackled with the aid of a network linking inputs (hypotheses about the variables I, V_{total}, R_{total}, etc. change) to outputs (statements about changes in triples of variables, such as those shown in the rows of the matrices presented in Tables 12.1 and 12.3. There exist positive or

Solution number	Solution	Per cent of occasions solution found by schedule A	by schedule B
1	$\begin{bmatrix} udu \\ udu \\ duu \\ ddd \\ duu \end{bmatrix}$	23.6	34.5
2	$\begin{bmatrix} uuu \\ udu \\ uuu \\ udu \\ uuu \end{bmatrix}$	16.4	1.8
3	$\begin{bmatrix} udu \\ udu \\ uuu \\ udu \\ uuu \end{bmatrix}$	12.7	1.8
4	$\begin{bmatrix} uuu \\ udd \\ uuu \\ udu \\ udu \end{bmatrix}$	10.9	3.6
5	$\begin{bmatrix} udu \\ udd \\ uuu \\ udd \\ udu \end{bmatrix}$	7.3	0.0
6	$\begin{bmatrix} udu \\ uds \\ uuu \\ udd \\ usu \end{bmatrix}$	7.3	14.5
7	$\begin{bmatrix} udu \\ udu \\ suu \\ sdd \\ suu \end{bmatrix}$	3.6	18.2
8	$\begin{bmatrix} uuu \\ uds \\ uuu \\ udu \\ usu \end{bmatrix}$	7.3	9.1
9	$\begin{bmatrix} usu \\ udd \\ uuu \\ uds \\ udu \end{bmatrix}$	5.5	1.8
10	$\begin{bmatrix} usu \\ udu \\ uuu \\ uds \\ uuu \end{bmatrix}$	5.5	1.8
11	$\begin{bmatrix} usu \\ uds \\ uuu \\ uds \\ usu \end{bmatrix}$	0.0	12.7

negative links between inputs and outputs, so, for example an increase in I at the input level is positively linked to all triples in which I is coded as u (going up) and negatively linked to all triples in which I is coded as d (going down). The fact that certain triples are impossible, because of Ohm's law etc., ensures that the ensuing pattern of activation conforms as nearly as possible to the constraints inherent in the problem, and, in ideal circumstances, a solution will appear, namely a pattern of inputs is found that is consistent with all the constraints of the problem.

The network for the Smolensky problem has 345 connections, and we have examined the effects of network degradation by randomly removing a number of connections between units, or randomly introducing connections between units where previously no connection existed. We conducted simulations with four degraded networks. In two of the networks nine randomly chosen connections (2.6% of all connections) were removed. In one network 14 randomly chosen connections (4.1% of all connections were removed), and in one network nine randomly chosen connections (2.6% of all connections) were added. Then 50 simulations were run, for each of the degraded networks, on Problem 1.

As is characteristic of connectionist models, such degradation does not totally disrupt the system, but it does produce a decrement in performance. This decrement is manifest in two ways, qualitatively and quantitatively. First, the correct solution is either retained or a minor variant is favoured. Sometimes two solutions are obtained: the correct solution and one that is substantially different. One such pair of solutions, for 2.6% removal of connections, is shown in Table 12.4. The correct solution we have already discussed: as you can see from the table, it makes correct assertions about voltages (V_1 goes down, V_2 goes up, and V_{total} stays the same). The alternative solution makes the wrong assertions about the voltages: as you can see from the table, it

TABLE 12.4
One of the simulations for Problem 1 when 2.6% of the connections in the network are deleted. Two solutions with equally high harmony are obtained. Solution I is the correct solution: Solution II is incorrect but fits the constraints of the degraded network equally well.

Matrix of changes			Solution I $H = 1.25$	Solution II $H = 1.25$
V_1	V_2	V_{total}	dus	sss
R_1	R_2	R_{total}	suu	suu
I	R_1	V_1	dsd	dus
I	R_2	V_2	duu	dus
I	R_{total}	V_{total}	dus	dus

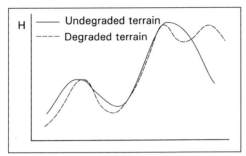

Figure 12.6. Schematic representation of changes in terrain with network degradation. Illustrated is the situation described in Table 12.4, where with an undegraded network there is a unique global maximum, but when some of the connections are removed from the constraining network two global maxima are created, one identical to the previous maximum, and one totally new.

asserts that all the voltages will stay the same. The degraded network has produced a re-shaped landscape in problem space, with two distinct peaks of equal height (shown in Figure 12.6), corresponding to the old (correct) solution and a second (incorrect) solution. Applying these ideas to memory, it is as if my original (accurate) memory of Martin-in-Bristol-in-July has become accompanied by a second (inaccurate) memory of Martin-in-Manchester-in-August, which feels just as authentic to me (both memories have the same H value in Figure 12.6). Note that different annealing schedules are differentially likely to become stuck with the incorrect solution or "false memory"; in particular, Schedule B, the constant low-temperature schedule is as likely to find the incorrect as the correct solution, but this is not true for the other schedules (Table 12.5).

Table 12.6 shows some quantitative measures of decline in performance. One useful measure is the percentage of occasions that the program fails to find a global maximum. This means the program has failed to find a solution with a maximum value of H: usually this is because the program has become stuck in a local maximum (a lesser summit with a smaller value of H). A 2.6% decrement in the number of

TABLE 12.5
Performance of the "harmony" model, on Problem 1, using various annealing schedules and a degraded network.

			Percentage of occasions solution found within 400 cycles			
Schedule	Change in T	Number of simulations	Solution type I	Solution type II then I	Solution type II only	No solution within 400 cycles
A	1 to 0.05 in 200 cycles	50	42	0	22	36
B	0.05 constant	50	24	0	22	54
E	0.05, except $T = 1$ every 50 cycles	50	52	30	12	6

TABLE 12.6
Performance as a function of network degradation. The cells of the table show the percentage of occasions the algorithm fails to find a solution within 400 cycles. Per cent degradation is the percentage of connections randomly added (+) or subtracted (–) from the network. All cells in the table are based on 50 simulations. The degraded networks studied had unique optimal solutions, i.e. the multiple solution data presented in Table 12.5 is excluded.

| Schedule | Change in T | Per cent degradation | | | |
		+2.6	0	–2.6	–4.1
A	1 to 0.05	10	8	12	18
B	0.05 constant	24	46	58	56
E	0.05, except $T = 1$ every 50 cycles	2	2	0	14

connections leads to decline in performance for Schedules A and B, but not Schedule E. When the decrement in connections is increased to 4.1%, all schedules show decline in performance.

When connections are *added* between units that had not previously been connected, somewhat different results are obtained. The aging process being simulated here is if connections become less well insulated (through demyelination?) and activation leaks to previously unconnected units. When 2.6% randomly chosen connections are added, such degradation makes little difference to the performance of Schedules A and E, but leads to an increase in performance, as measured by percentage of occasions a solution is reached within 400 cycles, for Schedule B. Adding connections to the network is effectively eroding valleys in problem space, making it less likely that the local and global maxima are isolated from each other: this enables the least energetic schedule, Schedule B (which always maintains the same low temperature), to move around problem space with less probability of being trapped at local maxima.

Relevance to memory retrieval
Connectionist models of memory have paid considerable attention to the encoding and storage aspects of memory and rather less to retrieval processes. For example, theorists have been concerned with how order information might be encoded in short-term memory (e.g. Burgess & Hitch 1992, Bairaktaris 1994) or how prototypes may emerge in storage following the presentation of diverse exemplars (e.g. McClelland & Rumelhart 1985). There are some ingenious models of retrieval in the literature, notably Metcalfe Eich's (1982) composite holograph associative recall model (CHARM) where encoding is effected by convolution and retrieval by correlation, and at least as far back as Atkinson et al.

(1974) theorists have considered the possibility that memory retrieval may consist of two components, one based on familiarity only and the other based on a more complex process that might involve search and/or retrieval of context. Nevertheless the complexity of this retrieval process has almost certainly been underestimated.

What we are attempting in this paper is to get some feeling for how a search process trying to satisfy multiple constraints might operate. In the previous section we took as an exemplar Smolensky's (1986) harmony model, applied to an electrical circuit problem. Table 12.7 represents our attempt both to summarize the results of these simulations

TABLE 12.7
A comparison of the electrical circuit problem and memory retrieval.

Electrical circuit problem	Memory retrieval
Task: Find solution, given a prompt	*Task*: Retrieve memory, given a cue
Type of problem: Satisfy multiple constraints (Ohm's Law, Kirchhoff's Law)	*Type of problem*: Ensure self-consistency of memory, with respect to context (who, what, where, when)
Solution strategy: Probabilistic search, with the aid of	*Solution strategy*: Probabilisitic search, with the aid of
(1) an evaluation measure	(1) a feedback mechanism giving information on the reliability and coherence of the retrieved memory
(2) an annealing schedule that economically finds the optimal solution	(2) a search strategy that attempts to avoid less than optimal states ("tip-of-the-tongue" (TOT) states, judgments based merely on familiarity, etc.)
Principal empirical results	*Corresponding results in memory retrieval*
(1) Efficiency of search depends on annealing schedule; in particular, a schedule with occasional resort to randomness is superior to a schedule involving gradual cooling	(1) Different retrieval strategies are appropriate for different contexts; in particular the subject may need to find ways round the "blocking" that sometimes occurs in TOT states
(2) In problems with multiple solutions different annealing schedules are best at finding different solutions	(2) Retrieval of general or specific memories will depend on the retrieval strategy adopted, which, in turn, may be influenced by emotional state
(3) Degradation of the network, either by removing connections or adding inappropriate connections, leads to decline in efficiency and, sometimes, to the creation of inappropriate "solutions". The low-temperature annealing schedule actually improves when inappropriate connections are added	(3) Old people may suffer retrieval problems because they are less able to utilize the most effective but resource-demanding retrieval strategies; low-cost (low-temperature) retrieval strategies might become more effective in an aging brain suffering demyelination and inappropriate cross-talk between neurons. "False" memories (inappropriate solutions) may emerge from a degraded network, and particular retrieval strategies may be particularly susceptible to them

and to draw parallels between the electrical circuit problem and memory retrieval. The general claim is that memory retrieval is a task involving satisfaction of multiple constraints, just like the electrical circuit problems.

Tip-of-the-tongue states

More specific claims are that local maxima in the electrical circuit problem may correspond to "tip-of-the-tongue" (TOT) states (Brown & McNeill 1966). It is a characteristic of these states that they include partial information and that "blocking" may occur, that is, the subject persistently keeps retrieving the inappropriate solution and cannot "escape" to a state of complete retrieval. The general advice to a subject stuck in a situation where they persistently retrieve the wrong item is to try to forget the current context and to try again later. (Yesterday I retrieved the name of Rex Stout's fictional detective as "Zero Wolfe": I was not happy about it, but repeated attempts failed to make an improvement; today I remember it is "Nero Wolfe".) Schedule E, the "frustration" schedule, that carries out careful low-temperature searches, but has bursts of high-temperature activity if it appears marooned in a local maximum, behaves in much the same way. The superiority of Schedule E on the problems we have examined suggests this is a schedule that deserves further study.

Emotional state and bias in memory retrieval

Problem 2, the problem with multiple solutions, where simultaneously R_1 is raised, R_2 is lowered and V_{total} is raised, the solutions for which are shown in Table 12.3, suggests some interesting analogies with memory retrieval. Note that what we have called the 0-match solutions (solutions 1 to 5), where an increase in one variable is not exactly matched by a decrease in another variable, occupy the bulk of problem space, in the sense that if we assigned numbers randomly to the changes in R_1, R_2 and V_{total}, while satisfying the constraints of the problem, the obtained solution is likely to be a 0-match solution. It is tempting to think of each of these as "general" memories, broadly similar to many other memories. The 1-match solutions (solutions 6 to 10, where a change in one variable is exactly matched by a compensatory change in another), and the 2-match solution (solution 11, where two pairs of variables match) occupy much smaller areas of problem space. They might be seen as "specific" memories, unlike any other memories. The results shown in Table 12.3 show that different annealing schedules differ in the range of memories they have access to and in the relative ease of access to "specific" memories. Schedule A has a good range, but with a strong bias towards "general" memories: this may be quite similar to suicidal subjects' performance, where it is often difficult to elicit specific autobiographical memories (Williams & Dritschel 1988). Schedule B has better access to certain specific memories, but lacks range: this might be characteristic of depressives, who exhibit biases to retrieving negative memories (e.g. Bradley & Mathews 1988) or panic disorder patients, who exhibit biases towards anxiety-related material (McNally et al. 1989). There are debates in this area as to whether such biases result from long-term structural differences (subjects with emotional disorders have different memory organization from controls) or from short-term mood differences (different moods differentially excite or inhibit different types of memory). The analogy we are pursuing here is that different annealing schedules (different retrieval strategies), which may be short-term mood-induced or long-term predispositional, lead to differential ease of access to different types of memory.

Aging and memory retrieval

The final analogy between the electrical circuit problem and memory retrieval has to do with changes in information processing with age. Our previous work attempting to model aging processes concentrated on prototype formation (Bankart et al. 1994). The technique was to remove connections from a supervised learning network that was trying to learn the classifications of distorted exemplars. The results were that in comparison to an undegraded network, the degraded network handled good examples of prototypes better, but distorted examplars worse, in line with the supposed inflexibility of old people's information processing. The present research has taken a different approach, in two different ways. First the emphasis has switched from storage of information to its retrieval, and, second, we have examined the possibility that aging might result either in decreased neural connections or in increased but inappropriate connections.

Our results for degrading the network show that modest amounts of removal of connections lead to modest decrements in performance, in line with the retrieval decrements observed in old people's memories. Throughout the range of degradation examined, the "frustration" schedule (Schedule E) maintained its superiority over the other schedules. The least energetic schedule (Schedule B, constant low temperature) performed poorly, but it is of note that its performance improved when a small number of inappropriate connections (i.e. connections not expressing the constraints imposed on the problem) were added to the network.

These results suggest two analogies with memory retrieval. One is that a contributory factor in the retrieval failures of elderly people may be their inability to utilize the effective but possibly effortful schedules that involve rapid changes in temperature (randomness of search). So independent of any degradation in the brain network itself, retrieval failure may result from ineffective retrieval strategy. This is entirely in line with the research reviewed in Light & Burke (1988), where performance on a wide range of memory and language tasks is impaired in the elderly if (effortful) retrieval is required, but relatively unimpaired if less effortful recognition or indirect (implicit) tests of memory are involved.

The other observation with implications for memory retrieval is the improvement of the low-temperature retrieval strategy when connections are added to the network: we might speculate that there is more cross-talk between poorly insulated axons in the aging brain, and, effectively, connections have been added. We might speculate that the low-temperature strategy is less effortful than other annealing schedules when there is more variation in temperature, and such a low-effort strategy might be favoured by the elderly. Putting these two observations together, the presence of additional connections in the aging brain enables a low-effort retrieval strategy to be more effective. In this way, memory retrieval in the elderly can be moderately effective despite a degraded network and a less than optimal retrieval strategy.

A final comment can be made about "false memories". Occasionally, degradation of the network leads to a quite distinct (and erroneous) "solution" being valued at least as highly as the correct solution (see Table 12.4). It will come as no surprise that "false memories" can emerge in this way from a degraded network. What is less obvious is that different annealing schedules are differentially susceptible to finding these erroneous solutions; in particular the constant low-temperature scheduled seemed particularly susceptible. In memory retrieval terms, a particular retrieval strategy is more likely to pick up false memories, and this strategy, the low-temperature search, is one we have already seen is consistent with data from emotionally disordered individuals (Bradley & Mathews 1988, from depressives, McNally et al. 1989, from panic disorder patients). We would be foolhardy to claim that this very modest amount of evidence establishes that emotionally disordered people are more likely to recover "false" memories, but it is consistent with the general claim in this paper that emotions can influence retrieval strategies and retrieval strategies influence the type of information that is retrieved.

CONCLUSION

This chapter has attempted to sustain an analogy between on the one hand, multiple constraint satisfaction and annealing schedules, and, on the other hand, memory retrieval processes and emotions. Its primary weakness is that the theorizing is still at the level of analogy and the correspondences we have suggested, for example, between the model's performance near local maxima and TOT states, or between a particular annealing schedule and an emotional disorder, need much more substantiation. But I believe a thoroughgoing working out of these ideas has the potential to unify several areas of contemporary psychology.

REFERENCES

Atkinson, R. C., D. J. Herrman, K. T. Westcourt 1974. Search processes in recognition memory. In *Theories in cognitive psychology: the Loyola symposium*, R. L. Solso (ed.), 101–46. Potomac, Md.: Lawrence Erlbaum.

Bairaktaris, D. 1994. The problem of temporal order in connectionist networks and its implications in short-term memory modelling. In *Neurodynamics and psychology*, M. R.Oaksford & G. D. A. Brown (eds). London: Academic Press.

Bankart, J., P. T. Smith, M. Bishop, P. Minchinton 1994. Feature representations in connectionist systems. In G. H. Fischer & D. Laming (eds) *Contributions to mathematical psychology, psychometrics & methodology*, 67–74. New York: Springer-Verlag.

Bradley, B. P. & A. Mathews 1988. Memory bias in recovered clinical depressives. *Cognition and Emotion* **2**, 235–45.

Brown, R. & D. McNeill 1966. The "tip-of-the-tongue" phenomenon. *Journal of Verbal Learning and Verbal Behavior* **5**, 325–37.

Burgess, N. & G. Hitch 1992. Towards a network model of the articulatory loop. *Journal of Memory & Language* **31**, 429–60.

Light, L. & D. M. Burke (eds) 1988. *Language, memory and aging*. Cambridge: Cambridge University Press.

Metcalfe Eich, J. M. 1982. A composite holographic associative recall model. *Psychological Review* **89**, 627–61.

McClelland, J. L. & D. E. Rumelhart 1985. Distributed memory and the representation of general and specific information. *Journal of Experimental Psychology: General* **114**, 159–88.

McClelland, J. L. & D. E. Rumelhart 1988. *Explorations in parallel distributed processing*. Cambridge, Mass.: MIT Press.

McNally, R. J., E. B. Foa, C. D. Donnell 1989. Memory bias for anxiety information in patients with panic disorder. *Cognition & Emotion* **3**, 27–44.

Oatley,K. & P. N. Johnson-Laird 1987. Towards a cognitive theory of emotions. *Cognition and Emotion* **1**, 29–50.

Simon, H. 1967. Motivational and emotional controls of cognition. *Psychological Review* **74**, 29–39.

Smolensky, P. 1986. Information processing in dynamical systems: foundations of harmony theory. In *Parallel distributed processing: explorations in the microstructure of cognition. Volume 1: foundations*, D. E. Rumelhart, J. L. McClelland and the PDP Research Group (eds), 194–281. Cambridge Mass.: MIT Press.

Ten Berge, J. M. F., H. A. L. Kiers, J. J. F. Commandeur 1993. Orthogonal Procrustes rotation for matrices with missing values. *British Journal of*

Mathematical and Statistical Psychology **46**, 119–34.

Williams, J. M. G. & B. H. Dritschel 1988. Emotional disturbance and the specificity of autobiographical memory. *Cognition & Emotion* **2**, 221–34.

ACKNOWLEDGEMENT

Parts of this chapter were presented as *Hill climbing: how do we know when we are past our peak?* at a conference on outdoor perception organized by Stirling University at Dingwall, 10–12 May 1995.

Index